To Bob FLANAGAN,

I am Sure that you'll enjoy my crazy
Irish Childhood Story!

THE BIG YANK

Memoir of a boy growing up irish

Cheers

J.P. Sext~~

Paddy Publicati~~

"Your battles inspired me – not the obvious material battles, but those that were fought behind your forehead."

— James Joyce

CONTENTS

FOREWORD

J.P. Sexton's foray into the world of commercial writing; "The Big Yank" is a fascinating tome about growing up in rural Ireland, where "nurturing" meant nothing more than survival. It is a raw, brutally honest, "take no prisoners" account of a dysfunctional Irish American family who reverse emigrated back to the old country from New York City. Like me, the author is a highly experienced investigator who has plied his craft around the world for several decades. His attention to detail and the clarity with which he can recall an incident and bring it to life more than 4 decades later, is a gift which will keep the reader turning the page and finding it difficult to put down.

When the author asked me to take a look at his finished manuscript, he did so in order to get an unbiased opinion as to how it struck me. He told me that he wasn't showing it to anybody with Irish heritage, but instead had created a group of readers with all kinds of mixed ethnic backgrounds, since they might be more likely to offer critiques which would help the overall project appeal to a wider audience.

His editor had told him that he did not feel it necessary to add a glossary of uncommon words and phrases, but he himself thought it would be a useful tool for readers with little knowledge of Irish slang and curses. Since my family name ended in a vowel, he was full sure that I was of Italian stock. He was shocked to discover that I had an Irish mother and that I knew as much about our Irish side as I did about our Italian side of the family.

What struck me the most about this well written, fast paced memoir was that it read like a novel and was written by somebody who had grown up in a similar time as I had, but who had an experience that one tends to associate with previous generations. Even though J.P. suffered much at the hands of his parents and in school, he injects so much natural humor into the retelling, that it is difficult to know if the readers' tears are of sorrow or laughter. We are introduced to a young lad who had to boot-strap his way through boyhood, unable to understand why his parents were never in his corner. Despite the constant put-downs and knockdowns, he always manages to pull himself up off the canvas and come out fighting in the next round.

I feel that when many Irish Americans think of Ireland, they tend to imagine an Ireland as depicted in "The Quiet Man." Make no bones about it, this is not "The Quiet Man" revisited. When punches are thrown and belt buckles are used for lashing, there are no stunt doubles, the likes of which John Wayne would have used, or special sound effects to make it seem like somebody was being hurt. From butchering the family pet pig, to living in a double-decker bus, this is a coming of age biography that takes place a stone's throw from the border of Northern Ireland in the 70's and 80's at the height of the "The Troubles" that made the Middle East at the time look like a school-yard brawl.

This is a real story of a life lived during troubled times and a troubled family. It is told in such a relaxed manner, that you will feel like you are on that farm with him or walking along the streets of Derry as the first British tanks made themselves known to the people of Northern Ireland in what would become one of the bloodiest periods in Irish history. Like most of us have, I had heard some stories about Ireland, but when I listened to J.P.'s telling of how life was back then, it made me feel as if I was being time-machined back to those days and seeing it clearly through his eyes.

Personally, I learned a lot from reading my colleague's story – some of which involved a slew of new curse words that only the lilting Irish could use in a way that sounds more like a poem than a damnation. It also gave me a new found admiration and a deeper sense of respect for the toughness of these people - my ancestors, whose Viking warrior DNA is shared with tens of millions of us all over the United Sates and throughout the world.

This is a book by a rare individual who is a man's man. He is the last of a quickly fading breed of men who know how "to take care of business." In our world today we are obsessed with being nice, being politically correct, being restrained in thought and deed. Sexton is not restrained in any shape or fashion. He tells it like it is. This is perhaps the greatest gift he bestows upon the reader. He is able to remain true to himself and still bare his soul without sacrificing his manliness and profound dignity that is laid bare upon these pages.

Paul Ciolino, author of; "The Company of Giants" and "Dead in Six Minutes" (December, 2016) – co-author of the best-selling and critically acclaimed; "Advanced Forensic Investigations and "Advanced Forensic Criminal Defense Investigations."

PREFACE & ACKNOWLEDGEMENTS

I started my writing "career" when I was around 10. I was something of a "Foreign Correspondent" back in those early days. Writing mainly consisted of letters to my Donegal Grandmother who was working in New York until such time as she could return to Ireland and retire.

The letters were all hand-written of course, on an International envelope, which when unfolded turned into your sheet of writing paper. After you had finished, you would fold up the letter, which would revert back into an envelope and get your mother to put a stamp on it. It had exotic phrases like; "Par Avion" written on the corners. To a 10 year old boy, there was something spy-like in the manner in which the information was hidden inside, camouflaged as an envelope, if it were ever to be held up to the light and examined.

It was the monthly corresponding and the weekly ceile sessions in neighbors' houses which instilled within me a love for storytelling and sharing. Even though I thought that I was too busy being a young boy to take any notice, I came to realize later in life that I had in fact subconsciously absorbed much of what was being said.

I never realized that "The Big Yank" was inside of me. One night in Bosnia during a period of heavy shelling, that was the genocidal Balkan wars in the mid 90's, I was spending a night in a bomb shelter in Sarajevo. As usual when working for the United Nations, I was surrounded by people from all over the globe. After a couple of hours, a South African guy turned to me and excitedly said; "tell them the story about "Barney the Pig." I knew right away who "Barney" was, but I could not remember having ever told the story in Sarajevo (which probably meant that it had happened during a late night session in the U.N. H.Q. bar).

I was surprised to learn that the story of a pig's journey in Ireland from family pet to breakfast products could be of interest to anybody outside of my immediate family. I was even more surprised that the "Barney Story" would prove to be a source of entertainment for people on the other side of the world.

Over the years I wondered how many times the story of Barney's demise was retold throughout places like South Africa, Australia, Germany, India, Singapore and other exotic locales. This thought inspired me a couple of years ago to share my strange childhood and crazy adult life stories with a wider audience.

I therefore raise a fork to the bold Barney and say; "here's looking at you pig."

To the many readers who volunteered to be part of TBY Beta readers group, I say thank you for your time and your encouraging feedback.

To E.J. who cracked the Beta whip – dishing out chapters all over the United States (and who I believe secretly looks upon Barney as a brother), thank you for the never-ending encouragement and belief that TBY was destined to be a NY Times best seller!

To M.J. for taking the time to enlighten me as to how my book resonates with female readers. There was me thinking I was clever in masking the pain with humor, but you saw through the "smoke and mirrors!"

To P.C., who is anything, but. Thank you brother for telling it like it is and for always being in my corner.

Finally, to the Big Yank himself. I'll always wonder what you would have made of this had you been around to read it. Maybe one day you'll tell me.

INTRODUCTION

Prior to "Angela's Ashes," I feel that Hollywood mostly romanticized life in Ireland. Feel good films depicted impish leprechauns, men and rosy-faced women drinking and singing merrily in the bars and pubs. Frank McCourt's skillful telling of a childhood destroyed by an alcoholic father, who left his family penniless and homeless, was a grim reminder of what an impoverished life really looked like in the "Emerald Isle."

Neither my father nor my mother drank alcohol, yet that did nothing to improve their relationship with their two eldest sons. As a matter of fact, I suspect that life might have been more bearable and I daresay even pleasant, had they sipped a wee whiskey or two every now and again. It certainly put my Grandfather in a good mood. He drank constantly and would sing songs and come out with funny stories all the time. I never once heard him say anything derogatory to any of us.

It's ironic that writing about growing up in Ireland, some forty plus years ago, has given me food for thought today as I ponder over this introduction. Writing a memoir obviously forces you to remember and I was surprised at how well memories can be preserved over a long period of time. I now wonder if repressing difficult memories somehow seals them in a vacuum packed mental vault.

Having said that, I did not set out to solicit sympathy from the reader. Many of the chapters you will read contain stark instances of physical and mental abuse. I know that I am not alone in experiencing this kind of upbringing. I am probably more alone in other chapters though that deal with the likes of a loveable, but most certainly certifiable grandfather, a blood thirsty mother – who did not seem to distinguish between her kids' blood and the blood from the kids of our mother goat, or a father who talked us all into living in a double-decker bus on the side of a Donegal mountain.

I would be the first to admit that I was no alter-boy and I am sure that I often tried my parents' patience, but looking back I realize that the crime did not fit the punishment. Brutal beatings would knock you down and leave physical marks, but the verbal degradation which dragged your inner being down, was soul-destroying and left mental scars.

A couple of Beta readers asked me how I survived living in that environment for so long. That is an easy answer – there was no alternative. You may have wished for it to stop, but you learned to live with it. It seemed like the price one had to pay for growing up. As I got older, the beatings eased off, but the verbal assaults continued and I was constantly reminded that I would never amount to anything.

I took their abuse and put-downs, but little by little, I started to push forward. I gained a little ground and kept "bucking the system." Obviously I didn't know anything about raising children, but having said that, I was being raised by a pair of chancers who seemed to know even less than I did. By the time I was ready to spread my wings and fly away, I had decided that I would take everything that I had witnessed from my parents and do the exact opposite.

My first order of business was to get my brother Jimmy to swear an oath that if we were to ever have children of our own that we would never lay a finger on them. I am the father of six wonderful children and to this day I have never raised a hand to one of them.

I have often times heard over the years that victims of sexual and physical abuse grow up to be abusers themselves and thereby continue the cycle. The message I would hope that people gain from my story is that this does not have to be the way. It is possible to break the cycle. I would like to think that my parents' method was something along the lines of "being cruel to be kind," but I know that is not true.

I found it within myself to "buck the system" and break the cycle. To this day, if somebody tells me that I can't do something or I have no chance of succeeding, they just gave me the fuel to propel myself forward and to prove to them that I have exactly what it takes.

Breaking the cycle may not come easy, but I am living proof that it can be done. It takes one to dig really deep and find that inner strength, which I happen to believe is something we all possess. It won't be easy, but then again, when has life ever been easy?

CHAPTER 1
BIRTH OF A SMUGGLER

I became a smuggler when I was 9. Before you start thinking that was fierce young, let me tell you that my brother Jimmy was also a smuggler—and he was only 6. You may well wonder how two young Donegal lads got into this line of work at such a tender age. The fact is, we never got paid a penny. We did it for fish and chips.

Our father, now that's a different story. He was definitely in it for the money. He ran the canteen in the shirt factory up in Buncrana. He had the franchise to feed all of the factory girls, and it didn't take him long to realize that he could make a hefty profit by smuggling Irish Free State meat and dairy products in from Northern Ireland. Cheese, butter, cream, hams, and bacon could all be bought for half the cost across the border in Derry. It had something to do with trade agreements—the Republic of Ireland exported the food to the North, and the people there could buy it at fifty percent off what it cost in the South.

Every Saturday morning we'd go up to Derry in my father's baby blue Morris Minor. He'd be driving, my mother would ride shotgun, and my two brothers and I would be in the back seat. The baby—he was two, the youngest criminal of the bunch—couldn't do much, but he made a great prop. After all, what kind of person would ever suspect that a father and mother would willingly endanger their young boys and baby by smuggling across borders in all kinds of weather, not to mention doing business in the middle of a virtual war zone?

Before we headed back across the border to the Republic, our parents would stuff bars of Kerrygold butter up the sleeves of our coats, and packets of Galtee bacon slices into the waistband of our trousers. (And while I never witnessed it, I suspect they sometimes jammed a few pounds of butter or a ham bone under the baby's blankets.) When the Customs and Excise officers at the Muff border crossing looked into the car, they'd see a normal—albeit puffy-looking—family, heading home after a day's outing. According to my father, the shirt factory girls he served breakfast and lunch to each day had every bit as much right to eat subsidized butter on their toast as did their neighbors to the North.

Not that he cared much for politics. My father was a capitalist, and a bartering capitalist at that. My brother and I eagerly awaited our weekly trips across the border. Once our parents were done with food shopping, they'd take us to The Dolphin restaurant for a feed of fish and chips smothered in brown vinegar. After the troops were fed and watered, it was off down the street to the Odeon cinema to see a matinee. To this day, I don't know if we were taken to the film as a family treat, or if our handlers were buying time in order to cross the border when the Customs and Excise officers would be coming to the end of their shift and anxious to have their tea. I always suspected it was the latter. At any rate, we were never caught.

There was one time, though, when the game could have been up. It was an unusually warm and sunny Saturday, and after the butter had sat in the car for several hours our parents proceeded to squish the gold-foil-wrapped bars up our sleeves in preparation for our journey to the South. As we sat in line with the rest of the cars waiting to be searched, I felt melted butter running down my arms. Part of me knew it wasn't my fault, but the other part of me knew how easy it was to catch a beating. I had enough sense to keep quiet—but Jimmy often spoke without thinking.

"Mommy," he complained, "the butter's gettin' on me."

"If you don't shut your mouth, I'll be gettin' on you," she warned him through clenched teeth. While we didn't fully understand the concept of why you needed to hide food inside your clothes and under the seats of the car, we knew enough to keep it from the men in uniforms when they held out their hands and stopped the car.

"But what if the man sees the butter on me?" he whined. He just couldn't let it rest.

"The butter's yellow, right?" her voice strained urgently. "If he sees it, we'll tell him you peed yourself."

Not a bad strategy, I thought. Not quite what my brother wanted to hear, however. "Ah, Mommy, sure he'll think I'm a baby."

I waited for a fist to come flying back at us from the front seat. You could expect fists to go flying when we went out driving.

Flying lefts always came from the driver. If you wanted to dodge his fist (and his were definitely the fists to dodge, as they packed a lot of punch), you sat yourself directly behind him. That way he'd have to stop the car and get out to give you a beating.

I always sat right behind him, and Jimmy sat to my left. Jimmy was his favorite, so he hardly ever got hit. Sometimes when Jimmy was acting the maggot and would make our baby brother cry, our father would reach back with his left hand like he was going to grab Jimmy, but he would get a hold of me by the hair or ear, and pull hard. I wanted to shout out, "I'm not Jimmy, I'm John Patrick!" I could never tell if he did it by accident or knew it was me he was hurting.

My mother, on the other hand, was a wild card. If she didn't have the time to pull over, or wasn't angry enough, she'd just lash out with a flying right from the front passenger seat. If you vexed her sufficiently, however, she'd turn around in her seat, get on her knees and beat the living shite out of you with both hands. I could always tell when she worked herself up into one of her fits of rage. Her green eyes burning in her head and her clenched teeth made her look like a wild animal going in for the kill. No need to stop the car for Sarah the Slasher.

With that, the car had come to a stop in front of the Custom man's outstretched arm. Our father wound down the driver's window.

"Good evening, sir. Anything to declare?" asked the man in uniform.

"Nothing at all, Officer," my father lied with a smile. "We just took the boys up to the Odeon to see a film." The customs man peered over my father's shoulder into the back of the car. He had to move around a bit in order to see in, though, as my father was a big, broad man, and he just about blocked out the view of the back seat. There was no fear of him attempting to move out of the way, either. The man in uniform caught sight of my brother's downcast face.

"What's wrong with the wee man?" he asked. "Did you not like the film?" My parents must have started to feel the pressure.

"Ach, they did," my mother assured him, turning around in order to convince us to back her up. "Youns loved *The Jungle Book*, didn't youns boys?"

By the age of 9, I had become an expert in reading faces—well, my parents' faces anyway. My mother's forced smile, squeezed out through semi-clenched teeth, said to me: "If you don't be nice to this hoor so that he'll let us through, I will beat you to within an inch of your lives; and when I'm through with you, I'll hand over what's left of you to your father."

"It was lovely," I assured the man in uniform. Had I known at that time what I found out later in life, that some kind of child protective services or social worker would have taken us away had they known what we went through at home, I would have claimed political asylum, or whatever it is that a 9-year-old can claim in order to get put into a witness protection program. Jimmy was still fidgeting with his fingers and mumbling about "butter bein' all over" him.

"Are you sure he's all right?" the customs man asked my mother, nodding back behind her at my brother.

"Ah, don't mind him," my mother smilingly replied, "he's just gone and peed himself," at which point Jimmy started crying and sobbing that it wasn't pee, it was butter.

"You can come in and use our toilet if you like," the man offered.

"Thank you, but we'll be getting out in a minute to get them some fish and chips anyway," my father chimed in. With that, Jimmy stopped sobbing and asked through teary eyes, "Are we getting more chips?"

"That's what it was," the Customs man chuckled. "He just needed a plate of chips." As we pulled off through the checkpoint, my brother again asked about stopping for chips. I knew it wasn't going to happen, and I nudged him to be quiet.

"I'll give youns chips," growled my mother. At that stage, even my butter-soaked brother knew there'd be no stopping for chips.

Our smuggling was done during peacetime in the early days. Then one Saturday as we drove down the Strand, we noticed Army tanks rolling down the streets and soldiers carrying guns. It was scary. I asked my parents about it, and they just did that grown-up thing of not wanting to answer. But I could tell they were scared too.

Also, there was barbed wire everywhere. Down home, the only place I'd seen barbed wire was in fields, where it was used to stop cattle from straying. I never liked the stuff myself. One time when we were playing "cowboys" in a neighbor's field, I nearly tore my mickey climbing over it. *Sure, there's no cattle straying in the middle of Derry,* I thought.

Our parents most likely knew right well about the dangers of doing business across the border in the North and in the middle of what was fast becoming a war zone, but they never said a word. After all, it's not a good idea to scare your employees. At no point did they ever show any fear or hesitation when it came to carrying out their mission. Far be it from them to be fussing over some bomb that could potentially be detonated as we were filling our trolleys with Free State dairy products.

Strange as it may sound, bombed-out buildings became a regular part of our weekend life. One week the store we shopped at would be boarded up after the glass front had been blown out, and the next week the window boards would have the words "business as usual" painted across them. A smuggler's patience was quickly rewarded in the North of Ireland in the late 60s and early 70s.

The summer after I had cut my teeth as an underage butter smuggler, my father decided it was time to bring me into the family business—well, at least the more legitimate side of the business. I helped around the canteen, took money from the factory girls (there wasn't a cash register, since we used a large biscuit tin for the money), opened cans, and stirred sauces and gravy. In exchange for performing these chores, I was paid one shilling a day. For the life of me, I have no idea if this was a fair wage or child exploitation. One thing it did teach me, though, was discipline when it came to saving. The auld fella made me save up the money and buy savings stamps at the Post Office.

The only real regret I have about those days is the fact that I was too young to fully enjoy the girls. The Buncrana shirt factory was any young man's dream. One hundred and fifty young women, probably no more than five or six of them older than 21, would hit the breakfast and lunch lines twice a day with a vengeance. Later in life, I would think back and imagine them all (the good looking ones, anyway) undressing me with their eyes as they waited to pay for the fruits of our smuggling. When I attended secondary school in Carndonagh a half dozen years later, and could better enjoy carnal thoughts about young lassies, Buncrana and Derry girls always made our Top Ten list. As a matter of fact, the Top Ten list was really a Top Two list, as no other girls compared to the ones from Derry or Buncrana.

I would venture to bet that if you were to take a poll amongst the priests working in the Inishowen peninsula area in the mid-70s, they'd have revealed that the majority of sins teenage boys spoke of in the confessional revolved around having immoral thoughts about those girls. In the safe, anonymous darkness of the confessional booth, we even told the priests where the girls were from. Our thought process on this was twofold. First, the priests were men themselves and *they had to see what we were seeing*, even though they probably wouldn't admit to it in a month of Sundays. Second, it placed the blame on our neighbors, making it appear as if they were the only distractions to which we succumbed.

Unfortunately, I heard the phrase "Isn't he a wee pet!" too many times to hold out hopes that any actual mental undressing occurred. Maybe that was a good thing; after all, those wouldn't be the healthiest of thoughts for a 20-year-old woman to be having about a wee 10-year-old boy.

Actually, that wasn't my only regret about my time working at the canteen. During one holiday period after I started working there, Jimmy was allowed in to "help." Even though I was probably still young enough to qualify as a UN poster child for under-age labor exploitation, I could see that my brother contributed nothing whatsoever to the overall operation. I didn't mind the fact that he was more interested in playing with a can opener instead of doing any real work, since I realized that he wasn't as close to manhood as myself. It was the fact that we were equally rewarded that got to me.

At the end of the day, our father gave each of us a shiny shilling. I may have been annoyed, but I wasn't stupid. I immediately saw an opportunity—not only to make a little extra coin, but also to readjust the balance of power so that seniority and a disciplined work ethic were once again assured their rightful place in the work force.

"You don't want that," I assured Jimmy, who was fondling the shiny shilling, "when you can have *this*."

With that, I took a golden thrupenny bit out of my pocket. Before decimalization was introduced to Ireland, there were twelve pennies to a shilling, and a thrupenny bit was worth three pennies. It was golden in color and had twelve angled sides. Every morning before he headed out to work, our father would come into our bedroom and drop a thrupenny bit into one of our shoes so that we could buy sweets on the way home from school.

"That shilling is no use at all," I lied. "You see how many sweets this one buys us every day."

"So this one is better?" he asked, holding up the gold coin.

"Much better by far. You know how we can get ten licorice Black Jacks for a penny? Well, with this gold one, you could buy thirty."

"That's a lot of blackjacks," he agreed, "but why did we get this shiny silver one if it's no use?" He wasn't as slow as he looked.

8

"It has some use, but it's not as good," I countered. "Remember when we saw that film in Derry the other week, about the old man Darby and the leprechauns?" The look on his face told me that I had him hooked, so I forged ahead. "Well, they had pots of gold just like this. And if the man had been able to catch the leprechaun and keep the gold, he'd have enough money to buy all the sweets in Ireland." His eyes bulged like a rabbit with maxymatosis.

"Can you give me the gold one and I can keep the shiny silver one as well?" he whispered. I was beginning to wonder who was taking advantage of whom here.

"I'll do better than that," I told him, fishing around in my pocket. "How 'bout I give you two gold ones for that one silver one?" The two-for-one deal was too difficult for him to resist. "Yes, please," he beamed. I walked away feeling a little disappointed that he didn't go for the straight swap. I hadn't done badly all the same, though. ; I had doubled my six penny investment by getting twelve pennies in return.

Then it hit me—it was actually all pure profit. I had pocketed the two thrupenny bits out of the money tin earlier when I was working the lunch line. I viewed it as a perk for risking my neck as a weekend smuggler.

Later in life, I would look back in amusement at the thought of skimming from my father, who had in turn been skimming from the Departments of Agriculture or Finance—one of those many grown-up organizations, anyway.

CHAPTER 2

DISCOVERING MY VIKING BLOOD

Y ou may be sitting there thinking to yourself that cross-border smuggling is not a common occupation for 6-year-old and 9-year-old boys. Truth be told, I'd have to agree with you now. At the time, however, it seemed perfectly normal.

You see, our father was anything but normal. He had the ability to turn the most absurd idea into a decent-sounding plan and convince people to go along with it. He missed his calling; he would have made a great salesman. He must have been very talented to talk my mother into going along with half of his wild ideas. Then again, I suppose she wasn't exactly the "normal mother" type. They were kind of suited, in much the same way as were Bonnie and Clyde.

The first big project that we all participated in fully was to uproot our lives from the United States and set sail for Ireland. That big idea, actually, I put down to my mother. My father, my brothers and I were all born in New York. My mother was a young Irish nurse from Donegal. After training and working in hospitals in

Scotland, she followed her sisters to New York, where she later met my father and they married.

I remember very little of my early years in America. Most of the crazy stories that we heard about this period came from my aunts or uncles, and sometimes from my parents themselves, doubled over with laughter over episodes that had happened in the past.

Like the time when my father, our mother, us wee lads, and our grandmother went to a restaurant in New York City. As I don't remember it, I must have been aged five or younger, which means that my brother would have been two or younger and would have had to be carried. Apparently, my father decided that instead of paying for our meal, like normal families do, we would all bolt out of the restaurant immediately after we had eaten. This would most definitely have been easier if masterminded and carried out by one individual, but having two small children and a maternal grandmother in tow was bound to have slowed down the "getaway" considerably. The fact that my grandmother was a conservative Irish woman from the Donegal countryside and not at all used to running out of a restaurant like a bank robber, also didn't help the speed factor.

I don't know how much significance running out of restaurants without paying had on my parents' decision to relocate to Ireland, but I did hear stories of debt collectors setting up surveillance on my grandmother's apartment in the Bronx, as we were known to hide out there. At some point, my father must have made the final decision to enroll us in his version of the witness protection program—a relocation to Ireland—and we set sail in late April 1968.

I know my mother was very much involved in that particular decision, since she taught us the Irish language and Irish songs to prepare us for school abroad. I suppose that she also prepared us for the many schoolyard fights we'd get into by beating the shite out of us almost from the time we could walk. Those are my earliest memories of my interactions with my mother—learning Irish and getting beaten. My father couldn't speak any Irish, of course, so he just concentrated on beating us.

When I say "us," I mostly mean me. For some reason I could never fully fathom, I seemed to bring out the worst in him. I thought of my parents as an "act," double teaming me on beatings; she warmed up the crowd and he delivered the main performance.

It didn't take much for us to get on my mother's nerves. After an initial bout of yelling about what she was going to do to us, true to her word, she'd grab a saucepan, frying pan or the broom and deliver on her promise. She was no lightweight either. Our strategy was always to run in different directions to tire her out. Initially, this strategy appeared to work, but looking back, I can see that it really only made things worse. It's hard to be stoic at five or six years of age and make the conscious decision to stand there and take a beating, but if we had been able to do so, we would have been better off in the long run. If we were successful in initially outrunning her, one of two things always happened: She'd either wait for us to let down our guard and then, without any warning, bring a broom or saucepan down across our head or back, or she would tell our father how terrible we had been as soon as he walked through the door. This, no doubt, is exactly the way he wished to be greeted after a long day working in a hot kitchen.

Not being a diplomatic or philosophical type, my father didn't seem to feel the need to hear both sides of the story, or stop to think for a moment that a 5-year-old and 2-year-old probably weren't the axe murderers that their mother had described them as. No—once he located us with that maniacal stare, his left hand would automatically grab the left side of his belt as his right hand pulled the buckle open. This usually all took place within two to three feet of the door, as he was given only the hastiest of briefings before carrying out his sentence. With one almighty pull, the thick black leather belt would be unleashed, and all hell would break loose. For the first few minutes, we'd "only" have to worry about getting walloped by the strap—which was no insignificant punishment, since the blows were being delivered by a 6-foot-2-inch 230-pound man in his prime.

Once he became more focused on the task at hand, however, he'd remember that he could inflict more pain and damage by grabbing the strap and hammering us with the buckle. Again, when I say *us*, I mostly mean me. In all honesty, if you were to ask me now if I ever *saw* my father smashing my head and arms with a heavy belt buckle, I'd have to say I did not. My strategy was to get as close to the corner of a wall as possible and cover my head with my arms. The welts on my arms and the lumps on my head were always an indicator, though, that he had been successful in carrying out his mission.

It's actually a wonder that none of the neighbors called the police to complain. All of this beating was not carried out in silence by any means. Once he got into his stride, he'd deliver the blows and attempt to tell you why you needed to get beat, all at the same time.

"You little trouble-making bastard—how many times do I have to tell you not to fight with your brother?" From what I could hear through the spaces of my fingers and under my armpits, he asked these types of questions like he expected an answer. It struck me that this was quite a strange way to have a conversation. I thought that it may have accounted for the fact that he didn't seem to have many friends. I couldn't imagine that his method of beating a conversation out of someone would have been very popular, since with us it always seemed to be a very one-sided chat. Trying to answer him in the middle of his rage would have been suicidal.

Next, I would hear my mother yelling at him from the kitchen: "Don't hit him in the head with the buckle. You'll hurt him." Don't hit me in the head with the buckle? That was easy for her to say; she stood safely in the kitchen while this psycho attempted to wallpaper the apartment with my skull.

Of course, the beating always stopped eventually, but the same could not be said for my crying. I remember crying so ferociously that I would go into convulsions, which would only make him come back. "You want to cry?" he'd ask me. "If you don't stop your son-of-a-bitching crying, I'll give you something to cry about." He threatened me in a tone that suggested that he had only been teasing me earlier. Over time, I learned to hold my breath in order to gain control of my breathing and slow down the sobbing.

Another trick I learned was to "double up" on clothes. Since beatings were almost an everyday occurrence, I figured that if I put on more clothes before my father got home from work, it might not hurt as much when he hit me with the belt and the buckle. There wasn't anything I could do for my head, but at least the rest of me would "soak up" the hitting a bit better. I learned how to time his arrival, and before he walked into the kitchen and was briefed on his duties as head executioner I'd put on an extra pair of trousers and an extra shirt over what I was already wearing.

Once my parents had apparently decided that we were sufficiently toughened up, they booked us passage on a massive liner called the Queen Elizabeth to sail from New York to Ireland. I read that name many, many times on the souvenir penknives my parents allowed my brother and I to buy. Although I was over the moon at being allowed to own the razor-sharp knife, it strikes me as odd now that my parents would allow two wild young boys to roam about with dangerous knives.

It also seems odd, several decades later, that my family crossed the Atlantic on a cruise ship. Today you'd have to be wealthy to be able to afford to sail leisurely from the United States to Europe, but in those days it was simply the cheaper option. I suppose not many people were interested in spending ten days traveling back and forth, unless they were either retired or making a one-way journey like us. Then again, it could also have been due to the fact that my father was afraid to fly. There was usually a method to his madness, although he was often too big and tough to admit it.

My brother cried as we boarded the ship. He'd wanted to bring our cat, Lucky, but we had to leave our pet behind. The ship officials said our cat would have to be quarantined in Ireland for several months before he could be brought in, so my father decided to give him to our Uncle Ritchie to look after. It wasn't until later that I understood why he laughed as he told the story about Uncle Ritchie dropping the cat off at the first Chinese restaurant he came to after leaving us by the dock. My father shook with laughter during the retelling, especially when he pointed out that poor old Lucky didn't have much luck after all.

One thing that struck me about our trip to Ireland was the complete cessation of violence; I don't remember getting beaten once. At first I thought it was because there were so many people on the ship, but my father had never seemed worried before about people watching him beat us or tell us how useless we were. When I was small, I used to think there could be nothing worse than his beatings; but when I grew older, I realized that I hated the way he would tell a complete stranger, or one of our relatives, how stupid we were and how he didn't know how I could be a son of his. I would feel my face burning red with embarrassment.

Thankfully, on the ship he was always in a great mood. He was up early every morning, ready to hit the breakfast table with whoever was hungry. That usually meant the three of us, as my mother was sick and lay in the cabin with the baby for most of the trip. My father found his sea legs as she lost hers. My brother and I didn't mind the absence of her watchful eyes and tough discipline, as this was a totally different world from anything we had experienced before, and we wanted to explore every part of the ship.

I'll never forget the first time I saw Ireland. Straining over the railing, wet salty air stinging my face, I watched the coastline of Cork appear as we drew alongside it from the southwest. I was amazed by the distant fields, rolling off as far as the eye could see in different shades of emerald and jade, divided and subdivided by spidery networks of chestnut-brown ditches. After we disembarked in Cobh, we began the long trip to Donegal, stopping at bed-and-breakfasts each night, and for meals and tea at various points throughout the day. My father had planned for the journey from Cork to Donegal to take several days. Although he had grown up in America and never been to Ireland before, he had a list of relatives scattered at various stages along the way, in places like Tipperary, Limerick, Galway, and Mayo.

I have no idea whether these people knew we were coming or if we just appeared, ghost-like, as their long-lost relatives from America. In those days most Irish households did not own telephones; there was just one communal telephone in each village. Our father didn't strike me as one who would have the patience to correspond with his relatives through writing, so the chances were slim that he would have bothered to mail out letters warning them of our arrival. Nevertheless, all of the people we visited had us in for tea, which was a far grander affair than just a cup of watery Lipton. They'd break out their best china, make sandwiches, and set out various cakes and biscuits. It was during one of these tea sessions that I was first introduced to Battenburg cake, with sweet little squares held together by marzipan icing. As soon as I saw it, I thought of my first glimpse of Ireland. The fields were the squares, and the ditches weaving through its green fields were the marzipan dividers.

Tea in Ireland was an exciting experience for Jimmy and me, mainly because we had never been allowed tea growing up, but more so because of the variety of biscuits. Biscuits are important to young boys. The biscuits in Ireland were exotic to us, their mysterious names—Java cakes, Kimberly Mikado, and Cadbury Chocolate Biscuits –seeming to conjure up images of the Orient. The only downside of having tea and biscuits in Ireland was that you had to eat them with old people. Our parents were old enough, but some of those people we dropped in on as we were driving through the countryside were pure ancient. Whenever we got the chance, we'd grab a few biscuits each and stuff them under our shirts and into our trouser pockets (this turned out to be good training for the roles we would later fill in our parents' smuggling escapades) and beat a hasty retreat to explore the hosts' farmyard buildings and trees.

We had a newfound sense of freedom, much like a couple of lifers who had been unexpectedly sprung from a maximum security prison. Up until this point, we had never gotten the chance to be out of our parents' view. Now that my father was learning how to ceile, he would get lost in conversation—as would the people we visited, since most had never been that close to a real-life Yank before. This worked well to our advantage. We used the hours to perfect our tree-climbing skills, torment whatever animals we came across, and—in our more adventurous moments—to climb the roofs of the houses of those we visited.

My interest in roof-climbing was as much a shock to me as to anybody else, and it soon developed into a cocaine-level addiction. There was just something about farmhouses in Ireland that seemed to scream "come mount me!" I remember being drawn, trance-like, to my first roof, the idea of scaling the walls quickly fermenting in my brain. Jimmy picked up on my fixation.

"What are you looking at?" he asked me.

"The roof on Mary Friel's house."

"What's wrong with it?" he wanted to know.

"Nothing. It's just lovely."

"How is it lovely?" It was obvious he didn't appreciate its beauty the way I did.

"I want to get up on it. I'm going to get up on it."

"What will you do when you're on it?" He was such a practical little bastard.

"I don't know. I'll see when I get up there."

Like many farmhouses in Ireland, Mary Friel's was built up against a large back field. This gave me a few different options for climbing up onto the roof. I found a plank of wood, jammed one end into the ground, and placed the other end against the spot where the house walls met the roof. I then walked *up* the plank, like a pirate in reverse. After reaching the peak, I perched on the gable end and rested one foot on the chimney.

"What is it like?" my brother shouted from the ground below.

"Like being on a pirate ship," I answered, still fixated on my walk up the plank.

"Can I come up on the pirate ship?"

"I think you're a bit small," I informed him imperiously, surveying the fields around the house for any sight of an approaching Jolly Roger like a first-time pirate captain.

I'd like to be able to claim that I fully mastered the art of tree climbing before I moved on to houses, but that wouldn't be true. It was still exciting to climb a nice knobbed, twisty tree every now and again, especially when I made it so far up that I was scared to come back down, but it couldn't compete. There was just something about climbing up on a house, knowing that other people were inside and underneath me, that made my heart dance in my chest.

My favorite type of roof was thatch. Thatch roofs had so much going for them. Strategically, I was much safer on them, since their thick padding meant that I could walk silently and had virtually no chance of getting caught by the people inside. Then there was the fact that they had wire mesh or fishermen's nets strung across the top to keep the flax in place. This made it easier to pull myself up and gave me something to grab on to if my footing slipped. Once I conquered a roof, I marked my territory. I didn't have to climb it every time I came back for a ceile, but I always knew I could if I felt like it, which was the important thing.

Our father used to smoke in those days: Woodbine cigarettes, unfiltered. Most homes did not have ashtrays back then, and he would come out the front door and throw the cigarette into the street when he was finished with it. We'd watch the door like hawks as we played. As soon as he turned his back and went in, we'd make straight for the area in front of the door and swoop down on the loose pebbles and gravel until we fished out the still-glowing cigarette butt. No matter who found it, I was always the first to suck on it, as I had seniority. After I had wet it and tried to make the smoke come out my nose like I had seen my father do, I'd pass it to my brother and he'd try to take a hit off it. He was always afraid of getting burned, and it was no wonder, as the end was always hot by the time we got to it.

⇥ ⇤

Whenever we'd visit the Glacken house their youngest son, who was around six, would play with us. The poor lad got a raw deal, as he was taught all of our bad habits. We'd use him as a scout, making him show us his sister's hiding places, bring us out food so that we didn't have to waste time going in for it, and be our lookout when we climbed his roof and stuck poles in it to hoist our ship's flag. The most he could expect in return was the chance to puff on the wet end of a soggy Woodbine butt and the privilege of being allowed to play football with us—using his ball, of course.

Although we didn't realize it at the time, we were known for leaving a visible trail of destruction behind us. The combination of attending an all-boys Catholic National school and being able to run wild around the countryside seemed to bring out the worst in us. We terrorized some families more than others, one such family being the Glackens. Although the young boy mostly enjoyed his time with us, the same couldn't be said for his sisters.

The first time the young Glacken boy showed us his sisters' "shop," we thought we had died and gone to heaven. Those girls must have spent years collecting jars and bottles to stock the shelves of their shop. The shop itself was in a sheltered little patch of garden. They had placed long planks of wood on big stones to make the shelves. There were cans of Coleman's mustard and jars of Bovril in one section, while bottles of Coke and Fanta stood in a corner near canisters labeled "Tea" and "Sugar." They had collected old cups and saucers that their mother no longer wanted and used them to serve tea to their "customers."

The first time we visited the shop, we infiltrated its walls under the guise of being customers. As soon as I saw the display, the wheels in my head started to turn at a ferocious rate. By the time we had walked out of earshot of the Glacken girls, I knew what we had to do.

"Right, lads," I commanded. "We are Vikings. We know what the Vikings did to the Irish—they plundered and pillaged. We will go to our Viking ship and get our swords, and we will return and destroy this Irish village."

"Will we have to kill my sisters?" young Glacken asked in a fairly unconcerned manner.

"Not unless they put up a fight," I assured him, "although we may have to carry them off to our ship and take them back to our land."

After we located some sticks that would pass for swords, we crept up on the unsuspecting sisters. With blood-curdling yells, we announced "The Vikings have landed! The Vikings have landed!" I am quite sure that they had no idea of the nightmare that was about to unfold.

Without providing any warning, or allowing them the opportunity to flee, we raised our weapons and began to demolish the shelves holding all things breakable. Glass flew, cups shattered, and tin cans were dented. The more things crashed and broke, the more worked up we became. None of us paused to catch a breath until everything had been annihilated.

The carnage finally subsided when we stopped to admire our handiwork. We decided that the Nordic swordsmen who had come before us would have been proud. The powder from the shop's busted flour jars whitened the shelves and ground like the dusting of a fresh snow. The jars and bottles, which had suffered the worst injuries during the battle, gave up the ghost as their liquid contents oozed and dripped all over the shelves and ground.

The Glacken girls stood frozen to the spot, watching in horror as the shop they had slaved to build and stock was decimated before their eyes. It probably would have been better for them (and definitely for us) if they had fled the scene when the level of our depravity first became obvious. It was not until our appetites for destruction had been satisfied and we took a minute to take stock that we realized that the girls had not taken advantage of the chance to escape. This, I decided, would prove to be a mistake they would live to regret.

"All right, men!" I shouted. "Bring the squaws back to our boat."

"What are squaws?" asked their young brother. "Are they crows?"

"No, they're not crows, they're the girls," I corrected him. "I heard John Wayne say that in a movie." Nobody bothered to question the correlation between The Duke and a Viking.

"So we are going to kill them, then?" their bother asked, with what appeared to be a glint in his eye. Fortunately, the girls were so horrified by what they had already witnessed that they didn't seem to hear their brother discussing their possible demise in such a casual tone.

"No, we won't kill them," I decided. "We'll carry them off as hostages. If their parents refuse to pay us to get them back, we'll throw them off the ship into the ocean. Now get some rope and we'll tie them up."

My two fellow kidnappers ran into one of the barns and reappeared with a loose bunch of twine used to tie up bales of straw and hay. I had them hold one end, and I ran around the two dumbstruck sisters until they started to resemble the unfortunate damsels from silent films who were bound with rope and tied to railway tracks.

"All right, we'll march them to our ship," I said, eying the metal gate that kept the cows corralled in the lower field.

We marched—well, the girls had to shuffle, as they were stuck on top of each other with little room to actually walk—toward the gate. I instructed them to back up against it and proceeded to tie them to the horizontal bars. Both girls suddenly seemed to reach their breaking point at that moment, erupting in screeching as soon as I finished tying the ropes. I hardly even got the chance to admire our handiwork.

"Let's get out of here," I shouted to my accomplices, who had already started to scamper away before I even got to the word "here."

We headed straight for the big field behind the house, making sure to run along the left side so that the old people would not see us. Unfortunately, in our crazed plundering of the shop, we had not stopped to discuss an escape plan, but running in the opposite direction from the screaming seemed a logical strategy. Running out to an open field, however, did not allow us any cover.

"Should we lay down and hide?" my brother asked.

"The grass is too short," I replied, as my mind raced to think of our next move.

I had a bad feeling that a beating could not be far away. I could feel it in my bones. Our hopes of coming up with a workable escape plan were dashed when we saw our father and the Glackens' father emerge from the house, yelling our names. We later found out that they were mainly concerned for the safety of the young boy, which seemed odd, as he was very much a part of the raiding party. Apparently his sisters had been so traumatized by the incident that their mother could not make sense of anything they were saying through all the sobbing.

We knew the game was up when the two fathers spotted us and raised their arms in a jerking motion toward the house.

"Look, they're waving at us," my brother remarked innocently.

"That's not a wave," I informed him. "A wave would be if they raised up their arm in a slow way and just moved their hand slightly, as if to say, 'Ah, there you are now, how's it going?' No, they're saying, 'Come down here now, right this minute, as I need to break your necks.'" My brother looked at me, then at the two men, then back at me, trying to analyze the significance of their beckoning.

I don't know if the two fathers had it planned, but each addressed their own delinquents in their own special way.

Mr. Glacken asked his son why he had tied his sisters to the gate. When the boy shrugged his shoulders and told him we were playing a game, his father shook his head, said he thought it was a strange game, and that was that. In contrast, Jimmy and I stood in front of my father, who shouted and roared. I listened to the exchange between Mr. Glacken and his son, in-credulous, while trying to take my mind off of my impending punishment.

The sight of Mr. Glacken merely shaking his head gave me some cause for hope. I started to think of a way to tell our father that it was just a game we were playing about Vikings and we had a ship. I was about to look up at him to tell him when I heard him spit, "You're not listening to me, you little fucker." The next thing I knew, one of his big hands had connected with the left side of my head, and the ground started moving up toward my face. I didn't know if he was still yelling. All I could hear was the ringing in my head.

I felt my elbows trying to pull my face up out of the grass as I tried to focus on him. It was important to my survival that I made it appear as if he had my full attention. The man wore size 14 shoes. I did not want to be on the ground at shoe level if he decided to use his feet.

He looked angry, and his mouth was moving fast, but the ringing in my ears was louder than anything he was saying. I knew I would be screwed if there was a question-and-answer ses-sion. Luckily, however, he must have been satisfied that he had gotten his point across, and stalked off back toward the house. I tried to stand up, but the ground seemed to be swelling and rocking, and I could not manage to straighten up.

"Did it hurt when he hit ya?" my brother asked. The little fucker escaped without as much as an ear-pulling. I was getting the shite kicked out of me when I was years younger than him. I wanted to tell the favorite son that it felt like my head was going to lift off my neck and go rolling through the grass like a football, but I needed to play the tough man.

"Not so much," I lied. "I think he's getting weaker now that he's getting older." I wished this was true. Being in his mid-thirties, he still had a lot of thumping power left in him.

"My dad wasn't so mad," young Glacken shared.

"I wish he was our dad," I replied. The two boys laughed, but I wasn't joking.

"Hey, let's go down and climb their roof," my brother suggested.

"Are you mad?" I asked him. "The old man's already on the war path. We don't need to do anything else to make him want to put the boxing gloves back on. Let's go down and wait for a smoke."

We walked down to the gable of the house and waited to hear talking at the door, which would indicate that someone was about to throw a fag outside. (Through all our visits, I never remember the Glackens closing their front door, even in winter.) We passed the rest of the afternoon turning over rocks and hunting for fat earthworms and roly-polies. My brother was mesmerized by how a worm could wriggle both ends independently when you cut it in half with a stick. I poked a roly-poly and watched it curl up into a ball. I wondered if it learned to do that from getting beaten by its father.

We hardly noticed that the afternoon had turned into evening and the evening was slipping into night until our mother called us from the doorway. We headed in, but I came slowly, dreading the coming conversation. Our father was always saying mean things about us to other people. Sometimes the other people would smile and say things like, "sure, they're only children," but that only seemed to make him worse. He would always say that he wished we were like their children, smart and well-mannered and not the little bastards we were. Luckily for me, this time he was sitting across the kitchen telling stories to the nice father and didn't seem to notice as we came in.

The three of us sat on chairs at the other end of the kitchen by the front door. The Glacken mother came over and told us she would get us something to eat. I was afraid that she might be angry with us for tying her daughters up, but she didn't let on if she was. I did think that she looked at me more closely than the other two, though. Word had probably gotten back to her that I was the head Viking.

Old Irish cottages never lacked bugs. Their owners hung up long strips of glue paper to trap flies. I wondered why I'd never see any other types of insects stuck to those strips. Either the glue was liked only by flies, or flies were the only ones dumb enough to get stuck on it. I figured they must be stupid, since spiders trapped them in their webs too.

Those glue strips must have cost a lot of money, because shops and houses would leave them up for a long time, until each had hundreds of flies stuck to it. Sometimes a strip would be pure black with flies, and I'd wonder how any more could possibly stick to it. I imagined flies stepping over other relatives, excusing themselves as they looked for a spot where the glue was still exposed so that they could press themselves on and never leave.

The bugs got worse at night, since they were beckoned by the light in the kitchen and wandered in freely through the door that never closed. In the summertime it was not unusual to see a gang of dragonflies, or "daddy longlegs" as we called them in Ireland, skimming lazily over the surfaces in the kitchen, taking their time as if they had nothing better to do. Not wanting to look near the adults, I started studying the long-legged pilots coming in the front door like they owned the place. After we had drunk our tea and finished the last of the sandwiches and biscuits, an idea began to swirl around my head.

"Did you ever catch a daddy longlegs?" I asked our young accomplice. The way he hesitated and then broke out into a grin made me think that he was either up for what I had in mind or had decided that I was completely mental.

"No. What would you do with one if you caught it?"

"Well, here's the thing," I replied excitedly. "What if we were to tie something onto it and then let it go again and see if he could take off and fly around with it?" I knew by the stare in his eye that I had him thinking.

"We could tie a spoon to him," my brother suggested idiotically.

"He couldn't fly with a spoon. Sure, that would be like 100 times his own weight. Could you walk around with 100 times your own weight on your back?" I asked him.

"Maybe we could tie a Polo mint to him," young Glacken offered, fishing a pack of Polo mints out of his trouser pocket. "It would be easy enough to tie a string around the hole."

"It might work," I said, "but I think it might still be too heavy. Can you find us some string?" The young lad took off to the lower room. I had never been down there but had heard it was a bedroom. After a while he came back with a spool of white thread.

"That's all I could find."

"Let's try it," I told my cohorts. "Let's pull off a chunk of it and then try to grab a daddy-longlegs when he flies past." Capturing flying bugs without drawing much notice to yourself isn't easy to do. My brother didn't have the height for the job, so he would jump at them and clap his hands together. After a few minutes he told us he had one. We were excited until he opened his hands and we saw that he had squashed it.

"Don't clap your hands on them," I instructed him as if I had been hunting them for years. "Cup your hands so you don't damage them." I watched another one flying by and went for him with cupped hands. The next thing I knew, I felt him moving against the cupped palms of my hand.

"Now tie a knot in the middle of the thread, but don't tie it tight all the way," I told young Glacken. He did as he was told, and I slowly opened my hands enough to see the wings and long tail.

"Right now, I'll hold him. You push his arse into the knot and pull the two ends slowly. Don't pull tight, though. Stop when the knot touches him all around." He did exactly what he was told, and in no time the big daddy-longlegs had two lengths of white thread hanging off his arse. I threw him back up in the air and, much to our surprise, he started flying. We laughed so hard at the big bug trailing the white thread that we nearly fell off our chairs.

The grown-ups didn't seem to notice the flying thread skirting around the ceiling, and had we stopped there they may never have been any the wiser. But we figured if one was that funny, then a bunch would be hilarious.

One by one, we caught, threaded, and released another half-dozen slow-flying daddy-longlegs until there were so many airborne that they passed one another as they flew around the kitchen light. We experimented with longer pieces of thread to test how much of a load these guys could pull to the ceiling. The result was that some now trailed nine to twelve inches of thread behind them. The nice father was the first to say something.

"Jesus, what is that at all?"

"What's what?" his wife asked.

"That there," he said, taking the pipe out of his mouth and using it as a pointer.

"It looks very like a daddy-longlegs with something hanging off it," she said, "and there's another one…and another one. Where are they all coming from?"

While they tried to figure out the stringed bug epidemic, we were working on our next launch. I decided to push the envelope, loading up my next victim with the longest piece of thread yet. I threw the poor fellow up in the air and he tried to make it to the ceiling, but the thread was too much for him. He flew toward the light, weighed down by nearly two feet of white sewing thread, as if in slow motion. Unfortunately, one of the sisters who had been tied up earlier was just passing under the light. The thread got caught up in her hair and the pilot was forced to make an emergency landing on her forehead. In so doing, he was propelled forward, and ended up dangling right on the bridge of her nose. She began flailing her arms and screaming just as she had done earlier. We froze in the corner.

Strangely enough, the grown-ups didn't go ballistic on us. They actually seemed to think the flying strings were funny. The girl's mother brushed off the bug and told her daughter not to get upset, as it was only a "harmless daddy-longlegs." The nice father was smirking as he puffed away on his pipe.

"How did youns think that up at all?" he asked us. We shrugged our shoulders, not wanting to take too much credit for the homemade circus act in case his query was a devious trick to lure us into admitting something that would later result in a beating. Our mother rolled her eyes and made a comment about the devil making work for idle hands. The young sister must have been too traumatized to remain amongst the terrible visitors. She fled to the lower room and was not seen again. I was quietly relieved when her young brother suggested that we play cards, and we huddled in the lower corner playing snap until it was time to leave.

CHAPTER 3
FROM CORK TO DONEGAL

Life is tough when you move as a child. You have to start over from scratch with an entirely new area, new friends, and a new school. It's even more difficult when you move from one country to another. Nothing could have prepared us for Ireland, not even the Irish lessons or the beatings.

The one good thing about making that transition at a young age is that boys live for adventure. I can't begin to tell you how many times I pitched a tent (blanket thrown over two chairs) under the stars on a Western prairie, or fired up a rocket ship and headed into deep space (via the tent conveniently turning into a spaceship). In comparison, the uprooting of our daily life was almost unbearably exciting.

In a way, the stories we'd heard had given us the wrong impression of Ireland altogether. We had prepared ourselves for leprechauns who were in charge of large pots of gold, and who would be forced to give you everything when you found them at the foot of a rainbow. It would seem, then, that any right-minded person would concentrate on bagging themselves a leprechaun and be set up for life. When we found out that we were moving to Ireland "for good," my brother and I decided that we would become professional leprechaun hunters.

"How long do you think it'll be before we can go hunting leprechauns?" he asked me.

"I'd say we can do it as soon as we get there. We'll have to save up for the stuff we need, though. Leprechauns are tricky, so we'll have to get some kind of cage or sack that we can put them into so they don't escape. We'll also need bags to put the gold in."

"Do you think maybe we are too small to hunt them?" he wanted to know.

"That's actually the best part. Because we're small, we'll be able to blend in and trick them that we're leprechauns too. You have no chance of catching a leprechaun when you get big, since they can spot you a mile away. You never hear of grown-ups catching them in any of the stories. Our mother always told us that they had no money growing up and had to walk to school in their bare feet. If her father could've caught a leprechaun, they'd have had enough money to buy shoes."

"That means we'll have to dress like them and act like them." My brother was definitely starting to get the picture.

"I don't think that will be hard. Everybody in Ireland dresses like leprechauns already. We just need to get shoes with buckles and those big green hats with the buckle in the middle. Leprechauns really like buckles."

Unfortunately, most of what we knew came from pictures and nursery rhymes—as well as from our mother, who told us ghost stories to scare us when she needed the extra leverage.

She also did her best to trick us, for entertainment purposes, on our long car rides. We knew of four places in Ireland—Donegal, Derry, Cork, and Kerry—and she tricked us by asking us to "spell that without a 'K.'" I had seen Cork and Kerry spelled out, so for the life of me I couldn't understand how it was possible to spell it without using a "K." I felt foolish when she told us the answer: "t-h-a-t."

Our long journey finally came to an end as we landed in a place called Cork. Our mother had told us that this is where they made the corks for bottles. We weren't going to live here, though. The plan was to head all the way north to Donegal, to a place called Malin Head where our mother and her family had all been born. Both my brother and I hoped that we'd be able to wear shoes when going to school up there. We weren't thrilled at the idea of going to a new school where we didn't know anybody, and the thought of going in bare feet made the idea that much worse.

My parents borrowed a car from someone and drove around. It felt like we were driving in circles. My father found it hard to get used to driving on the "small roads." But the toughest part for him was the placement of the steering wheel.

"Why do they put steering wheel on the wrong side?" he asked our mother.

"It's not on the wrong side here. It's on the right side. Don't worry, you'll get used to it after a while." He didn't. My father kept getting lost. He would stop in the middle of the road and ask people who were walking or riding bicycles how to get to the next town or to someone's house. Everyone seemed very smart to me, since they always knew exactly how to get to wherever we wanted to go.

"Excuse me, sir, could you help us find Tommy and Marge Harte, they're supposed to live just outside of Thurls?"

"You're looking for Tommy Harte in Thurls?" asked a thin man on a bicycle. He had a hat pulled down over his face, so that all you could see was a long nose and a cigarette sticking out of his mouth. He blew smoke out his nose and mouth simultaneously while he talked. My brother and I stared. "I know of Hartes living in Thur-less, would that be them?"

"I'd say it probably is," replied my father.

"Well, in that case," said the man—smoke pouring out both nostrils and a jet being pushed out the side of his mouth, still never taking his hands off the handlebars, and using his leg as a kick stand—"you go down a bit until you come to Betty's corner shop. You'll know it by the 'Sweet Afton' sign. Then you turn to your right onto the Togher Road—it has no sign, but you can't miss it. You go up that road for about two miles and you'll come to a fork in the road. Stay to your left—if you go to the right, you'll be going the wrong way. Go down that road a good bit and after a while you'll cross over railroad tracks. That means you're getting near to them. Their lane will be the second or third on the right. Look for a black and white gate. It's the only black and white gate on that road."

"And you're sure we can't miss it?" my father asked hopefully.

"You should have no bother finding it," replied the man, "just mind the cows."

"Mind the cows?"

"Aye, it's coming up to milking time and the Walshes drive their cows up to the house to be milked around now. They live just below the Hartes, so you might run into the cows. You don't want to actually *run into* them, that's why I said to mind them. Ye aren't from around here, I'd say?"

"No, we just arrived from America two days ago," my father proudly shared.

"Americans. They say it's a grand country, America. John Wayne and Jimmy Cagney, did you ever meet those boys?" The man reached for the little piece of cigarette that was sticking out of his mouth and took it between his thumb and nose-picking finger. What he did next was amazing. He rolled the lit cigarette between his fingers until it disappeared, and then he blew on his fingers. We watched the ashes drift away on the breeze.

"Ah...no, I never did, actually...but I saw a lot of their movies." Our father seemed to be as amazed by the man's cigarette trick as we were.

"And how is it that you know the Hartes, then?" Wherever he had been going on his bicycle could wait, by the looks of things.

"They're my cousins."

"Isn't that something. I never knew the Hartes had Yankee cousins."

"Well, thank you very much for the direction. We must be headed off now," my mother said, leaning across to the driver's window. As we pulled off, she told my father that these people weren't used to seeing strangers, and that "they'd talk the hind legs off a donkey" if they got half a chance. I puzzled over that. It sounded as if Irish donkeys weren't put together very well if you could just talk their legs off them. I figured that the smoking-nose man must have been responsible for a lot of crippled donkeys, the way *he* could talk.

A day or two later we drove to Mayo, where my father's mother had come from. We never knew our grandmother. She had been killed in a car accident before we were born, and our father didn't talk about her much. He seemed happy now, however, to be visiting the place where she had grown up.

"This is where your grandmother used to live when she was a girl," he proudly told us, "now her brother, Uncle Jimmy, owns the house."

"Is that the grandmother who is in Heaven?" my brother asked.

"Yes," replied my mother.

"And where is that other grandfather?"

"He also died before you boys were born," my father informed him. "He was poisoned in the war and he was sick when he came home. He married my mother and they had us children and then my father died when we were all young."

"Was he a spy?" I asked him.

"No, why would you think that?"

"Because you said he was poisoned. Sometimes spies poison each other and sometime when they get caught they have to swallow poison pills."

"He wasn't a spy. He was poisoned by gas during a battle in France."

It was hard finding our way around Mayo as well. We got to the town of Kiltimagh, but had no idea where to find the Gormleys' farm. The town didn't look that big, but where we were going was out in the countryside. My father stopped the car and called to a woman who was walking along the road with a boy about Jimmy's age.

"Excuse me, could you please tell me where I could find the Gormleys of Kill-tie-mag?"

"Kill-tie-mag?" asked the woman with a huge frown, "Kill-tie-mag...I'm sorry, I've never heard of it." My father pulled the map from the side of the seat and showed the woman.

"I thought we must be getting near, according to the map," he said.

"Oh, you're looking for Killshemock," said the woman with a smile. "It's right there ahead of you now."

"Okay," said my father, "Kill-she-mock. Would you know where we could find the Gormley farm?" He probably thought it was going to be something like a Texas ranch and that everybody in that part of the country would know of it.

"I'm sorry, I don't know it. Do you know any of the neighbors?"

"I believe that the Henry family lives next door or close by," he told her. The woman asked some more questions, but we lost interest in the back seat since she didn't do any fun tricks like blow smoke out her nose or squish fire with her fingers. We drove off and stopped at a small store to get more directions; they must have been good directions, because he came out with chocolate for us. We turned down a broken, potholed road that made the car bounce up and down, and stopped in front of a house standing alone in the middle of a field.

"I'll go to the door and see if it's the Henry house," our father told our mother. The chocolate was gone, however, and we started getting itchy feet. I elbowed my brother. That was our sign for him to ask for something we wanted. We both wanted to get out of the car and play.

"I have to pee," he announced.

"Hold it," she ordered. We looked at each other. We'd have to wait a while to make her think we were obeying her, as she accused us of disobeying her at least a few times each day. My brother waited all of a minute.

"I can't hold it any longer," he said, squirming in his seat. Either he was becoming a pretty good actor or he was actually about to pee himself; I couldn't tell which. As my mother turned around with a look that would put the heart crossways in you, I noticed a woman coming out the front door of the house and walking down the path toward our car.

"Maybe this woman can let you use the bathroom," I told my brother. The woman walked around to the side of the car and our mother rolled down the window.

Welcome to Mayo, Missus," the woman greeted her.

"Oh, hello..." we didn't often see my mother nervous, but she seemed to be at a loss for words.

"I'm Chris Henry's wife, Maureen. Won't you come in for a cup of tea?" A lassie dog came out and joined the woman. Our mother reached back and picked up our youngest brother, Kevin, who started pointing at the dog. He didn't look happy.

"Oh now, don't worry about Goldie," the woman told the baby. "She loves wee boys." We scouted out the area as we followed the woman into the house. My father was inside talking up a storm and didn't even notice us coming in.

"Look who I found outside," the woman announced. A tall man with a red face and big teeth stood up from the seat by the big fire and shook our mother's hand.

"Hello missus, and welcome. Your husband has been telling us about America. Maureen will wet the tea now, and then after we've had a wee cup, we'll go over to Agnes' place." I was glad to see a boy who looked to be my age, although he was playing with the dog and didn't seem to be interested in us. Jimmy was tugging at my mother's skirt. The Maureen woman caught him.

"What is it, wee pet?" I thought she was talking to the dog, but she was looking at my brother. Our mother bent down and he whispered something into her ear.

"He needs to go to the bathroom."

"Damien," the woman called over to the boy with the dog, "take the wee lad back."

I figured I'd go with Jimmy, as he'd be scared to go on his own with the boy. I was quite surprised when he led us outside, around the back of the house, and down toward a barn. My brother looked at me and I looked at Damien.

"Where does he go to the bathroom?" I asked him. Damien pointed to the barn. I stepped forward and beckoned to my brother to follow. We tiptoed into the barn, not knowing what we'd find. Turns out, it was a mess and stank to the high heavens.

"What do I do now?" asked my brother.

"Fish it out and do your business," I told him, all the while looking around for any sign of a toilet.

"But this place is very dirty," he complained.

"Well you came here to pee, not eat dinner—pull it out and let fly." After a few seconds he relaxed and started to pee, but had no sooner started doing the job at hand when he screamed "Something's moving in the grass!" and stuffed his still-gushing mickey back into his trousers, pissing all over himself. Tears began to flow down his face.

"What's wrong?" I asked him.

"There was something moving around on the ground when I was peeing—I think it was a mouse," he sobbed.

"So? You could have poisoned him or at least drowned him if you kept peeing," I berated him. "And what are we going to tell them inside now that you've peed all over yourself?"

"I don't know." Of course he didn't know. It was always left to me to get out us out of jams like this. Mind you, for the most part, I was usually the one getting us into them in the first place, so I really couldn't complain. I stepped outside to find Damien playing fetch with his dog.

"Excuse me," I politely interrupted, "but there's been an accident. Do you think you could bring us out a towel?" The boy looked at me, and then at the barn, and sauntered off toward the house without saying a word. My plan was to try and soak up as much of the pee as possible in the towel and hopefully dry out the trousers enough so as not to be too noticeable. It bothered me, though, that Damien never spoke. I wondered if he was the strong-and-silent type or if he had some kind of learning disability. Our mother used to tell us stories about "half-wits" in the area where she had grown up. By her account, you could have great fun with them, but you couldn't rely on them to do much for you.

Damien appeared from around the gable of the house as I was still trying to decide if he was a bit touched in the head. I had also considered the possibility of him not understanding us, as we definitely did not sound like they did. Thankfully, he was carrying a small white towel with blue stripes. Even though he had understood the part about getting the towel, though, I figured that I'd play it safe. I handed my brother the towel, and as he began to soak up the pee from his trousers, I turned to Damien and did my best to speak in slow motion.

"T-h-a-n-k y-o-u v-e-r-y m-u-c-h," I enunciated as clearly and slowly as I could.

"Why are you talking that way?" Damian asked. I was shocked. *It spoke.*

"Well we never heard you say anything, so I thought you may be one of those village half-wits and it would be easier for you to understand if we spoke slowly."

"You thought I was a fuckin' half-wit?" he screamed. I definitely had his attention now. "C'mere to me, Yank, so I can box your jaw." I had never heard the phrase before, but the way he held up his fists, I had a feeling that he was more than a little annoyed.

"I didn't mean to hurt your feelings," I assured him. "It's just that we heard a lot of stories about half-wits in Ireland and it seems that every village has a fair number, so we figured you might be one. It's great that you aren't, though, because now we can play and do stuff." He seemed to soften up a bit. My brother handed me back the towel, now damp with his pee.

"Just remember that there's no half-wits in this house," he warned me. I figured that a nod would be enough to show him I understood that his house was a half-wit-free zone. As I nodded, I attempted to hand him the pee-covered towel.

"What are you up to?" he growled as I held the towel by a corner, thereby limiting my exposure to my brother's urine.

"Sorry, I don't understand?"

"Why are you giving me the towel that's covered in the wee boy's pish?"

"Well, I don't know what else to do with it. Won't your mother want it back?"

"Let him take it into her," he instructed, nodding over at my brother. It seemed like a fair solution, so I tossed the damp towel at my brother. "Give that to Damien's mother when we go inside," I told him.

We followed Damien into the house and I nudged my brother, motioning for him to give the towel back to the Maureen woman.

He was reluctant, so I grabbed the waist of his trousers, pulled him up, and shoved him in her direction. When we were close, I let go and stepped to one side. The woman was talking, but when she caught sight of the towel she held out her hand.

"Oh, aren't you the wee pet," she smiled at my brother. "I was wondering where the tea towel had gotten to." Tea towel? What was a tea towel? She took the pee-damp towel and rubbed a chocolate spot off of my brother's chin. She didn't seem to notice how he flinched.

"Somebody's been eating chocolate," she said, smiling down at Jimmy, whose nose was scrunched up in disgust as his own pee was wiped across his face.

"Somebody's been pissing themselves," I said under my breath. I watched, entranced, as Damien's mother used the pee cloth to wipe off the plate before piling biscuits atop it.

I knew it was going to kill me to turn down those delicious-looking biscuits, but it did bring me a sadistic kind of pleasure to know that everyone in the house, except my two co-conspirators, would soon be munching on my brother's pee.

CHAPTER 4
PAIN IN THE ASS

It has often been said that every savage beast loves its native shore. Apparently, this was also the case for non-native beasts, like my father. For some reason he looked upon Donegal as his "promised land," and his arrival there was like a homecoming. At the time I was too young to fully grasp this fact, but I did have a sense that he had finally found whatever he had been searching for in life as we crossed the Sligo border into southern Donegal.

Of course, his happiness could also have also been due to the fact that he was running from the long arm of the law and figured that he had finally found somewhere remote enough to provide a safe haven. Either way, he finally seemed at peace with himself. Before you start thinking that he turned into some kind of Celtic Dali Lama, though, think again. Peace and himself made strange bedfellows. In his case, saying he was more at peace was akin to saying that Genghis Khan mellowed in his old age and killed only 1,000 people a day as opposed to his usual 5,000.

Among the first friends of my mother's family that we paid a visit to were a brother and sister named Eugene and Mary Friel. If I wrote about the Friels every day non-stop for a month, and filled all the pages between the two covers of a book, I could not come even close to recreating the experience of visiting their house as a young boy. Looking back, I am quite sure that you didn't even have to be a Yank to feel this way. A child from any large town, and definitely from any city, in Ireland would have been as shell-shocked as we were to discover this incredible brother and sister.

The Friels lived on a farm outside of Malin town. Their family had been friends of the Gillens (my mother's clan) since way back before my grandparents had married. Like a good deal of homes in rural Ireland at that time, they did not have many of the "mod cons," as they were called back in the day; they lacked running water, indoor plumbing, and heat. They did have electricity, though, which must have been more important to them than the other "luxuries" that they never seemed to miss. All their cooking was done on a black Stanley range which burned turf and seemed to stay lit 24 hours a day. The range also heated the house—well, the kitchen, living, and dining rooms. In order to stay warm in bed, they did what just about everyone did back then. They filled rubber hot water bottles with boiling water and placed them in the bottom of the bed a half hour before turning in for the night.

The first day we arrived in their yard, a sunny Sunday in mid-May, we were greeted by a bespectacled woman with rosy red cheeks and a grin on her face so wide that it made her eyes nearly disappear. My brother thought she was Chinese.

"Mommy, Daddy, is that Chinese woman going to cut me up with her knife?" he asked in a trembling voice.

"That's Mary, you eejit," my mother lovingly comforted him. "She's not Chinese."

I knew that my brother had a phobia of Chinese people. He had picked it up from watching martial arts movies in America. To add fuel to the fire, I elbowed him and pulled back the corners of my eyes to narrow them. I added to his fear by running a finger across my neck, indicating that he was about to get his throat slit.

"Then why does she have Chinese eyes?" he wanted to know.

"This is Ireland," I assured him. "There's no Chinese here, you eejit." I didn't know exactly what "eejit" meant, but I had often heard my mother use that word and it was always when one of us had screwed up.

"Welcome home, Sadie," Mary said warmly as she wrapped her arms around my mother. I saw something like dust on her hands, but lumpier; I had never seen this substance before. Now there were two dusty, lumpy hand prints on the back of my mother's sweater.

"It's been such a long time, Mary," my mother said. "This is my husband, John." My father went around the car to greet her. As she held out her hand, she realized it was dirty and began wiping it on her blue housecoat.

"Forgive me," she laughed. "I was stirring meal for the calves and I have it all over me. Come on in and we'll wet the tea." When it came to making tea, Mary could very well have been Chinese. She brewed it up like she had shares in the Lipton tea company. In Ireland in those days, it didn't matter if you were 5 or 95; you drank tea until it very nearly came out of your ears.

We visited the Friels' house most Sundays over the next ten years that I lived at home. I never left their house without having downed ten cups of tea at a bare minimum. Mind you, I was also a young boy who was running in and out of the house playing nonstop.

My father turned out to be the tea-drinking king. If I drank ten cups, he would easily drink thirty to forty. Of course, nobody ever seemed to consider the fact that tea had as much caffeine as coffee, if not more. If you were to give a 6-year-old and 9-year-old boy ten cups of coffee today, somebody would report you to the police, and social services would come knocking on your door before you knew it.

I will never forget that first cup of tea at the Friels' house. Not for the quality, although Mary's tea was as strong as iron and instilled a love of strong tea in me from a tender age. I remember it because I was struck by the fact that their house was an open forum for any barnyard animal that cared to wander in. Their door was always open for humans and animals alike. Of all the years that we ceiled at Mary's and Eugene's, I never knew the front door to close, not even in the middle of freezing winters.

Having traveled up the length of Ireland that past week, I came to learn that you were better off "paying your respects" as soon as you entered a neighbor's house. Most of the time they were old and no fun, but you at least had to allow them time to fuss over you a bit and say who they thought you looked like. There never had been a house that could hold our interest and tempted us to stay inside longer than was absolutely necessary until we met this sister and brother. Their house was a cross between a petting zoo, a museum, and an open-air asylum.

Mary was a salt-of-the-earth type, and there was no fear that you'd ever find pictures of her house in any beautiful homes magazine. The floors were cement, but not the smooth cement you'd see in other places in the area. Mary and Eugene's floors had chunks missing out of them, and you could see small seashells lodged inside the cement if you looked close enough.

Mary seemed to be always rinsing out basins, swirling the water until it was running around the top of the basin like a circus motorcycle driver racing inside a huge sphere. The best part was that, once she had built up enough momentum, she would casually flick her wrist and spray the water out right there on the kitchen floor. She would do this all the while without ever looking down once, and would carry on a full conversation as she swirled and flicked.

"Sit anywhere youns like," she instructed us as we made our way indoors for the first time. "Don't mind the place. It's as rough as a bear's arse right now, but we'll be doing it up for the Stations of the Cross one of these days." Once my eyes became accustomed to the dark, I started to make out someone hunched over by the fire. I couldn't tell if it was a man or woman, as all I could see was some sort of black blanket wrapped around them. Every few seconds a puff of smoke would come out from the front of the head, but the person never turned or looked in our direction.

"Sadie, you remember Grace Charlie Phil from the lower town?" The person in the black blanket turned around to the right, and I made out the outline of a terrifying old woman smoking a pipe. She looked for all the world like a witch. She had a bony face, and her jaw extended halfway down to her chest. All you could see was a long face with a man's pipe sticking out of the mouth.

"Oh, yes…" my mother stammered, trying to buy time until the memory of the old lady came back. "Didn't you live near Willy the Pet's place, Grace?"

"Aye," the old woman muttered, and returned to her original occupation of staring into the fire.

"Grace's house is fierce damp and cold," Mary explained, "so we had her stay with us over the winter."

My father and mother sat on chairs by the kitchen table, while Jimmy and I headed for a chaise-lounge type of couch with an arm that had stuffing poking out of it like wiry hair. My brother took long, squeamish looks at the old lady, not wanting to get too near to her.

"Who is that person?" he whispered in my ear.

"You do realize that I got here the same time as you and that I never saw these people before a few minutes ago, right?" I whispered hoarsely. Figuring I might as well give him something to worry about, I added, "I am quite certain, though, that she is a witch. She has all the right markings. Firstly, she is completely wrapped in black. She is hunched over, she has a huge long chin…and even though I didn't get a close enough look, I wouldn't be surprised if she had a big old wart on the end of it."

He was in a bad way. Not only did he have his doubts about whether or not Mary was part Chinese, he was also sure that he was sitting across from a witch. To make matters worse, he suddenly spotted something on the couch that caused him concern.

"What's that behind you?" he asked me under his breath. I turned around to see what looked like a person's knee sticking out from under a wrinkled newspaper.

"I don't know, but I'm not touching it." Even though we were shielded by the parents, Mary caught sight of our fidgeting and asked us what was wrong. Neither of us answered, so she came over to investigate. She pulled out a big dirty bone that seemed to have been half-chewed by somebody or something.

"Ach, that's just Blackie's bone," Mary chuckled. "He'll probably be coming in for it in a while."

"Who's Blackie?" my brother asked me.

"I don't know," I barked back, "but he sounds very much like an escaped convict." This made my brother worry even more. He got up off the couch and stood over by our mother. Mary was doing something else with a basin; it looked like it was time for her to water the floor again. We all heard whistling and singing coming from the front door area, then a loud scraping on the floor. A tall man with a crooked pipe hanging from his mouth walked in, a black and white dog following at his feet. When the man caught sight of my mother, he came toward her with an outstretched hand, exclaiming "well, hello Sadie Houton!" My brother, thinking this was Blackie, the escaped convict, tried to scramble up on my mother's knees, holding onto her legs for dear life.

"How are you, Eugene?" my mother greeted him warmly. "This is my husband, John, and these are our boys."

"Very pleased to meet you," Eugene said to my father. "When did youns arrive up?"

"We got into Malin town last night, and stopped for bed and breakfast," my father informed him.

"Well, that's a good one," Eugene commented as he walked over to the range. He reached down, tearing a strip off of a newspaper on the floor, and stuck one end into the front of the range. The old lady never budged, and he acted as if she was invisible. Within seconds, the newspaper had gone up in flames. Eugene pulled it out and stuck the flaming end into the pipe as he sucked hard, and a huge pile of smoke came out of his mouth. The paper must have been starting to burn his fingers, so he just let it fall on the floor next to the old woman. I jumped up to get a good view, as I was sure that she would catch on fire and was bound to burst into flames. This was by far the best house we had ever visited.

"So how's mom and dad, Sadie?" Eugene asked my mother. Before she could answer, we heard a loud grunting noise, and a huge pig waddled into the kitchen and looked up at Mary. This was the last straw for Jimmy, and he started crying and pulling at my mother like she had a special power over pigs. I couldn't say that I blamed him much, since the pig was at least ten times his size and looked like she could eat a 6-year-old boy as a snack.

"What's wrong, wee pet?" Mary asked my brother (not the pig). "Sure, that's only Molly, she'll not harm ya. She's come in looking for food."

With that, Mary grabbed the basin, bent down, and took a fist-ful of sawdust out of a burlap bag. She threw water on top of the sawdust and started mashing it through her fingers. I looked at my father; he looked as shocked as my brother. None of us Yanks had a clue what was coming next. Mary gathered up a handful of the grey stuff in the basin and, with a flick of her wrist, splattered a dollop of it right there on the floor in front of us.

Obviously Molly knew what to expect, as she had her snout buried into that mix. She filled her huge jowls as she snorted and grunted like the pig she was.

Eugene obviously saw the look of shock on our faces. "Aye, that's Molly's tea now, isn't that right, Molly?" he asked the pig, rubbing behind her ears.

Mary then went back to the ritual of splashing water into the basin, swirling it around, and dashing it on the floor. This time she took a step closer to the front door, but was still too far for any hope of the dirty water reaching the street outside. It only took the pig three or four gulps to finish her "tea" and, after sniffing around the floor for any stray bits, she turned on her trotters and strode out as comfortably as she had come in.

"The tea will be ready in a minute," Mary assured us. "Youns must be famished—I'll make some pancakes, I know the wains will love that." Jimmy, being the inquisitive type, started whispering into my mother's ear. No matter how many chores Mary was juggling at the same time, she never missed anything, and she spotted the whispering.

"Does he need to go pee, Sadie?"

"No, he's asking me what are; 'wains.' Mary started laughing so much that her cheeks glowed red and her eyes disappeared.

"Sure, you're a wain and your brothers are wains," Mary told him, in between gulps of air. "Wains are children." I decided that it would be interesting to keep an eye on these people, as well as toward the front door, in case any other wandering animal came into the kitchen for a visit. Mary never seemed to take a break from what she was doing, whether to wash her hands, find clean basins, or weigh out ingredients. She now began throwing handfuls of flour into the same basin that had been used to mix Molly's food. As she mixed it with a big wooden spoon, flour flew out the top of the basin, dusting the floor like powder on a baby's ass. If we had ever done something like that at home, we'd be beaten black and blue, but Mary took it all in her stride.

"So John," Eugene said to my father, "what will you work at now that you are in Ireland?"

"I'm a chef by training," he replied, "so I figured I'd contact the local hotels to see if they have any openings."

"You should try the Malin Hotel," Eugene suggested. "They do a lot of weddings, funerals, and other functions. I heard they were looking for a cook a while ago."

"It was renovated not that long ago," Mary added, "and they have been looking to get in more bookings now that they've made the function room bigger."

"Thanks for letting me know," my father replied. "I'll ask to speak with the manager tomorrow and see what they have to say."

"It just changed hands last year," Eugene advised, "but everybody still knows it as the Deerys' Hotel and a couple of the Deery girls still work there. Be sure to tell them that you are Sadie Houton's man. They all know Cassie and Danny Houton."

"Maybe you should be making the tea, what do you think, John?" asked Mary, "I don't think I can do as good a job as a famous American chef!"

"Not at all, Mary," he told her. "You can probably do better. After all, the pig really seemed to enjoy what you made her." This made everybody laugh. Even the old witch appeared to be laughing; I saw the blanket on her hunched-back moving up and down. Then again, she could have been coughing, as you couldn't hear much with everyone else laughing. I was hoping that my father would get up and make our food, as I couldn't get the idea of us eating out of the same bowl as Molly out of my head. Little did I know it at the time, but Molly wouldn't be the last animal to make herself at home in the kitchen.

True to her word, Mary did indeed make pancakes, and I have to admit that they were the tastiest pancakes I had ever had.

Mind you, I was no pancake expert, but as far as I was concerned they could not have been any better. Jimmy and I had been told we could go out and play after eating, so we took full advantage of the offer. We ran into the small field next to the house, where the Friels had built a huge turf stack. We were intrigued by the brown hard bars of dirt that the villagers put into their fires to cook with and stay warm. They piled the turf into huge stacks shaped like houses, and whenever they needed some, they'd fill a basket or bucket from one end of the stack and leave that next to the fire. To them it was heat; to us, it was another thing begging to be climbed.

I don't think we did too badly at overcoming new Irish obstacles like thatch roofs and turf stacks, especially when one considers that they were completely alien to us and we had to learn by trial and error. This first attempt at climbing a turf stack actually proved quite successful, if you overlook the blood aspect. Not having any prior engineering training, I was still able to work out that the manner in which the turf bars were stacked on top of one another. They appeared to give a bit of a footing to the climber, should one have half a mind to ascend to the peak, much the same way in which one would look to climb Mount Everest. Indeed, it was the thought of Mount Everest that proved to be my undoing.

The first few feet from the ground were no bother whatsoever. I merely had to wiggle the toe of my shoe into an opening, grab hold of the turf bars above my head, and pull myself up. That plan of attack worked well for the first few upward strides, but as I approached a higher elevation, I began to feel a bit shaky at the prospect of losing my footing and crashing back down without the aid of a safety net. I considered this problem, and then had the brilliant idea of mimicking a mountain climber using an ice axe. I had seen a show on television where climbers on Mount Everest had used this method with great success.

Of course, one of the major flaws with my plan was the fact that 6-year-old and 9-year-old boys do not generally go around carrying ice axes. That meant we had to improvise.

"I need an ice axe that I can stick into the turf and pull myself to the top," I shouted down over my shoulder to my brother.

"I don't think I have one," my brother innocently replied.

"I know you don't have one, you little eejit," I roared at him. "That's why we are going to need something that will do the same job." My mind was racing. I didn't know how far up the side of the turf stack I had climbed, but I knew that I was far enough up that coming down on one's back would not be a pleasant experience. Then it hit me.

"Do you have your Queen Elizabeth knife on you?" I shouted down desperately. I shot a glance over my shoulder to see him fishing around in his pocket. A minute or two later he had it out and opened.

"What are you going to do with it?" he asked.

"I'm going to use it to stick into the turf above my head," I informed him, as though I had been doing it for years, "then pull myself up to the top." I had not thought about how I would get back down, but right now my mind was firmly fixed on my ascent.

"How are you going to get the knife?" the little know-it-all bastard asked. I had not thought this part through either.

"I suppose you are going to have to throw it up to me," I replied, trying to sound like I knew what I was talking about so that he wouldn't know I was winging it. Had I given it some more thought, I probably would have realized that the odds of me catching a knife unseen behind my back were slim to none, even if the little prick could have managed to throw it correctly in the first place.

Over the next ten to fifteen minutes, I listened to the repetitive thud of the pocket knife hitting the turf well below me and knew that there was no way he was going to get it close enough unless we came up with another method. I held on with my left hand and slowly turned my upper body halfway to the right so that I could see him below me.

"Do you remember how the circus man threw knives at the woman on the spinning wheel?" I asked him. He looked confused, so I slowly took my right hand away from the turf to demonstrate.

"Hold the knife in your palm with the blade pointed straight out to the front. Now, point your nose-picking finger out front and on top of the back of the blade. Next, you are going to take the knife behind your head and back like this, and then bring your hand down fast to release the knife when it is just in front of you. Go ahead and try it."

In all fairness, it was way too much to expect from a 6-year-old, but my heightened sense of self-preservation was stronger than this reality. Jimmy's first attempt was half-decent, and the knife even nearly stuck into a bit of dried turf.

"That wasn't bad," I encouraged him, "but it was down by my shoe. This time aim it up at my waist and to the right a bit."

His second attempt was closer to where I could have reached it, but the side of the knife bounced against the turf and it tumbled to the ground. I could see that he was really getting into it, though; he stuck his tongue out the side of his mouth in concentration.

"That's it, concentrate," I said. I watched over my shoulder as he lifted his arm and brought it back down smoothly, releasing the knife. It was picture-perfect, just like the man who had thrown the knife in the circus act.

As I focused on the knife's release, time slowed to a crawl. The knife's three-second journey from brother's hand to turf stack seemed to last three full minutes. I remember thinking how perfectly the blade seemed to glide through the air and remain straight the whole way. As it grew closer, I began to think that this was the throw I had been waiting for. I could almost see it now, firmly lodging into a chunk of turf, offering its gleaming handle for me to use in resuming my climb.

I actually had part of the thought process right. It did strike perfectly, and did lodge firmly into something. Unfortunately, that "something" did not turn out to be a chunk of turf, but a chunk of my ass. The knife found its way in perfectly, as if I had a big red bull's eye painted on my backside. The shock of getting stabbed in the ass with a knife made me totally forget about where I was. I immediately let go of the turf and came crashing to the ground. Although I didn't feel very lucky at the time, I was very fortunate to have landed on my front. Had I landed on my back, that knife would have been pushed up God-knows-where, and I am fairly sure it would have involved a hospital visit to get it removed.

The other fortunate thing was the fact that the penknife had two blades—large and small—and my brother had opened the small blade instead of the big one. The small blade probably only went in a half an inch or less, taking into consideration that it first had to cut through my trousers. The big one would have gone in twice as far. The fact that I had a fairly chubby ass as a young lad probably also helped a bit. Once I got over the shock and started to feel the pain, I jumped up and started to do what probably resembled a Native American rain dance. My brother doubled over in a fit of laughter.

"What's so funny, you little fucker?" I roared.

"You look funny hopping around with a knife sticking out of your ass," he managed to share between gasps of laughter.

"You won't be laughing in a minute," I warned him, "when I pull out this knife and shove it up your ass." It dawned on me, even at that moment, that I sounded exactly like my mother. "Come over here and help me pull it out."

"If I do, will you stick it in me?" he wanted to know.

"Of course not," I assured him.

As I softly tried to remove the knife, it started to hurt worse than any bee sting, which up until that moment had been my marker for extreme pain.

"I'm going to have to pull it out quickly in one shot," I advised him like a surgeon telling his nurse. "In the Wild West they would pour whiskey on it, but we don't have any, so we'll just have to count to three and then pull."

On the count of three, I jerked out the knife blade. As soon as it had come out, I could feel something wet and sticky on the back of my pants. I tenderly inched my hand around behind me, and when I brought it back around, I saw that it was blood.

"Is that blood?" the little eejit asked.

"What else would it be, fucking ketchup?"

I was more annoyed at the site of the blood than afraid for my own safety. Well, in a way, it was all related, as I knew that I would be in for a serious beating altogether if my father found out that I had been cut with a knife. Life with our parents was a constant game of mental chess. You always had to think ahead a few moves to try and undo whatever it was that had the potential to lead to a beating.

"Go you to the car and bring back one of the baby's diapers," I ordered my brother.

"Did you pee yourself as well?" he asked with all sincerity.

I subconsciously started to make a fist with my right hand. I wanted to punch him in the head so badly I could taste it, but I knew that his cries would be the death of me if the old fella came out to investigate.

"No, I did not pee myself," I calmly assured him. "I want to stuff the diaper into the back of my trousers to soak up the blood. Whatever happens, you can't tell anyone," I reminded him. For good measure I added, "If they ever find out you'll really be in for it—remember, it was your knife that cut me."

I could see by the look on his face that it was sinking in. When he was gone, I finally screwed up my face in pain, as there was nobody there to see.

By the time he returned back with the diaper hidden under his coat, I had regained my composure and was leaning against the turf stack whistling like I hadn't a care in the world.

CHAPTER 5
FAT BELLY KELLY

When we first arrived in Donegal, we had no place to live, so we bounced around for a few weeks living with different relatives. The first place we stayed in was a bed-and-breakfast owned by my mother's first cousin in downtown Carndonagh. She had both a woman and a man's first name. Her name was Mary and her husband was called Paul and everyone knew her as; "Mary Paul". The best part of this place was that it was located two doors down from one of the best shops in town.

Back in those days, there were many small family-run shops selling loose sweets and biscuits. The sheer number of sweets, their colored packages stretching on almost infinitely down the counter, was enough to drive you mad with desire and insane with indecision. This is where I learned to become a sweet connoisseur. The "penny sweets" were every child's favorite. You might think that each sweet cost a penny, but you would be incorrect. The big ones such as the "jaw breakers" (huge gobstoppers that literally stopped your gob from being able to talk) cost that much, but the smaller Black Jacks actually came ten to a penny.

My brother and I took full advantage of this Aladdin's treasure trove of all things sweet as often as we could. When my mother's cousin discovered that our father was a chef, she decided it was time to start holding dinner parties. This suited Jimmy and I down to the ground, as the adults were too busy in the evening to keep an eye on us and one of us was always able to scrounge up a penny from somewhere. We lived the good life there for about three or four weeks, until it was time to move on to the next relative—Aunt Sadie, who was Mary Paul's mother and my grandmother's sister.

Big Sadie (as my father christened her) lived out in the countryside, her home surrounded by fields of cows. It was far from penny sweets, but it proved just as adventurous to my brother and me, who ran wild through the fields and ditches, climbing trees and barns from morning 'til night. I couldn't put my finger on it for certain, but I think we were a bit too wild for Aunt Sadie. The adults started to fall out, and it became obvious that we had to find a more permanent place to live.

Poor Sadie wasn't the worst of them. It must have been difficult for an older woman, her family raised and gone, to have three young boys dumped in her lap—and Yanks to boot. As they say in Donegal, she was no spring chicken; after all, she was my grandmother's sister. My father took a dislike to her waning patience in short time, and it wasn't long before we were packing up our belongings and hitting the road once again.

The place that the parents found for us turned out to be very nice digs. We rented half a house on a farm owned by the local veterinarian. It was a two-story house with so much room that the local weatherman and his family lived on the other side. This was to be the nicest house we would live in for many years to come.

As it was early May when we landed in Ireland, our parents figured there was no point in sending us to school before the summer holidays, so we had more than four months off from school that first year. Once we were settled in the new house, my father dropped the bombshell that I was to have a private tutor who would teach me Irish. It was a sound idea to prepare me for school in Ireland, but I didn't realize how inconvenient it would be until the young secondary girl started showing up in the middle of the afternoon to teach me Irish. Her presence totally foiled our plans to have a summer of exploration.

Two things helped me get through those lessons. First, there was the big fella with the size-fourteen shoes who was "paying good money" to see to it that I didn't fall behind in class. Second, they were paying her by the hour, which meant that I only had to feign interest for about sixty minutes before she was satisfied enough to close the books and let me run wild. It was extremely difficult trying to learn Irish that summer. It was nothing like the little phrases that my mother taught us, like "how are you?" and "I'm fine, thank you very much." This time around it involved loads of vocabulary, verbs, and the hardest friggin' spelling imaginable. Nothing sounded like it looked.

Apparently, though, I became quite good at mimicking my tutor. I was not only praised by her for sounding like a native Irish speaker, but the teacher at our new school used to single me out to read and show up the other boys at how well I could pronounce even the most difficult words. Of course, that went down like a ton of bricks, and I soon learned what my classmates thought of my talents. On one of the first lunch breaks after the teacher used me as a "shining example," I headed out to the yard to eat my sandwich. Within minutes, a ring of boys from fourth class surrounded me. One of them pushed his face six inches in front of mine and hissed, "So you think you're better than us, do ya, Yank?" Before I could reply, another one from behind hit me along the side of my head. I jerked around quickly to identify the culprit.

"You don't have fuckin' much to say now for yourself, do ya, Yank?" snarled the ring leader as he pushed me backwards. Someone else held out their leg so that I tripped back and fell.

Whatever was left of my sandwich went flying out of my hand as I tried to cushion the fall. It wouldn't have done me any good to hold on to it anyway, as the ring drew in closer and I had to use my hands to cover my head from the blows that poured down onto me. Within seconds, the gang worked itself into a frenzy, kicking and punching me wherever they could find a spot. It seemed to last for ages, but it was probably only a few minutes before one of the bigger boys from of the headmaster's class came over and pulled them off me.

"Are you all right, lad?" he asked as if he were genuinely concerned. I nodded, since I didn't feel like saying much. My lip felt like it was getting thick and I could taste blood inside my mouth.

"Don't mind them eejits," he consoled me. "We don't get many Americans around here. They'll be all right once they get to know you." I wondered how long it took people to get to know you in this school. I went in to the toilets and washed myself up so that the teacher would not notice the damage. I think the ringleader must have been worried that he would get into trouble if it was discovered that he had beaten the new boy, so he sent in one of his posse to give me a warning.

"Liam says if you breathe a word about what happened out there to a teacher, he'll fuckin' kill ya."

I stopped throwing water on my face and turned to look at the messenger. He was a watery-eyed looking wee boy, with buck teeth and a skinny face covered in freckles. I knew I could beat the shite out of him with no problem and part of me wanted to do just that. I felt like telling him that their beating was nothing compared to the beating I got from my old fella. All of their feet put together could not compare to his size-fourteen brogues. I moved closer in to him and felt like saying, "You haven't been stomped on 'till you've been kicked by my old fella." I actually felt a grin break across my face in a kind of sadistic pride at how violent my family life could be. I saw the look of terror on the skinny boy's face as he belted out of the bathroom; it must have been something I was thinking.

The end-of-lunch bell sounded shortly afterward, and as I returned to my seat, burying my head in my books, I could feel multiple sets of eyes on me wondering if I was going to tell. I looked across the room and stared down the skinny boy, whose eyes were now bulging out like his teeth. He quickly looked away as soon as he realized I had fixed my gaze on him. I didn't realize it at the time, but that was only the first of many fights I was to have in that schoolyard. I also didn't realize that I had earned my first stripe.

There was one thing I found out over the following months— it took those boys a long time to get to know you. Fighting seemed to be the only method of blending in, although there was little hope for a young American boy trying to blend in back in Donegal in the 1960s anyway. We were as alien to those locals as if we had come down from Mars. My brother was quite young, and while he did have his fair share of trouble, he was spared the cruelty that came with being in the senior classes. I started off in fourth class in the Boys Catholic Primary School in Carndonagh. My brother got to start in high infants, so he only missed the first official year of school. I missed the first five years; that was the problem.

Everybody else who was in fourth class had known one another since they were four or five years of age. I had to take a crash course—"crash" being the operative word. It dawned on me that, if I was to survive those early years, I was going to have to form alliances. There was bound to be safety in numbers. A 6-year-old brother would be of no use, so I started to look around to see what choices I had. I was highly unpopular, so I couldn't expect to be accepted by the popular set. The way I saw it, I had no choice but to throw my lot in with other renegades like myself. The best option would be to connect with the McLaughlin brothers. Well, their proper family name was McLaughlin, but everybody knew them by their nickname, "the Ducks."

Donegal, even more so than any other place in Ireland, has always been famous for nicknames. Up north, the majority of family surnames were either Doherty or McLaughlin. Of course every second, third, and fourth boy was called Patrick, Michael, James, or John, so it didn't take long for the country to become saturated with similar names. The only way to keep track was to give families nicknames. It was often a grandfather or great-grandfather's occupation that decided the nickname.

In the case of "the Ducks," the McLaughlin grandfather used to buy and sell ducks at Carndonagh livestock mart. The father of the boys we attended school with had fifteen brothers and four sisters. The men were all as mad as March hares, and were continually getting into fights and getting arrested by the Police on both sides of the border. As a result, although they had initially become known as "the Ducks," by the time three generations had passed, they were commonly referred to as "the Wild Ducks."

I quickly became familiar with the reputation of Seamus the Duck and Paddy the Duck. They were the two closest in age to me. It seemed that they did not discriminate when it came to fighting. They'd fight with anybody; they were truly their father's sons (and uncle's nephews). We met by way of a fight after school, when I squared off against Seamus, the eldest. Whatever grievance we had was not worth fighting over, but I knew that the fight was a chance to forge a relationship and get two allies into my camp for the price of one. After fifteen or twenty minutes of scrapping, Seamus and I knew we had both given as good as we had gotten, but neither of us would admit defeat. We agreed on a truce, and it was that truce which led to a coming-together of the two families.

Once we started to back each other up in the schoolyard, the number of fights others picked with us slowly started to dwindle.

The Ducks were not the biggest boys in the yard—they were all actually quite small—but they were wiry little bastards, and no matter how many times they were knocked down, they'd keep getting up for more. A lot of boys thought they were mad in the head and were afraid to go up against them.

The same could not be said for Fat-Belly Kelly, however. Mickey "Fat-Belly" Kelly was the biggest boy in school. Even though he was only in 6th class and had a full year until Secondary, he was the size of a man. His hands were like bear paws, and when he'd reach out to slap you, it felt like you were being hit by your father. We thought he was a freak of nature, but looking back, I really believe that he must have been held back several years for being thick or retarded—maybe a bit of both. Instead of being 12 years old in 6th grade, he was probably 16.

Unfortunately, Fat-Belly took a dislike to me. As I walked home from school one afternoon, he came up behind me and pelted me square in the back of the head, at close range, with half of an apple. He walked past, laughing his arse off and showing off to his friends. I felt the tears of pain well up in my eyes, but I fought them back so his friends wouldn't think I was weak.

When I got home, I made the grave mistake of telling my parents. I must have thought they would take pity on me.

"He's only a bully," my father proclaimed. "I've seen his type before." *Yes, every time you look into a mirror,* I thought to myself.

"What you want to do is go up to that bully and punch his lights out—that'll teach him a lesson," he continued. *Punch his lights out?* Would you tell your son to go up to a bull and *punch his lights out?*

"I want you to come home tomorrow and tell me you taught him a lesson."

That night, I played out the scenario in my head: I would saunter up to this man masquerading as a boy and punch him out. Try as I might, though, I could not imagine him stretched out on the ground after I had administered the knockout punch. However, that was the way my father told me it had to happen, and if there was one thing he knew, it was how to inflict pain and suffering. The next day I couldn't think of anything other than how I was going to manage to reach up to Kelly to punch him in the face. After all, I barely reached his shoulder. I even thought of jumping off the wall at the end of the school walk onto his back and hanging off his shoulders as I punched him from both sides. I knew that if I was going to survive that day, I had to use the element of surprise and hit him like I'd never hit anybody before.

The only ones I let in on my plan were Seamus and Paddy the Duck.

"Are you fuckin' mental?" Seamus asked me, with a terrified look on his face. His reaction did not provide the boost of confidence that I needed.

"The Guards will be scraping what little there will be left of you off the footpath this evening," Paddy chimed in.

"I think it can be done," I half-convincingly offered. "Our old fella says I need to teach him a lesson."

"Sure, Kelly the fucker is nearly as big as your old fella," Seamus reminded me. "Fat-Belly is going to eat you alive. Can I have your football cards?"

I was sorry I mentioned it to them at all. I was starting to think they were right. Nobody in their right mind would go up against Kelly unless they had a hammer in their hand and he was tied securely to a chair. Even then, I could imagine him gnawing his way through the rope, or bursting it into frayed strings by the sheer force of his immense bulk. The best I could do was to get the two Ducks to agree to walk alongside me after school as I made my big move on Kelly. I had to promise them half of my football card collection to get them to do so.

After the school bell rang for the last time that day, I hung off to one side and waited for the big boys to go out. In a few minutes, Kelly came sauntering out with his school bag flung over one shoulder, half of his shirt pulled out from his trousers and his arms swinging by his side. I could almost swear that his knuckles were dragging on the footpath. I took a deep breath and made my way slowly behind him. The Ducks were walking behind me with my brother. As we drew closer to the front of the school wall, I called out, "Hey, Kelly."

Kelly turned around and looked at me in disbelief. "What do you want, Yank?"

"I know it was you who pelted me with that apple yesterday," I blurted out.

"And what are you going to do about it, Yankee Doodle? Did you bring those wee mallards with you to be your bodyguards?"

One thing I *wasn't* going to do was to stand there and talk it over; I decided it was as good a time as any to make my move. I made a lunge for him. I figured I might be able to punch him in the belly, and if he bent over from that, I could punch him in the face. Hopefully then it would be lights out.

Unfortunately, Kelly had no intention of going along with my plan. He simply stepped to one side as I came forward to deliver my punch. Without having anything to connect with, my momentum started to carry me forward, but not before Kelly added to my grief by crashing one of his big ham fists down on the back of my head. The result was not pretty. I traveled about five feet forward and had my faced knocked into the dirt. Fat-Belly laughed so hard that he had to bend over.

"You know what, Yank, you look like a duck trying to fly in the mud...you need to stop spending so much time with those wee mallards."

Thankfully, the Ducks were standing by to help me to my feet. My legs felt like jelly, and I couldn't have stood on my own had they not each taken an arm and steadied me. I tried to look straight ahead, but everything was dancing around and making me feel dizzy.

"Not many have challenged Fat-Belly and lived to tell about it," Seamus told me excitedly.

"Am I alive?" I asked him.

"Sort of," came the reply. I looked at my brother.

"Don't breathe a word of this at home," I ordered.

The one good thing about getting hit in the back of the head, I figured, was the fact that my hair could hide the damage. If he had hit me in the face, I would have looked like a dog's dinner. We walked halfway home before we spotted the blue Morris Minor approaching. It pulled over and the passenger door opened.

"Well, did you teach the bully a lesson?"

"I did," I lied.

"I knew it," he said. "Bastards like that are all the same—just a lot of talk."

CHAPTER 6

GLASS EATING GRANDFATHER

As a young boy, I was not capable of figuring out my father. In all fairness, I don't think the task became any easier as I approached puberty, or even manhood, for that matter. I daresay there was never anyone who could figure him out; maybe not even himself. Later in life, I often wondered if he had ever undergone any type of psychological examination. I could imagine the psychologist or psychiatrist tearing their hair out trying to understand what made him tick. When my mind really got carried away, I'd imagine them using him as a medical experiment—strapping all kinds of electrodes to his head and chest and trying to make sense of the helter-skelter graphical lines that the machines spat out. There was no middle ground, no "grey area" with him: he was either brilliant or brutal. The Big Yank was truly unique.

My grandfather, Danny Houton, was also unique. Actually, "unique" is putting it too mildly; Danny Houton was a crazy bastard. One of his old friends once summed him up to me perfectly: "Your grandfather is one mad hoor." Danny Houton got married when he was sixteen and had fathered five children by his early twenties. He was supposed to have been the one to inherit the family farm in Malin Head, but his mother kicked him and his family out into the street after an argument and gave the farm to his older sister. With no place to live and no means of support, he decided to head to Scotland, where a lot of Donegal men went to work on farms, in forests, and the like.

The Houtons remained in Scotland for a number of years. The two eldest daughters, my mother and her sister Annie, became nurses, and when my grandfather decided to move to America, the entire family followed him and settled down in the Bronx. I don't remember seeing much of my grandfather. Although he and my grandmother had never divorced, they lived separately.

The summer we moved to Ireland was the first time we got to spend any time with Grandfather. He would have been around sixty years of age back then. He came over often to visit, and he always wore a black suit and tie with a white dress shirt when he went into Carndonagh to meet up with his old cronies.

We didn't see much of him, since he would head off early in the morning before we were awake. I remember the first time that my mother sent our father out to bring him back. My father came in from work in the evening, after working in the canteen in Buncrana all day, and found my mother upset. Thankfully, we were not to blame, and did not have to live in fear of a beating from either of them. She was complaining about how dinner was ready and would be ruined unless he could bring home our grandfather.

My father said he'd go into Carndonagh and bring him back out. He asked Jimmy and I if we wanted to go into town with him. We jumped at the chance, as we didn't get to see much of Grandfather. Neither our father nor mother drank alcohol, so we had not much of an idea what it was. Apparently, though, my father knew his own father-in-law, and started his search for him at the first pub we came to from the Moville Road.

The three of us went in together and my father asked the man behind the bar if he had seen Danny Houton.

"Oh aye," the man replied, "Danny was in here earlier, but he left a good while ago and said he was headed to the Persian Bar." My father thanked him and we got into the car and drove to the Persian. He same question was posed to the barman at the Persian.

He replied: "Danny was here before all right, but he and his cousin Packie left to Dever's."

We must have gone into another ten pubs over the next two hours. The same story was repeated in each one: Danny Houton had been there, but had left for yet another pub before we arrived. Finally, through the process of elimination, we hit pay dirt in the bar of the Carn Hotel, the pub that he had not yet left. It was nearly 9:00 pm when we came upon our long-lost grandfather standing on a table in the middle of the hotel bar, singing a rebel song. A group of people stood around him. Every once in a while, when he stopped to catch a breath, one of the onlookers would say "good man, Danny."

As soon as he saw us, our grandfather stopped singing momentarily and shouted to my father: "Buy those wains a drink!"

My brother and I were as proud as punch when my father asked us what we wanted to drink. We both opted for a bottle of Coke and a packet of cheese and onion crisps.

We had no sooner received our drinks, however, when our grandfather stopped singing, grabbed his chest, and wheezed, "Heart attack!" With that, he fell face forward and crashed down on the people standing around him. A woman screamed, "Call an ambulance!"

As they rushed to loosen his tie and make him comfortable, my grandfather jumped up on his feet and roared with laughter. "Jesus Christ, you don't think I'm going to die yet?" he asked them with a huge grin.

The woman, still holding her own chest, said, "Oh God, Danny, you're a fierce joker!" About two hours later (and another two bottles of Coke each), we finally managed to get our grandfather into the car and headed home.

"You boys better head straight for bed," my father warned us. "If your mother is still up, she's not going to be very happy to see us."

Grandfather looked over his shoulder with squinted eyes. "Are youns not coming in for a drink, lads?"

My brother and I looked at each other. "We live here, Grandfather," my brother reminded him.

Grandfather looked around, confused. "Ah, so you do. Well, I'm having a wee Powers myself." He had the door of the Morris opened before it had come to a complete stop.

"Sarah will fix you a bite of dinner, Danny," my father told him.

"No need," our grandfather replied. "I've got my dinner here in my pocket." With that, he pulled a fistful of something out of his pocket and yanked off a piece with his teeth. He walked toward the back door of the house singing "McAlpine's Fusiliers."

"Is he eating sweets?" my brother asked as we climbed out from the back of the Morris Minor.

"No, that's dulsce," my father replied.

"What's dulsce? Is it sweet?" My brother was a candy addict.

"No, it's salty. It's seaweed," my father informed him. "People gather it from the rocks by the sea at low tide and they take it home and dry it out."

"Yuck."

By the time the three of us had made it into the house, our grandfather was standing at the kitchen table pouring yellow stuff into a glass from a bottle with a gold label. "What's that stuff?" my inquisitive brother asked.

"This," my grandfather replied, raising the glass up in front of him so that the bright light from the kitchen bulb shone through and the contents of the glass sparkled like gold, "is uisce beatha—the water of life. God made Heaven and Earth, but the Irish make the best whiskey." At that very moment, my mother walked into the kitchen. She didn't look happy to hear that sermon.

"This is a fine time of night to be coming home after being out drinking all day," she said to no one in particular.

Adults were strange. If we came in an hour late home from school because we stopped to eat blackberries, we'd get yelled at, but when they got home late, she thought the time was fine.

"Why is it a fine time?" I asked, only half-aware that I had said it out loud. I looked over at my grandfather, who had a cheeky grin on his face as he put the glass up to his mouth to have a drink.

"What are you two still doing up?" came her reply. "Get up those stairs at once." We didn't have to be told twice. As we slunk out of the kitchen, our grandfather called out after us, "Good night, men."

"Did you hear that?" my brother whispered. "He thinks we're men."

"Don't be so thick. He knows well we're not men. He's just pulling our leg." The Cokes we had knocked back earlier had us still half-full of sugar, making it difficult to think of sleep.

"Let's sit here on the stairs," I instructed my partner in crime, "and listen to what they're saying."

"But mommy told us to get up those stairs," came the voice of reason.

"Where did we just go?" I asked him.

"Here."

"And where's here?"

"On the stairs."

"Where are you sitting?" I continued the interrogation.

"On my arse."

"And where's is your arse plonked down?"

"On the stairs."

"So, we were told to 'get up those stairs,' and that is just what we did. We are 'up' and on those stairs. We're doing what we were told to do. Now shut up before you get us into trouble."

In the kitchen we could hear our grandfather mumbling. He seemed to be singing a song. We heard pots rattling as our mother fixed him dinner. Then her voice got louder, and she was nearly yelling at our grandfather about his drinking and how she was afraid that something had happened to him and that he was lying hurt in Carndonagh hospital.

"Is she giving out?" my brother asked.

"Sounds like it."

"If we gave out to our daddy, he'd kill us. Is her daddy going to kill her?"

"I don't think he'd be able," I told him. "She's as tough as nails."

I decided that we shouldn't push our luck any further or grandfather wouldn't be the only one getting yelled at. We headed up the stairs and got into bed. The Coke was still running through my veins as I lay there wondering how any person could eat salty seaweed. I figured it was the dulsce that made Grandfather drink the Powers. I decided that I would get up early, sneak into his coat pocket, and eat some of it. It seemed like a long time later that our mother and father came into the room to make sure we had gone to bed. I made believe I was asleep, even though I was wide awake.

"Did you see that crazy old man eating the glass?" my mother asked my father in a low tone.

"How could I not?" replied my father. "After he finished his whiskey, he bit a chunk out of the glass like he was eating an apple. How could he eat glass like that without cutting his mouth wide open? Was he ever in the circus?"

"He can do it because he's Crazy Houton," she told him. "Don't say anything about it—just act like it's perfectly normal. If you make a big deal out of it, he'll only go and do something worse to see your reaction."

"I don't know what could be worse," mumbled my father as they turned from the room and headed back downstairs.

They must have been doing the strange adult talk again. There was no way that our grandfather was down there eating my mother's crystal like some kind of crazy werewolf. The next morning I was up bright and early, slipping downstairs to try and rummage through my grandfather's pockets. I was concentrating so hard on the treasure hunt that I didn't realize someone was behind me.

"How's the head, young fella?" asked our grandfather.

I searched around my brain, but couldn't recall what had happened to my head...unless he had heard about Fat-Belly Kelly. I didn't think it was possible, but then again, it was starting to seem that anything could be possible with Danny Houton. He saw the confused look on my face.

"I was wondering if you had a sore head this morning. You drank a brave sup of whiskey last night," he said, pointing at the bottle he had been drinking from the night before.

Before I could say anything in my defense, he picked up a brown bottle and bit the top right off. He handed me the top of the bottle as he swigged from it.

"Never been to a dentist in my life," he proudly announced, bending down to me and flashing a mouthful of teeth.

The conversation my parents had had the night before came back to me. *Jesus, he really does eat glass.* I wondered what kind of blood I had in me. On one hand, I had a father who, if he wasn't beating me himself, was encouraging me to get hammered by the school giant. On the other hand, my mother's father liked to eat glass and bite the tops off bottles.

I had heard that the Ducks' grandfather had a glass eye. I prayed that if my grandfather ever met him that he wouldn't try to eat the glass eye. It would be hard to stay friends with them if that happened.

"What are you up to today?" he asked me.

I couldn't tell him that my only plan was to look around in his pockets, so I just shrugged.

"Would you like to learn to smoke a pipe?" he asked, as casual as you'd say to a cat, "Can I get you a saucer of milk?"

I couldn't believe my ears, and was about to jump at the offer, but it occurred to me that it could be a trap. I quickly weighed up the situation at hand. He may have been put up to it by my mother to see if we would do something as mental as smoking a pipe, but then again, he was Crazy Houton. He *did* make believe he was having heart attacks, and he *did* like to eat people's drinking glasses.

"Should we bring my brother?" I asked him.

"You may as well," he replied. "Sure, he's going to have to learn how to do it sooner or later."

It didn't strike him as the least bit odd that a 9-year-old and 6-year-old should be getting ready to smoke pipes before their breakfast. I ran up the stairs, quickly but stealthily. My father had already left for work, but if our mother woke up and found out what we were planning, she would blame everything on me. My chances of making it to my 10th birthday in that case would be very slim, despite the fact that it wasn't very far away.

I shook my brother awake and put my hand over his mouth. His eyes started to bulge and dart back and forth. It must have been out of fear, since his oxygen couldn't be running out *that* quickly.

"Get up, but don't say a word," I mouthed to him.

I crept back downstairs. My grandfather had laid two pipes on the kitchen table, and was taking tobacco out of a pouch and putting it into a little sweet can. There was nothing to connect me to this so far, which made me happy since my mother had a way of just appearing out of nowhere like a spirit. *Father, Son, Holy Ghost...and Sadie.*

"When the wain comes down, we'll head out to the shed and light up," my grandfather announced.

A couple of minutes later, the wain came tiptoeing down. He could follow orders when he put his mind to it. The three of us headed out to the turf shed behind the house. My grandfather had a lovely crooked stem pipe carved out of shiny brown wood with a metal ring in the middle. He handed me a yellow pipe that he called a "corn cob," and gave my brother a white clay pipe like the men used to smoke in Ireland during the famine when everybody died from eating bad potatoes.

"This is how you fill your pipe with tobacco," he instructed us, pushing the pipe into the pouch and scooping up the tobacco. "When you grab a good scoop full into the bowl, you pull it out and tap down the tobacco with your thumb."

We watched the master, and then took turns at scooping and tapping. We must have done a good enough job, since he told us it was time to light the pipes. We watched like hawks as he struck the wooden match along the side of the box and let the flame hover just above the bowl. The he started sucking on the pipe until his cheeks looked like they were going to meet on the inside. Within two seconds, he was pushing big clouds of smoke out of the side of his mouth, and the tobacco in the bowl started glowing red. He grabbed the end of the pipe between those teeth that had never seen a dentist and handed me the matches.

"Fire away," he said with a nod of his head.

I had no idea how it would turn out, but there was no backing down at this stage. I did what he did, and soon I too was sucking in and blowing out smoke.

"Remember not to breathe in the smoke," he advised.

There was more to pipe-smoking then I thought. I passed the matches to Jimmy as I tried to hold the pipe between my teeth, but it was too heavy so I had to hold the bowl with my left hand. Jimmy was scared to light the match and bring it close to his face, so our grandfather volunteered to help.

"You concentrate on holding the pipe and sucking. I'll light it for you," the pipe master told Jimmy. "Just remember to blow out the smoke and don't breathe it in."

My brother closed his eyes as the match came over the bowl and started sucking once he heard the command "Suck!" Small clouds of smoke started to come out of his mouth, and I was just about to congratulate him when he jerked back, yelled, and started to cough and splutter. The pipe fell to the ground, spilling hot tobacco on the turf mole on the ground.

"It's burning, it's burning," he began yelling, choking at the same time.

In between gasps and coughs, he flailed his arms, as if the circulated air would clear the smoke. Well, it might have done if I hadn't been standing next to him blowing my smoke in his face. I didn't do it intentionally, mind, but there wasn't that much room in the wee shed, as it was nearly full of turf. I don't know whether it was my smoke or the stuff he swallowed. He pushed past us toward the half-opened door.

"Where are ya going now?" our grandfather asked in a rough whisper.

"I need a drink, I need a drink," he shot back, feeling his way out, as his eyes were still closed.

Grandfather looked worried. "Hold your whisht and come back in here a minute," he told him. My brother was rubbing his eyes, but he stopped trying to escape.

"I have a bag of Licorice Allsorts in my pocket," our grandfather informed him.

My brother perked up right away. Telling him you'd be back with a bag of sweets was like telling a heroin addict you'd return with a syringe. "Wait here 'til I go get them." As an afterthought he added, "No smoking 'till I get back."

"Can't I not even smoke?" I asked him.

"You're all right. Just be careful not to set fire to the turf."

After he left, I made a seat for myself out of the turf and sat down to better enjoy my smoke. Truth be told, I didn't find smoking all that enjoyable. You had to keep sucking on the pipe so that it wouldn't go out. The more you sucked, the hotter your mouth got. The hotter your mouth got, the more you had to spit. It was basically all about sucking, blowing, and spitting. I figured that was the price you had to pay to be a man.

"Do you like pipe smoking?" my brother asked. I took the pipe out of my mouth and held it in front of me as I pondered his question. It's not that I had to think too deeply about the question, but I knew that holding a pipe as you appeared to be thinking was a great look.

"Indeed I do."

"Does it not burn your mouth?"

It did, but I wouldn't admit it to the little bastard.

"It doesn't if you do it right," I replied, pulling out the pipe to eject a burning-hot spittle.

Our grandfather pushed the door in. He had his pipe in his left hand and a small white bag in the right. I bit down harder on the pipe when I realized that I could have grabbed a handful of those sweets if only I had had a few more seconds to go through his pockets.

Licorice Allsorts were not just sweets. They were *magical* sweets. Some of them were solid black licorice, while others were formed into licorice pipes filled with a sweet white icing. Still others were pink and blue, round and squishy. Those ones rolled around between your teeth as you bit down on them, as if they were trying to get away from being eaten. My favorites, though, were the wee square stacked ones. They had a tan or yellow layer on top, a flat layer of black licorice under that, then a sweet white soft layer, followed by another tan or yellow square. They were just like a licorice sandwich.

"Have a sweetie," our grandfather said, holding the bag out in front of my brother, whose eyes grew larger (though not as big as when I had had my hand over his mouth). He stuck his hand in and fished around as if he was looking for the perfect specimen. When he had chosen, our grandfather bent down, picked up the cooled-down clay pipe, and handed it back to him. He then turned to me with the bag.

"Will you have one yourself?"

"Ah, no," I replied, "save them for the wain." It was painful not to reach in and pull out a handful, but I was a man now, and Irish men did not sit around smoking pipes and eating sweets.

"You may as well have them all," Grandfather said, handing the remaining contents of the bag to my brother.

You jammy wee bastard, I thought to myself. *Now I'm going to have to come up with a plan to get my hands on those sweets.* A big smile broke out on my brother's face. He looked odd, I thought to myself, standing there holding a bag of sweets in one hand and clay pipe in the other.

"All right, men. When you don't have tobacco for your pipe, you can always use this," said Grandfather, bending over and picking up a handful of turf mole.

"Turf mole?" I asked. It didn't seem right that you could smoke turf mole.

"Well, you can hardly ask Sadie or John to buy you more tobacco for your pipe, can you?"

He had a good point there.

"Better than the turf mole, though, is tea." Back then, everybody in Ireland drank loose tea. Only the very well-off, or people who were trying to be fancy, used tea bags.

"Which is the best," I asked him, "tea or turf mole?"

"Definitely the tea," he replied without hesitation, "but when we were young, we didn't always have tea. There was never any shortage of turf mole."

"You pour tea into your pipe?" asked my half-wit brother, a big black licorice stain forming around his mouth. Our grandfather laughed.

"No son, it's not wet tea. It's dry tea that's in the tea-box. Same thing with the turf mole—it's got to be fierce dry. With the tea and the turf mole, you have to rub them until they get very fine before filling your pipe. Then make sure to pack it down tight. They'll burn up fast if they're not packed well."

I was very happy that our grandfather was taking time out from visiting his friends to each us how to smoke and what to do when your tobacco ran out. Our father never taught us these things; they must be the type of things that only grandfathers teach their grandchildren in Ireland, I thought.

"J.P.! Jimmy!" Our mother was calling out the back door for us.

"Hide those fecking pipes," our grandfather whispered. "She'll have our guts for garters if she ever finds out I had youns out here smoking."

Maybe it wasn't something that grandfathers regularly taught their grandchildren after all.

"We're in here, Mommy," called Jimmy.

"Don't breathe a word," our grandfather reminded us. "If she asks what we were doing, tell her we were looking for worms for fishing." He grabbed a sweet from the bag and stuck it into my mouth so fast that I couldn't even see what kind it was.

"We're going fishing?" asked my brother with a wide grin.

"We are now," said Grandfather. The three of us walked over to the back of the house, where our mother was standing holding the baby brother.

"What's that on your face?" she asked the licorice-licker.

"Sweeties," came his reply.

"What are you doing eating sweets at this hour of the morning?" She was asking Jimmy, but the question was clearly directed toward our grandfather. *You wouldn't be half as annoyed with him eating sweets if you knew that five minutes ago he was choking on a clay pipe,* I thought to myself.

"Ah, it's just a few sweeties I had in my pocket, Sadie," sighed Grandfather as we walked past her and into the kitchen.

"Where did all the smoke come from?" she retorted.

"I was just having a wee puff before breakfast," he replied innocently.

"Sit youns down so and I'll fix the breakfast," she told us as she held baby Kevin in one arm and reached out with the other to fill the kettle with water. She looked over her shoulder at our grandfather and asked, "Will you be headed into town?"

"No," replied Jimmy before Grandfather had a chance to say anything. "We're going fishing."

CHAPTER 7

THE POPE AND J.F.K

My grandfather wasn't one to let the grass grow under his feet for very long. About a fortnight after he provided us with pipes and lessons on alternative smoking fuels, he was gone back to America. He wanted to come home to Ireland to retire for good, they said, but he had to work a bit longer in America before he could get his Social Security pay. We looked forward to seeing him again, as he was bound to have many more grown-up things to teach us.

As I've mentioned, nobody we knew had a telephone back then, but news travelled fast all the same. Once word got out that the two little Yankee boys had pipes, we started getting visits from lads from around the area. At first, we were the only ones to have pipes, and that made us feel like kings. We didn't even light them. We just kept them in our pockets, and every once in a while we'd stick them in our mouths like it was the most natural thing in the world. One day, though, Terrence Logue pulled out a pipe and stuck it in his gob as we were choosing sides for a kick-around football match.

This was an awful shock; we weren't willing to share the kingdom. Then, before the two sides had been chosen, another wee boy that everybody called Tinker sat down on the football he had brought with him. He fished around in his pocket, pulled out a shiny brown crooked-stem pipe, and popped it in his cakehole. This changed the dynamics of the game instantly.

"All right, then," ordered the Logue lad, "never mind those other two sides. It'll now be the pipe-smokers against the rest. Me, Tinker, and the two Yanks will take on the rest of youns."

I was surprised that my brother was even allowed to play. He was usually the youngest and nobody ever wanted him. He seemed to have a different status now that he was a pipe-smoker. We kicked the football around for about a half hour, and then during the halftime break, Logue announced that he was "dyin' for a smoke." He had brought matches, but none of us had any tobacco.

"We have shop tobacco back at the house," I volunteered. Everyone turned to stare at me. Logue's jaw hung open. The pipe fell out of his mouth, but he caught it in midair.

"Can you go get it?" he asked, wide-eyed.

"No bother," I assured him, wondering how I would make it out of the house without getting caught with the contraband or if I'd even be allowed back out again.

Then it hit me. If I made my brother stay behind, our mother would have to release me so that I could go get him and bring him back home.

"You stay here, young fella," I instructed my brother with all of the authority I could muster, "while I go back and get some tobacco for the lads."

I ran back to the house as fast as my legs could carry me, heart pounding in my chest. My plan was to try and avoid my mother seeing me at all, since I had hidden Grandfather's pouch of tobacco in the turf shed behind a loose wall stone. I crept inside and was wriggling the stone frantically from the wall when the door swung open.

"Jesus, what are you doing in here?" my mother seemed more startled than angry. I had not banked on getting caught, though, and I could not think of even a half-intelligent excuse that might be acceptable.

"Let me help you fill the turf bucket," I offered in an attempt to buy me enough time to cook up something believable.

"Where's your brother?"

"He's over by the shed."

"You didn't leave him alone, did you?" I could sense a flying fist was not too far away, unless I came up with something to save my skin.

"Ah no, he's with Tinker. We're, uh, playing hide-and-seek… and they're counting. I was going to hide in here." This actually seemed to work. As she bent down with the baby brother under her left arm, topping off the bucket with sods of turf with her free hand, she nodded.

"Well, don't wander off too far from your brother," she warned me. "He might fall into a well or a ditch. And don't youns be running all over the countryside. Your dinner will be ready in about an hour."

She picked up the bucket and walked out of the shed. I knew I had just had a close call. I wriggled the stone out as fast as I could, pulled out the pouch, stuffed it into my pocket, and jammed the stone back into the wall. I considered leaving the stone out to save time, but that might give away my hiding spot, and it was too good to lose. I darted out of the shed and raced back to the lads, feeling like a king again as I pulled out the tobacco pouch and told them to line up for a "fill." Logue was first in line, of course, and he pulled a good pinch of shredded tobacco out of the pouch between his fingers and stuffed it into the bowl of the pipe with his thumb.

"Have you smoked before?" I asked him.

"Been smoking for years," came the reply.

Tinker took only a little pinch, and by the look on his face, it was probably his first time. My brother didn't want to take any, so I nodded to him that it was all right to sit this one out. I was the last to fill my pipe, and waited for Logue to be done with the matches. For a man who had been smoking "for years," he was not making much headway with getting lit up. He had easily burned through half a dozen matches from the time I started watching him. I figured that he had packed in the tobacco too tight and as a result couldn't get it to light. Grandfather had told us not to squash it in, but to gently tap it.

Finally, a little trickle of smoke wafted up from his pipe, and I reached out for the box of matches. "There's only two matches left," I muttered to myself. Meanwhile, Logue was sucking on his pipe for all he was worth. At his feet lay the remnants of at least a dozen spent matches. I took one out, struck it on the side of the box and sucked in 'til my cheeks nearly touched together. After about four sucks, I was coolly exhaling more smoke than Logue could muster after nearly ten minutes. I passed the last match in the box to wee Tinker.

"Make it count," I warned him. "There's no more."

The poor lad wasn't that much younger than me, but he *was* younger—probably around seven or eight. He obviously didn't have much experience, and was a bit shaky as he took the match from the box. He could have done with a grandfather like we had. The match went out when he was on his first suck. I turned to Logue.

"What will we do now?"

"Did the Tinker get lit up?" he asked, focused on his puffing.

"It went out," replied Tinker with a sad look on his face.

"I know what we'll do," announced Logue. "We'll go on over to old Bridey's house. She'll have matches."

Old Bridey lived in a thatch house over the lane from where we lived. Everybody knew her. She looked like she must have been 100 years old. As my grandfather would say, "She looked like she'd been around since Christ was a carpenter."

Logue and I led the posse to Bridey's. He was puffing out big clouds of smoke and I was doing the same. To keep them lit, we had to constantly suck on our pipes. After a while, my mouth started to get very hot, and I had to keep spitting. I took a break, and by the time we reached Bridey's house all the pipes had gone out. Her door was open, and Logue called out her name as he knocked on the door.

"Hello, boys," Bridey greeted us as she came up from the lower room.

"Hello, Bridey," Logue replied. "Would you have any matches for us to light our pipes?"

After he asked her for matches, he put his pipe into his mouth. Now Logue was the eldest of the bunch and definitely the biggest, but Tinker and I were, by most people's standards, too bloody young to be smoking men's tobacco pipes. This did not seem to bother Bridey in the least.

"Sure, there's no need for matches as I have the fire lit," she said as she waved us all in and made for the open fireplace.

This was the first time I had seen a thatch cottage open fire. It was huge. If it wasn't lit, I could have easily stood up inside it and looked out at the boys without bending down.

"And who are these boys, then?" Bridey asked Logue, pointing at myself and my brother.

"Thems are the Yanks that moved into the vet's house in Fodden," Logue replied.

Bridey started to smile. "Do you know who that is up there?" she asked us, pointing to a picture of a smiling man dressed in a suit that was perched on a ledge atop the fireplace. Next to that was a picture of a man in a white dress and cap. I shook my head; I wasn't sure if I had ever seen them before.

"On top of the mantel, there is your President, John Fitzgerald Kennedy. And next to him is the Pope." She didn't have any other pictures, so these men were either related to her, or she was fierce fond of them altogether.

"Matches, Bridey," Logue reminded her.

"You don't need matches," she told him, tearing off long strips of a newspaper that was folded up by the side of the fireplace.

She gave myself, Logue and Tinker a strip each and told us to twist them before sticking them into the open fireplace. I had no bloody idea how this operation was going to work, as I had only seen Eugene Friel do it one time before and he nearly set a witch on fire back then. I waited for Logue to lead the way. He twisted the paper around and around until it looked stiff. Next he stuck the end into the open fire. When the paper started to burn, he pulled it out, stuck the burning end into his pipe and sucked and puffed. Within seconds he was smoking like a train, and he tossed the still-burning paper back into the open fire.

I was next up to twist my chunk of newspaper and light the torch. It didn't look too hard; at least Logue made it look fairly easy. I bit down hard on the stem of the pipe and thrust my hand into the fire. My arms were shorter than Logue's, so I had to step in closer to the flame. Had I looked up, I would have noticed that I was actually standing fairly much inside the fireplace. What I noticed, quickly, was how fast my paper torch had started to burn. Logue was able to relax, suck a bit, and then puff a bit before throwing away his burning paper. By the time I had pulled mine out to start lighting my pipe, half of the paper was burning. I pulled it up to my face and stuck it into my pipe as best I could. I started to suck on the flame, but it had started growing and climbing, charging toward my face.

I was so fixated on the flame, which seemed intent on baking my eyeballs, that I only barely realized that the others were shouting and waving their arms. When the flame reached my fingers, I instinctively dropped what was left of the newspaper. By this time, everyone was shouting and pointing. At first, I thought they were happy for me having lit my pipe like this for the first time. Then I noticed that they were pointing above my head. I looked up to see that the mantel was on fire. I had not noticed, as I focused on my pipe, that the flame from the paper had grown high enough to light the framed photos on the mantel.

"Get out before the house comes crashing down on top of us," Logue shouted at me.

The younger lads had already run out the front door. Bridey was running in circles looking for water, but I don't think she really knew what to do. She probably wasn't used to having her house set on fire. As I headed for the door, I looked back to see Bridey throwing the contents of her teapot up toward the mantel. Smoke rose up to the low ceiling and rolled down into the rest of the house.

"Shouldn't we help her?" I asked Logue.

"Sure, we're not firemen, what do we know about putting out a fire?" came his reply. I couldn't really argue with that. It seemed like we knew more about starting fires than putting them out. When we caught up with the rest of the group, I could see that my brother was pouting.

I nudged his shoulder. "What's wrong with you?" I asked.

"You burned the President," he mumbled. For a while I had no clue what he was talking about, until he added, "and that old man in the dress."

"Those were pictures, you little amadan, sure President Kennedy is already dead. Some eejit shot him in the head."

"What about the Pope?" asked Logue.

"What about him?" I retorted. "That was a picture too...are youns all mad in the head?"

"I know it was a picture," Logue shot back, "but it couldn't be a good thing to burn a picture of the Pope. I think you're going to have seven years bad luck for that."

"I didn't burn him on purpose, and besides, seven years bad luck comes from breaking a mirror. Nobody ever said that mirrors and a man in a dress carry the same punishment." We had learned all about superstitions and old Irish sayings from my mother growing up.

"All the same," Logue continued, "if I were you, I'd tell the priest everything the next time you go to confession. Maybe he'll let you off with it."

"But I've never gone to confession."

"You never what?" Logue asked, as if I had just said that I never shit myself as a baby.

"I never talked to a priest. That's for grown-ups."

"Have you not made your First Holy Communion?" he demanded.

"Not that I know of. What is that all about?"

"Jesus, lad, are you a Protestant? I bet all Yanks are Protestants, aren't they?" Logue kept getting closer to my face. Protestants must have different skin, or maybe there was some smell or something you could only see about them up close, I thought. "Have you got nits?" he asked me, inspecting my hair.

"What are nits?" I asked.

"You don't know what nits are. You don't know what a Protestant is. Jesus, man, what did they teach you went you went to school? Nits are bugs that live in your hair, and when they hatch out, they turn into lice and they start eating into your head and making you scratch like you want to tear your head apart."

"I had them," offered Tinker.

"We all get them," admitted Logue. "When you get them, your mother shakes DDT powder on your head and that poisons them. Any that survive get combed out with a fine-tooth comb. I didn't see those nits before. I wonder why you have them now?" pondered Logue. He got closer to my hair and started sniffing. I was hoping I didn't smell like a Protestant, since he didn't seem to have much time for them.

"Your hair is singed!" he exclaimed. "It's not nits, but wee pieces of burned hair!"

"My mother will kill me," I blurted out. There was no way I was going to get past her on this. There was just no good way to explain how your hair had gotten burned unless you were a fireman.

"I'll take care of it," announced Logue, fishing around in his pocket.

He pulled out a penknife, only it wasn't like our Queen Elizabeth penknives; Logue's knife looked like he could use it to be a butcher.

"What will you do with the knife?" I asked. Things weren't good as they were, but the sight of this knife didn't help to make me feel better.

"I'll cut off the ends of your hair, so that your mother won't know it was burned in a fire." This sounded like a good idea to me, but my brother started to get agitated.

"What's wrong?" I asked.

"That big boy is going to cut off your head," he whimpered. Logue looked at me and shook his head. "Is he related to you?" There was no use in denying it, since everyone knew we were brothers. We were probably the only Yanks in Donegal. We might have been the only Yanks in the whole of Ireland, actually.

Logue grabbed hold of my hair and started to saw off the ends. "Next time, I think you should bring matches with the tobacco," he advised.

I thought this over and had to agree that it would be best next time not to try to light our pipes from an open fire. Strangely, I didn't give a thought to what happened to the old woman. I was more concerned about how much bad luck I might get for burning a picture of the Pope. He seemed to be a lot more important than a mirror. If a mirror brought seven years bad luck, I might be cursed by the Pope for the rest of my life.

Looking back years later, I'd often wonder if I had had the "Pope's Curse" on me. As it turned out, he might have been the first man in a dress to be mad at me, but he wouldn't be the last.

CHAPTER 8
BIKERS

The vet's house had been the home of a lot of firsts for us. As I already mentioned, it was the first place we learned how to smoke a pipe, though I am not 100% sure that my brother had fully gotten the hang of it before we left. It was definitely the first place where I set a house on fire, or part of a house, anyway. I don't think anybody died in the fire, but then again, we didn't hang around long enough to make sure.

The other thing about living in that house was that it really toughened us up. School did that too; we had school fights wherever we lived. But we got into a lot of trouble that had to be kept from our parents for the sake of our continued health while at the vet's house.

One such time was when I got hold of a man's bicycle, decided to go for a joyride, and tore off down the lane. I probably would have survived the ride better had my brother not insisted on coming along.

In theory, bicycles have not changed much in the past forty years—they have a saddle, handlebars, and a front and rear wheel. What they don't really come equipped with is accommodation for a passenger. Not that it was uncommon to see a passenger being transported on a rider's bike; young lads were famous for letting a smaller passenger sit up on the front handlebars back in those days. If the lad was a bit bigger and could be trusted to balance themselves, they could be carried on the crossbar.

Any person with at least an ounce of sense could see where that might not be the safest mode of transport imaginable. When you carried a passenger on the crossbar of your bike, you did not have a clear and unobstructed view of the road. You would therefore be forced to squint over someone's body perched up in front of you. The person riding on the crossbar had to hold onto the handlebars for dear life, and if they got nervous and started to fidget around, they could easily change the flight path of the two-wheeled machine, bringing ditches and oncoming traffic suddenly into play.

Of course, there was no such thing as a bicycle helmet back then, so if you came off the bike at any speed there was a very real chance that you could get seriously injured. Bad and all as that would be, it would have been even worse if you had the misfortune to have a parent with the sense to see how a helmet could be a good idea. You would be laughed at from a height if anyone you knew saw you riding a bike with a helmet. I had heard tell of a wee lad, an only child, whose parents made him ride his bike wearing a motorbike helmet. All the other lads said he was soft in the head, thinking he was riding a real motorbike.

Now on top of those other natural hazards, the thing that made our fateful bike ride such a bloody disaster was the fact that it was the first time I had ridden a man's bike. When I first saw the big black Raleigh, leaning up against the wall minding its own business, I knew I had to have it. I didn't have a clue as to whom it belonged—maybe one of the workers in the fields that day or a visitor passing by—but it didn't matter. I stress that it was a man's bike because those bikes had a cross bar running from the saddle to the handlebars. Women's bikes (which I probably wouldn't have looked upon as big a challenge, but likely would have made off with just the same) didn't have crossbars, and the frames were smaller.

I had seen some other lads around my size ride a man's bike, so I knew what had to be done. When you were small, you had to stick your right leg through the opening under the cross bar and plant your right foot on the right peddle. Then you planted your left foot on the left peddle as you were too small to sit on the seat *and* reach both peddles. The trouble with this method was that nearly all of your weight was on the left side of the bike. In order to keep the bike upright, you had to peddle fast and throw your weight back and forth between the right and left sides. On your own, this was quite doable. Problems only arose when you had a brother who needed to balance on the handlebars.

Unfortunately, when Jimmy started gurning about being carried on the handlebars, I did not realize just how difficult it was for a small boy to maneuver a man's bike alone, never mind with a bloody passenger. I had to bring him along, though, or face the risk of him ratting me out to our mother. In order to properly set the scene, I have to describe the lane that ran from our house down to the main Carndonagh/Moville Road. It was made up of dirt and stones—not just pebbles, but big chunky stones that jutted up and stood out sideways along the whole road. There were even holes—not potholes, but craters that when a small boy stood in them, it looked like he had no feet. In the summertime, when it was dry, you'd know someone was driving up from the main road, as there'd be a big cloud of dust making its way up the lane. The ditches on either side were high, so you couldn't make out who it was, but a slow-moving dust cloud meant that it was a tractor and a fast-moving cloud meant that it was a car.

I would soon regret my decision to ride the man's bike down this mess of a road. The only good part about it was that my brother got the fright of his life, and most likely would never ask to be my co-pilot again. Once we determined that the coast was clear and nobody was watching, I grabbed the bike by the handlebars and took off running toward the lane.

The first thing that struck me was just how big the machine was. The top of my head barely came to the top of the handlebars. As I grabbed it and made off with it, I felt like Jack from *Jack and the Beanstalk* making off with the Giant's treasured possessions. As soon as we reached the rough gravel of the lane, I tipped the bike toward me and shouted at my brother to climb onto the handlebars. If the silly wee bastard had had any sense, he would have realized that it was a bad move, but he was determined to take the maiden voyage with me. He didn't realize the height of the bike or his perilous position until I forced the bike upwards and outwards.

"It's very high," he whimpered.

"No use crying like a girl," I reminded him. "It was you who wanted to ride it with me."

With that, I stuck my right leg through the opening under the bar, found the right peddle with my right foot, and used my left foot on the ground to push us forward and gather enough momentum to keep us upright until I could peddle with both feet. I soon realized that there was no way I could peddle and throw the bike from left to right with the little prick on the handlebars. Since the lane went downhill to the main road, I concentrated on keeping the bike upright by pushing it out to my right. We started to gather speed, and in no time we were flying down the road at a pace that felt as fast as my father's driving. The wind felt good on our faces.

Then the unthinkable happened. My brother moved his leg and his foot got stuck in the spokes of the front wheel. As soon as his foot got jammed, the front wheel came to an abrupt stop. About the same time that he started to scream, the back of the bike decreed that the ride was over and it was time for all riders to depart. My departure came in the form of an ejection that sent me flying out over the handlebars and onto the lane. I tumbled through the dirt, finally using the stones and gravel of the lane to bring me to a stop. My brother was a bit more fortunate, although you would never have guessed it from hearing him scream like a stuck pig. He didn't even skid, but just caved in like a lump, the bike somersaulting over his head.

The fact that we did not break any bones was nothing short of amazing. This miracle did not exactly thrill me at the time, however, since I had left a good deal of skin from both of my palms and knees strewn among the rocks and stones of the road. There was blood everywhere. I didn't even realize how cut up I was until I saw it splattered like a red river across the road. I looked at my brother, and despite the fact that he was roaring like a banshee, I didn't see any signs of physical damage. Then I looked down at myself. My legs were covered in grey dust, and my knees were shiny and red. I didn't understand why they were shiny at first. When I got my wits about me, I saw that the skin had been completely torn off both kneecaps, and the new layer of skin underneath was pulsing with blood. Then I felt my hands stinging. They were a mess of dust and blood and pieces of skin hanging off.

"We have to get back to the house," I called hoarsely to my brother. He was crying and mumbling something that I could not make out. I tried to get to my feet, but I couldn't push up on my hands, so I used my elbows. My knees felt like they had locked up after the crash, and they were reluctant to straighten out and help me get up. When I finally stood, I realized that it was too painful to walk normally, as this involved bending my knees. I had to walk straight-legged, like a young Frankenstein.

"How are we going to get the bike back?" he wanted to know. I was dusty, bloody, skin-deprived, throbbing with pain, and the only thing that little fucker could think about was how we were going to return the bike?

"You must have been dropped on your head when you were a baby," I told him. "We're lucky as fuck to be alive, yet all you can think about is how do we get the bike back?"

"Well, the man you stole it from is going to need it," he replied, looking down at the ground.

"Jesus Christ, don't go around saying I stole the bike. If our mother hears that, she will break the bones that didn't break when we crashed. My friggin' leg is only hanging together by a wee bit of skin as it is."

I realized at that moment that it was hurting me to talk, as my face had taken a fair beating as part of the overall effort my body put into trying to get itself to stop. To keep the peace, I slowly pulled up the bicycle and leaned it up against the side of the ditch. There was no way that I was going to get caught wheeling that thing back. My mind was racing to try and come up with a story that would sound in any way believable. It would only take one look at my torn, bloody knee caps and skin scraped face for my mother to know that I didn't get this way from playing hide and seek.

Thankfully, we had to walk slowly due to the pain, and that gave me more time to think...except that my mind had suddenly started to drift uncontrollably. One thing I could never quite fathom was why parents needed to beat you. If you came back to the house looking like you had just returned from the front lines of a World War battle, was that not punishment enough? You would think that they'd be worried that you hurt yourself or that you might need medical attention, but *no,* not our parents. *Our* parents seemed to be inspired by our misfortune. The more pain we seemed to be in, the more additional pain they felt like they needed to inflict.

There was a water faucet at the back of the vet's house, and I figured it might be safer to try and wash off some of the dust and blood. We might look more presentable if we cleaned up a bit. At first, the cold water felt good—at least when I splashed it on me.

Splashing was not going to get the blood washed off, though, and when I started to rub my face, hands and knees, I had to bite my lip from yelling out with the pain. My brother's pain was not that bad, as he had been fairly much shielded by the big bike. When I couldn't take any more, I decided it was time to go in and face the music.

"Whatever you do, make sure you never mention the bike," I warned him. "Remember, we were running down the lane chasing after a rabbit and we tripped on the stones and that's how I got cut and dirty. If you say anything about taking a bike, they'll beat us to a pulp."

I knew that I could withstand any amount of interrogation, but I was afraid he would break. My body was way too damaged to take on a beating from either one of them, never mind both of them. I didn't feel good having to rely on Jimmy not to spill the beans, but I had no bloody choice. My mother was feeding baby brother when we went in.

"Jesus, Mary and Joseph, what happened to you?" she asked me. I was about to tell the story about chasing after a rabbit when my brother beat me to it.

"There was a rabbit and a bicycle and then the rabbit tripped on the stones and we cut our legs and hit our heads," he blurted out.

"What is that Amadan saying?" my mother asked me.

"He's just excited because he saw a rabbit. A man was riding down the lane on a bike and he must have startled a rabbit in the ditch. When it ran out, we ran after it and then we ran too fast and we fell on the stones." Even as I told it, I felt that it was too weak and that she would see right through it.

"Let's get you some ginger violet and hydrogen peroxide to put on those cuts and clean them," she said.

I stood frozen. She didn't curse at me or take a swing at me. Was I becoming such a good storyteller? I was still reluctant to count my chickens before they were hatched. She could be sneaky when she wanted to be. I was afraid that she might be tired and was just being nice to keep me from running off. I stretched my neck to try and see if she was coming back with a belt or a stick. I was relieved to see her carrying two small brown bottles and some cotton wool.

"Drop your trousers so I can see where the cuts are," she instructed.

I did as she said, and then she dabbed the first piece of cotton wool onto the neck of the bigger bottle and turned it upside down. She pressed the wet cotton wool against the dirty cut on my right knee, and it stung like a bastard.

"Holy fuck," I shouted out, unable to contain myself.

She looked at me with a stern face and asked me, "Where did you learn language like that?" If it wasn't for the pain, I probably wouldn't have been able to keep a straight face. *Definitely not from Father John or Sister Sarah*, I thought to myself.

"It's a wonder youns aren't getting into trouble at school for using bad language, if that's the kind of things you are saying." I looked at my brother. He was bent over looking at my knee like an assistant surgeon during a life-or-death operation.

"It's foaming all up," he shrieked.

"What's foaming up?" I asked him.

"Your knee." I looked down to see a big patch of foam on my cut. The little fucker was right.

"That's the hydrogen peroxide doing its job," my mother informed us. "It'll suck out any dirt or foreign objects from the wound, and then I can dress it."

True to her word, she waited until the knee was dry, and then she dabbed cotton wool into the smaller brown bottle and rubbed that on the cut. This stuff made my knee turn purple.

"I want purple skin," my brother shouted.

"Be thankful that you don't have any bad cuts that need it," she told him.

I was just grateful that my purple skin was coming out of a bottle this time. The purple, yellow, and blue colors that I usually sported on my skin didn't come out of a bottle. They were earned the old-fashioned way.

CHAPTER 9
GETTING THE HANG OF CURSING

I think, generally speaking, that children have a knack for picking up curse words. Having said that, my brother and I (although admittedly, it was I who displayed a higher level of fluency) took to cursing like frogs take to jumping. Mind you, we received excellent tutoring along the way.

Firstly, there was my mother herself. What that woman did not know about cursing was not worth knowing. To give the Devil her due, she didn't really believe in cursing just for the sake of it. Most of the time she could talk without using any profanity at all. When she got worked up, though, she could make a sailor blush. The two times when she was guaranteed to lose her cool were when my brother and I were beating the shite out of each other, and when she had company coming over.

Now, there was virtually nothing I could do about the first instance, or for that matter the second, as I played no part whatsoever when it came to inviting people around to the house. If you're thinking to yourself that we could have avoided a lot of hassle by just not fighting—well, that was impossible. You may as well tell a fish that he could no longer swim in water as to try and tell Jimmy and I that we could no longer fight one another.

While my mother definitely taught us a useful selection of curses, we could not recite them as artistically as she could. She basically saved all her cursing for times when her anger and frustration were at their boiling point. Her cursing at us and beating the living (I never could understand why it was called "living") shite out of us was conducted in a sing-song fashion. When she managed to trap you in a corner, she'd smash down on whatever body part was exposed with whatever she was holding in her hand at the time. The curses then would come out in rhythm to the blows being struck. For example: "How many/*punch*/ times have/*punch*/I told/*punch*/you little Bastard/***double** punch*/..."

I don't know if the boys we met along the way also had mothers who sang their curses, but they taught us a plethora of words, the like of which we had never come across while being beaten at home. Logue's favorite word was "hoor." If you got on his bad side, you could bet on getting called a "wee hoor," or a "dirty hoor," or even a "hoor's melt." I just couldn't get the hang of "hoor" being a bad word, and as a result I started using it in everyday conversation. The "melt" part did throw me a bit. I decided to wait until the perfect opportunity presented itself before slipping that into a sentence.

At the time we had no idea what half of those words meant, or if indeed they had a meaning at all, but it wouldn't be long before we were to learn how the teachers of St. Patrick's Catholic National School for Boys felt about their students' grasp of all things vulgar. Funny enough, the one with the best grasp was the most prolific curser of them all—Master Seamus Quigley, my first teacher when I started in 4th Grade in Carndonagh.

At first sight, Master Quigley seemed like a fairly normal teacher. I had no clue what age he was, but his hair was half-dark and half-silver, so he must have been getting long enough in the tooth.

He wore tweed coats for the most part, and always had a shirt and tie. One thing a little strange about him, though, was the fact that he had orange fingers on his right hand. I spotted it close up one day when I handed over my homework to the Master's desk. When I asked one of the lads in my class why he had orange fingers, he told me that was because he smoked 100 cigarettes a day.

"Seamus smokes like a fucking chimney," another one remarked.

"Why do you call him Seamus?" I asked.

"Because that's the hoor's name," he replied, "but don't ever let him hear you call him that, or he'll have your guts for garters. We call him Seamus behind his back, but never let him hear you call him anything other than 'Sir' or 'Master.'"

"Then who is the old man who teaches the big boys next door?" I asked, trying to form a mental picture of this mysterious hierarchy.

"That's Headmaster MacCafferty," Liam the saddler told me. "He's not well. He has to drink medicine all the time."

"Medicine, my bollocks," replied a tall thin lad with a nose like a bird's beak. "The bottle his 'medicine' comes in says 'Jameson.'"

I knew what Jameson was, as my grandfather used to drink it and he was never sick.

"At any rate," continued Liam, "never get close enough to him to let him breathe on you—he's got T.B." The bird-beak boy nodded at me in agreement.

I hadn't a clue what this meant. "What's T.B.?"

"T.B. stands for tuberculosis. Auld fellas get it from smoking too much and walking out in the rain. T.B. turns your lungs into mush. If old MacCafferty ever breathes on you, he'll rot the lungs out of your chest." That sent a shiver down my spine.

"Many of us will catch T.B. off him next year when we move into his class," the bird-beak boy shared, with a sad look on his face.

"Maybe the hoor will be dead by then," I told them excitedly.

"Good man, Yank," said Liam with a big grin. "The old hoor just might have croaked by then."

Elementary schools in Ireland back in the day used to house two classes in each room. If the school was in a very remote area, with a small population, a teacher may even have to teach more than two years in the same room. Although it was a little strange at the beginning, it soon became very normal to stand in a semicircle in front of the Master's desk as students from the other year sat at their desks doing lessons. We studied everything in this fashion—from English to history, from Gaelic to geography. The Master's desk sat at the very top of the room, right in the middle. When we formed a semicircle in front of him, the rest of the class was out of sight—in theory. In reality, though, Seamus had the ears of a Serengeti lion in its prime.

I'll never forget the first time I witnessed him going into "Fucking Jesus Meltdown," as the boys had christened it. We had formed a semicircle in front of him and were discussing the major rivers in Ireland when he started to peer between the cracks of the boys who blocked his view of the third class down at their desks. Apparently he had heard one of the boys behind us acting the maggot. Unchecked, it grew louder until such time as we could hear it as well.

I watched as Seamus ran his orange fingers through the front of his hair, pulling the strands backward as he muttered something to himself. At first, it seemed as if he was praying, since I thought I heard him say "Jesus." Being the new boy, I was the only one who interpreted this as prayer. After a few moments, his stare became more focused and his chanting grew louder.

That was when I clearly heard him muttering, "Fucking Jesus Christ, Fucking Jesus Christ," all the time yanking backward on his hair. The more he stroked his hair, the louder he cursed Jesus, until such time as the volcano erupted and he jumped to his feet, flinging the big wooden chair behind him and grinning as he tore through the middle of our fourth class semicircle to get to the troublemakers behind us.

As dangerous as I figured it was to be a witness to what might follow, I couldn't help myself from stealing some sideward glances, as it sounded like bones were being crushed behind us. I was shocked by what I saw. I thought that school was something of a safe zone, a sanctuary where we could go to *escape* getting beaten, and here I was witnessing our teacher ripping through the boys seated on the right side of the classroom like a human tornado.

His method was calculated. With his left hand he would sweep one boy out of the way so that he could reach an instigator seated in close to the window. He would raise his right fist overhead, then pound it down onto the boy's body with a heavy thumping sound. Most boys would whimper or shriek when a blow landed—especially the younger third class—but we had a few hard cases in our fourth class who would let out the odd "Jesus!" or even "Fuck!" when they got pounded by Seamus. Such a boy was Paul Sweeney.

Paul Sweeney was a smart lad. He probably figured that, with his intelligence, he didn't need to work as hard in school as the rest, so he turned his attention to making us all laugh. He was always telling some joke or playing a prank on his classmates. The only time I saw him *not* smirking or sniggering (two things that our father regularly accused me of doing) was the day that Master Quigley caught him in the act.

In those days, every young boy was mad about English footballers (who in America are called *soccer* players). Every penny we got our hands on wound up being spent on penny sweets or on football cards, which came in a packet with a piece of chewing gum. We spent much of our free time during lunch or walking home boasting about the cards we had or trying to swap one footballer for another.

One day after lunch, our fourth class was lined up in a semi-circle as Master Quigley went around correcting a lesson that we had completed earlier. He would check each boy's work, and giving it a "good" check mark or a "bad" X. We watched in horror as Sweeney handed Seamus his copy book for correction while simultaneously reaching around behind the teacher's back to stick a football card of Manchester United's Georgie Best on the back of his tweed coat. All the while he distracted Seamus by asking a question about the lesson.

As we began to wonder if he had really just pulled off the practical joke of the century, Seamus felt the hand touching his back. He spun around to his left, catching Sweeney flattening out the football card on his back. That was the first time anyone had ever seen Paul Sweeney look scared. His face immediately turned beet red. Master Quigley grabbed his left ear and a good chunk of his hair, dragging him up to his desk as he repeated, "Fucking little bastard."

Next to the Master's desk was a tall wooden press that had a key sticking out of it when class was in session. Seamus let go of Sweeney, flung open the door of the press, and pulled out a tattered looking bamboo walking stick. The ends were all frayed and split apart. This was the first time I had ever seen a boy being caned. Apparently Sweeney was familiar with the punishment, though. He held out his right hand, palm facing upwards.

Seamus was still cursing as he brought the cane down onto Paul Sweeney's palm. Being the hard case that he was, Sweeney took it like a man, wincing only slightly each time the cane was brought down onto his skin. This must have frustrated the teacher to some extent, since he started to go wild after the fifth or sixth blow, adding a sideways action to the blows and hitting Paul on the arms.

The boy was obviously afraid of getting hit in the head, so he raised his arms up to protect it. Master Quigley responded by beating him about the head with the cane. I have no idea how many lashes were landed, but I felt like I was going to throw up the butter and jam sandwich I had eaten for lunch.

At our next break, we all gathered around Paul to see how he felt.

"It was like getting stung by a wasp," he told us, making light of the huge welts on the front and backs of his hands.

"You're a mad hoor, that's for sure," admitted Liam, and we all laughed as the bell announced the end of the afternoon break.

The next day was Friday, and the last day of my first week in school. I say *my*, but I really mean *our*, as Jimmy had started first class the same day I started fourth. Of course, I refused to have anything to do with him. I was going into the seniors' room next year, and I couldn't be seen around someone from the "baby" classes, even if he *was* my brother.

Classes began at 9:30am as usual that Friday. Fourth class was the first class to go up in front of Master Quigley. We had only begun our lesson about ten minutes when there was the sound of a loud commotion outside our door in the shared hallway.

Glancing sideways, I saw the elderly woman who taught the younger classes, Mrs. Doyle, running down the hall. She seemed to be exchanging shouts with a boy. After a few minutes, a school bag went flying past the glass windows of our class door, and Mrs. Doyle went running in the opposite direction. After another few minutes, a knock sounded and Master Quigley went over to open the door. It looked like he was speaking to the older teacher.

What happened next surprised me. Master Quigley returned to our group and told me to go out and meet with Mrs. Doyle. I walked to the door, opened it and stepped into the hallway.

"Your brother has gone mad," Mrs. Doyle informed me. At first I wanted to assure her if anyone was going mad, it was definitely not my brother. He was a troublesome little bastard all right, but mad he was not. Then I saw it for myself. My brother was peering around the corner of the wall with his jacket half hanging off him and his hair sticking up in several places.

"You need to talk sense to him," she instructed me. I went over to my brother and told him that he had to go back into his classroom.

"I'm finished," he told me.

"What do you mean, you're 'finished?'" I asked him.

"I'm finished with school," he said. "I went and now I am finished—I don't have to go anymore." *Maybe the hoor* is *mad,* I thought to myself.

"You take your brother into the teacher's staff room right now," Mrs. Doyle ordered.

I put my arm around his neck and dragged him as if I was choking him—something I wouldn't have minded doing—down the hall after Mrs. Doyle. Mrs. Doyle joined a younger lady teacher sitting behind a round table. I turned to go.

As I walked toward the door, Mrs. Doyle called out, "Where do you think you're going?"

I turned to discover that she was talking to me. "I'm going to class, Miss."

"Oh no you're not. You stand right there next to your brother. What do you have to say for yourselves?"

I looked to my brother for guidance, as I had no idea what had happened between the two of them, other than the fact that he had apparently been trying to escape and Mrs. Doyle kept blocking his way. He was no help either; he just looked down at the ground.

"Where did this young man hear the kind of language he was using?" Mrs. Doyle demanded. "I have never heard such filthy language in all my life."

"He picked up some of it from our mother," I answered honestly, "and more from the boys we play with." The two teachers looked horrified.

"I am quite sure he did not hear that kind of language from his mother," the younger teacher assured us.

"I did," admitted my brother. "She always curses whenever she gets really fucking angry."

The younger teacher tried to say something, but only stammered. "But, how….who….I never…." She turned to Mrs. Doyle for help.

"I blame you," Mrs. Doyle said, pointing a finger at me. "As the older brother, you influence the younger boy. He acts like you, and therefore you must have taught him these terrible things."

"He hears most of it from the boys near where we live," I honestly explained.

"What boys?" she wanted to know. At that stage, I figured it would be bad to get the others involved, so I decided it was safer to tell her that I did not know their names.

"Even if that were true," she shot back, "that kind of dirty talk is not tolerated in this school. We are a Catholic National school and there is no place for talk like that here. Maybe the heathens in America let you talk that way, but it won't be allowed here. Will you really stand there and continue to tell me that 'some boy' you don't know taught you these words?"

I didn't know what a "heathen" was, but it seemed that she didn't believe me, and that she was happy to place the full blame for my brother's bad behavior on me.

I persevered in my innocence. If I told her how things really were, she would have to understand. "The other way I learned these curses was from Master Quigley."

Now it was Mrs. Doyle's turn to stammer. She and the younger teacher looked at each other in shock, and then both turned to me as if they must have heard wrong.

"Seamus is all the time saying things like 'Jesus Fucking Christ.'" I didn't mean to call him Seamus—it just kind of slipped out—and as a result, I couldn't be sure if they were more shocked to hear me calling Master Quigley by his first name or at their discovery of the words he used when talking about Jesus.

"Sea-mus?" the young teacher stammered.

"Aye," I replied, "that's the hoor's name." I added, for good measure, "The boys say he smokes like a fucking chimney."

I don't know if it was something I said, or whether Mrs. Doyle had simply been tired out from chasing Jimmy up and down the corridor, but she sat back in the chair and started to open the collar of her shirt. She wasn't making a very good job of it and started waving her arms all around. The young teacher looked scared and she ran out.

I thought about helping, but as Logue would say, I wasn't a doctor. The way things were going, I'd probably only get myself into more trouble if I helped her take off her clothes. After a moment, the young teacher rushed back into the room with a glass of water. She held her hand behind Mrs. Doyle's head as the older woman drank some.

"Keep them here until we can contact their parents," Mrs. Doyle told the younger woman.

"Thanks to you, we didn't even last one whole week in school," I told my brother.

"I don't care," he informed me. "I'm all fucking finished anyway."

CHAPTER 10
GETTING AN EARFUL

Despite his erratic, dysfunctional and maniacal behavior, my father had a streak in him that allowed him to deeply believe in the people of Ireland. Not just believe in them, but actually *trust* in them. As I got older, I figured that he must have put his faith in Irish people as a result of his romantic view of Ireland—the island of saints and scholars. No point in telling him that heroin addicts in Dublin shot junk into their veins every day in alleyways, or that more than one Catholic priest got turned on by an altar boy's chubby arse.

One thing was for certain: he didn't pick up his views due to his mild and gentle demeanor. More than likely, he had heard feel-good stories about Ireland from his Irish mother, the same way my brother and I had. He would have been exposed to yarns about mischievous little fairies and singing Irishmen who never fought or beat their wives when they got drunk, but just broke into combustible song like the any-excuse-to-sing-and-dance actors in a Bollywood film.

His mother-in-law, my grandmother, came from the Malin area of the Inishowen Peninsula in North Donegal. He would have had to spend time around her when they all lived in the

Bronx and he was courting our mother. She was always a very gentle, sweet old lady to my brothers and I, but something must have happened between the two of them to make him turn against her. Even as a boy, I noticed his attitude change at the mere mention of her name. He had great time for her husband, my grandfather Danny Houton. That can probably be explained by the fact that they were both a bit touched in the head.

I say her husband, but to this day I do not fully know the legal status of my grandfather and grandmother's relationship. We often stayed at my grandmother's place in the Bronx, but I can only remember visiting my grandfather's apartment as a young boy once. He was a wild character by all accounts, and the stories that my father used to tell about him made him seem larger than life. It seems that we all went out together a fair bit, though I was too young to remember. One of my father's favorite memories was of a time my grandfather had a few whiskies in him as they walked down a street in New York City.

Suddenly my grandfather got the urge to start jumping over old people walking on the footpath. Apparently he would spot an old man or woman walking along, minding their own business, and he would start running toward them. Just before they collided, he would hurdle the old person, who had no idea why a crazy man was jumping over their head. Mind you, he was a grandfather at the time, so he was no spring chicken himself, but he must have been very spry.

I remember the time when he decided to retire and come back to live in Ireland for good. My mother seemed genuinely scared for his well-being. It seems that one of her spies passed the word to her that her father had gotten into a bar fight the night before he was to leave for Ireland (probably over a woman). She was perplexed to find out that the fight had been with a Puerto Rican, and that knives had been used. She was also scared to hear that the guy he fought with was only about half his age.

Apparently, though, she had no need to be concerned. Her sources went on to describe how her father pulled the man into the street, pulled an ice pick out of his sock, and stabbed him multiple times. He then flung the weapon under the wheels of oncoming traffic and jumped into a yellow cab, after which he was never seen or heard from again in New York.

After his icepick-wielding departure from the city, Grandfather arrived back in Donegal, but he wasn't the type to slip into retirement gracefully. Even though he had emigrated from Ireland to America in his late twenties, he returned forty years later with the same sense of devilment and energy. By night he was drinking the local bars dry, and by day he was building his own house from scratch, as he was an accomplished stonemason. His eldest daughter had bought back the family farm, which they had formerly lost during a blood feud, and now he was determined to build a house with his own hands on its land and spend the rest of his life there. Every time we visited him, his house had reached a higher level. Slowly but surely, he was getting there.

"You'll never find 'til the roof is going on," my mother encouraged him one Sunday about a year after he had been back.

"Not before time," grandfather replied. "I'd need to hurry it along if I am to be laid out in it one of these days."

"What are you talking about?" my mother asked him. "Sure you'll outlive the lot of us. You're as healthy as a horse."

"I don't know about healthy," he replied, "but the whiskey has the insides fairly well-preserved, I'd say."

He lived in a little tin caravan at the head of one of his fields. The whole thing was made up of only one room. It wasn't meant to be lived in for any length of time—more like a short holiday stay by the shore —but he lived in it nearly a year at that stage. Anytime a decent wind blew in from the Atlantic Ocean, which was about 90% of the time in Malin Head, the whole place shook like a leaf on a tree. His eldest daughter, the private nurse in

Manhattan, had commissioned the building of three big new houses during the time he was erecting his little house. There was one for herself, one for her bachelor brother, and another one for her mother. Grandfather could have lived in any of the houses—well, any of the two houses anyway—but he was far too independent to rely on someone else for his shelter.

Shortly after our grandfather's house had reached the roof stage, his dreams of living in a house built by his own hands came crashing down. The house was built solid, so it wasn't coming down of its own accord, but the local authorities contacted him and told him that he did not seek planning permission and he would have to cease work immediately. When we came to visit him that Sunday, he was fit to be tied.

"So what were you told about the house, Danny?" my father asked him.

"Those fuckers in the County Council told me that I needed a wee piece of paper to build on my own land. Can you believe that?" It actually wasn't that hard to believe, but there were probably fewer rules when he had lived in Ireland nearly half a century before.

"So will you look for planning permission now?" my mother wanted to know.

"I will in me arse," he shot back. "This land has been in our family for the past 100 years, and we never had to ask any fucking pencil-pusher where we could make a house."

"I heard of a case in Clonmany, where some people built a house like that without planning permission, and when they wouldn't stop after being warned, the Council came in and had the house knocked down," his daughter informed him.

"Let the useless hoors try that with me," our grandfather warned, "and I'll open up on them with both barrels of my shotgun." My mother looked fierce worried. She knew her father was crazy enough to try something like that.

"Sure, what harm would it do to see what you'd need in order to get the permission?" asked the child-beating peacemaker.

"They can wipe their arse with their paper," he told her. "I'll get the roof on and then I'll move in. Let's see them try to tear it down with me inside it."

Unfortunately, Grandfather was no match for the authorities. He was forced to concede that if he were to lay another block without having the proper permission, they would level his dream house. Too stubborn to apply for the planning permission, he left the house in its half-finished state as a testament to his independent spirit. He continued to live out the rest of his life in a little tin box that did not allow him to swing a cat (if he were ever to feel so inclined).

The local authorities may have been able to keep Danny Houton down when it came to the building code, but there was no force on Earth that could dissuade that old man from pulling other stunts. Mind you, I witnessed his carrying-on when he was well past his heyday. God only knows what had been capable of doing during his thirties and forties.

One of his favorite props was chewing tobacco. Like many men of his vintage, he enjoyed a good chew. My brother and I would watch intently as he pulled a big lump of plug tobacco out of a coat pocket. In contrast to most men, who would cut off a civilized piece with a penknife they carried mainly for that purpose. Danny Houton would shove one end of the plug into his mouth and sever a big chunk of it with his teeth.

My brother and I watched like hawks, full sure that since it was the spitting image of licorice, it must taste like it. Our belief was further reinforced by the fact that my father always joined in chewing tobacco when he was around our grandfather. His claim to fame was that he could leave in a big wad of tobacco as he drank cups of tea. Even though the old people warned us that the stuff was horrible, we could not believe them. Who in their right mind would go around chewing on something that tasted so hateful?

The Fifteenth of August was always a huge day in Malin Head. For some reason or other, nobody else seemed to celebrate it like the folks in "the Head." There was a big field right in the middle of the Parish, conveniently situated right beside Dock's pub, where the Fifteenth of August Sports Day was held each year. There was the egg and spoon race for children, as well as the three-legged race for all. (Every sports day worth its salt in Ireland had to have those two events as part of its program.) The adults had relay races and sprints, as well as feats of strength such as "Tossing the Sheaf of Corn." This was like pole-vaulting with a pitchfork and a sheaf of corn. The men would stick the fork into the sheaf and then hoist it up over a horizontal bar that kept getting higher until there was only one man who could throw it high enough to clear the bar. Needless to say, all of that physical activity worked up quite a thirst, and Dock's pub did a roaring trade that day and through the night.

Apart from the sports and the drinking, it was also some kind of religious occasion. When we traveled to downtown Malin Head, we started off the day by going to mass. Just as everything about that part of the world was unique to the rest of civilization, so too was the church experience. All of the women and the old men would go into the chapel, but many of the younger men and older bachelors would huddle in the back and listen to mass through the open door.

The reasons for this were many. Firstly, if they arrived a bit late, nobody inside would be any the wiser. Secondly, they could have the craic without worrying about interrupting the priest. Thirdly, and probably most important (although it might be a neck-in-neck photo finish with reason number four), it allowed them to make a quick getaway once the mass was over. The fourth reason was because some of them needed a smoke so badly, and it gave them the freedom to light up as soon as communion was over and done with.

For some reason—probably because he wanted to be more like our grandfather – my father also took up a position outside the back door, and was one of the first ones to light up a non-filter Woodbine as soon as the last of communion was dispensed. My brother and I were the youngest members of the back-door gang by about a dozen years.

We went up to the "Fifteenth" the first year our grandfather returned. After mass he asked us to bring him to visit an old friend from his younger days. We were probably related to this man, since just about everyone throughout Malin Head seemed to be either our second or third cousin. As usual, our grandfather had a big lump of chew in his mouth as he went up to the house and knocked on the front door. There did not seem to be anybody home, and the only sign of life was a black and white cat that sat on the front door stoop.

We watched our grandfather bend down as if he was going to pet the cat. He held out his hand to call the cat to come closer to him. When the poor cat was only about a foot away, he moved his head forward and spat into its face. The cat's eyes were burned by the tobacco juice, and it furiously wiped its eyes with its paws.

My father burst out laughing. "Did you see that crazy shit?" he asked my mother. "That crazy old bastard of a father of yours spat tobacco juice in that cat's eye. Unbelievable!"

"Stop laughing," my mother ordered. "You'll only encourage him, and he's bad enough as it is. He's coming back—say nothing."

"There was nobody at home then?" my mother asked him as he got back into the car.

"No, they've probably already left for Docks," he replied without mentioning the poor old maimed cat, which was still rolling around the front stoop, pulling the face off herself.

"Where to now, Danny?" asked my father, barely able to contain his grin.

"We may as well head over to Dock's field and see who's over there. Maybe along the way we can stop in the shop in Bree and get the wains some ice cream." Looking back at my brother and me, he added, "They look like they could do with ice cream." I felt my brother pull back away from our grandfather when he turned around from the front passenger seat to look at us.

"What's wrong with you?" I asked him.

"Did you see the way he was looking at us?" he whispered back. "I think he was about to spit tobacco juice in our eyes."

"Don't be daft. Sure he'd never do that to us," I assured him. But part of me was not all that sure.

When we arrived down at the field, the festivities were in full swing. Our grandfather jumped out of the car like a young fella, followed by my father. My brother and I took up the rear. My mother said she had to stay in the car to change the baby. Everywhere our grandfather turned, he met someone he knew. I've never heard so many nicknames in one day. There was Willy the Pet, Charlie Mickey Tom, David and Tess the Carpenter, Packie the Butcher, Paddy Joe Willy, the Garetts, John Toey, Shauney the Teacher, and Paul, Tom, and Eugene the Mason (our grandparents neighbors), to name but a few.

The man that Grandfather had stopped to see on the way down was Paddy Monagle's father. After about a half hour, he spotted him over near the sheaf-throwing area. As we drew closer to the man, I couldn't help but notice that he had a perfect bite-sized piece missing from his left ear. Without thinking, I pulled on my grandfather's sleeve and asked him about it.

"Some say he was bitten by a horse, while others say he had cancer on his ear and the doctors had to cut it out in a half-moon shape to remove it," answered my grandfather. "He's had it for as long as I can remember. Paddy told me one time that he told him he got it in a fight in London when he was young. The way he told it, his father had a hold of this big guy by his balls and was afraid to let go, as the Englishman was more than twice his size. In the end, the big man had to bite a chunk out of Monagle's ear in order to make him let go of his grip."

Our grandfather turned back to look at the action, but after a couple of seconds he turned around, looked down at me, nodded toward Paddy Monagle's father, and winked at me. I knew something was going to happen or had happened, but I hadn't a clue, other than the fact that our grandfather seemed to be chewing harder on the big lump of tobacco in his jaw. I elbowed my brother and nodded toward Grandfather, without taking my eyes off the old man, afraid to miss whatever was about to take place. What I saw next surprised me even more than seeing the cat get tobacco juice spat into her eyes.

Our grandfather kept looking forward, but screwed around his face, puckered up his lips, and spat a big mouthful of brown tobacco juice into Mr. Monagle's ear hole. He did not aim for just any ear, but the ear that had fallen victim to a horse, or cancer, or from an Englishman that he had had by the balls. Once the brown juice shot into his ear, Mr. Monagle immediately stuck his finger inside it. When he realized that it was wet, he looked up at the sky, seemingly wondering whether it had been a large raindrop of some sort.

When the man realized that the sky was as clear as a bell and it had definitely not rained in his half-eaten ear, he stuck his finger back inside, twirled it around a bit, and then examined the brown liquid coating it. Even though I could only see the side of his face, I could see that he was completely bamboozled as to how this liquid had entered the side of his head. Meanwhile, our grandfather could have won an Academy Award for his acting. He kept staring straight ahead, watching the sheaf-throwing and talking about who was doing the best.

After a moment he turned around and asked Jimmy and I, "How are the men?" He fished around in his pocket, pulled out a shilling, and told us to go get some sweets for ourselves. He looked at me, grinning, as he nodded behind his head at the poor old man who had gotten his ear hole flushed out with tobacco juice. I knew that my mother wouldn't have approved, but I smiled back at him. As I did so, he winked again at me. It looked like he wanted us to wait before running off to buy sweets.

My brother wanted to go spend our fortune in the wee shop that was attached to Dock's pub, but I had a feeling that Grandfather was up to no good and his antics were not to be missed. By this time a few more of our grandfather's old cronies had joined the circle around him, and Mr. Monagle had rotated to the other side. Paddy Monagle, the old man's son who lived and worked the family farm, was standing in front of our grandfather. He had the type of cap that most of the other men wore, only his was pushed further back on his head and tilted to one side. He had both hands buried deep in his pockets as he sucked on an unfiltered cigarette, blowing smoke out of his nose and mouth at the same time.

I tried to predict what devilment Grandfather was plotting so as to keep a closer eye on the action. There was no cat or dog around, so the chances were slim that he was planning to abuse an animal. The men were all facing him and talking away, so he could hardly spit straight in their face. God knows, poor old Mr. Monagle had already been terrorized; and besides, his son was in the middle of the action now. Surely our grandfather was not mental enough to try and fill Mr. Monagle's good, uneaten ear with tobacco juice right in front of his son.

Then it happened. I watched as Grandfather twisted around his face and puckered his lips. Almost instantly, he shot a big gob of tobacco juice into the old man's right ear. Not only was it an amazing feat of precision spitting, but he must have had balls the size of cabbages to do this right in front of the man's son. I watched with bated breath as old man Monagle shot his right finger into his right ear and pulled it out in total disbelief. The poor old bastard once again looked up to the sky. One can only imagine that he expected drops of tobacco juice to be raining from above.

He looked behind him, and for good measure, looked up once more. Two earfuls of tobacco juice later, he still never suspected his childhood friend of abusing his listening devices. The men who had witnessed the spectacular feat of spitting were bent over in laughter. Some were holding their sides. I looked between the men to see what kind of expression was on Paddy Monagle's face, as I was full sure that he would take a swing at our grandfather for making an eejit out of his father. As it turned out, he was laughing harder than any of the other men. He was laughing so hard that he could no longer balance the cigarette in his mouth. He had to hold it in his fingers as he laughed, sputtered, and coughed himself senseless.

All the while, our grandfather stared straight ahead as if he was in no way connected to whatever was taking place. Poor Mr. Monagle had finally seemed to come to the realization that whatever had invaded his left ear had now made its way around to his right one as well. As he stood there plunging a finger into each ear and spinning them around, I remembered the poor old cat back home on his door stoop. I thought it ironic that both owner and pet were probably rubbing eyes and ears at the same time as they fell foul to the same tormentor.

I was beginning to see that nothing or nobody was off-limits when it came to Danny Houton's need for entertainment. Man and beast were both fair game, and it paid to keep your eyes and ears open when he was around. Actually, on second thought, it was probably safer to keep both closed.

CHAPTER 11

HOUSE BUS

My father's restaurant in the canteen of the shirt factory didn't have a cash register. In its place was just a biscuit tin where the factory girls would throw in their silver and coppers. This is why I could pocket a couple of extra shillings on Saturdays—there were no receipts, so there was no way of knowing exactly how much was being taken in during the breakfast and lunch-time breaks. If you think *that* was a bad system, wait 'til you hear what comes next.

During the week—all five days and ten feedings—the factory girls were trusted to put in or take out the proper amount of change from the biscuit tin on their own. He didn't have anyone in place to collect the money, but relied instead on the "honor system." The result was that those bitches robbed him blind. He only had two things going for him. First, his smuggling meant that he was buying much of the raw ingredients at a deep discount, and second, he had me to charge the proper price on Saturdays. Those dishonest girls also taught me a couple of lessons. Firstly, that even though they appeared innocent and sweet, they were still thieving bitches. And secondly, through overhearing their conversations, I was able to piece together from an early age what was going on across the border in Derry.

In 1969, things were heating up across the border. I heard how Catholics were marching for their civil rights and how Protestants did not want them living near them or working with them. I found that hard to understand, as there were a few Protestant families living around us and we were all friendly. Every Saturday, the factory girls would talk about riots in Derry and Belfast, and speak about how Catholics in the North were being burned out of their homes and being shot and killed by the local police, the RUC. I asked my father about it, but he didn't want to talk about it.

"Don't be listening to those girls," he would tell me. Later in life, I would come to know that the girls really knew what they were talking about, as many IRA men on-the-run would come to live in Buncrana in safe houses. Some had brothers, and even fathers, who were active in the IRA.

I am sure that if our auld fella did not have the benefit of smuggling, or me to charge the right prices on a Saturday, that he would have gone bankrupt in his first year.

As it was, he lasted two years.

At first, we didn't notice anything different. The first thing to go was the thrupenny bit coin that he used to drop into our shoe before he left for work. Next, we started to hear the parents talking about moving to save on rent. I don't know at what stage all caution was thrown to the wind, but at some point my mother gave in to the insane idea that we should all live in a bus. That was the thing about my father; he could talk a stripper into becoming a nun, or vice-versa, if he set his mind to it.

Mind you, for a young boy, the idea of living in a double-decker bus was quite exciting. Despite the planning we overheard between my father and his father-in-law, I didn't think it would amount to anything. But one day we were told to get ready, as we were going up to Derry to buy a bus from Lough Swilly, the company that provided bus service for that part of Ireland.

My father was tickled pink when he discovered that it was possible to buy a bus after it was too old to use on the road. He didn't care about the road-worthiness of the bus anyway; he intended to park it in a field so that we could live in it. Being a bona fide head case, he could be excused from making rational decisions. Grandfather seemed to be more traditional, as he was building a stone house on his land and didn't seem like the type who would embrace living in a double-decker bus. Then again, he *was* the same grandfather who enjoyed doing things like spitting into men's ears and jumping over elderly pensioners in the street.

The day that all six of us travelled up to Derry to visit the Lough Swilly bus yard was one of the best days we had had in a long time. It was, in fact, the first time we went into the city without having to smuggle anything out (or so I had thought). We even got fish and chips to boot. Grandfather was no eejit, and he used the trip to visit a pub in the Bogside area of Derry that was owned by a friend of his. My mother wasn't happy about bringing him (and us) to a pub, especially in the Bogside; but she knew that without him, the bus would stay a bus.

"We need to get out of here as soon as we can," she told my father. "The rioting is starting to get out of control, and the Bogside is the most dangerous place we can be."

"I know," my father replied, "but we can hardly tell him that he can't visit with his friends."

"Friends? Don't you know that they are in the IRA? Next fucking thing you know, he'll have a gun, and get it into his head that he needs to go and shoot a cop or a soldier."

My father didn't respond, but I could tell he was worried. For some reason, he never talked about the war that was going on across from us. I wanted to learn everything I could, and I figured that asking our grandfather about what was happening was the best way to find out. Looking back, I realized that my father was only in his early thirties when Derry was being burned and bombed, and that he was young enough to join the IRA if he had wanted.

Grandfather was "happy as Larry" making his way up to the bar. "A large bottle of Smithwick's, and a rum and pep," he ordered. Then he turned to us and asked, "What are youns having, men?"

"Coke and cheese and onion crisps," Jimmy replied. Grandfather didn't even bother to ask my mother and father what they wanted. Since they didn't drink alcohol, they didn't count. We didn't drink due to our age, of course, but he figured there was a chance for us to follow in his footsteps one day.

"Is your boss about?" Grandfather asked the bartender.

"Ah...no, he's out and about," replied the barman cautiously. "Who should I say is asking for him?"

"Danny Houton from Malin Head," came the reply. My mother looked worriedly at my father.

"Wasn't that a great deal we got on the bus, Danny?" my father asked him.

"Ten quid? I'm bloody sure it was," replied our grandfather. "How will you get it up the mountain?"

"I've hired the Masons' lorry and winch. They said they'll meet us at the Lough Swilly bus yard around 5:00 pm. They'll tow it across the border and park it at the bottom of the field. I've already got the road up the mountain scraped, and the limestone is set to be delivered tomorrow for the roadway. Once it's been packed in good and tight, they'll come back and tow the bus up to the top with the winch."

I don't know how they finagled it, but my parents had become friendly with an old Protestant man who had a farm on the side of the mountain, on the Buncrana Road overlooking Carndonagh. I can remember old Sam being fond of my mother, and I think that's the angle my father worked. They bought about half an acre at the very top of one of Sam's fields for a few hundred pounds. It was the last green field before the rest of the land turned into hillside heather. I was a bit unsure of Protestants after listening to the factory girls talk about how the Protestants were burning down Catholics' houses, so I was still somewhat suspicious of old Sam. What if he wanted us to live there so he and his friends could burn down our house, or in this case, bus?

My father said that after the contractor came and made a road up the far end of the mountain and the bus was pulled to the top, they'd tie it down somehow and then convert it into a house. I think the whole idea would have been a complete disaster if it had not been for the fact that our grandfather was a very good stonemason.

"Have you applied for the planning permission yet?" grandfather asked, which was ironic as all fuck, since he had fought a raging battle over the same thing with the County Council and staunchly maintained that he didn't *need* permission.

"That's the beauty of it all," my father replied proudly. "Since we're not building a house, there's no planning permission needed. Nobody has ever thought to live in a bus before, so they have no category for planning permission on something which is, in theory, a mobile vehicle." It was little wonder that nobody had ever looked to live in a bus before, as the Council had likely not come across as mad a bastard as my father prior to this point.

"That's fierce handy that you're sticking it up on the Buncrana Road," Grandfather added. "It'll be a straight drive in to the shirt factory for you."

"I'm worried about the wind," my mother announced to nobody in particular.

"What about it?" asked Grandfather.

"It's going to be fierce windy up there with no shelter around it. I'm afraid that it will blow over."

"The view from up there is going to be amazing," my father chimed in. This did little to alleviate her fear of the bus rolling down the mountainside and pulverizing all of us as we slept soundly in our beds. My mother caught my attention, though, when she talked about our new house blowing over. It made me think of the moment in *The Wizard of Oz* when Dorothy's home was caught in the tornado and swirled up into the sky. I looked over at my brother to see if he was concerned but realized, when I saw his face buried inside the bag of crisps, that he didn't have a care in the world.

"Once we have built the stone foundation and poured in the concrete, that thing will be as stable as the Rock of Gibraltar," Grandfather promised her.

"When you are ready, Danny, we'll go for a bite to eat and then do some shopping. We may as well kill two birds with one stone." Our father seemed anxious to get out of the pub.

"Sure, we have plenty of time, what's your rush? That lorry won't be getting up here for another three hours. Another round there, men?"

Jimmy and I didn't care how long we stayed. It was a treat to be in a pub, and guzzling cokes and crisps. We eagerly nodded our approval to getting more food and drink. Grandfather went back up to the bar and this time talked longer to the barman, but he was quieter so we could not make out what he said.

"After this one so," our father said, not sounding too sure if there would only be one more round. "I have to stock up on supplies for the canteen while we are here."

"Do we have to stick more butter into our anoraks?" asked Jimmy.

"Actually," replied my father, "today we are going to put all of the food on the bus!" Our grandfather had just sat down with the drinks and caught the last bit.

"You are going to smuggle a bus full of food across the border?"

"I was looking at the engine compartment," shared my father, "and there are two big empty spaces on either side of the engine. We'll have to pack the food into boxes, as it would fall down through the opening at the bottom if we didn't. I figure that we can jam at least four weeks worth of food in the engine alone."

"Jesus, they'll arrest us all, and confiscate the food as well as the bloody bus itself if we are caught," worried my mother.

"Hold on, Sadie," her father told her, "your man has thought this out and his plan sounds good. Sure, you'll make a killing if this works out."

"That's not all," my father promised. "There is a built-in closet under the stairs where the conductor might have kept a broom and dustpan. I reckon we could jam another couple stone weight of meat and butter in there."

Grandfather started to rub his hands together and smile. "Drink up men, we are on a mission, there's no time to waste." He seemed the most excited of all of us. After we wolfed down some fish and chips, we headed to Littlewoods supermarket where we bought loads of food. Whatever we didn't get there, we found in a couple of other nearby shops. We had so much food, that there was hardly any room in the car for us. We were plastered up against the windows, trying to make room. Kevin was even put into one of the boxes of bacon, as if it was a cot. Thankfully the drive to the bus yard took only a few minutes.

"Right," said my father, "Sarah will go with the boys into the office and pay for the bus. I got five pounds in change—shillings and sixpences, so it will take them a good while to count it out. If they are not as slow as I think they should be, have one of the wains complain about needing to go to the toilet. That will buy Danny and I more time to load up the food and hide it as best we can."

"Will you put Kevin in the engine too?" asked Jimmy.

"Of course not," replied our father. "Why do you think we would do that?"

"Well, you put him into the box with the bacon, and you'll be putting that into the engine."

"Don't worry, son," Grandfather comforted him, "your brother will ride back with all of us in the car. It would look fierce funny all the same if they happened to open the engine of the bus at the border and saw a wee boy sitting in a box of bacon, staring back out at them!"

"So you think there is a chance they might look inside the engine?" my mother looked worried.

"No, of course not. Your father is only pulling your leg. They have no reason to look when the bus won't even be running."

We followed my mother into the ticket area to pay for our bus. It took a long time—so long that we didn't have to make believe we needed to go to the toilet. I was bursting for a pish. When we came out, our father and grandfather were standing by the bus smoking cigarettes and looking happy with themselves.

"That looks like the Masons' lorry now," observed my father. He and grandfather walked over to the driver, and they spoke back and forth. It took a while for the driver to hook up the bus. When it was ready to go, we followed behind.

"I told him that I will get out when we stop at the Muff border crossing, and bring the paperwork into the Customs Officers to show that we just bought it and are towing it back to Carn." My mother was biting her nails. Grandfather was whistling a tune. We had never been caught before, so I wasn't sure what we should do if they opened the bonnet of the bus and saw all of the food. I figured that we should probably get out of the car and run, but where? Derry wasn't a safe place to be running. There were soldiers with big guns everywhere you looked. I didn't know if they would shoot young boys, but I knew they could shoot the old people in the car. After a few minutes we saw a Customs Officer walking with our father back to our car. The bus still sat in front of us.

"Jesus, Mary and Joseph, he looks like he is going to arrest us all," said our mother, to nobody in particular. Maybe she was praying. The Customs man looked into our car. Grandfather rolled down the front passenger window.

"Fine day now," he told the Customs man.

"'Tis. So ye are going to make a house out of this bus and live in it?" the Customs man asked. You could tell from the way he looked at us that he thought we were all mental.

"Aye, that's what we are doing alright," agreed Grandfather.

"Well, that's a good one," shared the man in uniform. "I have never seen a bus being brought down across the border to be turned into a house. How did ye think up that one at all?"

"It was my son-in-law's idea," informed Grandfather. "The man is full of interesting ideas."

"Well, I'll let you be on your way," said the man. "Good luck with your bus-house or house-bus, or whatever you'll call it."

"Thank you," said my father, and he waved at the lorry driver to drive off. "That was a close call," admitted my father, when we were driving and safely away from the men who could arrest us. "They started to ask me if the bus drove, and if I would be driving it did I have insurance on it." Grandfather started a fit of laughing.

"If the hoors only knew," he squeezed out between fits of laughter, "that the feckin' thing was more of a mobile butcher shop than it was a bus." Everyone laughed at that. Everyone except for our mother. She was still staring ahead and biting her nails. She mustn't have thought we were out of harm's way yet.

"When will you unload the food from the bus?" she asked.

"We'll wait until the lorry driver unhooks the bus and leaves. There's no point in him knowing that he could have been arrested and had his lorry impounded for smuggling a bus full of Free State food across the border."

"By Jesus, that would have left a bad taste in his mouth," Grandfather said, laughing. "Probably would have been enough to put him off bacon and butter for the rest of his life!"

Three days later, we watched as the Masons' lorry towed our new bus-home up the side of Sam's mountain. It looked strange sitting at the bottom of the hillside, parked like it was waiting to pick up people. As predicted, they could tow it up only a small part of the way, but the lorry was able to make it up to the top, where they winched the bus up with little bother. The top of the mountain had already been cleared and leveled. Loads of limestone had been dumped on it.

It was very strange to see a double-decker bus going up the side of the mountain. The driver of the lorry must have told the story for the rest of his life about the time he towed a Lough Swilly double-decker bus up the side of a mountain for a Yank. I would say that my father was as excited as a little kid, but he was actually far *more* excited than we were. We watched from the bottom of the lane as the bus was brought to dock in its new home. As soon as it had come to a complete stop, my father tore up the side of the mountain on foot.

We struggled up behind him, but he never once turned around to see if we were able to navigate the steep incline. His size fourteen shoes were able to cover much more ground. By the time we had made it halfway up, he was already at the top and speaking with the lorry driver. My mother had a tougher time than my brother and I, since she had to struggle up the mountain carrying a baby. We reached the top as my father was handing the lorry driver money. The man said "Good luck," but he had a funny look on his face and it seemed like he was shaking his head.

"Would you look at that view," my father said to us after the driver headed back down the mountain. I looked down to see the whole of Carndonagh town, its big stone chapel looming in the distance. I could also see my mother still struggling to make it up to where we were, baby in tow. I figured she would not be in the best of moods once she made it to the top and witnessed her lords surveying their new manor. She finally reached the summit, where my father asked her eagerly, "What do you think of this view, Sarah?"

"*View?*" she asked, her voice at a noticeably higher pitch than when we had all been down on the laneway. "Did you not see me crawling up the fucking mountain like some kind of pack mule?" It was obvious that she was not as mesmerized by the view as was her husband.

He either thought that ignoring her was the best way to respond, or else he was really so smitten with the view from the top of the mountain that he failed to feel any empathy for her whatsoever.

"There's no place anywhere around that has this view," he continued.

I couldn't understand why he was so preoccupied with a view when my brother and I just wanted to get inside the bus and play. Whenever I wanted to get something and was afraid that I would be turned down, I talked Jimmy into asking.

"Ask him if we can go inside the bus," I whispered.

"Daddy," asked Jimmy, tugging on our father's sleeve, "can we go inside the bus to play?" His request was totally ignored, as our father's gaze was still drawn to the Donegal countryside.

"Please Daddy, please," he begged. Our father looked down when he felt the tugging.

"All right," he conceded, "let's go see how it looks from the inside."

My father opened the rear door of the bus, and was followed in by my mother and the baby. Jimmy got tangled up in their legs as he tried to squeeze in at the same time.

The inside of the bus looked...well, just like a bus. I was a bit surprised by this, as I thought for some reason that it would look more like a house. There were rows of seats along both sides of the bus as you went in the narrow door. There was only a narrow walkway between both rows, big enough for one person at a time to walk through.

"It's very narrow," my mother accurately pointed out.

"Don't worry about that," my father shot back. "There'll be much more room once we have taken out all of the seats. Right here," he said pointing to the area inside the door, "is where I'll put the range. The heat will rise up the stairs naturally," he said, as he walked toward the winding metal stairs, motioning for us to follow him like some kind of double-decker bus tour guide.

The stairs were also very narrow, and they went round and round like the stairs must have done in a lighthouse. His big body filled up the whole stairway, and his feet were so big that the tops of his shoes hung over the footing. Upstairs there were two more rows of bus seats. All four walls—well, they weren't exactly walls, but the tin sides of the bus – were covered in glass windows.

"I'll never have enough curtains," muttered my mother to herself.

"Can you imagine waking up every morning to this view?" asked my father. His obsession with the view knew no bounds. I was quite sure that he was starting to annoy my mother's arse.

"I hope you're right," my mother replied.

"Of course," my father shot back loudly. "Look at that view—it's going to be wonderful."

"I'm not talking about the friggin' view," she barked. "I'm talking about this bastard of a bus getting blown over by the wind. If it ever breaks free, it won't stop rolling until it reaches Malin."

Once again, she had me worried. I started to imagine the wind ripping the bus up, throwing it down the hill, arse-over-head, all the way to Malin Head. All of those windows would break, for one, and probably cut us all to shreds. Then there was the metal to consider. One time I cut my finger on the jagged edge of a can and I bled like a stuck pig. Whatever part of us the glass didn't cut to pieces would surely be ripped apart by the jagged tin edges.

"It can't happen," my father assured her. "Your father and I will tie this bitch down so that she won't budge an inch. Now let me show you where I'm putting your kitchen."

Once again he led the way, and we all obediently followed him downstairs and toward the front of the bus.

"Since we won't have too much room for cabinets, I'm going to build a table that will have two brick sides," he said, pointing to two bus seats toward the front left of the bus. "But it won't be an ordinary table," he assured her. "This table will have hinges, and the top will flip up so that you can put your pots and pans inside it where they'll be out of the way." I didn't know if he could actually do this or he was just bullshitting her to keep her quiet, but I had to admit that it did sound clever.

"Where's your brother gone?" my mother suddenly asked me, in a tone that suggested I was in charge of knowing where the little bastard was at any given moment.

"I don't know," I replied, shrugging my shoulders.

"Don't shrug your shoulders at me, you little fucker. Go find your brother." I looked under the seats in our make-believe kitchen, but he wasn't there. I had seen him come down from upstairs. He had to be on this floor, as there was no other place to go.

"What are you doing in there?" my mother called up toward the bus driver's seat. Inside the driver's wee room sat my brother, pulling the steering wheel to the left and right.

"I'm driving the bus," he told her. "Where do you want to go?"

"I'll *go* you," she hissed back at him. "Get down from there before you make the bus roll down the hill and we all get killed."

"That's where I'm putting the toilet," said my father, completely oblivious to the fact that my brother could accidently set off the handbrake at any moment and take us all for a ride on the bus.

I think that all this talk about make-believe kitchens, bedrooms, and bathrooms was starting to get the best of my mother. "Sure there is only room for one person to sit and barely stand in there, let alone do anything else," she said. "Where would you put a bathtub in that little space?"

My father didn't have an answer for that one.

"But it would be a lovely view as you were taking a shite, all the same," I chimed in. My father was still speechless, and my mother looked as if she were suddenly realizing that this had not been such a good idea after all.

"I'm going to the car—the baby needs feeding," she shot over her shoulder as she walked toward the door. We walked after her in silence, with no more talk about the view.

Over the coming weeks, my father spent all of his free time working on making the bus livable. He and Grandfather built a massive stone foundation for the bus to sit in, and they poured concrete into the bottom of the bus, covering the wheels and everything underneath. One Sunday about two months after the bus had been driven up to its final resting place, we drove up the mountain to see what kind of shape our new home was in.

My father was excited as he rushed to the front door. The tin-and-glass bus door had been replaced with a real wooden door, just like a real house. Strangely, the door opened to the outside, not inwards like normal house doors do in Ireland. It was the first thing to catch my mother's attention.

"Why does the door swing out and not in like other doors?" she asked him.

"There was not enough room to swing in," he said. "That's why the bus had a collapsible door before. Don't worry about that, though. Come in and see what I've done."

The inside of the bus had been massively redone. All of the seats had been taken out, and there was enough room for two people to walk past each other. Up toward the front sat a red brick table with a shiny black top.

"Look at this," he said, lifting up the top of the table to show a large space underneath where pots and pans could be stored.

At the end, under the stairs, was a little black Stanley Number 7 range, just as he had promised. My brother and I ran upstairs to see what it was like up there now. All of the seats were gone up there too; it was just an open space. It would make a great playroom. We bound back down the winding stairway, making believe that we were Batman and Robin heading off to fight crime after getting a call at the Batcave. I was Batman, of course.

"Where's the bathroom?" asked my mother.

"Well, there isn't one yet," my father admitted. "I'm going to have to build a bit on to the driver's cubicle somehow."

"Is there electricity?" she wanted to know.

"The Electricity Supply Board will need a few weeks to run the line up," he told her. "In the meantime, Sam said we can borrow a couple of Tilley oil lamps for light at night. We can move in next week if you want."

I put the idea of going out to play into my brother's head so that he could ask. For some reason or another, our mother agreed to let us out.

"Stay around where we can see youns," she instructed us.

The top of the mountain had a bunch of whin bushes. We made believe that we were cowboys out in the Wild West and the whin bushes were tumbleweed.

"Watch out for Indians and rattlesnakes," I warned my brother. He peered at me with a very worried look on his face.

"What happens if I see one?" he asked.

"Nothing, you eejit. Sure, everybody knows there are no snakes in Ireland." The worried look left his face and he crouched over, making his way through the bushes.

"Watch out for the Indians, though. We do have *them* running around."

The terrified look on his face as he came running back to me was priceless. There was a big hole dug behind the bus. We stared down into it and looked at the muddy water at the bottom.

"What made the hole?" he asked me.

"Probably some kind of mountain monster," I answered casually. Scaring him was way too easy.

Just then the door of the bus swung open out and my mother and father both stepped out.

"I had the water diviner man from Clonmany come out, and he said that this would make a good well," advised my father, pointing at the hole with the muddy water.

"I suppose we can wait a while for the ESB," conceded my mother. "It'll be hard doing without a bathroom, but hopefully you'll get one made soon."

"That's it then, boys," said my father, rubbing his hands together. "We move into our new house next week."

"Where's the new house?" my brother whispered to me.

"This is it," I told him.

"But this is a bus."

"That's the whole point," I reminded him. "We are turning a bus into our house. Why did you think we brought it up here and put a cooker into it and took out all of the seats?"

"I thought they were making a play house for us," he replied, as serious as a heart attack.

I forgave him for being stupid. After all, he was still young, and nobody would come up with such a mental idea as living on the side of a mountain in Ireland in a double-decker bus, except for our mad father. Nor would it be the last idea he would have that would make people look at us like we belonged in a mental asylum. When it came to mad ideas, the Big Yank took the biscuit.

CHAPTER 12
WATER AND PISS POTS

In all fairness, I don't think parents set out to deliberately embarrass their children. But some, like our parents, seem to have a real knack for it. Looking back, I can see how nearly everything they did (and when I say *they*, I mostly mean my father) made others laugh at us, fight with us, or make life uncomfortable for us in some other miserable fashion.

Take moving to Donegal, for example. It is hard to imagine a more remote, isolated environment than the Inishowen Peninsula in the late 60s. Not that I didn't learn to love the place as if I had been born there, for I did. But from the get-go, we were going to stick out just by being Yanks. The crazy shit that my father got up to only added fuel to the fire.

He was very proud of his idea to live in a bus on the side of the mountain. He would tell everyone he ran into about it. I thought it was all right, but I wasn't about to go telling the whole school about our new living arrangements. It wasn't as if we were a bunch of hippies, or he was some kind of famous writer or painter the likes of which could be forgiven for his eccentricity. He was a cook, for fuck's sake. Unfortunately, it didn't take long for word to get out around the school. My classmates began to quiz me nonstop.

"Is it true that youns are living in a double-decker bus?" Paul Sweeney asked with bulging eyes.

"It used to be a bus, but our father turned it into a house," I explained. Liam Sullivan was standing next to Sweeney, though, and I knew the little bollix would have something to say.

"But your house has four wheels, Yank," came the smart reply.

"My grandfather and father built a foundation, and it is the same as a house now," I replied in defense of my father's decision.

"Why can't youns Yanks just live in a normal house like everyone else?" continued Sullivan. "*We* don't get the notion to drive away in our houses." This drew a laugh from several of the boys who had gathered around to listen in on the conversation. I felt the anger swelling up inside me, and I knew that my efforts to resolve this discussion in a diplomatic fashion were coming to an end.

"Shut up, Sullivan, you little hoor."

"Why don't you make me, Yank?"

"I *will* make you shut up, you skittery little shite."

"Oh aye, you and whose army? Are you going to call in the American army to help you, Yank? Calling John Wayne, calling John Wayne—you're needed to save a Yank from getting his arse beaten."

That was the straw that broke my back. I made a fist with my right hand and was about to lunge at Sullivan when he pushed me back and I fell arse-over-head. One of his friends had gone down on his hands and knees behind me, and I fell backwards over the obstacle. Before I could get back up, Sullivan had jumped on me, pinning my arms back with his knees. I flailed out as much as I could, but he had gotten the upper hand through sneaky tricks and was now punching my face. My pipe-smoking friend Logue pulled him off when my nose started to bleed. I didn't have much time to clean up either, as the bell was ringing, which meant that lunch was over and it was time to get back to class. Once inside, it didn't take long for Master Quigley to notice that I was worse for the wear. He called me up to his desk.

"Who did this to you?" he demanded.

I was reluctant to rat out Sullivan, even if he was a little prick. I tried to think of a way to get out of this so that it wouldn't have any repercussions, but I could see a fire starting to burn in Quigley's eyes. Sullivan had landed a few decent blows on me and had done a bit of damage, but that would pale in comparison to Seamus' fists if I made him beat the answer out of me.

"Liam Sullivan, Sir," I replied, staring at the ground.

"SULLIVAN!" roared Quigley. "Get up here *now!*" Sullivan wasn't in a hurry to face the music, and he took his time putting away his paper and pen as he climbed from his seat.

"If I have to go down there and bring you up..." Seamus didn't need to finish that sentence. We all knew it wouldn't be a pretty sight. Sullivan took heed of this added incentive and hurried himself up.

"What's the meaning of this?" Master Quigley asked Sullivan, motioning toward me.

"We were just messing, Sir," the wide-eyed boy replied.

"Who started it?" Seamus asked, looking from one of us to the other. Neither of us particularly wanted to volunteer.

"We were arguing about the Yank living in a double-decker bus and we got carried away," Sullivan offered. I figured that Master Quigley would have taken the cane to Sullivan, as this was tantamount to admitting responsibility. Instead, he looked over at me with his eyebrows raised and forehead wrinkled.

"You live in a *double-decker bus?*" he asked, his mouth hanging open.

"Yes Sir, but our father has turned it into a house."

"Where...how...do you turn a bus into a house?" It was the first time I had ever seen our teacher at a loss for words.

"We towed the bus up onto the mountain on the Buncrana Road and then we built a stone wall around the wheels." I was actually starting to enjoy telling the story again, as Master Quigley seemed to be genuinely interested.

"So you don't drive around in the bus and live in it at the same time?" he asked.

"Oh no, Sir, it's not for driving anymore. Besides, we took out all the seats and put in a range and a kitchen table."

"And...you sleep...?"

"Yes Sir, we sleep in it. The seats for the bus riders have all been taken out, and we have two big beds up on the top deck."

"Well, that's a good one," replied Quigley, shaking his head, just as the lorry driver had after he took the bus up to the mountain.

In the months that followed, that bus was responsible for more fights than any other single argument-starter could ever have been. Countless bloody noses—both my own and other boys'—occurred in the schoolyard during breaks and on walks home.

After many months, I learned to ignore the comments in order to avoid a punch-up, but they still got to me. It also didn't help that the fun of living in a bus was beginning to fade. The ESB took weeks to come out and connect us to a power line, and with winter on its way, it soon started getting dark shortly after we got home from school. My father's well was less than a raging success, and until someone could be found to fix it we had to carry buckets of water up the laneway from old Sam's well. I started to wonder why we couldn't have been more like the other families who lived in normal houses.

I learned a lot of things living in a bus that I had never had to think about before. For instance, people use much more water than I had ever imagined. Getting water used to be as easy as turning on a tap, but now that it had to be physically carried, it seemed that we were always running out. At first we tried to carry the water up in buckets using the car, but between the bumpy lane from Sam's house and the steep hill up to the bus, half of the water would splash out into the car. For some reason or other, my mother decided that I was to be the official water carrier of the family. Once I became the water boy, I quickly realized something else about water—it's fucking heavy. Hercules himself could have hardly carried full buckets of water up our steep hill.

With my official duties came the realization that going out to play after getting home from school was no longer an option. This was tough to deal with, since school was made all the more bearable when you could look forward to coming home and playing before dinner or doing your lessons. As soon as I walked in the door after school, I was told to fetch a bucket and bring up water.

When you are a young fella, there is no such thing as a direct route to anything. Walking down the lane was a daily adventure. If there were blackberries to be seen, they would be picked and eaten. Spotting a rabbit in one of Sam's fields meant that further investigation was needed, in order to discover where the rabbit's hole was located in case I should want to make a snare and place it there later.

When the well was finally reached and the water scooped up, the long journey back to the bus would begin. It was not too bad walking along the laneway itself, unless it was raining. When it rained, however, it became muddy and slippery, which was a treacherous condition for a water boy. More than once I had to go back and start all over again when I lost my footing and the bucket went flying. Whenever a bucket fell into the mud, the whole process was excruciatingly delayed. I'd have to go back to the well, wash the inside and outside of the bucket until not one speck of mud was to be seen, then start dragging it up the hill again.

Even without the rain to contend with, hauling water was just plain hard work. The last few feet up the hill were always the worst. The reception I got once I brought the water into the bus-house did nothing to encourage me either. My mother was usually in a bad mood, and God help me if she had run out of water and was waiting for it to start cooking dinner or do the washing.

"Where have you been all this time? Off gallivanting when you should have been doing your chores?" was a typical type of greeting. Another was, "You must have been making the water for the time it took you to bring it to me."

If she ever just thanked me, I'd probably have had a friggin' seizure from the shock. The worst of it for me, though, was having to turn around and do the same thing all over again.

"What do you call that?" she'd often ask when I opened the door and left the water offering at her feet.

I looked down at the water in the bucket and was fierce tempted to say "water," but I knew that would only lead to a beating. After I had simply stared into the bucket for a few seconds, she would answer her own question for me.

"That's only half a bucket, what do you expect me to do with that? Sure I could hardly wash your little brother's arse with that bit of water."

Then only wash half of his arse, I wanted to say.

"Get back down the hill and bring up enough water for everybody," she barked, pulling me out of my smart-mouth dream state.

On days like that, I cursed my father for coming up with the mental idea of living in a bus, Grandfather for helping to make it work, Kevin for needing his arse washed so much—hell, I even cursed Lough Swilly for selling us the fucking bus in the first place. Being a Yank in Donegal was tough enough without adding to the hardship by living in a bus.

⟨+ +⟩

Another thing we soon came to realize was that there was not much room in a bus when two parents and three children had to live in it. Most people just get on a bus and after a short while get off it again. But we had a one-way ticket.

Adding to the difficulty was the fact that the bus was plopped down on top of a mountain. Even on days when the weather was calm down below in Carn, the wind whipped against our tin walls. Most of the time it felt like living in a continual storm. The longer we lived up there, the more moody my mother became. She and my father were fighting more and more, and it only became worse when he told her that he was closing the canteen.

"How are we going to live if you close it?" she demanded.

"Well, I can't keep losing money," he told her. "I owe the bakers, the butcher, the mineral people—hell, I haven't even been able to pay the rent for the past month. The factory manager told me that they can't let me keep running the kitchen without paying rent. If I can't come up with the past month's rent and a month in advance, Friday will be my last day."

"What are we to do?" she asked him, continuing on before he could offer up a possible solution. "We have all of these mouths to feed and now another one on the way." Another one on the way? Were we expecting visitors? If we had some relatives coming over from America to visit us, I didn't know where they were going to sleep.

"Don't worry," he told her. "I'll find something. We've always been able to make a go of it."

"I wish you had been able to make a go of that bathroom you promised to build for us six months ago," she shot back.

I have to say, she did have a point there. Like running water, you'll never appreciate a bathroom so much as you will when it's been taken away from you. It also introduced me to something we would use for many years to come: the "piss pot." If you've ever lived on a bus without a toilet, or in a thatched cottage, you will know *all too well* the importance of a piss pot. I say "a bus without a toilet," as I've discovered decades later that people in places like America live in camper homes fully outfitted with kitchens, living rooms with televisions, and bathrooms with toilets. I also learned later in life that tour buses and the like normally have a toilet on board. No such luck with Lough Swilly buses.

The piss pot is a very unassuming device. Its humble appearance is deceiving, for it wields incredible power, especially in the dead of night. When your house—or in our case, your bus—doesn't have a toilet facility and you wake up in the middle of the night busting for a piss, you have little option but to go outside and relieve yourself, unless you had the presence of mind to leave a bucket at the end of the bed for that purpose. Before bed, nobody would ever consider pissing into the bucket. That just wouldn't be proper. On those occasions, you would step outside and make your water, or whatever you had to do, in the bushes. It might sound simple enough, but taking a pee atop an Irish mountainside on a winter's night was anything but simple.

The first obstacle was that fucking door which opened out instead of in. With the winter wind outside whipping in every direction known to man, as soon as you'd open the door the smallest crack, the wind would get in around it and under it. Eight times out of ten, it would pull the door straight out of your hand and smash it against the side of the bus. If you didn't make a mad dash out into the gale force and body-slam the door closed behind you, the whole house would be shouting abuse at you until such time as you did.

If you've never lived in a bus on top of a Donegal mountain, you might not realize how relentless the gale force blows. The wind up there has a mind of its own and it changes its mind like a swallow changes its flight pattern. It made me laugh to hear a weatherman on the local news talking about a "south-easterly" wind. I couldn't be a weatherman unless they would let me add a disclaimer: "Disregard if you live in North Donegal—then all bets are off, since the wind up there is a crazy drugged-out bitch who will blow anything that crosses her path."

Dealing with the wind was only the beginning of the journey. Officially, we were instructed to go out behind the bus and make our water in the whin bushes. The man of the house didn't really think that one through too well, considering that we had no outside light and this route involved walking by a well with enough water in the bottom to drown all three of his sons at the same time. Those of us who didn't drown right away would probably have died from exposure to the cold before anybody even realized that we were missing.

I tried doing as instructed for a time or two, but quickly realized that it was a hopeless task. Even if you did manage to negotiate the dangerous trek to the bushes, you had to try and guess which way the wind was blowing so that you didn't relieve yourself into it. I did that one time and was so concentrated on making it back into the relative comfort of the bus that I had no idea what had happened until I got back in and my mother asked me why I had pissed all over myself. On another occasion I got too close to a whin bush and it stabbed my mickey with its needle. The advantage of getting close to the bushes was that they provided a wee bit of shelter and made it a tad easier to go without ending up drenched in your own piss.

After I learned that you literally took your life into your own hands every night that you stepped outside with your mickey out, I decided to play it safe. All of my future nocturnal pissing would be done from the front doorstep. There was no danger of the urine building up and leaving the front door area smelly, since it rained every night. On those rare occasions when it didn't, I'd bring a cupful of water out with me and throw it over the area I had just sprinkled. Nobody ever seemed any the wiser. Maybe they figured it was not right to ask what I was doing with the water, since it was me who was carrying the shagging stuff up the mountain in the first place.

If the night was particularly hateful and if the rain was lashing too hard, I would try to hold it in and wait until bedtime, since that was the one time when it was acceptable to pee inside. It was always called a piss pot, but in actual fact we never used anything as small as a pot. With four people relieving themselves all night long, you definitely needed a bucket. Thankfully, I was still too young to be allowed to empty the bucket. I think that parental decision was reached after they saw me slip one too many times with the water bucket. If I could spill half a bucket of water all over myself, I shudder to think what kind of an unholy mess I would make negotiating a full-to-the-brim bucket of piss down the winding metal bus stairs and out the door.

While the emptying duties usually fell to my father, I didn't have to wait too long to be chosen for the job. I soon found out that there was no breaking-in or official training period associated with becoming a piss pot-emptier. All tips were picked up on the job, so to speak. There was one unwritten rule regarding emptying the pot: The last one to pee into the bucket had to empty it if it was filled to a point where somebody else could possibly make it overflow. The last thing you would ever want was an over-flowing piss pot.

Carrying an overflowing bucket was tempting fate. I've done it, so I know. Even if you made it out the door without spilling any of the contents inside, you had to have a firm grasp of the bucket. The only way to really do this was to stick your thumbs inside both sides and squeeze the outside of the bucket tightly with your other eight fingers. Of course, the wind would be blowing like a bastard once you made it out the door, and there was no way to escape the piss spray coming off the top of the bucket.

The "two-thumbs-in-the-piss pot" method of carrying the bucket worked just fine as long as there was not a lot of pissing going on that night. On those nights when there was, whoever had the misfortune to grab hold of the bucket had no other option than to plunge their thumbs into everybody else's piss. It wasn't a very pleasant experience, but it sure got me out of the habit of biting my nails.

My mother went on, day in and day out, about my father building a toilet where the bus driver used to sit. I think that it was too tall an order to ever be carried out. Even to this day, when I ride a bus, especially a double-decker bus in Dublin, I often steal a glance at the driver and wonder how in the name of God you could fit a sink, toilet bowl, and bathtub into that seat.

My parents began to argue more about using up all our savings, so I knew money was getting tight. However, I never knew if we were on the verge of becoming destitute, or if my father just wanted to get away from my mother's nagging when he decided to go to Scotland for work.

⊨⊣⊢⊨

My father soon dropped the bombshell on us that he would be heading off to Scotland to plant sapling trees in a forest in a few days' time. He said he would be gone only a few months and he'd be back before we knew it. He told me that during his absence I would be the "man of the house," and that I was to look after my mother and brothers.

At first thought, I was kind of excited to be thought of as the man of the house. But being the practical little bastard that I was, it soon dawned on me that a lot more work was bound to come along with this promotion. I got that right. One of the first things I discovered was that I now had to pick up where my father had left off in his piss pot-emptying duties. (At least we were a man down, so the bucket would not fill as quickly.) The other chore added to my growing list of responsibilities was the gathering of firewood. When my father had the canteen running, we would always buy coal or turf for the fireplace. Now that we no longer had money, we had to scrape and scrounge for fuel for the range.

During the day my mother would collect pieces of whin bushes to burn. Sometimes Sam down the lane would tell her to take turf from his shed. My job during the weekend (for I was a full-time water carrier during the week) was to troll through the fields looking for tree branches that had fallen in stormy weather, and carry or drag them back. If they were large and needed to be carried, my mother would saw them into little pieces, as she couldn't trust me with a saw. She had stopped trusting me, perhaps understandably, the day she watched from inside as I chased my brother around the outside of the bus threatening to saw off his legs because he had touched my football cards.

I don't remember the exact time that I noticed it, but at some stage I realized that my mother was going to have a baby. Her stomach was getting bigger, and it wasn't because we were eating a lot. In fact, the opposite was true. We brought sandwiches to eat on our lunch break at school, but they were always the same thing: bread and strawberry jam. The jam would soak into the bread, turning it red. If you left any of it in your bag, by the time you got home from school the bread would have become hard. I once made the mistake of taking the old bread I had not eaten back home, and I thought my mother was going to have a fit when she saw it.

"What's this bread doing in your bag? Was it not good enough for you? Do you think I'm made of money?"

"I was saving it for the walk home, but we ate blackberries and I forgot to have it."

"Then you can keep saving it," she growled, "and you can bring it to school tomorrow."

I knew that the bread would be rock-hard the next day. Hopefully I could talk my brother into sharing his lunch. It would still only be jam, but at least it wouldn't be two-day-old jam. We did have a little fridge in the bus, now that we had electricity, but we didn't seem to have enough money to buy much. Apart from milk, leftover scraps and sometimes butter, there was hardly ever anything to eat for lunch besides jam sandwiches. Things were so tight that it was a treat to have both butter and jam on our bread. Butter kept the jam from soaking into the bread as badly, and as a result the bread didn't become as hard.

I don't know how I came up with the idea, or the name, but after we moved into the bus I started to take chocolate milk to school. It wasn't chocolate milk like they would sell in a shop. I don't believe they even sold chocolate milk in shops back then, so I don't know where I got the notion. My chocolate milk was made by adding cocoa powder to ordinary milk. In the beginning I carried it in a little glass bottle in my school bag, but the first time I used the bag in an afterschool fight the glass broke. It was the last time I was allowed to carry glass in my school bag. After that I was forced to put the milk into an old World War II soldier's canteen made of tin and covered by a green canvas pouch. The top screwed on, but had a little metal chain fastened to the canteen that kept it from falling off after it'd been opened.

Having seen my strange choice of beverage, one of the neighborhood boys asked me what I was drinking. I didn't want to say milk in case it made me sound like a baby, so I said the first thing that came into my head: "Dog's milk."

"Dog's milk?"

"Aye, dog's milk."

"That's disgusting as all fuck," he informed me.

"It's supposed to make you strong as fuck," I enlightened him, "and what's more, it makes your teeth strong and sharp like dogs' teeth." I could see his mind working on that one. Since he hadn't completely shot down the possibility that I was really drinking dog's milk, I figured that I'd have a bit of craic with him.

"Do you want a slug of it?" I asked, holding up the bottle of brownish-colored milk. He gingerly sniffed the contents of the bottle and looked at me like I had two heads.

"Does it make you feel any different?" he asked.

The fish had bitten the hook, and now it was time to reel him in.

"Not really, but every once in a while I do feel the urge to chase after a cat. I don't remember if I felt that way before, but I definitely get the craving this last while."

He stared at me with his gob hanging open. "How do you get the milk?" he asked. Good friggin' question.

"My mother gets it for me. I think she milks our dog for it. Blackie had pups a while back, so she has milk for them."

Not a bad effort, considering I had to pull it out of my arse without warning. I thought no more about this incident until a few days later, when more boys came up to me asking me to show them my dog's milk. Most of them turned up their noses at the idea of drinking milk which had come from a dog, but I noticed a few of them began staring more closely at my teeth.

⚓ ⚓

The longer my father was away in Scotland, the harder life became. My mother's stomach grew bigger; and the bigger it got, the more she found reason to yell at us.

Also, she was not able to do as many things as she could before my father left. Bending over for firewood was the latest thing to be taken off her list of chores. Of course, being the man of the house meant that I had to do all the things she could no longer do. I was in charge of water carrying, firewood collecting, piss pot emptying, dog-milk making, and anything else that could not be done by a woman with a huge belly.

One day when we came home from school, she told my brother and me that we had to help her clean the house/bus as my father was on his way back from Scotland.

"The two of youns are going to help me clean up this kip before your father gets home," was how she put it.

He was due to come across on the ferry to Belfast the next day and take the train down to Derry. Jimmy was excited to see Father and was wondering what he would bring back for us. I was looking forward to his coming home as well, but for different reasons. I was fed up with this "man of the house" shite and eagerly looking forward to handing back the title.

The night Father returned resulted in one of my better memories of him. He brought us back Scottish berets that he called "Tam O' Shanters" and a strange Scotch food called haggis. The prospect of eating haggis for dinner did not thrill my mother. She said she had eaten it before, when she studied nursing in Scotland, and it disgusted her. My father boiled it up as he told us stories about his time working in Scotland planting trees. My mother said that haggis was a load of sheeps' guts. But it tasted delicious, so I figured she had to be wrong about that.

The night that my father returned from Scotland was one of the few times—maybe the only time—that I actually felt sorry for him. He was not the type to do well with manual labor, yet that made up his work in the mountains of Scotland. He lived in a workhouse with a bunch of men, mostly Irishmen, and was given a sack of saplings and a spade each day. The ground had been turned over, and their job was to stick the spade into the turned sod and plant the young tree in the opening they had just made.

He said they worked "piecemeal," which meant that the harder you worked, the more they paid you. I really hoped that he had used his feet on the spade as well as he did when he was stomping on me with them, for if he did, we would surely be eating well for several months to come. But otherwise, even if we had to go back to eating jam sandwiches for lunch, at least he'd be able to resume his job as the chief piss pot emptier.

My father and mother did a lot of talking about "the hospital" after his return, and while they never said anything to us directly, I knew that my mother was soon going to have another baby. My brother didn't pay much attention and just thought she was getting fatter. She was not as vexed anymore now that my father was back. She was even able to laugh about some of the things that had happened while he was gone that she had definitely not laughed about when they happened. For instance, there was the time she had opened up the top of the table and saw a rat sitting down below with the pots and pans. I thought she was going to go totally mad. She slammed down the top of the table and shouted at me to go down the lane and get Sam. I didn't know what rat catching or fighting abilities old Sam had, but none of us knew what to do, so it seemed like a fairly decent idea.

Sam was a nice old man. He looked like he had to be at least 100 years old; and whatever his age, his wife was even older. He was always so calm and pleasant. I don't know if he had hair, for I never saw him without his cap. His face was pink like a baby's, and all of the skin that could be seen around his cap was the same color. The closest I ever heard him come to raising his voice was when he had to yell at his dog to herd the cows into the barn as they came in from the fields in the evening.

The one thing that bothered me about Sam, though, was that the poor old man had T.B. It wasn't just that I thought he looked like he *might* have T.B. He admitted to having had it. He told us stories about the time when he was in hospital for it. Every day he used to drink one bottle of Guinness, because the doctor told him that it was good to keep up his strength. I was always afraid that he would breathe on me and give me T.B, because anybody who had T.B. couldn't breathe well, and that meant that you could never play rugby for Ireland or football for Manchester United.

I was half out of breath by the time I reached Sam's house, as I had run the whole way. He was standing outside of his front door feeding his dog. "What's happened, lad, is everything all right at home?" he asked, moving closer to me.

"Rat," I sputtered, "rat in the kitchen. Our mother told me to come and fetch you."

I tried to pull back a bit so I wouldn't catch his T.B., but with the trouble I had breathing, I was afraid that I might already have it.

Sam calmly reached for his walking stick and said, "Let's see what we can do."

As we walked up the lane together, I tried looking at him out of the side of my eye to see what he was going to use to trap the rat. I didn't want to ask him, since he seemed to be having a bit of bother breathing. When his chest wheezed, it sounded a bit like my father's accordion. He'd take two steps and then tap the end of the walking stick down in the dirt.

When we came to the foot of our hill, he turned to me and said, "You run on up and tell your mother I'll be there shortly. I just need to take a wee breather."

I belted off up the hill and was nearly at the front step before Sam finished his wee breather. My mother was sitting in a chair by the range, holding a broomstick in her hands.

"Was Sam not at home?" she asked me worriedly when I walked in alone.

"He was, aye," I replied. "He told me to run on ahead. He'll be up shortly." She looked relieved. Several minutes later there was a knock on the door. I opened it and let Sam inside. "I hear youns have a visitor, Sadie," he said in his calm voice.

My mother didn't say anything, but pointed to the table. Sam had seen the bus at various stages as it was being turned into a house, so he knew that the table lifted up. He opened it up and said, "There he is." With that, he turned his walking stick upside down and stuck the part he held in his hand down into the bottom of the table. It looked like he only gave it a wee tap before he took it back out and said, "That'll do him."

"Did you get him?" my mother asked.

"Oh aye," said Sam. "I just needed to tap him on the back. Rats have fierce weak backs. The slightest little tap at all will break it, and they die right away."

Then he turned the walking stick around again and stuck the end that had been tapping the dirt back down into the bottom of the table. He wiggled it around a bit and pulled out the rat, who seemed to be hanging on to the stick by its long tail. Sam must have twirled the rat's tail around his walking stick, like you would do with spaghetti on your fork.

"I'll get rid of this for you, Sadie," Sam said, walking toward the door.

"Can I get you a cup of tea, Sam?" my mother asked.

"Ah no, don't bother yourself. I'll have to get the milking started soon. You know where I am if you need anything."

I was glad he wasn't going to stay. God knows how much T.B. he could have spread throughout the bus if he'd sat down and drank a couple of cups of tea. We might have all been rotten with it by the time my father got back from Scotland.

Now that we were able to eat a feed of haggis, wear our Scottish caps, and laugh about funny stories, life didn't seem too bad. While we lacked a proper bathroom, we did have electricity. Even the water carrying didn't seem as hateful—and I might not even have to carry it for that much longer, since my father said he was getting in a man to fix the well.

Just as things were settling down nicely, my father made the announcement that our mother would be going into the hospital the next day to have the baby. For some strange reason, he seemed happy. I was wondering to myself, *where are we going to put this baby?*

"Where will we put it?" I asked, not even realizing that I had said it out loud.

"Put what?" asked my father

"The baby. Where's it going to sleep?" I was finding it difficult trying to work this one out.

"With your mother and I, of course," he replied. "You three boys can all sleep in one double bed and the three of us will sleep in the other one. Not right away, of course," he added. "For the first few months the baby will sleep in a cot, like you all did."

Fucking great, I thought, *one more obstacle to get in the way when I empty the piss pot.* I resolved not to piss inside anymore. If I didn't use the bucket, I wouldn't have to empty it.

The next day my father picked us up from school and told us that my mother was in Carn hospital.

"Did she have a baby yet?" my brother asked.

"She did," my father replied with a big smile. "You have a baby sister. We're going to go and visit her for a few minutes now so you can meet her."

Neither my brother nor I were that into babies, but we did enjoy going shopping with my father for food after we left the hospital. He bought all kinds of goodies that we had not seen in a while. He said that he wanted to have the house nice and warm (he always called the bus a "house") for my mother and the baby when he picked them up from the hospital in a few days. He cooked pastries, and made two loaves of soda bread with raisins. The day she was coming home, he planned to make steak and baked potatoes.

I remember that Saturday like it was yesterday. I woke up early and looked over at my father's bed, but he wasn't there. The bus was filled with the smell of cooking, and the upstairs was warm and toasty. Downstairs I could hear someone moving around and knew it must be my father getting the place ready. About an hour later he came back upstairs and woke us up.

"Who wants pancakes for breakfast?" he asked us.

I raised my hand, as that was the drill we had been taught in school. He told us the food would be ready by the time we had dressed. After we were fed, my father filled the range with coal he had bought when he got back from Scotland. He wanted to make sure it would be nice and warm for the baby when we got back. We all piled into my father's Morris Minor and headed to Carn hospital.

Unfortunately, picking up a new baby did not turn out to be a quick job. I don't know if the hospital got our baby mixed up with someone else's, or what caused the delay, but my two brothers and I sat in the waiting room for a couple of hours. My father was with my mother and the nurses, and he only came to check on us once.

Jimmy wanted to play tag. "Don't be such an amadan," I told him. "We can't go running around a hospital playing tag."

"Why not?" he pouted. "There's plenty of room to do it."

"This place is full of old people," I reminded him. "God knows what they'd break if we went running into them."

Luckily, I didn't have to talk him out of any more daft ideas, as my father soon appeared. He was carrying a baby's basket and walking alongside my mother, who was being pushed in a wheelchair by a nurse.

"Hello, my boys," she greeted us in a way that almost sounded like she missed us. "Wait here with me until your father brings around the car." A few minutes later, we were all cramming into the Morris Minor.

"The house will be very warm. This little girl will be as snug as a bug in a rug," he told her as we drove down the Mill Brae on our way to the Buncrana road. "We are going to have steak with creamed carrots and baked potatoes for dinner to celebrate."

"Oh God, that will be a welcome change from the prison food they serve in that hospital," my mother remarked.

As we made our way around the Carndonagh Cross, just past Ard Colgan, the fire brigade overtook us and screamed past us with their lights flashing. "Some poor devil is in trouble by the looks of things," said my mother as we motored on up the hill, all quietly looking forward to our welcome home party.

Our bus stood at the foot of the big mountain behind Sam's fields, and it made a strange backdrop against the sky. There was never any mistaking that it was a double-decker bus. I'm sure that many a person who saw that silhouette for the first time did a double-take when they saw it parked up on the side of a hill.

As we rounded the bend just past the Ducks' house, I spotted what looked like smoke pouring out of the bus. It sat way up on the hill, so it was hard to see clearly from my spot in the backseat behind my father as we drove up the Buncrana road. However, as we got a bit closer, I could see the big red fire brigade on the laneway at the foot of our driveway.

"I think the bus is on fire," I said to nobody in particular.

"Stop acting the maggot," my mother told me.

"All right, but look for yourself," I said, pointing up at the bus.

"Jesus Christ, I think it *is* on fire," my mother screeched.

"It couldn't be," said my father, trying to keep the car on the road as he stole glances to his right.

He started driving faster, and took the right hand turn onto Sam's road so fast that I thought the car was going to topple over onto its rounded top. Everything still looked normal as we drove past Sam's house, but as we came to the clearing in the laneway hedges, we could suddenly all see clearly up to the bus. Flames were shooting out of the windows by the door, and black smoke was pouring out of nearly every other window. The fire brigade had only made it up the hill part of the way, and it looked like the firemen were trying to put out the fire the best that they could. My brothers started to cry.

"Wait here. I'll go see what they have to say," my father told us.

He walked up the hill toward the firemen. Fifteen minutes later, he came back down. He looked very white, and his lower lip seemed to be twitching, but no sound was coming out of his mouth.

"What did they say to you?" asked my mother.

"They said it was a lost cause," he replied slowly and softly. "They told me to come up tomorrow and see if there was anything that could be salvaged, but it was unsafe to try and look this evening. They will keep putting the fire out. They're afraid of it spreading to the whin bushes, and maybe even traveling down to Sam's house."

"Dear Jesus, what are we going to do now?" she asked him. When he didn't reply right away, she asked him again. "What are we going to do, John? We're homeless, with a new baby. Where are we going to live?"

"We'll have to ask your cousin if she has room in her B&B." His answer was solid enough, but he appeared to be in a bit of a trance.

"Can I go up to get my football?" Jimmy asked. Everybody ignored him. I suppose the question was too stupid to deserve an answer. My father slowly reversed the Morris Minor back down the lane and turned around in Sam's yard. Sam's wife came out and approached the car.

"I'm fierce sorry about what happened to your place," she said with tears in her eyes as she leaned on the driver's door. "Sam went into town. He should be home shortly. You can stay here the night. You need a place to stay, with a new baby and all."

"Thank you, Violet," said my father, "but Sarah's cousin has a B&B in town and she more than likely has a room we can use until we decide what we are going to do."

What a relief that he didn't take her up on her offer. Bad enough that our bus had burned down and everything we owned in the world was now gone, but catching a dose of T.B. with the new baby and all would have made things a lot worse.

It probably doesn't sound right, but I was actually looking forward to going to the B&B. We had good fun playing with the cousins when we first came over from America, but the biggest selling point for me was that they had bathrooms. Bathrooms meant no more emptying piss pots, at least for a while.

The next day my father, my brother, and I drove up to look at the damage. Nobody wanted my mother to go in case it vexed her. She had to stay and mind the baby. I was the spotter, looking out the front window, as I was sitting in the passenger's seat. As soon we rounded the bend by the Ducks' house, I saw the frame against the morning sky. It was still smoking. My father stole glances to his right but never said a word. We drove slowly up our road and got out to take in the grim scene.

The front door looked like it had been attacked by somebody with an axe. The whole place smelled smoky. My father told us to stand by the car as he looked around. He slowly stepped inside the front door. We couldn't see him inside since the windows were all black. A few minutes later he came back out and told us that it was too dangerous to go inside, as both floors were all burned up. He said you could see upstairs by looking up from the floor down below.

"Did you see my football?" asked Jimmy. The little fucker had to be part half-wit.

"No, I didn't, son," my father answered. "I'll get you a new one tomorrow." *That jammy little bastard,* I thought to myself. I suppose he wasn't that much of a half-wit after all.

CHAPTER 13

ONE FIELD FARMER

I don't know exactly how long we stayed at our cousin's B&B, but it was good while it lasted. My brothers and I had our own bedroom, while our parents shared another room with the new baby. It was such a pleasure not to have to go out into the cold and dark when I needed to pee. Television was also a novelty. We got used to not having it in the bus, but my brothers were lapping it up now. I swear, those little bastards could watch cartoons until the cows came home.

All good things come to an end, however, and about a week after getting burned out, my father made the announcement that he had found a new house for us. Jimmy asked him if it was a real house or a bus, which made him smile. It was a fair question, though. Knowing my father, it wouldn't surprise me if he told us we were going to move into a covered wagon and take to the road.

"Will we have to go to a new school?" I asked him.

It would be a right hoor having to go to a new school and get into a whole bunch of fights all over again. Not that we totally stopped fighting at our own National school. It was just a bit easier now, as I had a good number of scraps under my belt, and there were plenty of boys who knew I could beat them and had stopped challenging me. Also, we were sort of fitting in—as much as could be expected, at any rate. For some reason or other, my teacher seemed to like me, or at least like me enough that he tended to beat me much less often than he did the other boys. Headmaster McCafferty had died at the end of my time in 4th grade, and Seamus had moved in to teach the senior classes.

"No, we're staying here in Carn," he reassured me. "The house is just down the road from where we were, but closer to town. It's a little thatched cottage with neighbors around it and only a few minutes away from your school."

It sounded like a good deal—a new house, not a bus, and it was closer to town. Then I remembered that we had moved out of a house because my parents didn't have the money to spend on rent. I wondered how they'd afford it now.

It was difficult trying to settle in anywhere when you were always moving. One thing I did come to realize, though, whenever you went from a good place to a bad place, it really made you miss the good place. The house where we learned to smoke pipes was a good place. Actually, I now ranked any house that had a bathroom and electricity as a good place. I didn't care if the roof leaked. We could always put a bucket under the leak to catch the water.

I would say that life became strange after we moved into the thatch cottage as a result of our bus burning down, but our life was always pretty strange. It might be more accurate to say that it became *stranger.*

I wondered what escapades and new adventures we could expect from the new house. I also wondered about whether there were neighbor boys our own age. Our closest neighbors at the bus were an old man and woman near enough to age 100, we figured. Maybe now there would be others around our own age with which to play football and climb trees.

A few days later we were introduced to the "new house." It was an old thatch cottage with just two rooms and no bathroom. It did have electricity, though. As soon as I realized that it didn't have a bathroom, I knew that it was back to the piss pot for us. Six of us in two rooms didn't leave much space. But then again, after losing everything in the fire, we didn't have much to bring with us.

"Who are the neighbors?" I asked my father after we took the grand tour of the inside, which lasted all of two minutes.

"One family is Protestants," he answered, "and the other house is owned by people who live and work in England, but come over to the house for a month in the summer." There must have been more Protestants around than we thought, or else my father just had a knack for finding places to live where Protestants were already living.

"Do the Protestants have any children?" asked Jimmy.

"I think they have two daughters." That didn't exactly fill my heart with joy, as the last girls we tried playing with found themselves tied up, which in turn led to me getting the head knocked off myself.

"It's very strange how the house sticks out on to the road," my mother chimed in. She was right. The house was built on a sharp bend of the road, and cars coming off the Buncrana road would pass by within a couple of inches of the gable end of the house.

"They must not have had any planning permission back in those days," my father said, "as I don't think it would be allowed these days."

I was wondering where we would empty the piss pot when it got full. Up at the bus we had the whole mountainside, more or less.

"Where will we be emptying the piss pot?" I asked nobody in particular.

"Jesus, but you do have the strangest thoughts," my mother replied. "Most children would be thinking about playing or having chips for dinner, but you're thinking about piss pots." I held my tongue, but I felt like telling her that it was me who was in charge of emptying it every night and morning when my father was off working in Scotland.

"He's right, though," my father told her. That was strange—him taking my side. "We don't want to wait until the middle of the night to think about where we will throw it."

"We'll have to empty it in the ditch by the gable end of the house. Sure, where else is there?" she asked.

"We'll have to be careful of cars, then," he said. "They'll be driving close to the gable when they round the bend, and they won't see you until they are right on top of you." Every time he said "you," I wondered if I was being made the official piss pot emptier. Again.

Our aunt in New York City took to sending us parcels on a fairly regular basis. I remember when the first parcel came along; it was like something magical. It was a big brown box covered in brown paper and smothered in fancy American stamps. Our aunt must have thought that the Post Office in Carndonagh would look at only one side of the box to see who was supposed to get it, for she put our name and address on every spare space she could find.

We were all home when it was opened. My mother was in charge, and she put it in the middle of the floor. We all stood around watching over her shoulder as she started to pull out clothes. They weren't new clothes, so she must have told people in America about our bus burning down and made them feel sorry for us. I don't know who would have worn those clothes, but if you saw what they looked like, you would feel sorry for whoever had to wear them. Unfortunately, the person who had to wear them turned out to be me.

The trousers were the worst eyesores of the lot. When I first saw them, one pair was shiny with gold stripes and another had blue stripes. I knew that there was no way they could be worn in Ireland. Well, maybe in Dublin, since it was said that "anything went in Dublin." Unfortunately, these crazy clothes were more or less my size. The legs were probably about a foot too long, but nothing that a needle and thread could not cure. For some reason I could not fathom, my mother didn't see anything wrong with them, and handed them to me like some kind of prize.

"Aren't you the lucky one to be getting these lovely trousers?" she asked as she handed them to me. I couldn't make myself take them and left her holding them draped over her outstretched arm.

"How can I wear them to school?" I asked her.

"What's wrong with them?"

"Sure, they're like a clown's trousers," I told her. My brother started laughing, and I was suddenly afraid that this would come back to haunt me.

"Would you rather look like a clown or go to school with your arse hanging out? You know very well that we don't have money to be buying new clothes."

I actually would have preferred to have my arse hanging out. "Can I just wear them around the house?"

"You'll wear them to school, and there won't be any more lip out of you. You should be very grateful to your Aunt Annie for going to the trouble of buying all of these clothes and then spending money on posting them all the way here."

"She must have bought them at a circus," I mumbled under my breath, reluctantly taking the multi-colored clothes.

"I'll circus *you* if you're not careful," she barked. She had the hearing of a ninja. My parents kept pulling clothes out of the box, but no matter how many items they pulled out, nothing came close to looking like the clothes that the other boys wore. Just when it seemed as though the contents had been completely depleted, she found something else.

"These look like sweaters for you and your brother," she said, removing the sweaters and shaking them out. They appeared to be about our size, except that the sleeves were as long as a trouser leg. "Put them on," she ordered. I pulled the jumper over my head and lost my hands. The end of the sleeves came nearly down to my knees.

"That's grand," she assured me. "You'll grow into it."

"Only if I turn out to be an orangutan."

"Why do you always have to act the fool?" she wanted to know. "You roll up the sleeves a couple of turns, and as you get older and your arms get longer, you roll them down again to fit you. There's a note in here that says she hand-knitted them both when she was working on Fifth Avenue minding a rich old Jewish woman during the night."

She must have knitted them with steel wool; they weighed a ton. I had only been wearing it for a few minutes and I was already sweating. I looked down at the cuffs that my mother had rolled, and noticed they seemed as big as the tires on the old fella's Morris Minor. I was full sure that my arrival at school wearing this getup would start a whole new round of fistfights.

In theory, we should have arrived at school on time each day after we moved, as the cottage was closer to school than the bus had been. In fact, though, we began to arrive much later. National school started at half nine in the morning, and while it was only about two miles down the road, my father got into some kind of rut where he wouldn't leave the house with us until around a quarter to ten. We'd be ready and waiting for him to take us down by a quarter after nine at the latest, but he always found some last-minute thing to do that would hold us back.

My brother trotted off down the corridor into his classroom (he had long since worked out his internal struggles with his teacher), but I couldn't face walking into the classroom alone. I hung outside the door hoping that someone would come out to knock the dust out of the chalkboard erasers or go to the bathroom so that I could sneak in behind them. The first time I suppose I got lucky, as I only had to wait about fifteen minutes before one of the boys came out. When he went back in, I ducked in behind him. Fortunately, my class was sitting down, so I quietly slid into a seat. I'm sure the teacher saw me, but I refused to make eye contact.

I didn't know that being late would turn out be a daily occurrence, so when it happened again the following day, I knew what I had to do—wait and listen for movement toward the door. If I could have just summoned up the courage to go in when he dropped us off, I would have been "only" a half hour late at the most, but my stomach was so tied up in knots that I couldn't make myself turn the door handle. The longer I waited outside the door, the more sick to my stomach I felt.

This time, however, I stood outside the door listening for an hour before I heard any noise whatsoever. The noise wasn't even a boy coming out. It was the conversation between the semi-circle of standing boys and the teacher. I peered around the doorjamb, and my heart sank when I saw my class standing up in front of Seamus. Holding my breath, I grabbed hold of the doorknob and turned it as slowly and quietly as I could.

It must not have been as quiet as I had hoped, however, judging by the way most of the boys turned around to witness me creeping into class, nearly an hour and a half late, in my "pajamas" (as they had taken to calling the Yankee trousers). I walked slowly toward them and joined the circle, trying not to look at anybody.

"What's your excuse for not coming to school until nearly lunchtime?" Seamus asked me.

"Sorry Sir, it's the car—it was giving problems."

"And where is it that you are living?"

"Maheramore, Sir."

"Sure, that's just up the hill," he informed me, with a half a grin that could turn vicious at any moment. "A young lad could walk down in no time. Does your car have wheels?" The other lads loved the questioning. It was an excuse to laugh and get away from their lessons.

"It does, Sir."

"The road from Maheramore to our school is all downhill in the morning. If you sat in the car and let it roll down, it wouldn't take more than ten minutes—even if it was out of petrol." The boys started to laugh harder, but I knew better than to answer Seamus. I just stared at the floor and hoped he would give up soon.

The late rut kept up for the rest of the month. There was no way to get my father out of the house on time. And worse still, there was no way I could force myself to go in late—although it would have been far better to have gone in twenty minutes late instead of the sixty to ninety minutes it took to psych myself up in the hallway. I was at my wits' end by the time I suggested to my father that I be allowed to walk down to school in the morning.

"Why don't you want to get a lift down with your brother as you always have done?" he questioned. I knew better than to suggest that he was the problem, so I had an answer ready. I knew full well that he wouldn't grant my request without an argument.

"When we play football at lunchtime, I'm always the last to get picked for a side because they say I don't run fast enough. I want to walk down in the morning to help me get fit so I can be a better football player."

"Who is saying that you can't run fast enough? Is it one of those Duck fuckers across the road? If it is, I'll go over to their house right now and straighten them out."

Jesus, that's all I needed was for him to start a row with the Ducks' father. The next thing I knew we'd be in the middle of a foul war.

"No, some other boys said it, but they are right. I need to train to get fit. If I walk down to school and then back up some days, I'll be able to do better."

This seemed to appease him for a bit. I knew that if I could come up with a half-decent reason not to wait for him in the morning, he'd soon fix his attention on something else and I could go about my merry way. I had enough to deal with in my classmates, who continued to break my balls every day about wearing pajamas to school.

⸎ ⸎

The house in Maheramore had only two rooms. As you entered the front door, you walked in to the kitchen/living room. At the head of it was a big black Stanley range—like the one that burned down the bus, only bigger—that heated the house and cooked all of the food.

To the left of the front door was the bedroom we all shared. We had two big beds, like on the bus. My two brothers and I slept in one bed; the youngest brother had to sleep with us now that he had been replaced as the baby, which he still wasn't happy about. My mother and father slept in the other, and our new sister slept in a cot next to them.

There was just one door serving as both entrance and exit, so we were pretty much screwed if a fire broke out and we couldn't get through there. (I began giving more thought to fires after the bus burned down.)

Although our living quarters were fairly cramped, we didn't feel overcrowded—that is, until Paddy Mooney came along. Paddy Mooney was an ancient man who was somehow related to us. I had never heard his name mentioned until our Aunt in America sent word that Paddy Mooney had nowhere to live and we were to take him in. The Aunt was like that. She was kind of like the Wizard in *The Wizard of Oz*. Nobody ever saw her, but when she sent word that something was to be done, it was more than your life was worth to stand in her way. I had seen it first-hand with the sweaters and trousers. If the Aunt sent it, you had damn well better wear it.

At first, Paddy Mooney was a novelty, and quite good craic. I don't know where he moved from—maybe his house had burned down too—but he was given the lower room all to himself. This meant that we had to move both of our big beds into the kitchen. The one good thing about this was that our bed was always warm. In an old thatch cottage, the range was responsible for heating the whole house, and the only way to heat up a lower room was to open the door and let the heat wander down into it. If you got the kitchen hot enough, you would get a bit of heat down there, but you still had to stick a couple of hot water bottles into the bed so you wouldn't freeze in the winter. I'm sure Paddy Mooney had to use a couple of hot water bottles every night, but at least he got to have the whole room to himself.

I don't remember how soon it started, but early in his stay with us, Paddy Mooney's mind started to wander. The first night it happened, we were all woken up by a terrible commotion in the lower room. Things were being knocked over and the old man was shouting. Father got up and went to see what was wrong, and a few minutes later Mother went down after him. We heard them telling Paddy that everything would be all right, that he was in his bedroom, and that he needed to go back to sleep. They sounded like they did whenever Jimmy had a bad dream.

"What was he saying about going to the bog to cut turf?" asked my father.

"He's doting," she told him. "He doesn't know here he is. That's why he had to leave the place he was in—they couldn't take care of him." I didn't fully grasp the idea of an older person's mind slipping, and thought it very funny that he wanted to go out in the middle of the night to cut turf.

"Sure, everybody knows you don't cut turf at nighttime," I chirped up. "He must be mad in the head."

My mother obviously did not find this as funny as I did. "Don't you be so smart," she scolded. "That could be you one day. He's very old, and he's doting. We don't make fun of people like that. Why are you awake, anyway?"

I turned over and stared at the wall in front of my face. She knew I was awake because Paddy Mooney's raving had woken us all up, but I knew better than to try and answer her.

Paddy Mooney's nightly wanderings around his bedroom continued to entertain me. I never knew what he would be doing. One night he got up to milk a cow (which neither he nor we owned), and another night he got dressed to go to the mart to buy sheep. One of the funniest nights was when he got up to go courting. He put on his shirt and jacket, but forgot to put on any trousers. My father grabbed him as he was trying to get out the door.

"We can't keep doing this every night," Father told Mother. "The poor old bastard was on his way out to meet with the woman he married probably fifty years ago."

"Ach, I know," she said, "but Annie asked us to look after him because he has nobody else."

"Easy for *her* to say," he replied, "living 3,000 miles away."

I don't know exactly how long Paddy was with us after he went off without his trousers, but the night he pissed himself proved to be the last straw. He must have drank a lot of tea that day, for my mother reckoned that he "pissed up one wall and down the other"—and that was after he had soaked the bed from one end to the other.

The following day, some people from a hospital came and took him away. The good news was that we got our bedroom back. The bad news was that our bed got shoved up against a wall that reeked of piss.

For some reason or other, my father began thinking of himself as a farmer after we moved into the thatched cottage in Maheramore. He rented a small field about thirty yards from the house and bought two young heifers. His plan was to raise the heifers to cows and then sell them for a profit at Carn Mart. According to him, the plan was simple and foolproof: buy two baby cows, put them in a field, and watch them grow. When they were big enough to sell, he'd get a local farmer to take them down to the mart on Monday and sell them for a tidy profit. In the meantime, we got to pet them and visit them every day, just as if they were part of the family. Jimmy christened them Tom and Jerry after watching cartoons at the neighbors' house.

Unfortunately, many of my father's plans turned out to be less than foolproof. After a few months of feeding and babying the calves, they started to fail. Whatever it was they had, they didn't want to eat. We would go up to the little barn that they stayed in at night during the winter and sit with them like you would keep watch over a sick patient. My father would take handfuls of hay and hand-feed each calf, who would in turn chew very slowly, just like children who didn't want to eat but knew they would get in trouble if they refused.

We didn't know that they were seriously ill, since their bellies were full-looking and stuck out. I think this confused my father as well, and he didn't call in the vet until it was too late. The vet took one look at them, shook his head, and told my father that they were bloated and would die. He said they had something I heard as "liver fluke." It must have been hard for the auld fella to tell my mother he had botched this plan up as well, since she was still sore with him for the bus burning down on the day she was released from the hospital.

"Is that what Grandfather has?" asked Jimmy when he heard the bad news about the calves' livers.

"What are you talking about?" replied our mother.

"You always say that Grandfather will die because he is killing his liver. Will his belly swell up like Tom's and Jerry's bellies?"

"Don't be daft. Your grandfather does not have liver fluke— and besides, that's grown-up talk. You shouldn't be listening."

"Maybe it was because they were calves," said my father to nobody in particular. "Maybe if I got a pony, it would be all right."

"So you go from being Old McDonald to John Wayne, is that it?" my mother snapped sarcastically.

"Well, I was thinking," he said, "that if we got a young filly pony and raised her until we could take her to the stud, that we could then sell her ponies for good money, since they would have pedigree lineage documentation."

The idea of having a horse sounded like much more fun than having calves. "Can I ride the pony?" asked my brother. "I want to ride it and wear a cowboy hat."

"I don't see why not," replied my father, who seemed pleased with himself for coming up with the new idea.

"Jesus, what will come after the pony," asked my mother, "a friggin' camel, or maybe a giraffe?"

"Don't be daft, woman," he told her. "Sure there are no camels or giraffes in Ireland." He thought a moment and added, "But that might not be a bad idea. People would probably come from all over and pay good money to see them."

There was no more said about ponies—or camels or giraffes, for that matter – until my father made the announcement a week later over dinner that he had bought a horse from Harry the Blacksmith.

"For the love of Jesus, please tell me that you didn't give money to Harry the Blacksmith," beseeched my mother.

"I did, and the deal is done," replied my father, grinning from ear to ear.

"Sure, he is the biggest crook that ever stood in a pair of shoes," she told him.

"Well, he met his match this time," he assured her. "I gave him five guineas less than he was asking for the pony."

"That's probably because he already added on ten, with you being a Yank and all," she said, shaking her head.

"Yippee!" shrieked my brother. "I'm going to be a cowboy!" Mother looked at him like he was mental, then turned her focus back at Father.

"Did you look him in the eye when you were striking the deal?" she asked him.

"The man wears glasses as thick as Coke bottles. Sure you can't even tell if he has eyes."

"How the hell could you buy a horse from someone if you couldn't see his eyes?" She wasn't giving up in a hurry.

"I reckon I got the pony for a good price."

"How do you even know if the horse is worth anything?" she continued.

"The man comes from a family of blacksmiths. I'm sure he knows a thing or two about ponies."

"His grandfather was a blacksmith," she shot back. "Squinty-eyed Harry wouldn't know what to do if you put him in front of an anvil and stuck a hammer in his hand."

"I'm sure it's in his blood." His method of self-defense seemed only to be getting him deeper in the hole.

"I'll tell you what's in his blood: Guinness and whiskey. And after today, he'll have a lot more of it in his blood, since now he's gotten a sucker to buy some nag that was probably headed to the glue factory."

"She's a fine wee pony, I tell ya."

"Well, there's no use trying to get your money back, since half of it will be drunk by tomorrow morning. Get Eugene Friel to take a look at it. He'll let you know if she's worth anything or not."

When Eugene examined the "pony" the following weekend, he had bad news for my father.

"Well, she's in good shape…for her age," said Eugene.

"For her *age?*"

"Aye, well you know she's been around a bit, this one."

"How can you tell?" my father asked with a shocked look on his face.

Eugene reached over and pulled the horse's lips up, revealing her yellow teeth and pink gums. "You tell a horse's age by her teeth. This mare's suggest that she's at least ten years old, maybe as much as twelve or thirteen."

"The bastard conned me. He told me she was less than two years old."

Eugene let the mare's lips fall back over her teeth and took the crooked-stem pipe out of his mouth—something he apparently hadn't needed to do during the entire previous examination.

"If it was anyone else, you might say that they didn't really know. But seeing as how Harry the Blacksmith sold her to you, I'd say you're right—you got conned."

"What do you think I should do now?"

"I don't think there's a whole lot you can do. I'd say most of what you paid him has already changed hands over several bar counters in Carn."

"You're not the first one to say that," admitted my father.

"She's a decent looking Connemara," said Eugene, "which means that she should be a good work horse."

"That gives me an idea," said my father with a gleam in his eye. *Him and his bloody ideas,* I thought, inwardly rolling my eyes.

"She should be able to pull a sidecar or a trap, right?" he asked Eugene.

"Aye, she should...but you don't see many sidecars around these days. They're a thing of the past."

"If I could get my hands on an old one and do it up," continued my father, "I could take it into Carn on a fair day or maybe give the wains horse rides on a Saturday."

"I suppose you could do that," Eugene agreed, but he had the same look on his face as my mother did when she looked at Jimmy who wanted to be a cowboy.

Incidentally, my father had the same grin on his face as my brother had when he thought about being a cowboy.

I had a bad feeling about this one. This wasn't Wyoming, and there was no bloody way that Donegal was ready for cowboys.

CHAPTER 14
EROTIC MONOPOLY

Every day when we came home from school, my father seemed to have a new piece of cowboy equipment. He was on the dole, which meant that he got paid for not working. I never really understood how that worked. On the one hand, it seemed like he left the factory canteen because the factory girls were eating food and not paying for it, but I also remember hearing him complaining about a pain in his leg and how he was unable to carry large pots of sauce or hot water, and he soon started limping. If my father could get money from the government for limping, I knew that in short time he would become a limping master.

Since he was not working and therefore free all day to tour the countryside, he picked up carts, wheels, and horse harnesses that he came across in barns and fields all over the Inishowen Peninsula. Fair play to him, though, he had great vision. He could look at a woeful heap of shite of a cart, and in his mind he'd visualize it with new wood and fresh paint to make it a carriage fit to pull a king.

I came home one day to see what looked like a heap of rotted wood on splintered, blackened wheels. He proudly told us that this heap of old boards, which had been riddled by woodworm and looked much like a bullet-riddled gangster's car from an old film, would become the finest jaunting car in Ireland by the time *he* was done with it.

This claim was made more unbelievable by the fact that my father had no experience whatsoever with restoring old horse carts. It was as if he woke up one morning and thought, *Today, I am going to become a rotted-wood restoration expert.* I wouldn't have backed him to pull it off, nor would my mother, and though Jimmy was as excited as a young puppy, he seldom had a good grasp on any situation so his vote didn't really count.

Don't ask me how it happened, or where the old man even got any tools, but before any of us knew it the old jaunting car had been completely transformed. Our old fella had decided to paint the jaunting car purple and black—or as he emphasized, *lilac* and black. Dr. Seuss would have been proud, I thought. *I will not eat green eggs and ham out of a hat...l will eat it off a jaunting car painted lilac and black.*

The first Saturday after the purple people-puller was ready to be tested, he made the announcement that he would be giving horse rides to the children of Carndonagh after he finished his tea and scone.

"Can I come?" asked Jimmy.

"Of course you can. Sure, you and your brother will be helping me." I had a bad feeling about what the boys who saw me would say Monday morning in school.

After breakfast, the horse was harnessed to the jaunting car and we took off down the road. My brother and I sat on either side of the cart on seats that folded up when they weren't being used. My father had a kind of throne in the front. Sitting atop it proudly, he used the reins to slap the horse on the back to make her go faster. She rocketed forward, nearly launching us from our seats. Just like my teacher said, it took us almost no time at all to get down the hill and onto the main street of Carn.

The town was fairly busy, but the streets were not filled with wains, so I was wondering how we were going to find enough of them to make it worth our while. My father already had a plan. He made that horse run back and forth through the town as he shouted out, "Horse rides! Come get your horse rides!" I could tell by the way peoples' heads turned to follow us that they had never seen the likes of this before—probably not even in the days when everybody used horses and carts to get around.

For the first couple of passes, I got away without seeing anybody I knew from school. As long as none of my classmates saw me, I didn't really care about everyone else who looked at us like we had just driven out of a mental asylum.

"Horse rides...giddyup, giddyup! Come get a horse ride," the old fella yelled even louder, just in case somebody in the next town had not heard him.

That's when I spotted them: Donal and Liam the Duck. Those bastards *would* have to be on the street when John Wayne decided to wake the dead with his "horse rides" shouting. I tucked my chin down into the collar of my coat in hopes that they might not recognize me. That was a stupid idea, since everybody for miles around knew us. There wasn't exactly a deluge of Yanks pouring into the area.

"Look at the Big Yank," squealed Donal the Duck as we passed by. "Sure he thinks he's in the Wild West...ride him, cowboy!"

Liam also seemed to be grinning, but he had such a mouthful of buck teeth that he always looked happy. My father ignored them and charged forward, yelling "Step right up and get your horse ride right here!" Step right up? Now he was sounding like a circus ringmaster. Just when I thought I would die from embarrassment, I saw two young boys standing outside the Persian Bar pointing toward us. Since the bar hadn't opened yet, and I assumed they weren't drinking, they must have wanted a horse ride. Seeing the opportunity, my father rolled over to them.

"Who wants to be the first one to feel like a real cowboy?" he asked them. They looked at each other and giggled.

"Come on," he coaxed, "It's just like being a cowboy. Who wants to feel like a cowboy?" *I know that I feel like a right eejit,* I thought.

Then one of the wains stepped forward. "How much is it?" he asked.

"How much have you got?"

The boy held up a sixpence. *Surely he wasn't going to charge the wee boy half a shilling for a poxy ride on the cart?* Sixpence was a small fortune.

"Is that your little brother?" my father asked. The boy nodded.

"I'll let both of you have a ride for sixpence," my father bargained. That was a bit better, but it was still way too much to pay. That amount of money could keep you eating sweets for two straight days. The boy nodded and reached up to my father, the money in his hand.

"Help those boys up," he called to me over his shoulder.

As I hoisted the little boys into the seats, I wondered if they would be able to hold on well enough. We had very nearly slid off, and the younger brother was a fair bit younger than my brother. If that poor wee hoor fell off and landed under the big wooden wheels, it would flatten him like the sixpence he had paid to ride.

My father didn't seem a bit bothered by the possibility of the boy's death. He rattled through the streets, shouting "giddyup!" as loud as he could. The tour took the boys down the Malin Road, where he turned by the hotel and then back up and out the Moville Road, coming to a stop outside the Persian. By the time we docked, there was a group of four or five boys and a couple of girls waiting.

"Who wants to ride the Lilac Lightning?" he asked them. All of their hands shot up into the air. "Who has money?" was the next question. Half of the hands went down.

"Everybody who has money can give it to the conductor and he'll help you on. Those who don't have money should go and get some from your mothers and fathers."

Conductor? Did I get a promotion? Next thing I knew he'd be getting me to punch tickets. Every time he made the loop around, there would be more wains waiting by the bar. I was starting to think that he was on to something. Maybe he *could* make a living as a cowboy in Donegal. He had been making a living doing nothing, after all. I envisioned my future, but could not see myself staying on as a conductor forever. Being a bullfighter in Spain was much more to my liking.

I "conducted" for about four or five hours before the line of children waiting to ride dwindled to one or two stragglers. I didn't realize how much money we had collected until my trousers nearly fell off from the amount of pennies, thrupenny bits, and sixpences weighing them down. However much we made, it was enough for my father to decide to treat us to fish and chips at McGroddy's chipper on the way home. I poured so much brown vinegar on those chips that the wax bag held a puddle of vinegar after the chips were gone. Then I drank the vinegar. It had been so long since we had had fish and chips—probably not since we stopped smuggling—and I had forgotten just how good they were. If we could eat like this every Saturday, maybe being a conductor on Lilac Lightning wouldn't be so bad.

When we reached home, my father couldn't wait to get the harness off the horse and put her in the field so he could run in and tell my mother how much money we had made. It took us over an hour to get the coins all sorted. At the end of it, we had nearly three pounds. *An absolute fortune,* I thought.

As we walked in the door, shouting about our profit, my mother interrupted, "How much did you spend on fish and chips?"

"How do you know we had fish and chips?"

"Sure, it's reeking off youns."

"About four bob," my father answered sheepishly.

"Well, the rest of it can go toward the car insurance," she reminded him.

"I already had plans for it."

"What plans?"

"I was ahh…thinking, that, ahh…I could use it to help build a covered wagon."

"A *what?*" she shrieked.

"You know, a covered wagon—the kind that the settlers rode in when they traveled out West to stake their claim."

"Jesus, you really *do* think you're John Wayne. If you don't pay the bloody car insurance, you'd better hope there's no claim, or no Garda stopping you for insurance either."

"If worst came to worst, we could always get rid of the car and ride in the covered wagon."

"Are you out of your tree?" she asked him. "You must be bloody bonkers if you think I'm going to ride around in some covered wagon like a squaw."

"You wouldn't be a squaw. You'd be a settler's wife. Squaws are Indian women." She threw him a look that could curdle milk. In most cases, I did my best not to agree with my mother, but in this case, I was on her side. I didn't want to ride around in a covered wagon either.

I don't know what kind of agreement they reached—maybe we rode around without insurance for a while—but he did start working on his covered wagon. Once again, he picked up a cart in some field for next to nothing, then he welded bars of iron into hoops. Over these hoops he tied a white canvas, and in no time we were the proud owners of our own covered wagon.

The day he drove the covered wagon into town was a sight to behold. Most of the children would have seen such a wagon on an old black and white Western film, so they knew what it was, but they had never seen a "real" one.

What surprised me was just how popular the wagon became. It turned out to be a veritable license to print money. Since the body of the cart was large, my father could fit seven or eight children in the cart at a time, and since it was covered, he could continue giving rides even when it rained.

Word spread like wildfire. Soon young children would pour out of doorways and alleyways as soon as we pulled into the Diamond. They came running to the covered wagon, shouting, "Here comes the Big Yank!" God knows where they found the money to ride, but they always had available funds. My father even introduced a "frequent flyer" program, allowing anyone who paid for two rides on the same day to be given a third for free.

I had to hand it to him, it was quite a brilliant idea. As he didn't pay a lick of insurance or road tax, and his help (me) was free, his only expense was feeding the horse.

Of course, as I collected money in the canteen, it didn't take me long to slip back into my old ways. I would siphon off about a sixpence every hour. I think he still got a good deal. There was no way anybody else would work for less than a sixpence an hour.

My father would not sit in the cart himself, as he was afraid that his added weight would tire the horse out too quickly. He took to running alongside the cart, holding the mare's bridle as he ran. After a few runs, his limp became very noticeable. I think he exaggerated it, because I used to hear him tell stories about neighbors who were "on the sick." Every now and again, an inspector would catch them working and they wouldn't be able to claim the sick money anymore.

His favorite joke was even about a man claiming the sick:

A man claimed that he had hurt his arms on the farm in some kind of machinery accident and as a result could raise his arms only waist-high. The examining doctor agreed that it was a terrible affliction not to be able to raise up one's arms anymore.

"Tell us this," quizzed the doctor. "How high could you raise them before the accident?"

"Jesus doctor, I could raise them this high," answered the man, raising his hands above his head.

"Claim denied," replied the doctor.

I didn't think adding a limp would help much, though, since the inspector could easily see that we were charging money for the rides. I began to think that maybe there actually *was* something wrong with his leg, and not just with his head.

"You've been running a long time," I said. "Why don't you ride on the wagon for a while?" He looked at me as if he were trying to figure out if I was working some kind of con on him.

"Maybe I will," he said. "There's still plenty of wains, so we won't be quitting for a while yet." He had actually agreed with me about something.

⊷⊰⊹⊱⊶

That evening as we rode home up the hill to Maheramore, I wondered more about the Big Yank. I wondered if this was what he had wanted to do with his life—give children horse rides in the arsehole end of Donegal. It was all right for me, for a while anyway, and I was young. There was no way I wanted to be in his place when I was his age. I wanted to be famous—an Irish writer, perhaps. Maybe my plays would be showing in Dublin, or my songs would be sung by bands from London to Liverpool. If I had a banjaxed leg, I'd at least have the money to get it fixed, and I wouldn't have to worry about a Garda stopping me for not having insurance on my car.

"Good evening, Garda," I would say, as I rolled the window down in my Rolls-Royce, sipping on champagne. "Insurance, you say? But of *course* I have insurance." I would then turn to my

driver, ordering, "James, show the nice Garda our insurance certificate, like a good man." I would turn back toward the window,
laughing, "Of course it's in order, Garda. Now, can I interest you
in a glass of bubbly?"

The strong smell of fresh horse shite snapped me back to
reality. We had pulled up to our yard, and the Connemara was
emptying her guts out onto the street. I had a fair idea who
would have to clean it up. Little did I know it at that time, but
I would reign as shite-scooper in the not-too-distant future. My
teenage years would prove to be long, tough, and shite-filled.
Destiny's plans for me were far removed from riding around in a
Rolls-Royce and sipping champagne. More like walking around
in Wellingtons and shoveling shite, really.

"Good lad, can you grab the spade and bucket from the shed
there and throw her shite into the ditch?" my father asked me.
It sounded like a request, but it wasn't. There was no way I could
have replied, "Do you know what? I think I'll pass on the shite-
shoveling this time around, but thanks for the offer anyway."

That friggin' ditch was a multi-use waterway—it was also
where we dumped a full bucket of piss every single morning.
When I first took over bucket-emptying duties, I was just glad
to get it out of the house and across the street without dropping
it or spilling half of it all over me. The strange thing about that
drain was the fact that it was covered in grass and weeds, and I
never did see any water in it.

That actually made it a strange choice for a place to throw a
horse's shite. If you aren't familiar with how a horse takes a shite,
let me tell you that it is much different from, say, a rabbit or a
sheep. There is nothing pellet-like about horse shite. It comes out
in big steaming lumps. A drain would need to be in the full of its
health to carry a horse's dung downstream.

And then there were the potato skins. Although we usually
ate potatoes skins and all (as goes the popular Donegal saying),

there were times when my mother or father would make mashed potatoes and would peel about a dozen and a half spuds for dinner. Where else would the skins be dumped but in the drain?

≒⊹ ⊹≓

As houses go, our thatch in Maheramore was not the worse place you could be stuck. At least it wasn't out in the middle of nowhere, which is where we would find ourselves when we left it and moved out the Moville Road. Our first Christmas there saw us getting the board game Monopoly. I didn't realize it at the time, but there was something ironic about playing a game where you spent hours on end buying properties, building hotels and bullying the other players with your wealth whilst barely having a pot to piss in yourself (I say "barely" because we did, in fact, have a pot to piss in. I should know.)

We shared a small cul-de-sac with two other cottages. There were no boys our age in any of the other houses, but somehow or other, we managed to become friends with a couple of Protestant girls across the street. The strange thing was that they were all grown up and both had jobs. When you are nine and twelve, a couple of girls in their late teens and early twenties seem like much older women. The younger of the two was probably nineteen or twenty, and she had a pair of tits on her that could give a man writer's cramp just from groping them. As a matter of fact, I think it was my daydreaming about fondling those tits that prepared me for milking cows when we moved to our farm a few years later.

Our parents invited the girls and their parents over one Friday night to play Monopoly, and from that first night, it became a weekly ritual. Those game nights would go on until one or two in the morning. I didn't care if we sat up all night as long as I could steal sidelong glances at the younger sister's huge knockers. The more I looked at them, the more I wanted to grope them. One night we were playing for hours, as usual, and the young sister went out to relieve herself. I waited a moment or two and slipped out after her. When she turned the corner, I propositioned her: "If you let me feel your tits, I'll let you off paying rent the next time you land on Grafton Street."

"Are you mad?" she asked. I was afraid that she might tell the parents about my breast obsession, but she continued on: "Sure the rent on that is only a few quid. You'd have to have a hotel, or at least a house on the street, to make it worth my while."

It didn't take me long to seize the opportunity. "I was just about to put hotels on the whole street after our tea break," I lied. "Now can I feel your tits?"

"How do I know I can trust you?" she asked me.

I had myself worked up and didn't want to have to wait to get a handful. "If you let me feel them now," I promised, "I'll let you off for two goes around the board."

"So you'll let me off if I get you off?" I didn't know what she meant, but I knew her smirking was a good sign. "Let me go three times and it's a deal."

"Right so," I agreed.

Little did she know, but I would have given her six goes around—three per tit, if she had asked for it. It was cheap at half the price. I moved in closer and started to feel through her jumper.

"What are you doing?" she asked me.

"Getting to your boobs," I replied, as you do.

"Jesus, you can't be pulling and hauling at me out here, sure it's freezing. Put your hands up under."

I plunged both hands up under her heavy jumper and thrusted my way up to the promised land. My efforts were road-blocked by her bra, which I had not counted on. I groped around a bit trying to find a gap to make my way through, but they were well-sealed. Then I got the brilliant idea to go over the top. That was a major coup, as the tops were unprotected. Her breasts were so big and full that I needed both hands just to cover the top of one of them. I gave them a big squishy squeeze and she jumped.

"Did I hurt ya?" I was afraid I had done something wrong.

"No, you did not," she reassured me, "but your hands are fucking freezing—you'll have to warm them up a bit."

She then reached around the back of her jumper and fidgeted with something. When I put my hands under her jumper this time, I felt that the bra was hanging off and I could get a proper grip. She moved in closer and pulled me by the waist so we were touching up against each other. I started to feel my young cock stiffening, and my hands started squeezing harder and faster.

"What's that I feel?" she asked me, bouncing her pelvis off my groin. I could feel my face reddening.

"It's the cold," I lied.

"So it's frozen?" she asked with a grin.

I couldn't believe what she did next. She grabbed for my belt buckle, and before I knew it she had shoved her right hand down the front of my trousers. I was glad that it was so dark that she couldn't see the look of shock on my face. She then grabbed my stiff cock and started squeezing and pulling it up and down. It felt so strange to have someone else touching my mickey, especially a girl, but it felt like nothing I had ever felt before. I had no idea what she was going to do next, or what I was supposed to do, so I just stood there holding on to her big breasts for dear life and waiting to see what would happen.

What happened next was an explosion in my damned underwear. I had no control over it. Before I even knew what was happening, I started to pee myself, but the strange thing was that I wasn't peeing. When this explosion happened, she stopped moving her fingers up and down, but kept squeezing my mickey very tightly.

"How did that feel?" she asked as she pulled her hand back out.

I literally didn't know what to say. "It felt good," I assured her. "How did you do that?"

"It's my magic touch," she laughed.

At that moment, our front door started to open. I pulled my hands down from her breasts before the crack of kitchen light gave us away. She moved toward the door. The older sister stepped out.

"What are youns doing out here in the cold?"

"I came out for a fag," the younger one lied.

"Are you smoking now too?" the sister asked me.

"No, I came out for a pish." I started to fiddle with my fly to back up my alibi.

"Well, we're waiting for the two of you to come back in so we can finish the game," the older sister informed us.

"I'm ready," said the younger one, walking toward the light.

"I'll be there in a minute," I told them as I headed toward the turf shed.

I didn't know what had happened a minute before, but my underwear felt wet, so I decided to drop my trousers in the turf shed and remove them. There was no outside light, so I had to feel my way around. I didn't want to stay out too long in case it aroused suspicions.

Never let anyone tell you that it is easy taking off your underwear in a turf shed at night, with no outside light. Once you kick off your shoes, you have to be careful not to trip over lumps of turf as you take off your trousers. I know this because that is exactly what I did—I stepped on a rock-hard piece of turf, and then lost my balance as I tried to massage my foot. Stepping on a bunch of angled turf is bad enough, but falling over backwards is a total pain in the arse. Literally.

Once I got my underwear removed, I had to get quickly re-dressed and make my way back into the house. I tossed the underwear into a dark corner of the shed and felt for my trousers. I didn't have much trouble finding them, as they were close to where I had been standing. I figured that the shoes would be close by too, but they weren't. One had gone missing: I must have kicked it too far when I was tossing it off and it went flying in amongst the turf.

I couldn't afford to spend any more time looking for it, so I put on the one shoe I did have and hopped out of the shed toward the house. When I opened the door, I walked in as normal as possible and tried to get into my chair before anyone noticed I was missing a shoe. I quickly stuck both feet under the kitchen table.

"It's my turn," Jimmy informed us. He rolled the dice, moved his silver terrier seven spaces and handed the dice to my sex trainer. She landed on my street. I grabbed the dice quickly and rolled, doing my best to ignore it, but my brother spotted it right away.

"Look there," he prodded me, "she landed on Grafton Street—she owes you rent."

"Ah, it's too late now," I replied, "sure you have to spot it before the next person rolls the dice again."

"That's not what you said when I landed on your street and you wanted rent after two rolls."

"Well, that's different," I told him.

"What's different about it?" I wanted to tell the little bastard that he didn't have a huge pair of tits.

"You live here, but the girls are our guests." I knew it was weak, but I couldn't think of anything else to say at such short notice. Big Knockers grinned over at me. I swore to myself that I would kick the shite out of the little prick the next day if he came between me and her girl-mountains again.

With all of the Monopoly commotion going on, I didn't even realize that my mother had gone out for turf. My heart sank when she opened the door and walked in with the turf bucket. I didn't want to look obvious, but I was anxious to know if she had found my shoe. She didn't say anything, so I figured that was a good sign, until I stole a sideways glance at the turf bucket she was carrying. My heart sank when I saw my shoe sticking up between the pieces of turf.

I couldn't take a chance on my mother discovering the shoe. She probably hadn't seen it yet in the darkness of the turf shed. I immediately jumped up, went up behind her, and reached for the bucket with my right hand.

"I'll put turf into the range for you," I told her, trying to hide my sock-covered foot so that she wouldn't notice it. She gave me a strange look; she wasn't used to me volunteering for work. I held her gaze as I slowly felt for the shoe with my left hand. I pulled it out of the bucket, dropping it onto the floor while simultaneously pulling out a piece of turf for the fire. I thought I had gotten away with it, but Sarah suspected something.

"Why are you only wearing one shoe?"

"I took off my shoe to get rid of a stone," I told her, as I turned away from her to open the lid of the range. I could feel her eyes burning into the back of my head. As nervous as I felt, I was grateful that she had picked up my shoe instead of my underwear. Nothing I could have told her would have explained *that* one away.

CHAPTER 15

SWINEICIDE

I don't know how long we stayed in the Maheramore house, but I do remember that it was long enough for everyone to get the flu one Christmas, and that the weather was warm when we moved out, so we were there at least a year. It seems that my father had convinced himself and my mother that what we needed was a real farm. Our "pony" was going to have a foal, and he said we needed space for the horses to run around several fields. He also wanted cows and chickens so that we would have fresh milk and eggs.

Little did I know it at the time, but his plans did not necessarily include him doing much *work* on the farm. Unfortunately for me, I was the eldest and the heir apparent to these chores.

Now if you're wondering how we managed to buy a farm without actually having any money, I can understand your bewilderment.

We didn't actually buy the farm. My mother's sister in America, that crazy aunt who persisted in sending over parcels of hippie clothes, bought it for us. She must have taken pity on us. She did have a huge heart, so she probably felt sorry that all of us children were living in such dire circumstances.

She most likely believed that the farm would be the answer to our prayers, but for me, it was nothing short of a curse. Not only did it mean that I would never have a minute's rest, and that I would eventually have to go into exile from Donegal just to escape it, but of all the land in Inishowen, our Father had to pick a godforsaken parcel of rushes and bog in the wilds of Gleneely.

I was 13 and finished with Primary school when we moved. Frank, the local postman, owned the farm. To give you an idea of how desirable it was, neither he nor his two sons wanted anything to do with the land. In fact, he built a new cottage alongside the roadway that ran down from the Moville Road, as far away from the main farm as he could get. The deal was that he would keep his house and patch of land out by the road, and sell us the remaining twenty acres plus a dilapidated old thatch cottage to live in. For some reason I could never understand, my father thought that those neglected fields and that run-down cottage were the greatest purchase he had ever made. The rest of us felt as if we were sliding backwards in time, as the farm and cottage did not have any electricity or running water. We had to use Tilley lamps for light and carry the water in buckets from a well down the road, and had to cut turf and save it all summer for heat in the winter.

I don't know where the money came from (probably my aunt again), but cows suddenly started to appear on the farm. I think we started off with two. The only one who knew how to milk them was my mother. At first it was good craic learning how to squeeze milk out of the cows' tits into buckets. We had a tiger cat who would sit right behind the cow's tail, and once every six or seven squeezes into the bucket my mother would squirt a long line of milk out into the air toward the cat, who would catch it on her tongue in mid-air. My mother was no fool, and to this day I swear that she worked that trick out with the cat to get me interested in milking. It worked, too. Mind you, milk production took a right nose-dive as I perfected the art of squirting milk into the cat's mouth on every third squeeze.

After a while this became less entertaining, so I decided to mess with the cat. I would aim a stream of milk at her mouth, then readjust my wrist so that the milk squirted into her eyes. This drove the poor old cat mad, but she had such a severe milk addiction that she refused to turn away. Instead, she would rub her eyes with her paws and watch through squinted eyes, hoping that my aim would fail and that the next squirt would find its mark. I'd mix it up so much that she never knew when she would get it in the mouth or eyes. By the time I was finished milking, the poor bitch would be so soaked in milk that it would take her an hour to lick it all off herself.

As you may have already guessed, I was easily bored, and was always on the lookout for the next victim with which to entertain myself. Living out in the middle of nowhere meant that the victim was usually Jimmy. As he was a bit too young to do much work and was also my father's favorite, he never had any responsibilities. This didn't excuse him from being screwed with by me, though. I therefore hatched a plan for him to take the cat's place.

"Come into the byre and see what I do with the cat," I invited him. He knew me well enough to be skeptical.

"What...do...you...do...with...the...cat?" he asked, looking at me like I was a parish priest who had just invited him around the back of the church to polish off a bottle of altar wine.

"I just have the craic with her," I reassured him. Curiosity must have gotten the better of him, for he followed me into the byre and stood behind the cat as I placed the bucket under the cow's udder. The cat also took her place behind the cow and waited for the spraying ritual to begin. Once I got into my stride and the milk started flowing, it was time for the cat to get drenched in cow juice. My brother bent over laughing as the cat did her best to keep the jet stream of milk out of her eyes and lap it up with her tongue. The more he laughed, the wider he opened his mouth. I found it difficult to hold myself back from filling his gob with warm milk there and then, but I knew that if I took my time, it would be worth it.

"Watch this," I told him, as I grabbed a handful of the milk-full tit and shot up the cat's eyes, nose, over the top of her head, and under her arms as she tried to wipe off the milk with her paws. He moved closer to the cat (which made his pending dousing all the more promising), bent over to grab his knees, and laughed so hard that his eyes disappeared. His mouth was so wide open that he could have swallowed the bloody cat. I knew that this was my opportunity to strike, so I grabbed another big tit and twisted it around so that it was aimed at my brother's face. With a squeeze that made my teeth clench, I pressed on that fleshy tit with all of my might and aimed it right at the back of my brother's tonsils.

He never saw it coming. Next thing I knew, he was gurgling like a drowning man in a pool of milk. As soon as his mouth was filled (which happened immediately, since this tit was one which I hadn't milked yet and was so full that it was dripping), he spewed out a spray of warm milk. In so doing, he bent his head forward and moved even closer to me. Not one to miss a golden opportunity, I quickly re-aimed the tit so that it was now pointed squarely at his right eye. During the time he was spraying the cow's arse with her own liquid, I released my grip so that a fresh supply of warm milk would flood back into my milk-pistol. As I started to pump the stream of warm milk into his eye, his eyes bulged in surprise, making it even easier for me to make a bulls-eye. As soon as I completed the bombardment of his right eye-ball, I aimed for the left.

The poor bastard didn't stand a chance. Blinded and half choking on the milk, he stumbled forward with his arm out in front of himself for guidance. The only thing it managed to guide him to was a steaming pile of cow's shite in the trough be-hind the cow. The drain was supposed to let the cow's pish run out to the midden. It would have if it had been cleaned out, but since I was the chief cook and cow-milker, I hadn't got around to shoveling shite, and the build-up meant that nothing was going anywhere.

When he got back up on his feet, he was a sight for sore eyes. His face was drenched in milk, he had snot running out his nose from bawling, and he was covered in warm cow shite, from his fingertips to his elbows. He ran out of the byre as I sat under the cow laughing my arse off. If I was a bit smarter, I would have re-alized that I was going to get severely punished once he told his story back in the house.

A few minutes later, my father came roaring into the byre. "What the hell did you do to your brother?"

"I didn't do anything." I had learned that telling the truth got you nowhere with the Big Yank.

"What do you mean you didn't do anything? Sure, he's cov-ered from head to toe in milk and cow's shite."

I had to physically bite on the inside of my lower lip to keep from laughing. I felt the pressure of a massive laugh coming on, and my eyes started to water a little. I was able to hide my face from him by burying my head into the cow's belly, milking her methodically into the bucket.

"I showed him how I squirt milk into the cat's mouth. He bent down to see, and he got too close."

I watched the auld fella out of the corner of my left eye and saw that he was pacing around, probably deciding whether to give me a beating right there in front of the cow. He made an attempt to cross over the trough, but his left leg didn't seem to want to go, so he backed away.

"I'd break your neck if I thought you did it on purpose," he assured me. "Your mother is right. You're a crazy bastard, just like your grandfather. Keep it up and you'll be in trouble the rest of your life."

With that, he stormed out of the barn. It sounded as if he had just tried to give me some kind of advice. Of course, it was off-handed and fucked-up, like everything else he did, but for a minute there, it had nearly seemed as if he cared. The thought was too disturbing, and I actually had to stop milking in order to ponder it.

What the fuck had just happened? Did he say what he said because he was frustrated that he couldn't break my neck? And why couldn't he break my neck anyway? Did he *really* just give me the benefit of the doubt? No way. I saw him trying to get at me. He stepped his right leg over but it was as if his left leg had said, "Are you fucking codding me? There's no way I'm crossing over that heap of shite just so that you can break the young fella's neck." *Thanks, left leg. I owe you one.*

I began to wonder why his left leg refused to go along with the program. It surely wasn't out of loyalty to me. It's not like me and the auld fella's left leg had a great love for each other. Many were the times it and its twin had stomped the living shite out of me as I lay on the ground, arms wrapped around my chest and head. No, there was something else going on. He knew it too. I saw the way he seemed to freeze when he couldn't get the left leg to move. More and more people were now asking him about his leg. We had gotten used to his limping, as we saw it every day, but anybody who had not seen him in a while seemed surprised. He told them all the same thing: "I hurt the back in the bog cutting turf and it's thrown off the leg a bit. I'm seeing a chiropractor from Derry now and he'll make it right."

This was the one good thing about the limp (and God forgive me for calling it a "good thing")—he was no longer as deadly as he used to be. That hoor had the biggest feet I ever laid eyes on. His feet were so fucking big that he couldn't get shoes to fit him in Ireland. When he needed new shoes (which was no more than once every six to seven years), he had to write to his sister in New York and get her to send them to him.

I have no idea how she decided what style of shoes she should send, as it would take a letter weeks to get to America and months before you would ever get a reply. I suppose he had to judge when he might need the shoes and then start planning several months out. We always knew when the shoes arrived, however, as there would be a brown shoe box the size of a small coffin. I'm sure there were many a leprechaun who could have set up house in one of the Big Yank's shoe boxes.

In case you have not experienced it firsthand, big feet can cause a lot of hurt. Unfortunately, big feet and big hands tend to go together, and my father had hands like shovels. I can't really remember a time when he didn't work me over with his hands and then finish me off with his feet.

I remember a time, when I was four or five, that he was walloping me with his big hands. As I protected my head with my arms, I instinctively reached out and grabbed on to his forearms. At that moment he began to draw back in order to get a full swing at me. As he swung back, gathering momentum for the crashing blows which he expected to reign down on my head, he took me with him in the air. It was a comical moment, if you took the violence out of it, like something from a *Tom and Jerry* cartoon.

I looked at him with eyes as large as dinner plates, and he looked back with a confused look that said, "What the fuck are you doing riding on my arms?" I would have jumped there and then, but a four-foot drop when you are 4 years old is akin to plunging into the Grand Canyon. For a split second, neither of us knew what to do with the other. Then he started to shake me off his arm as you would with a bug. I was so shocked that he was trying to drop me that I held on with even fiercer determination. The more I held on, the more he tried to shake me off.

Eventually his shaking was too much for me, and I fell to the floor. For a split second, he looked down at me and I up at him. When I realized how vulnerable I was under those big feet, I scurried backwards like a crab, pushing like mad with my heels and the palms of my hands in an effort to find a corner to squeeze into for shelter.

Much to my surprise, he didn't kick me. He simply stared in silence, looking shocked. It may have been one of the few times in his life when he realized that what he was doing was wrong. Most times his temper was too out of control to entertain any thought other than the desire to inflict pain.

⊷⊷ ⊷⊷

There really was a chiropractor who came down from Derry. Although I was only a young fella, I could see that whatever Mr. Cooper was doing for his back wasn't worth a shite. Every Tuesday morning he would land in the yard before we left for school and go to work on the auld fella's back. Half an hour and ten shillings later, he would pack up his ointments and head off to see his next victim.

The Big Yank thought Mr. Cooper was doing him a world of good. He would hobble about the kitchen saying how much better he felt, and we would all have to agree that his walking was improving. I watched this go on for years and couldn't say what I really felt. *Cooper is doing nothing for you—you're dragging your leg worse now than last year.* As I got older, I figured that the ten shillings he gave to Cooper every week was more to ease his mind than to fix that which couldn't be fixed.

I vividly remember the day we drove down to Letterkenny hospital, where my father had an appointment to have his leg examined. We were all left in the car, as usual, while he and my mother went in for the exam. After what felt like several hours, they both returned to the car. My father was in a foul mood, and he and my mother were arguing.

"What does that bastard know?" he barked at her.

"Well, he is a doctor," she replied sheepishly.

"Doctor, my ass—he's a Pakistani fucking student. Couldn't be a doctor in his own country, so he comes over here and talks shite to the Irish." He was so worked up that he had trouble getting the key into the ignition.

"Wait a wee minute before you start driving," she advised him.

"Fuck him and his multiple sclerosis. That's a *disease*. I don't have a *disease*. They should send that bastard back to where he came from," was his reply.

"You've got myxomatosis, Daddy, like the Friel's rabbits?" asked my brother. For a moment there was silence, and I thought how lucky it was for my brother that my father's mind was pre-occupied and he probably hadn't even heard this ridiculous question.

"Mommy, is Daddy like the rabbits now?" *Jesus Christ*. That boy was begging for a belt in the jaw. My father seemed to snap out of his daze long enough to catch the last bit of what the eejit was asking.

"What the hell is that half-wit saying?" he asked her.

"Ah, I think he got multiple sclerosis mixed up with myxomatosis," she realized.

"I must be going mad," my father muttered to himself as he pushed the key into the ignition. "I have a Pakistani telling me I have a disease, and my own son thinks I'm turning into a rabbit. It's like a bad dream."

Although he did not seem to have any notion of accepting the Pakistani doctor's diagnosis, my father started to change after we got back from Letterkenny hospital. I had no understanding of what multiple sclerosis was, so I didn't know whether he had just gotten a fright or if he realized down deep that there was something seriously wrong with him (medically, at least). Before, he was always pulling or hauling at something, but he seemed to have lost the desire to tinker that used to inspire him to build jaunting cars and covered wagons.

The last major farm project that I remember him getting involved in took me by surprise and had a very bloody ending. "You are going to stay home from school tomorrow and help me with a job," he informed me one Thursday evening. Although I was curious as all hell to know what he had planned, I thought it best not to seem too anxious. Whatever it was, it was bound to involve a fair amount of physical exertion on my part. And since it was only five or six weeks before Christmas, it was bound to be cold, and most likely miserable.

The next day, after my brothers had been sent off to school and my mother had taken my sister out in the car with her, I learned what he had in store for me. Well, l should rephrase that; nothing could have prepared me for what he had in store for me. He did tell me, though, that he and I were going down to the small barn next to the cows to kill our pet pig, Barney.

I don't remember feeling sad or shocked. Looking back, it's safe to say that I had an idea Barney was never meant to live to a ripe old age as the family mascot. My brothers and sister were a different story. The two youngest boys looked upon Barney as a brother. Most days Barney would get a visit from one or both of them as soon as they arrived home from school. It wasn't odd for them to go down and talk to him during the course of the weekend as well. The pig seemed to appreciate it, too. The fat little bastard would stand up on his hind legs and rest his front trotters on the half door that kept him inside the barn. It was as if he wanted to appear more human and try to communicate with them when they came to talk.

I don't think they had a clue where bacon came from, since it was classed as a delicacy in our house. Meat, in general, was a delicacy for us. If you unexpectedly found meat on your dinner plate at the farm, there was a good chance that somebody in the area had shot it, snared it, or run over it with a car. Pickings were very slim. I wouldn't say we were "living off the fat of the land."

I was hoping that the auld fella didn't have a plan to sell the pig to the local butcher, or trade him against a bullock or some other animal. I shouldn't have worried—by the time we were finished with Barney that day, he was a sight for sore eyes. The breakfast table was about the only place he would ever fit in again.

"So this is what we are going to do," my father instructed me as we came to a stop in front of Barney's place. "I'm going to tie a rope around the pig's neck and then pull the rope through the rafter in the roof. Then I'll hoist him up on his back feet and hand you the rope."

"He's good at standing on his back feet," I informed the auld fella. He looked at me like I had lost my mind. My father, not the pig.

"What the hell are you talking about?"

"He stands on his back legs when the wains come down to talk to him," I told him.

"Well, I hope he is as obliging for us, since we need to get this job over with before they come back home." Barney didn't seem a bit bothered when my father went in to his little shed and slipped the rope around his neck. He looked like he was about to be taken out for a walk. He even seemed willing to get up on his back legs when my father started to hoist him up.

"How long do you think it will take to hang him?" I asked.

"Hang him? Jesus, we're not going to hang him—you're going to hold on tight and keep him from trying to get away."

The concept was still lost on me, even as my father began backing out of the shed and placed the end of the rope in my hand. If we weren't going to hang the pig, how were we going to convert him into bacon? At that moment my father bent down and opened up a piece of burlap that he had carried out of the house along with the rope. He opened the sack and produced a knife, the likes of which would have made a Viking proud.

"Right," he said, "hold on tight, he's not going to like the next part." I looked at the pig, standing up on his back legs, and he looked back at me with what appeared to be a confused look on his face. He was used to the wains throwing pieces of lettuce on his head like a hat, and must now have thought that we were playing a new game with him. Without a word of warning to either Barney or myself, the auld fella lunged at Barney's chest with the knife. It all happened very fast, so I can't be sure if his aim was off, or if Barney sidestepped the knife to dodge a bullet, so to speak. At any rate, the knife only punctured the pig's skin enough to make a small cut and draw blood.

I don't know who was more shocked—me or the pig. It seemed to take him a second or two to digest what had happened, but as soon as he got the picture, he started to squeal like a banshee and danced on his back legs like he was doing a jig. Thankfully I had kept a good hold on the rope, but he was still able to twirl about and voice his displeasure at the way he was being treated.

"Hold on tight," my father barked. "I just need one good jab into his heart and it will be all over." In theory, that sounded like it should work. The trouble was that Barney was not what you might call a willing participant. I think he quickly realized after the Big Yank drew the first blood that his true calling was not to be the family pet. Every time my father would lunge at him, Barney's eyes would grow bigger, and just as the tip of the blade was heading for his chest, he would give a little hop to the side or pull back. We must have stabbed at him for about half an hour, and left more than a dozen puncture wounds all over his chest. I suggested to the auld fella that we should blindfold him so that he wouldn't see the knife coming.

"It doesn't take a fucking firing squad to kill a pig," my father roared at me. He lunged at Barney, but completely missed him, nearly landing under the animal's belly.

By the way you're going, I thought to myself, *the poor bastard will die from exhaustion before he dies from blood loss.* I think the auld fella felt like the pig was trying to make a fool of him, though, and it made him all the more determined to bury the butcher's knife inside the bold Barney.

"Put everything you have into holding that rope tight," he snarled. "This pig is not going to make a monkey out of me any longer." I did what I was told and laid back on the rope with my feet stretched in front of me. With that, my father roared and lunged at the pig, who squealed, quite literally, like a stuck pig. He must have got him square in the heart, as a big stream of blood jetted out of Barney and covered my father's face and clothes.

It didn't bother him in the least, though. He laid into Barney, their snouts nearly touching each other as the pig gave his last dying kicks, and he didn't break away until the pig had come to a complete stop. Now that he didn't have any life left, Barney's full weight hung on the rope. It Indian-burned my palms as I lost my grip on the heavy animal, causing him to come crashing to the floor.

"Take a hold of that back leg and I'll take the other," my father ordered. We pulled the dead pig out of his shed, into the street, and all the way to the front door of the house. My father put a pot of water on the range and, when it was hot enough, half-filled the basin that my mother used to wash the dishes. He then took his bristle shaving brush, a stick of shaving soap, and the silver razor that popped open when you twisted its bottom.

"Come out here and I'll show you what you're going to do next," he said as he walked out the door. I followed. He put the basin of hot water next to the pig, dipped the shaving brush into the water, lathered up the brush with the stick of soap and then slapped the brush up and down the side of the pig. Once he had the pig's side soapy, he took the razor and ran it up and down the pig's carcass. After a couple of strokes, he dipped the razor back into the basin. The water in the basin turned red from his hands, which were still covered in Barney's blood.

"Keep that up," he told me, "and I'll get this blood off me before the other children see it." I did as I was told. At the beginning, it was kind of entertaining to be shaving a pig. Like most young teenage boys, I was anxious for the day when I could start shaving. Little did I think that my first shave would be with a pig. The novelty wore off as my hands got colder and colder from dipping the razor in hot water and then crouching over the pig until it was time to re-dip. After what felt like hours, I was delighted to see a hairless pig lying in front of me. I stood up and took the basin of water, along with the tools of the trade, into the house. My father had removed all of Barney's blood and was making a scone.

"Are you finished already?" he asked me.

"Yes, and my hands are frozen to the bone."

"Let's see how you did then," he said, walking toward the front door. I felt a sense of achievement at seeing the white hairless skin of the pig again.

"What about the other side?" asked the auld fella.

"The other side?" I asked him.

"Yes, the other side. Did you shave the other half of him?" It slowly started to dawn on me that I was only halfway through.

"No. I wouldn't be able to lift him up on my own."

"All right, then," he replied, "let's roll him over so that you can shave the other side. I'll put on more hot water and change the razor blade." I looked down at the side of the pig that needed shaving—and not only shaving, but washing, as he had been lying in the mud of the street and his own blood. The auld fella came out with the basin full of hot water, throwing it all over the pig.

"That'll soften up the bristles a bit," he assured me. "Give me another couple of minutes and I'll bring you out the shaving water." I drastically changed my style of pig-shaving on the second go-around. The first time, I had been careful to go up and down in long controlled strokes, making sure that I had every bit of old hair off the razor before applying it to a new patch of skin. On the second go-around, I scraped the hair off vertically, horizontally, and diagonally, and nicked the skin left, right, and center. I figured that the pig was past caring how his hide looked, and if the Big Yank was so fussy, *he* should be out here freezing his balls off making the pig look pretty.

As soon as I was done, I gathered up everything and darted into the house. I stood over the range, turning first my arse to the heat and then my front, so that I looked like I was a pig roasting on a spit. My father took a hatchet from around the back of the range and headed toward the door.

"You stay here and get warm," he told me, "I'm going to chop him up into cuts we will be using over the coming months."

He didn't have to tell me twice. I had to pry the razor out of my right hand after I finished shaving him; and even when I did, my fingers were bent up like those of an old-age pensioner with a bad dose of arthritis.

Once I had thawed out, I was able to wrap my fingers around the kettle and make a pot of tea. I loaded the range up with half a bucket of turf, buttered myself a nice thick piece of scone, and poured a steaming hot mug of tea.

Luckily, the auld fella had been down to the shop and bought the *Derry Journal,* so I could catch up on all of the local news. When you grow up without electricity, it doesn't leave much room for entertainment—you can't watch television, listen to the radio, or even read at night. You look forward to reading the local paper on a Friday evening when you get home from school. Being able to read it "fresh" during the day was a special treat.

I paused to daydream about where I could be at that moment. I wished I was riding my bike. When we first moved out to the farm, bicycles were our main source of entertainment. I had saved like a miser in order to be able to buy myself a bike. I literally stuck aside every penny I came across. I don't even know how I managed it.

Of course, Jimmy and I also stole some money along the way. Knocking around with our grandfather whenever he would come home from America was a good source of revenue. He always seemed to have an endless supply of money. He'd throw us a few bob every time we were with him, especially if he had been drinking (which was all of the time). Then when we'd go into Carn to find him and bring him home, his old friends would feel sorry for us and would often give us a shilling or two as well.

Of course, the bicycles were second-hand. Everything we ever bought was second-hand. Some boy at school would pass the word around that he had a bicycle for sale, and you would then make an arrangement to view the bicycle and take it for a test drive. It never struck either one of us as odd that we had to buy the bikes ourselves. I suppose there was no point in asking our parents. They would have just turned around and cried the poor mouth.

The only thing I ever remember being bought new were a pair of shoes just before my first year of secondary school. I don't think the parents would have bought them either, if it wasn't for some government program that gave poor families money for buying shoes for going back to school. If it hadn't been for the government, I might have been going to school barefoot, like our mother told us she did when she was growing up in Donegal.

Talk about history repeating itself.

CHAPTER 16

THE BIKE WARS

As I waited for my father to finish chopping up Barney, I smiled to myself at the thought of pulling the wool over Jimmy's eyes. Not that I could assume full responsibility for the killing of the pet pig. After all, I was merely but a co-executioner (and shaver). There was, however, something extremely satisfying about knowing what I knew and knowing what he did not. It was as if this knowledge put me into a separate league. I was a member of a special type of club—a club whose members were killers, but more importantly, a club whose members had relatives who did not know their dark secret.

From as far back as I could remember, Jimmy and I were having a go at each other, always trying to get the upper hand. He'd climb a tree and I would have to climb higher. He'd smoke a bit of my father's discarded cigarette butt and I'd have to smoke it down further, even if it meant burning the shite out of my lips. I usually had the upper hand. It must have bothered him more than I knew, and I only realized how far it had escalated when he openly declared war on my bike.

⊫‡ ‡⊨

To fully grasp the importance of a bike back then, remember this was Ireland in the early seventies. The country had only two national TV stations; and we didn't own a TV anyway. There were summer evenings when we'd be so starved for entertainment that we'd look out across the bog toward Derry and try to figure where the bomb had just exploded and how much damage it had caused.

I saved for several years to buy my bike. I had to raid my savings account, which I had started to build up when I worked as a smuggler and cashier. When I found the bike I was later to buy, it was love at first sight. It was a black (all men's bikes were black back then) Raleigh, with three gears on the handlebars. It had a wee metal saddle on the back, over the rear mud guard, that I christened the "wain's seat." In peace times, before the outbreak of the bike wars, I used to let my brother ride on the wain's seat, since he couldn't afford to buy himself a bike. It took him a while to work up the courage to ride with me at all, as he still had some memories from a few years back when we nearly killed each other on our joyride.

Fortunately I was tall, but it was still a bit of a challenge to ride a man's bike, so I was a bit shaky for the first few months. I was more proud of that bike than anything else I had ever owned. To me, it might as well have been a Ferrari. This made what he did a year later all the more hateful.

I don't remember what started the war, but I have a feeling it arose mainly from the fact that I slagged him off about riding a girl's bike. He pestered our parents so much after I got my bike that they eventually gave in and bought him a cheap girl's bike. He tried for the longest time to deny that it was a girl's bike, but it didn't have a cross bar, and any eejit could tell you that a man's bike has to have a cross bar. Of course, the first thing you want to do when you get your wheels is to race someone else, and I didn't really even need to use the gears to beat my brother. My longer limbs and extra power beat him every time. I told him, though, that the reason he could never win was because he was riding a girl's bike.

To this day, I have no clue where the little bastard found the paint. The fact that it was lilac, though, told me that it was left-over paint from the father's jaunting car. I will never forget that Saturday morning I went down to milk the cow and discovered that my black bike had been painted lilac. I knew right away that it was him. When I had parked it in the shed between the byre and the house the night before, it was still black. Mind you, it wasn't that the color scheme did not go together—it matched very well, actually. It was the fact that my prize possession had been violated. My bike had been in pristine condition, and now nothing could bring it back to its former glory. I couldn't touch him in the house. But when there were no witnesses later on in the day, I grabbed him by the throat and squeezed down hard on his Adam's apple.

"Why did you do it, you little fucker?" His eyes were bulging, and he made some gurgling sounds in his throat.

"Don't be making believe that you can't talk. I will push the last breath out of you, and then I will throw your body into the river. Everybody will believe that you fell in and drowned by accident."

He really did look terrified, but I couldn't pay too much attention to that, as he was a slippery wee fucker and used to squirming his way out of trouble. The more I pressed down on his throat, the less I cared about his answer. I was mesmerized by the bulging of his eyes. I think I could have finished him off if he didn't start shaking his head. The shaking of his head got me to wondering. *Why the fuck was he shaking his head?* I looked behind me, but there was nobody there.

"What do you mean, *no?*" I asked him, pressing down harder on the lump in his throat.

"Do you mean, 'No, I didn't do it,' or 'No, I'm not talking,' or 'No, now go and fuck yourself'? Do you see my predicament? You'll have to explain yourself a bit better if I am to understand you."

Later, I realized that his head-shaking was a way of saying, "No, please don't kill me." Apparently I had a somewhat deranged look on my face. I can't confirm that part, but I am quite sure that I really did want to kill the little bastard. In hindsight, I am quite sure I would have gotten away with it, too. An Irish jury had never previously been asked to determine the guilt of a 13-year-old accused of strangling his 10-year-old brother. The most I would have gotten would have been a few years in some type of juvenile facility, which would probably have been an improvement on the quality of life I had experienced thus far.

It was not the jury I was afraid of, though. I am quite sure I wouldn't have survived long enough to go to trial. My father would have strung me up, there would have been two fewer mouths to feed, and that would have been the end of it.

I sensed there wasn't a whole lot of time left before my brother checked out, so I decided to let him go. That didn't mean that all was forgiven by any means, though. It just meant that I would bide my time and strike when I was good and ready. As soon as I released my grip, he pulled away from me and sucked in air as he coughed out.

"You're...mental," he wheezed, stumbling away from me.

"I'm mental?" I roared at him. I was starting to feel stupid for letting him go. "What do you call some little half-wit fucker who paints a man's bicycle purple?"

My mind raced as I thought of ways to get even, but I could not come up with a decent solution. It would be a right bastard trying to top painting a bike lilac. The more I thought, the darker and more devious my thoughts became. I'd be lying if I said I did not think about doing him a grave bodily injury. I had no moral problem with that. It was just that it needed to be done in such a way as to not be able to come back on me.

No, my revenge would have to be taken out on his bike: a tooth for a tooth and all that jazz. He had already gone the paint route, so I couldn't go there, or else it would look like I lacked imagination.

Suddenly, it came to me. I'd set his bike on fire and make it appear to be a sectarian attack, the like of which was happening daily down the road in Derry. I was so consumed with rage that I never gave a moment's thought to the sectarian angle. What kind of mad hoor of a Protestant would sneak on to the farm and set fire to a boy's (or girl's) bike?

Well, far be it from me to let common sense get in the way. For the next few days, I went about gathering the ingredients I would need to make a Molotov cocktail. I squirreled away all types of bottles, from wee ones to large milk ones. I tore up pieces of rags and hoarded matches. The fuel was easy, since the auld fella kept a big fifty-gallon tank of diesel at the end of the shed for the tractor.

Two Saturdays later, I finally got the chance to try my arm at being a Freedom Fighter. The rest of them were going up to Derry shopping, and I volunteered to stay behind to foot turf in the bog.

My mother suspected that something was not right. "You'd rather stay here and foot turf than go into Derry and shop with us?"

I had to think of my answer fast and make it believable, since she had a mind like a police detective. "No, of course I would rather go with youns, but it is a fine day and God knows when we'll get another. I don't want to have to be working in the bog when it's raining." She looked at me as if she didn't quite believe me, but there wasn't much arguing with my reasoning.

As soon as I watched them turn around the bend of the lane and head up the road, I retrieved my stash from the stone ditch that joined the first field to the byres and sheds. As I was root-ing around for the equipment, I came a across a rubber bullet I had bought from a lad at school. He claimed to have picked it up off the street in Derry's Bogside after a skirmish with the British Army. I didn't know what would happen if the rest of them knew I had bought a rubber bullet, so I hid it well in the ditch to keep them from finding out.

I filled two bottles three-quarters of the way with diesel, soaked some of the rags in it, jammed them in the necks of the bottles, and put them aside until it was time to set them alight. I decided to try out my homemade bombs on the gable end of the house. Being an inexperienced youth, both in the ways of the world and in organizing bombing campaigns, I figured it would be safe enough to torch a stone gable.

I should have also considered the fact that the roof was made out of sticks and covered in flax—highly combustible materi-als. I had not. What I *had* considered, though, was leaving some kind of note or slogan. The first thing I thought of was the usual mantra of the day, "Brits out!" Fortunately, I did have enough sense to realize that a Protestant was very unlikely to sneak onto a Catholic farm in broad daylight, petrol-bomb a child's bike, then leave graffiti on the wall exclaiming "Brits out."

I continued to think. *And what the hell are they going to think when they pull into the yard and see black smoke from a bicycle's tires wafting up from the sheds?* They sure as hell were not going to think that it was an electrical fire, since we didn't have any friggin' elec-tricity. Also, the broken bottles and smell of diesel were bound to be some kind of clue. Then there was the fact that I had stayed behind. The bog was only a few hundred feet behind the house. Could a fire really break out without me noticing?

At least I was not too concerned about them calling the police. My father was most likely on the run from the police in America. I didn't know if the Yankee police and the Gardaí talked to each other, but I figured that my father wouldn't be the type to go running to the police anyway.

After this brief weighing-up conversation with myself, I decided that the pros definitely outweighed the cons, and my brother's bike was to be diesel-bombed.

It took me seven matches to get the rag in the first bottle lit. *Jesus,* I thought, *you wouldn't want to be in a hurry bombing some fucker.* In hindsight, the problem was most likely due to the rag not having been soaked enough in diesel. When I finally got it lit, I stood watching it like an eejit. I had seen Derry lads on the news throwing petrol bombs at the Brits. They made it look so easy. I suppose they were used to making bombs.

Now that I had a lit one in my hand, I wanted to take some time to enjoy it. At some stage, though, I realized this was a foolish thing to do and I let the bottle fly at the stone gable. It hit the side of the house, broke...and that was it. Where was the explosion? My parents would definitely not have to call the police about *this*.

I decided to make my next attempt more dramatic. I talked myself into a scenario. It was a Saturday night in Derry and I was with a bunch of lads looking for action. Word had it that the Provos would be active in the Bogside after the pubs closed, and we were going to show our support and hopefully throw a few petrol bombs at the soldiers. I put so much swagger into this attempt that I was able to light the fuse on the second match. I pulled my t-shirt up over my mouth so as to cover my face and not get caught on the Brits' cameras. Holding the lit bottle with my right hand, I extended it behind me like some kind of Olympic javelin-thrower. With my left hand pointed at the target like a sight, I took three half-steps forward with my left foot and shouted, "An Phoblacht Abu!" ("Up the Republic!"), as I flung the flaming bottle against the wall.

I expected all hell to break lose. Instead, the feckin' thing fizzled out like the first effort. It was then that it dawned on me.

The reason it was called a "petrol bomb" was because it used petrol. I never once heard a Molotov cocktail referred to as a "diesel bomb." The bloody diesel wouldn't ignite. All that planning for nothing.

⊨ ⊫

"All right, I think I have finished him," my father informed me as he came through the kitchen door. "He should last us a good few months."

I went out to the street and saw Barney all cut up into sections. It was actually quite funny; he looked like a jigsaw puzzle. Maybe he should be called a *pigsaw,* I thought, struggling to hold in my laughter. I don't know where my father had learned to cut up a pig, but it really looked like he knew what he was doing. Now he was gathering up sheets of brown paper and twine.

"What do you need all the paper for?" I asked him.

"First, I'm going to rub brown sugar and saltpeter into the skin, and then I'll wrap him up tight with the brown paper. We should be able to slice off our first breakfast in about four weeks."

For the next two hours, we wrapped that pig in brown paper and tied him up to the rafters of the ceiling. I'd never seen anything like it. By the time we were finished, there were a dozen surprise packages hanging from the ceiling. I say "surprise" because if you walked into the kitchen after we finished hanging the pig, you wouldn't have a bloody notion that these packages signified poor Barney had met his maker. How was he going to explain the roof-hanging parcels to the young ones when they came home?

I wouldn't have to wait long to find out. Five minutes later, the car pulled up outside. The wains came into the house and at once noticed the brown parcels hanging from the ceiling.

"What's in the parcels?" asked Jimmy. There was a moment of silence. I looked at the auld fella. It was definitely his duty to explain.

"We're getting ready for Christmas," he said.

"So Santa has come early?"

The little bastard was conniving enough to paint my bike unbeknownst to me, yet he was stupid enough to think that Santa was hanging presents from the ceiling rafters this year. Never mind that we were only in mid-November. And what was the prick doing still believing in Santa Claus anyway?

"Ah, no. We were just experimenting to see how the decorations would look if we hung them from the ceiling," replied my father. If he pulled this off, he should be awarded the World's Best Bullshit Artist Award.

The wains actually seemed to buy it. Jimmy shrugged and glanced over at our youngest brother. "Let's go down and visit Barney," he said.

I looked over at the auld fella. He looked at me pleadingly, his eyes begging for help. I covertly followed the wains down toward Barney's shed and grabbed the spade as I passed the cow byre. I started to clean the floor of cow shite, keeping an ear open for the conversation next door.

"Barney isn't here," said Jimmy.

"Where's he at?" asked Kevin.

I walked over and pulled the door closed behind me. There would be a lot more questions asked if they saw the gruesome, wadded-up straw where Barney had begun to bleed out.

"He's always here when we come home," lamented Jimmy. "Where is he now?"

"It looks like he must have opened his door and left," I offered.

"Left? Where would he go? Why would he leave? Sure, this is his home." *If the poor bastard had known what was in store for him today,* I thought, *he would have been well-advised to get as far away as possible.*

"Maybe he decided he wanted to see the world. You know, he probably felt caged up living in this little shed and decided to, ah...spread his trotters."

"So you're saying he ran away from home?" Jimmy demanded.

"Looks that way."

Part of me wanted to tell him what I really knew. I had to bite my tongue to stop myself from blurting out, *"He didn't run away from home, you stupid wee bastard. The Big Yank and I stabbed his fat ass, and then we chopped him up into small pieces. Every time you walk into the kitchen, he'll be looking down at you."* I knew I couldn't do it, though; it would break little Kevin's heart. He had such a sad look on his face.

The two of them walked out of Barney's shed and headed out into the field behind. I knew they were hoping to spot their pet in the distance.

I felt sorry for Kevin. He really seemed heartbroken. He could gaze across the fields as long as he wanted, but the next time he'd catch sight of Barney would be as he looked down on his breakfast plate in about a month. I headed back to the house and let the auld fella know what to expect.

"They are fairly upset that their pig has gone missing."

"Do they have any idea what really happened to him?"

"Not a bit. I've convinced them that he must have knocked down his half-door and then took off for parts unknown. I made it sound like he was having the adventure of his life."

My father started laughing, which I didn't expect at all. "It's a good thing they didn't walk in on us when we were trying to kill that pig," he said between laughs.

I would have liked to bring the fact to his attention that it was *he* who was "trying" to kill the pig. I had been trying to hold him up on his back legs. It was never good for one's health to contradict the auld fella, though, so I let him amuse himself.

"When he started to twirl around after getting a few stabs, it looked like he was dancing a jig on his hind legs," he continued.

I actually found the thought amusing myself. "It must have been a pig jig," I added.

"That's a good one," he conceded, slapping his knees. "Aye, a pig jig!"

"When you two have calmed down a bit from your comedy routine, maybe somebody could tell me how long it will be before we can have some bacon and ham," said my mother.

"About four weeks' time," replied my father.

"That's a long time to wait," she shot back. "I think I'll kill one of the kids tomorrow so we can have some meat in the meantime."

My heart sank in my chest. Jesus Christ, were we turning into cannibals? I knew we were not your average family, but surely she wasn't mad enough to kill one of the wains for meat? She must have read my mind easily when she caught me staring at her, my jaw hanging open.

"What's wrong with you?" she asked.

"Kill...one of the...kids?"

"The goat's kids, you eejit."

We had gotten a goat to have goat's milk for my sister, who had a bit of a chest condition. Goat's milk was supposed to be powerful for a dodgy chest. Then the goat went and gave birth to four kids. The kids sucked milk from their mother. This was not part of our mother's original plan.

"You don't really think I would kill one of my own kids for meat, do you?" she asked.

When it came to Sarah the Slasher, it was hard to say. I think she got her answer when I simply stared at her in reply. She probably would have been much better at killing the pig.

"You can help me tomorrow to kill one of the kids," she told me.

What the hell had I got myself into? I had been co-executioner of a pig on Friday, and was to be co-executioner of a baby goat on Saturday. Good bloody thing we were Catholics, so that I could be guaranteed one day of rest from the killing spree on Sunday. At least it wouldn't be as traumatic a killing as the poor old pig had experienced.

Or so I hoped.

CHAPTER 17

GUNS AND GOATS

The next day I got up and went about my business feeding and milking the cow and cleaning out her bed. Nobody mentioned anything about killing baby goats, and I sure as hell had no intention of bringing up the subject. Then around noon, when other Irish lads were going out to kick around a football with their mates, or watch a match on the telly, my mother turned to me over her mug of tea and asked, "Are you ready to help with this goat?" There I had been thinking it had gone out of her head.

Something to remember with my parents—there was never a choice involved. A question might be asked in a manner which would lead you to believe that it had a democratic nature about it, but you could bet your life there was only one acceptable answer.

"Whatever you say," I responded, dying to add, "Mein Führer."

I followed her out to the garden behind the house where the goats roamed. The mother goat was tied with some rope that gave her about twenty yards to move in any direction. Her babies ran free, never straying too far from their mother. On her way, my mother picked up a length of two-by-four that had been propped up against the gable end of the house. As we approached the goats, she motioned to me to grab the biggest of the kids. I did as she asked, wondering what type of execution she had in mind.

"Hold it by the hindquarters," she instructed.

I held the little goat by the waist, wondering how this was going to get the deed accomplished. Next thing I saw was my crazy mother raising the two by four up behind her head and then bringing it down crashing onto the little goat's head. Unfortunately for me, her aim was off a bit, and she cracked the wood against my wrist before it made contact with the animal's spine. I heard a crunch sound, but wasn't sure whether it was my wrist or the goat's backbone that was breaking.

"FUCK ME," I roared.

"BAAAAAAAAAAAAA," bleated the goat.

A two-by-four? Really? What kind of maniac would choose a lump of timber as a murder weapon? James Bond had his Walther PPK; Russian spies had poison-tipped umbrellas; Mafia hitmen had their tommy guns; and our old lady had a lump of fucking wood. As soon as she brought it down on my wrist, I let go. I think it was just enough of a breather for the little goat to get an inch or two out of the kill zone and narrowly escape being creamed.

"She's getting away," shrieked Sarah. "Go after her and bring her back." *Bring her back…to stand trial for desertion?* Now that my mother was highly agitated, there was no knowing who or what she would crucify when the wood started flying. I ran after the little goat, but my heart wasn't in catching her. That was a real problem. If Sarah the Slasher thought I wasn't putting my whole heart into it, she was more than capable of turning the murder weapon on me. I pounced when I was close enough to be sure of a capture and carried the goat back to the would-be killer.

"OK," she said, "hold her so that I can finish her off."

Not a fucking chance, you crazy bitch, I said to myself. Slowly, I carried the poor unfortunate kid over to the executioner and held on to her as Sarah took a big backward swing. I watched her like a hawk. I watched the muscles in her arms as she brought the timber back. I watched the deranged look in her eye as she contemplated the kill. I even watched her breathing. As she clenched her teeth and brought down the hammer (so to speak), I let go and fell back in the final two seconds. The wood came crashing down on the animal's neck, right where I had been holding it before I made my escape. Once again there was a crunching of bones, but the kid ran off, bleating like a stuck pig.

"What did you let her go for?" the madwoman screamed at me. You'd think she hadn't eaten a piece of meat in years.

"I saw the way that wood was headed, and I didn't fancy losing another hand."

By that time, my wrist had ballooned up to four times its normal size. I could tell she was as frustrated as all hell. The look in her eye told me that she would as soon clobber me over the head with the two-by-four as the goat.

"I'll get Houton to take care of this."

Now she was going to get my grandfather to come down from Malin Head to finish off the baby goat that she had maimed and half-killed? By Jesus, I had been born into one weird tribe (the very fact that all of his children referred to their father by his surname was a good indication right there.) I followed her back to the house in order to find out what was going to happen. She walked in to the kitchen and spoke to my father in what sounded more like an attack to me.

"Go get Houton and tell him we have a goat to kill."

In those days, there was no way you could pick up a phone and call someone to tell them you were coming over. You just arrived on their doorstep and hoped they would be there. If you were the Big Yank, you would get in your car and do what your wife ordered when she was in one of her moods. If he couldn't find my father-in-law, he would have to drive around until he did. Finding our grandfather could be like looking for a needle in a haystack. God knows how many bars and hotels there were in Innishowen, but there was a chance he was in any one of them at any given time.

"What if he's not at home?"

The auld fella knew this might turn out to be a wild goose chase. He might be out combing the countryside for her father until the wee hours of the morning.

"Then you know what to do. You've done it before," she barked at him. "Start off with the Malin Hotel and then search all the bars in the Head one by one. Everybody knows him, and someone will be bound to know where he went after he was in that place."

My father took Jimmy and headed off in his car. There was a good chance that they would find him, as it was early yet. If he had been out drinking the night before, he might be knocking around his yard. He was also building a chicken house around that time. When he helped our auld fella build the bus foundation on the hilltop, he worked as hard as anyone half his age. He never even stopped to eat. He'd just stop every hour or so to smoke an unfiltered Sweet Afton cigarette.

I made myself as scarce as possible so that I could devote some time to the project, which I had since named "Get Even." I was fairly obsessed with getting my own back on my brother. Painting his bike was now out of the question, and bombing it had not gone as well as expected. I would have liked to have placed it under the tractor wheel in the hopes that my father might drive over it and crush it, but the little prick might not realize that I was the brains behind it. I really wanted him to know that, whatever happened, I was the one responsible.

That's when I decided that I would take on a germ warfare solution. I would piss into bottles and save them up over several weeks. When I had enough, I would soak the bike with the pish. Frame, leather seat, rubber wheels—every single part of his bike would be doused. I am quite sure that I was the first one ever to construct a "dirty bomb" in Ireland (even if it was incapable of exploding.)

I had three plastic gallon oil jugs filled with my urine. I opened the tops to see how the fermentation process was coming along. I had no sooner exposed the contents (which had been sitting for a few weeks) when the most putrid smell I have ever experienced wafted up from the jugs and assaulted my nostrils. The stench was indescribable. You'd have to do it yourself in order to have any idea how awful it smelled.

I knew that the time was right for his bike to "take a bath." I wheeled it out of the small shed and propped it up against the wall of the ex-pig shed, which was sheltered by a big stone wall that gave me a good amount of privacy. I was about to christen it when I had another thought—it would be better to turn it upside-down and get the underside done first. I was able to fully soak the seat from every angle. I let the air out of the tires so that the piss would get under the tire and between the rubber and inner tube.

Once I was satisfied that all of that was taken care of, I flipped it right-side up using the handlebars, which were still dry. I was extremely thorough, if I do say so myself, especially for having to do it all one-handed after being crippled by the madwoman. I didn't just throw piss over the handlebars, but eased off the rubber grips that were on all bikes' handlebars back then. I filled each grip up with my stale, fermented pee and then slipped them back on the handlebar on each side. I figured that he would clean the bike, but never suspect that the insides of the grips were rotten. The smell would always be with him when he rode.

Fortunately it was a fair enough day with a little sun, so I left the finished product against the wall to "bake" in my special concoction. I was probably working on my "project" for a good couple of hours, and was lucky to get as much time to myself as I did. Eventually, my mother came out looking for me in her usual state of mind— a bad mood.

"I need you to go and milk the goat so I can give it to your sister. Her chest is acting up again."

I thought, *Ah, do you not want to milk the goat, since you tried to kill her child with a lump of wood right in front of the poor bitch?* The goat wasn't very large, but she did have a sharp set of twisty horns, and if she turned on you while you were pulling on her tits, she could knock your lights out. These thoughts reeled through my worried head as I walked into the house to get a small pot for the milk.

I'd opt to milk a cow over a goat any day of the week. Cows are big, and they just stand in the one spot. You nearly always milk them in their byre, but I had gone out to the field and grabbed a couple of quick pints as they were grazing on grass. A goat, on the other hand, is usually tethered outside and left to scrounge around eating leaves from bushes, rough grass, weeds, and just about anything. They are also very alert creatures. You'd have to be James Bond to have any chance of sneaking up on a goat. Milking one is a mobile effort.

The goat doesn't care that you need to milk it, and she keeps moving around and picking out things to eat. Your best chance of getting a few cups of milk would be when she stands for a few minutes chewing. If she is on the go, then you must be too. This makes it difficult to safeguard the milk in your pot. You have to get down on one knee, place the pot, squirt, grab the pot, and move to the next stopping point, whereby you continue to repeat the process until you have enough. This is the reason why goat's milk is so scarce.

As I closed in on the goat, I thought she gave me a strange look. I hadn't been the one directly trying to kill her kid, but I was at the scene of the crime. I was full sure she knew it was me and remembered the part I played, holding down her offspring as the crazy woman from inside the house tried to kill it. Cow's eyes are big and dark and sad-looking, but goats have crazy eyes even at the best of times. They are the eyes of a tiger, terrifying and psychedelic. If you stare into them for too long, you feel as if you are going into some kind of a trance. That's where I now found myself—staring into her eyes, feeling as though she was putting a spell on me.

I don't know how long we were staring at each other, but I only snapped out of it when I heard my mother scream: "Are you going to ask that goat to dance with you or are you going to milk it?"

Strange how she would mention dancing with the goat when not too long ago I watched the jigging pig. I inched my way up to the goat and talked softly to it to relax her. "Good girl. Who's a good girl, then? Are you going to give me some of your milk?" Her kids surrounded her, and I wondered how much milk she had to spare after they had sucked her. I saw the black and white spotted one that we had tried to kill. The poor thing seemed to hang her head to one side as if she had a broken neck, or as if she was some kind of goat half-wit.

The mother goat stopped chewing as she watched me looking at the kid. At that stage, I knew all too well that she knew what we had tried to do. I eased myself down onto one knee under her hindquarters and grabbed one of her tits. It didn't have much milk in it, so I had to release my grip and try to get more of it in my hand. I aimed at the small pot and hit it first time. I had no sooner gotten one decent squirt than she started to wander off. I followed her. When she stopped to eat, I got in another squirt. I had managed to get about a dozen and a half decent squirts into the pot when I heard our car coming over the lane. I stood up and waited to see if they had Grandfather with them. They pulled up into the street and got out.

"What are you doing there, young fella?" my grandfather asked.

"Milking the goat for my sister's chest."

"Is that the one your mother wants me to kill?"

I didn't know what to say. Knowing her, she could have decided to line them all up against the wall and get rid of them, one after another. My mother came out of the house.

"So which one of them do you want me to kill, Sadie?' he asked her.

No beating about the bush for Grandfather. No need to come up with a story about how the baby goat ran away. I was anxious to see which method he would use. If it was the two by four again, I hoped he had a better aim, or that they could use somebody else to hold the intended victim.

"No, it's one of the kids," she replied. "They're a bit small yet, but we could do with the meat. We'll knock one off every month after this." He walked over toward the goats and staggered unsteadily.

She looked at my father. "Is he drunk?"

"I'd say he has had a few, all right. He made us stop at a ditch, and he pulled something out of the stones and put it in his pocket. It was probably a bottle of Poteen."

Grandfather was over at the goats calling them like you would do to a cat: "pishwwwwwa, pishwwwwwa."

Kevin looked confused. "Why is grandfather calling the goats like they are cats?"

Nobody had an answer for him.

After he got close enough, Grandfather pulled a gun out of his pocket and aimed into the middle of the goats. I thought it was a toy gun. Nobody could have a gun like that in Ireland. I didn't know all of the laws, but I knew that if the police caught you with a hand gun you were automatically arrested and would be put in jail for twenty years.

It sounded real when he started shooting it, though. BANG! BANG! BANG! The goats began to run around like crazy as he shot into the pack.

"He's got a gun!" shouted the auld fella. "Did you know he has a gun?"

"I didn't," Sarah replied, "but he did come to kill a goat."

"I didn't know he would have a gun," shouted my father above the noise of the gunfire. "If the neighbors call the Guards, we could all go to prison for the next twenty years."

I was focused on Grandfather, suddenly realizing that he wasn't even aiming at the kid with the broken neck. He was just blasting away at anything he could hit. There was so much shouting and shooting going on that nobody seemed to care which goat got shot. I walked toward Grandfather so that I could point out the goat that needed to be shot. I only half-realized that I was still holding the pot full of goat milk.

The goat family was in mayhem. The mother goat was running around the length of the tether trying to get out of the kill zone, and her kids were bleating and running helter-skelter. As I tapped my grandfather's elbow, I heard my father yelling "Jesus, get him out of there before he gets shot!"

Grandfather looked around to see what the yelling was about. He was wearing a black suit and a white shirt. He reminded me of an Italian Mafia guy I had seen in a film on old Tess's telly one Sunday.

"What's wrong with them?" Grandfather asked me, nodding at my parents.

"I think they are afraid you will shoot one of us, or maybe yourself," I told him, trying to sound casual. In fact, I had no fear of him doing something like that. This was the same man, for Christ's sake, who could spit in a person's ear as they were standing right next to him and never be suspected of a thing. He didn't *make* mistakes.

That made him grin. Whenever he had been drinking, he would wrinkle up his nose when he grinned. He turned around and faced my parents.

"What, are they mental?"

"Pretty much," I replied. He looked at me, and his lip started to curl up. He wrinkled his nose.

"Tell him to put down the gun, for the love of sweet Jesus," shouted my father to my mother.

This made Grandfather look down. When he realized that he was pointing the gun barrel squarely at them, instead of at the ground, he began to laugh.

"Why is he screaming like a wee girl?" Grandfather asked me, bending over now as his laughter started to get the better of him.

I figured that I should reply, but in doing so I would be definitely signing my own death warrant with the Big Yank. Laughing would be no better, maybe even worse, but I couldn't help myself. What started out as a snigger became uncontrollable, until I too was bent over, grabbing my sides. The parents stared.

When Grandfather and I had finally regained our composure, he handed me the pistol and nodded toward the goats. "Here, you shoot the damned goat then." I slowly held out my right hand and took the gun from him. It was small, but it felt heavy. It also felt oily. I hesitated. I was new at killing animals, after all.

"Go on," he encouraged me, "shoot whichever wee fucker you like."

I was in a state of shock. Here I was holding a highly illegal gun, the likes of which would send a man to jail for a lifetime, and all I could think was, *There are men across the border who haven't been this close to a gun.* Yet here I was, a young pup, holding a killing machine in one hand and a pot of fucking goat's milk in the other. It made my attempt at making Molotov cocktails pale in comparison.

Behind me I could hear my father getting excited. "Do you see what he just did? Your crazy goddamned father just gave his gun to the boy. Jesus, somebody's going to get killed or go to jail today."

I ignored the commotion behind me. When you are a young fella and holding a gun in your hand, you can feel your own power. With that kind of might, you can ignore whoever you want.

"So what do I do now?" I asked Grandfather.

"Just stretch out your arm and raise the gun up until you can see who or what you want to shoot," he calmly explained.

"I'm going to shoot the wee one with the crooked neck."

"Be careful. Don't get your fingerprints on the gun," shouted my auld fella.

Don't get my fingerprints on the gun? Who the fuck was he? What kind of father tells his 13-year-old son to be careful about leaving his fingerprints on a gun that he should not have come within an ass's roar of in the first place?

"All right then," continued Grandfather, ignoring his son-in-law. "You're right-handed, so close your left eye, aiming with the right. When you see the goat at the end of the gun barrel, hold your breath and squeeze the trigger."

In the background I could faintly hear someone chanting "Jesus, Mary, and Joseph help us all." Like Elvis sang, it was "now or never." I spotted that poor wee kid with the crooked neck. It was not running around as daft as the others. They had all settled down a bit now that the shooting had stopped. It looked like old Crooked Neck was trying to get close to its mother in order to get a suck from her.

I didn't know what I was doing, but I knew enough that you had to point the gun at whatever you were going to shoot. I pointed the end of the barrel at the damaged goat, held on tight to the pot of milk, held my breath, closed my left eye and started to pull the trigger. *Don't breathe, or you'll lose your aim.* I didn't know how long I should wait to get the perfect aim or how long I could last without breathing. Apparently I waited just a little too long. Everything started to get dark.

That was the last thing I remembered—falling—and night coming so fast.

CHAPTER 18
VEHICULAR PIG SLAUGHTER

The explosion of the gun in my hand jerked my eyes open before I hit the ground. I was immediately aware of Grandfather bent over, howling with laughter, and my mother shouting something at me. I couldn't make out what she was yelling because of the loud ringing in my ears. My right hand was shaking and my big swollen left hand felt warm, wet, and sticky. *I've shot myself.* The last time my hand felt like that was when I had Barney's blood on my hands. I slowly looked down, expecting the worst.

White liquid was running down my wrist. White blood? Shite, it was goat milk. I looked over at the parents. The auld fella was holding his head in his hands. My mother was shouting at me and pointing at the ground behind me. I focused in on her to try to understand what she was saying. She was really mad. She was definitely mouthing "fucking"—something about me and fucking. I moved a couple of steps closer to her in order to see if that would help me hear her better. That did the trick.

"You shot the fucking goat," she said. Brilliant. That is what I was trying to do! At least we would be having some decent meat for a change. Although, actually, I had never eaten goat before, so I didn't know whether it would be decent. I turned back to look at my handiwork, expecting to see that Crooked Neck had been dispatched to meet her maker. Instead, I saw wee Crooked Neck standing over her mother, nudging the goat's udder with her nose. The mother lay flat on her side, her legs stretched out on the ground in front of her, twitching. The poor bitch was having a seizure. *A goat seizure?* I looked down at the pistol in my right hand. I had shot the wrong fucking goat. No wonder the old lady was yelling at me.

I tried to make things better. "At least we'll get more meat out of her," I shouted back at my mother, my ears ringing.

"Meat? Meat?" she shrieked. "We were supposed to eat the *kids* for meat. The mother supplies us with milk, don't you remember? What will you shoot next, the fucking *cow?*"

I turned back toward the downed goat, hoping I had just "winged" her and she might be back up on her feet. Not only was she still down, but Grandfather was now also down on his hands and knees, laughing his arse off. I heard crying behind me. Kevin had witnessed the goat slaying and couldn't believe that I had shot our "pet." Part of me wanted to divert attention away from myself by telling him that his father had killed the other pet. Grandfather slowly rose to his feet and reached out for the gun.

"Who do you have to shoot around here to get a cup of tea?" he asked, sticking the pistol in his trouser pocket.

"Just please don't ask for goat milk in your tea," I half-whispered. We walked into the house, and I was glad that Grandfather was there to take the heat off me.

"Have you got some tea there, Sadie?" he asked, winking at me.

My father was sitting in his chair at the end of the table, staring out the window into the fields. The great thing about having Grandfather around was there was no question he was certifiably insane. It didn't matter what crazy shit he got up to. Nobody could be surprised or afford to say anything. My mother threw a fistful of loose tea into the teapot and poured boiling, steaming water from the kettle over the leaves. (You never had to wait long for a cup of tea in an Irish house. The kettle spent its entire life sitting on the cooker, waiting to be called into action.)

"You wouldn't have a wee bit of scone there, would you, Sadie?" he asked his daughter. "All that killing has made me hungry."

She went to the cupboard, pulled out half a scone, and began slicing it in silence. For a bunch of hoors who had a lot to say ten minutes ago, my parents now resembled an order of monks and nuns who had taken a vow of silence. Grandfather looked at me.

"Do you want some scone, Killer?"

"Aye."

"Give the lad some scone, Sadie. Sure he hunted dinner for us, he must have worked up a hunger."

She threw me a look that could curdle fresh goat's milk.

"Is that the first time you've shot and killed something, lad?" Grandfather asked. I took my time answering, for I knew there was so much going unsaid as to be dangerous.

"Sure, where would he be getting a gun, if not from you?" asked my mother. My father was still looking out the window, and shaking his head back and forth slowly.

"For all you know, he's up in Derry shooting British soldiers on the weekend," replied Grandfather.

"That's a fine idea to put into his head. Sure, he's bad enough without making him worse."

"It is a fine idea," replied the crazy man. "It's every Irishman's duty to drive those bastards out of our country."

"That'll do," scolded my mother. "I don't need to be going up visiting a son of mine in Long Kesh." Grandfather looked over at me and winked like a bold schoolboy when she mentioned the prison. They didn't know it, but I could tell he was trying to get a rise out of them. He loved messing with people.

"So, John," he shouted over at my father, "what will you do with the goat, chop her up like you did with the pig?" My father looked up and then quickly over at the wains, but was caught off-guard and speechless. I looked at my brothers. Their eyes grew as large as dinner plates, and their eyebrows jerked downward in horror.

"What are you talking about?" Sadie asked, warning him with her eyes. "He never chopped up a pig."

"Of course he did," persisted the old man, "and a fine job he made of it too. That man of yours could get a job in a butcher shop in Carn any day of the week."

My father looked nervous. "Ah, no," he replied, "sure the pig we had, Barney, he ran away one day. Got over the half-door and took off through the fields, never to be heard from again."

Grandfather wrinkled his nose, and I knew that trouble was not far away. "Ran away, you say? Aye, I hear that's on the rise. I was driving the tractor down the Black Mountain a lock of weeks back, coming back from mart day, and I saw one of those run-away pigs myself."

I could tell that my father hated his life in that moment. He had no idea where the story might go, but he was strapped in now. All he could do was hang on and go along for the ride.

"How did you know he was running away?" asked the gullible-but-curious Jimmy.

"Hard to say, really. I think it was the look in his eye. You know how they have those red eyes. Well, when the tractor head-lamps hit them, I could see that determined look on his face. Now if he had been walking away from me, I would never have known, as his arse would have been lit up and that wouldn't have told me anything."

"Go on," encouraged my brother, hanging onto every word.

"Well, as your man gets closer to me, I'm thinking to my-self that's one of those rebellious runaway pigs, like your father talked about. Of course he doesn't have any markings, or any-thing to say who he belongs to—there was no knowing how far he had come. He could have even swam across from Scotland if he caught the tide just right." He was on a roll now and not about to be stopped.

"So then what did you do, Grandfather?"

"Well, what else *could* I do? I swerved at the last minute when I realized what was going on."

"So you saved the wee pig from getting hurt on the road?" asked Kevin, glowing with innocence.

"Christ, no," shot back Grandfather. "I swerved and hit the little fat bastard. I brought him down to Malin the next morning to have him cut up. That wee fucker will feed me for the next three months, at least."

My brothers sat in stunned horror.

Actually, everyone did. They just stared in shock.

"Any more tea in the pot, Sadie?" asked Grandfather, as he pulled a lump of plug tobacco out of his jacket pocket and bit off a chunk. "There's something about shooting goats that makes me fierce thirsty."

My mother brought over the teapot and poured him another mug in silence. She went to pass him the milk, but he held up his hand.

"Ah no, I'll drink it black. Sure milk will be scarce around the house now," he said as he blew on the hot tea with a wrinkled nose and a half-smirk.

CHAPTER 19

ROBBING RELATIVES

As strange as my life felt up until this point, I had no idea that things were to become even stranger. I don't know why this came as such a surprise. The fact that I was a 13-year-old trying to balance running a working farm with attending secondary school should have been enough to sound warning bells. I don't know whether it was part of his grand plan, or if Mother Nature was just playing a cruel joke on me, but soon after my father had delegated all of the backbreaking farm chores to me, he announced that he was becoming a writer.

That in itself would not have been so unbelievable—Ireland was home to countless writers, and I myself had been writing poetry for a couple of years by that point—but we had never seen my father write anything other than letters to America asking others to buy him new shoes. Surely letters based on his oversized feet could not lead to a literary career? At any rate, he determined that he was destined to be a writer.

His first major project was to be a three-act play entitled *The Herder*. It was about a farmer who basically spent his life moving a few cows and calves from one field to another, each as run down as the other. The inspiration for the play was an actual farmer who lived nearby with his wife in an old thatch cottage similar to ours. To this day, I have no idea if the play had any merit. It could have been an Irish masterpiece or a total heap of shite. It did keep the Big Yank out of our hair for a time, though.

Now that I was officially the man of the house, I decided that we had suffered for long enough without a television and it was time to set things right. I had my brothers on my side, but our parents were opposed. I don't know whether they looked upon TV as an evil distraction to students, or whether they just didn't want to have to find the money to buy one. Either way, the result was the same—they were not bringing a telly into the house.

My father decided to counteract our desire for television by distracting us with reading. Six months before, the auld fella had bought a set of encyclopedias from a travelling salesman. "I didn't waste money on these books for them to sit on a shelf," he informed everyone within earshot, though I knew it was aimed directly at me. "I want youns to pick out a topic each day and learn about it, and then I will quiz you later."

Little did he understand that threatening us to learn was the wrong way to go about it. By making it sound like a prison chore, he would force us to do it begrudgingly, but our hearts would not be in it. As usual, I did enough to get by. In my remaining free time, I began to teach myself to play chess. Every time I would give a good chess player a run for his or her money, I would take extra pride in knowing that I had taught myself to play and that my first games had been against myself.

Although my father and I had always got along like oil and water, the arguing became fiercer and more frequent when I started secondary school. In order to plant the seed of a telly into my parents' brains, I knew it couldn't come from me, so I turned to the tried-and-trusted method of brainwashing Jimmy into doing my dirty work.

I couldn't have asked for a better partner. The little bastard never gave up, and his whining was as annoying as a goat's bleating when it was getting its brains knocked out by a two-by-four.

"If we told you once, we told you 100 times, we are *not* buying you a television. If you want to learn something, go open one of those books and read."

"But we can't watch football matches in a book. All of the other lads in school talk about football, but I don't know any of the players."

"You want a television? Fine. Go and buy it yourself," barked our father.

"We're fucked now," Jimmy reported back to me.

"Not at all. Sure, all we have to do is find the money to buy a telly," I told him. "That's the way I bought my bike."

"How do we do that when we have nothing?"

"Well, we can steal some of it, and for the rest we can work at something to give us money."

"Who will we steal from, and who will give us a job?"

"Jesus Christ, can you give me a minute to think?" I exploded. "You're involved in this too. Why do I have to come up with all of the answers?" After I asked the question, I saw the sadness on his face. I realized that the poor wee prick was only 10 and I was always the master planner.

"Don't worry," I reassured him. "Give me a few days to think it over, and I'm sure we will find a way. Why don't you go outside and ride your bike, and I'll think about it for a bit."

"I don't like riding it anymore," he informed me. "It always smells like pee."

I remembered the thorough dousing I had given it. No wonder it still smelled. I felt bad about project "Get Even."

"Get a basin of soapy water and give it a good wash," I advised him, "and don't forget to take off the handle grips and wash them too. You never know what kind of animal peed all over it when it was sitting outside one night."

The wheels inside my head were always turning. And anyway, I had half an idea of where we could lay our hands on some easy cash. The problem with the plan was that it was very dangerous. It would be better if there were no witnesses, but if I got him in really deep, I hoped that he would be too afraid to ever tell anyone and we'd bring the secret to our graves—or at least keep it until such time as everyone who could have harmed us would be dead already.

The next day after school, we met in the byre as I was milking the cow. He stood behind the right side of the cow's arse, by the door, so I had no chance of squirting him.

"So here's the deal," I said. "You know how Uncle Daniel always has a lot of American dollars on him?"

"Aye, mommy says that he must have brought enough money over from America to buy everybody in Donegal a drink when he came to stay with us."

"Exactly. Well, when he comes in from the pub tonight, one of us will sneak up to the kitchen and go through his pockets for money after he has fallen asleep."

"What if he wakes up and catches us?"

"If he comes in late, like he does sometimes when he crashes into the chairs and trips over the turf bucket, it will be nearly morning. He'll be so tired and drunk that he'll never hear us."

"Maybe he'll miss the money." The little bastard was always thinking of things that could go wrong.

"I'll bet that he won't have a clue how much he spent. Anyways, how could he prove it? Nobody is going to suspect his poor innocent nephews, with hardly a pot to piss in, of having robbed him."

"So who will sneak up and take the money?" Jimmy asked.

I thought about this quickly and came to the conclusion that if I wanted to get something done, I would have to do it myself.

"Don't worry about it; I'll do it. Just make sure you never breathe a word about this, or we're both dead men." I ran my forefinger across my throat to emphasize the importance of secrecy. I knew by the way he gulped his Adam's apple that he understood.

"How much do you think you'll get?" He wasn't done with the questions yet.

"How the hell do I know? Maybe a couple of quid. With a bit of luck, maybe as much as a fiver."

"Five pounds? That's a fortune!"

"It's not going to be enough to buy a telly," I told him. "There was one for sale in last week's *Derry Journal* and they were asking twenty quid for it."

"So who else can we rob?"

"Nobody. It's too risky. We're going to have to work to make up the difference."

"Who will give us a job? Sure, we can't do anything."

"What are you saying? Weren't we smuggling Free State food across the border when we were only wains and never got caught once? And then we were working in the shirt factory canteen. We're businessmen, never forget it. I wouldn't be one bit surprised if we don't wind up having our own shop selling televisions in a few years' time."

I didn't let on, but I was a bag of nerves for the rest of the day. I knew damn well that there was a good chance of getting caught. Daniel was like our grandfather—he slept with one eye open. Before I even made it up to the kitchen to go through his pockets, I had to successfully get through the bedroom obstacle course. Six of us slept in the same room, in two beds that faced one another. Somebody was nearly always getting up to take a piss throughout the night. It would be just my luck to be headed to the kitchen and get caught.

I had to stop worrying myself, though. Daniel would be headed back to America next week, and our best chance at getting a few extra pounds would be gone.

That night I lay in bed and kept telling myself that I wouldn't sleep. I was full sure that I wouldn't, either, until Daniel knocked over the kettle in the dark and woke me up, and I realized that I had nodded off.

I peered over the blankets to see if anyone else had heard the noise. Nobody moved.

Next came the waiting game. I hadn't a bloody clue how long I should wait for him to fall asleep. I cocked an ear to one side in case I heard him snoring.

Jesus, he was talking to someone! Who the hell was he talking to? I strained harder, but his was the only voice I could make out. We didn't have a phone, so he couldn't be calling anyone. Maybe he was talking to himself. Grandfather used to sing to himself when he was drinking.

I waited for what felt like ages. Finally the talking stopped, and I thought I heard snoring.

I eased myself out of bed, being careful not to step on either brother. I hunched down and crept across the floor toward the bedroom door. I squeezed it like it was an egg, but that didn't stop the fecking thing from creaking. I had never heard it creak before. For a second I considered whether this might be a warning to cancel the mission. I'd come that far, though, and was going to see it through.

My eyes became used to the darkness, and I could make out Daniel stretched out across the sofa. He was easy to spot, as he always wore a bright white t-shirt. His clothes were hanging on a chair, which sat directly in front of where his knees would be.

I crept up alongside the sofa, and reached over for the trousers and coat. I slid my right hand into his trouser pocket, and felt a bunch of coins and keys. I was tempted to grab some of the coins, but I was afraid it would make too much noise; if I dropped even one on the cement floor, I'd be totally bollixed. I couldn't afford to pay too much attention to the clothes, either, as I was watching the Uncle in case he turned around and saw me.

I removed my hand from his trousers and felt inside the pocket of the coat he had been wearing. I felt a big bulge, and my heart started beating faster. This could be the place where he kept his big money. Then again, him being a Houton, it might also be a gun. I pushed down deeper in the inside pocket and started to feel paper. I didn't want to pull out the whole thing, as I would be screwed if he turned over to face me and I couldn't get it back in.

I decided to use both hands, and to remove some of the paper notes by prying the pocket open with my right-hand fingers and slipping out the notes with my left hand. It was scary slow, but the notes started coming out. Some of the paper felt like it might have been a bit shiny. Maybe he had got new bank notes. I kept pulling until I could feel the paper in my left palm, and I wrapped my fingers across it so as not to drop anything on the floor.

I carefully removed both hands, balled up the paper in my left hand, and tried to make the coat look as if it had never been touched. I walked backwards to the bedroom in case he woke up. If he suddenly turned, I planned to start walking toward the table as if I were just hungry and getting myself a piece of bread. When I retraced my steps back into the bedroom, I got down on all fours and stuffed the balled-up paper I had just stolen into the toe of my shoe. I then stuffed my sock into the shoe. I managed to crawl across my brothers without anyone being the wiser. I waited for morning to come, and for the chance to hide the money properly inside the hole in the stone wall where I kept my rubber bullet.

"You've got nits."

I opened one eye to see my youngest brother bent over my head, searching through my hair. Daylight stumbled through the window like a drunken uncle looking for a sofa. Even when it was raining, the morning light was always in my face, as none of the windows had curtains. Neither bed had a plentiful supply of blankets either, as we supplemented bedclothes with heavy winter coats. I was too tired to throw Kevin off me or to open my other eye. I should have at least covered his mouth with my hand, as we always did when he started crying and was in danger of attracting the auld fella's attention.

"Mommy, Mommy, he's got nits. If I sleep next to him, I'll have them too."

"Shut up, you little half-wit," I muttered under my breath, as I pulled the collar of a coat over my head.

"I'll check his head after breakfast, and if he has them, I'll douse him with DDT."

Jesus, the old lady had heard him. I thought she was already up. I hadn't been doused in DDT since Elementary school. At that time, me and Jimmy had to get "the treatment" at least once a fortnight. This involved my mother digging out the lice with a fine-toothed comb and snapping the baby nits with her thumbnails. Once you heard the snap, you knew the nit was destroyed.

Just to make sure, though, she would have us strip to our underwear and then shake half a can of DDT powder on our heads, shoulders, chest, back, and arms. Since we didn't have back or chest hair, it was only needed on our scalps, but when she got to shaking that white shite, it covered anything within a quarter mile.

I was the last one to leave the bedroom. I don't know how much sleep I had gotten, but it wasn't near enough. I was hungry, but the idea of getting covered head-to-toe in lice powder killed my appetite. My short-term memory recalled nothing of the night before. I pulled on a pair of jeans and threw a jumper over the shirt I had slept in. When I tried to put on my shoes, I discovered that one of my feet had grown during the night and now my shoe was too small. Then I realized that this would have been ridiculous. As they would say in Inishowen, "as sure as there is shite in a goose," something in my shoe was stopping my toes from going forward.

I plunged my hand into the darkness of my shoe and almost immediately felt a lump of paper at the top. Now I remembered. What kind of an eejit was I, forgetting that I had stuffed what I pulled out of Daniel's coat pocket into my shoe? I looked toward the bedroom door before I withdrew the stolen paper complete-ly, looked into my hand, and saw green American money with a "20" printed in the corner. It was *twenty American dollars.* Behind it was another one that said "10." I was holding *thirty American dollars.* I felt like a bank robber. There was some other paper there too, but it didn't look like money; it looked like a ticket. The top featured a picture of a horse running and said "Irish Sweepstakes" in gold lettering. I had no idea what it was, but I balled it all up together and stuffed it way down into the corner of my pocket.

I slowly opened the door of the bedroom and then made a quick dive for the kitchen door, intent on hiding my treasure in the stone wall.

"Where do you think *you're* going?" asked my mother.

"I thought I was going out for a pish."

"Well then, make sure you empty the bucket."

I had been emptying piss pots for that crowd for years at that stage. You would have thought that now, when I was about to go into secondary school, my piss pot emptying days would be over. What was wrong with Jimmy taking *his* turn? I was handed the piss pot emptying duties when I was exactly his age. Seething, I turned around and went back into the bedroom to retrieve the communal piss pot. At least it would provide me a clear and unobstructed path all the way down to the byre. The one thing that could be said for being the piss pot carrier was that nobody wanted to get in your way. When you were hunched over a five-gallon pot of overnight pish, struggling to keep control as your thumbs did their best to keep above the yellow water line, there was no fear anyone would stop you on your quest to ask, "So, who do you fancy in the Ulster football final, Donegal or Tyrone?"

As soon as I dumped the contents of the bucket, I headed straight for my stone wall. For now, I'd just stick the notes and the sweepstakes thingy in the cracks, but later I would find a piece of wax-paper bread wrapping and make the money waterproof.

I felt much better after I had made both deposits. I sauntered into the kitchen, grabbed a basin, and threw in a couple of inches of boiling water from the whistling kettle. Then I collected a bar of soap and brought it all outside to add rainwater so that I could wash my hands.

When I returned back inside to look for a towel, I saw that Daniel had made an attempt to rise. He sat on the edge of the couch in his underwear, scratching his head and looking for a match with which to light the cigarette that hung out of his mouth. He looked a bit like I felt. I don't think that mornings were ever his favorite time of the day—definitely not in our house, anyway. No matter what time of night the poor hoor came home, he could be guaranteed of one thing: there'd be no lay-in. When you slept in the kitchen, your sleep was pretty much over when the kitchen came to life. As I banged the door shut, my father was making a scone and my mother was feeding the wains, adding to the racket.

I think Daniel might have had an easier time of it if he had stayed with his father (our grandfather), but he was seeing a girl in our neighborhood when he came over to visit from America, and it would have been very far to drive to Malin Head after he had been drinking all night.

"What would you like for your breakfast, Daniel?" my mother asked him.

Being asked what they wanted to eat was a dead giveaway that our guest was a visitor from far away. The rest of us had to eat whatever was put in front of us. We'd probably have had to get out a dictionary to see what the word "choice" meant.

"Oh, just a cup of tea for the moment, Sarah."

I watched as he reached for his coat and searched around for something. What if he discovered the missing money right now? My heart started doing jumping jacks in my chest. I was relieved to see that he was only getting a cigarette lighter.

After he lit his fag and took a couple of puffs, he started to search his pockets again. Jesus, Mary, and Joseph, what was he looking for now? I was full sure it was the money. I felt my knees getting a little weak. I didn't know if I could lie well enough to pull it off. What I saw next made me feel better, but sick at the same time. He pulled out a big lump of dulsce and started to chew on it.

I don't know if the salty seaweed snack existed in other parts of Ireland, but it was a big thing in North Donegal. I could see chewing it in the bog as you worked the turf, or in a hay field, but to watch a man eat it in the morning for breakfast and then wash it down with tea was enough to make the strongest of stomachs want to puke. Like father, like son.

"Come over here, you, and get some scone and tea so I can check your hair for lice," my mother ordered me.

Here I was thinking she had forgotten. I turned my back on the seaweed-eater and ate a chunk of scone, washing it down with steaming-hot tea. Luckily, I never found out what DDT would do to you if you swallowed a rake of it, but it couldn't be good, as it had the word "poison" on the label. Not swallowing any was just about impossible, though. You'd hold your breath as Sarah the Lice Killer started to shake the powder all over your head, but just as she was mid-frenzy with the shaking was when your lungs would be bursting for air. You'd have no other option but to spit out whatever ounce of air was left and quickly inhale a white cloud of DDT. One thing is for certain: there were no lice living inside of my lungs. I think that was one of the reasons why we never had any money—either us or the cattle were continually being covered in DDT. That stuff couldn't have been cheap, and Sarah used it like it was going out of style.

She sat me down at the head of the table, right in the middle of the breakfast and the baking. There was a window at the head of the table, and she wanted to use its light to see the bugs. She peered through her glasses and into my hair.

"Where did you see nits?" she asked Kevin. He came over, hoisting himself up on a stool, and joined her in rummaging around my scalp.

"There!" he shouted. "See that white nit."

"That's not a nit, you wee eejit. That's a piece of dandruff. I'm not going to waste DDT over dandruff."

What a close escape. I looked at my small brother, who seemed disappointed that he had not found creepy crawlies in my head. He was turning out to be a bigger bollix than Jimmy. For some reason or other, it was to be my lot in life to be surrounded by little pricks who were intent on making my life as miserable as possible.

I looked over at Daniel, who was peacefully slurping his hot tea and sucking on his fag. No wonder he hadn't a care in the world; he didn't have one shagging brother.

He had four sisters, and they probably all thought the sun shone out of his arse. Just once, I would love it if somebody thought the sun shone out of my arse as well. "J.P. is a bright boy, all right," my mother could say. "He is so bright that I swear the sun shines right out of his arse."

I had to shake the thought from my head, as it just didn't sound right when it was put that way. After escaping a DDT dousing and safeguarding my night's thieving, I felt fairly relaxed, so I poured myself another mug of tea and sat over by Daniel.

"Don't youns be getting too comfortable," the auld fella started shouting at nobody in particular. "I have a last verse to write for the Eurovision song contest, and I'm going to need peace and quiet to concentrate."

If he was going to become a great songwriter, I wondered, then why the hell didn't he get a big house overlooking the ocean, with a loft maybe, or a garage that he could turn into a studio? It would have made life a damn site more bearable than us all trying to cram our arses in a two-room cottage with a grass roof, and no water or electricity.

Not to mention the fact that he just wasn't just trying to write something that you could hum or whistle as you worked in the bog. Damn dapped, he was entering a pop song contest where his song would be picked above all of the other entries in the country. His song, as he saw it, would represent Ireland. In fact, he was full sure it would be chosen as the best song in all of Europe.

At the risk of sounding pessimistic, I could see a couple of problems with that train of thought. One of the most obvious, or so it seemed to me, was that he didn't have a bull's notion what a pop song should sound like. He had grown up listening to Irish folk and rebel songs from his mother. The only music he seemed to have in him was the ability to play a few bars on the accordion.

Another challenge was that he didn't have a clue what was popular or who the modern-day singers were, since he refused to get a telly. The "song" that he was writing was a bunch of words sung to the tune of "Danny Boy."

"So John," Daniel spoke, "tell me about your song. What kind is it, what is it about?"

"Well, it's pretty much a love song type of thing."

A love song? That really took the biscuit. I was dying to ask him what the hell he would know about love that could possibly qualify him to write such a song.

"It's very catchy," added my mother.

Jesus Christ. It was like living in a mental hospital, only the staff were the lunatics. I couldn't take any more. I finished the last of my tea, dropped the mug into the basin, and headed out the door. My brother followed me out a few minutes later.

"What did we get last night?"

"Jesus, would you ever keep it down? If those crowd in there find out what we did, they'll have our guts for garters. Let's walk down by the byre and I'll tell you." When we got a safe distance from the house, I turned to face him.

"I don't know exactly how much we got, because it was all Yankee dollars."

"How many Yankee dollars?" he asked.

"Thirty."

"That's a lot!"

"Well, we'll have to wait and see. There was a bunch of other important-looking papers that said 'sweepstakes' on them, whatever that means."

"Maybe it means that we can swap those papers for steaks." This didn't sound quite right, but it did seem possible.

"Can you go to the bank and get Irish money for them?"

"I can *not*. Sure, that could get me caught red-handed. We will have to get a middleman or fence to cash them for us."

"What's a middleman?"

"When a cat burglar or international thief breaks into a museum or a very rich person's house and steals their jewels, he doesn't want to get caught by trying to sell the stuff himself, so he gets somebody else to do it. That's a middleman."

"Who is our middleman then? Uncle Daniel?"

"How the hell could it be Uncle Daniel, you silly bollix? I might as well just ask him to cash in the dollars that we stole out of his pocket. I think I know who we will use—Frank the postman."

"What about the fence? Will he be waiting by the fence to take it?"

"Do you know what? You are as thick as two short planks. Do I have to spell everything out for you?"

"Well, I don't know who you have waiting by the fence. If you just tell me, then I'll know."

"You feckin' eejit, there is nobody waiting by the fence. The fence is the person who gets rid of stolen things. Here is an example: somebody must have stolen your brain and given it to a fence."

"Who'd want my brain?"

"Excellent point. I couldn't have put it better myself."

CHAPTER 20

IN MICK JAGGER'S SHOES

As I mentioned earlier, the only time we had ever gotten new shoes was when the government ran a program to provide shoes to poor children going back to school. It was a strange feeling, then, going into the men's clothing shop in Carndonagh to try on shoes. Up until that time, everything we ever wore seemed to come out of a brown box from America. In case you haven't experienced getting your wardrobe outfitted from a brown box, it teaches you to set your expectations very low. According to my mother, nothing that came out of one of those boxes was ever too big.

"What do you mean, it doesn't fit?" barked my mother.

It was no use telling her that the sleeves of a jumper hung down to your knees. In her mind, that was a positive thing; it meant that you would get even longer wear out of it.

"Sure all you have to do is to turn it up a few times and you can get a few winters out of it."

It was the same story with shoes—not that I ever once saw anything remotely resembling a normal pair of shoes come out of those Yankee boxes. The most you could expect would be a white pair of runners that she called sneakers. "Sneakers" were the perfect name for them: nobody in the whole of Ireland had anything like them, and when you wore them, you'd want to sneak around so as not to arouse anyone's attention. The fact that they might be three or four sizes too big was never a problem for my mother.

"What do you mean, they're too big?" was her usual question when it came to shoes.

Once she had uttered it, you were doomed to wear a four-sizes-too-big shoe for the next few years, or at least until you kicked the shite out of it enough and it fell apart.

"Sure, all you have to do is wear a large pair of socks."

"It's still slipping up and down," whined Jimmy.

"Then stick another sock up in the toe and it will fit just fine."

I tried to hide my laughter as my brother moped off in his massive white sneakers, but what I saw and heard next sent the heart crossways in my chest. My mother pulled out a hateful-looking pair of white shoes with big rounded tops. She nodded as she held them out toward me.

"These look like they'll be a good fit for you."

"What...*a-a-are*...they?" I stammered.

"What do you mean, what *are* they? They're shoes, of course. Why do you always have to be acting the eejit?"

"I can't wear them," I proclaimed, without even stopping for a second to consider that I would soon be wearing them on my head if she got close enough to clobber me with them.

I didn't know what they were, but they bore no resemblance whatsoever to any footwear I had ever seen before. At least the sneakers had some kind of sporting look to them. These horrible white things looked like the big shoes the astronauts wore when they landed on the moon—except that they didn't even look like a man should be wearing them.

"Well?" she said, holding out the shoes for me to take them. I just looked at them. At that moment, my father very unexpectedly came to my rescue.

"I think they're probably nurse's shoes," he told her. "We can get him new shoes in Carn next week when the shoe coupons come out with the dole."

"Fine," she replied, dropping the shoes on the floor and stepping into them. "Some of us aren't so spoiled. These are *grand* shoes."

Strangely enough, they didn't look as hateful on her. That's when I realized that they were women's shoes. Jesus, Mary and Joseph—the crazy bitch had intended to send me out to school wearing women's nursing shoes. My father hadn't really ever shown me any kindness before that, but if it hadn't been for him, I'd probably still be getting into fights over those shoes.

Not only was it a thrill to be getting proper new shoes in a shop, but the thought of what would have happened if I had been forced to wear the nurse's shoes sent a shiver down my spine even as I sat in the shoe section of the men's shop.

"What size are you, lad?" asked a man who worked in the shop.

"I don't know," I told him.

"What was the size of the last shoes you got, then?" he asked.

"I don't know. I never got new shoes. My aunt always sent them over from America."

"Ah, that's the problem then," he nodded. "Yankee shoes are a different size. You look like you'd be around a nine or nine-and-a-half. You have fine big healthy feet, God bless you." With that, he walked over to the wall of shoes and took down a box.

"Here you go. Try these on for size."

I opened the box and pulled out one of the black brogues. It looked like the kind of shoe that a priest would wear, or the local Guard. It was hard and shiny, and it smelled brand new. I could see my reflection in the toe cap. I put on the right shoe first and laced it up tight before putting on the left one. *These would be great boots to have in a fight,* I thought.

"How do they fit?" asked the clerk.

"Grand!" I told him.

"I see you are a man of few words," he observed. "Will you take these?"

I looked around to locate my parents. I had never bought shoes before, so I had no clue how it all worked. They were on the other side of the store looking at clothes that might fit Jimmy. The little bastard had better not be getting new clothes. I wasn't getting new clothes when I was his age.

"Are these the only ones you have?" I asked the clerk.

"No, we have a couple of other styles. Most parents prefer the boots, though, as lads are rough on shoes and these will take a fair beating. Take a look and see if there is anything you fancy."

I followed him over to the shoe wall area and immediately set my sights on a pair of shoes that looked like something the lead singer of an English rock band would wear. They weren't quite black or brown; they were black *and* brown at the same time, with a square toe. Best of all were the laces, striped in brown and orange. These shoes were fit for a star.

"Would these fit me?" I asked him, fingers crossed.

"You've got good taste! We just got these in from Dublin. Mick Jagger wears the exact same shoe."

He handed me the box, and when I looked at those shoes, I could barely make myself take them out. I handled the first shoe with both hands. This was a dream come true. I slipped in my foot. Well, it was more of a shove than a slip.

"They're a bit tight," I told him.

He reached down, felt the sides of the shoe, and then told me to raise my big toe. After bouncing my big toe off the inside of the shoe a few times, he came to the conclusion that they were a "wee bit tight."

"Unfortunately, we don't have any bigger sizes," he advised me, "but we could order them from Dublin, if you want to wait a month or so." Wait a month? I wanted the hoors there and then.

"Do you think they'll stretch at all?"

"Och aye," he shot back, "all new leather stretches. Just make sure not to wear heavy socks."

Heavy socks, my bollix. I wanted these shoes so bad that I'd put polish on my feet and wear them without any socks at all if that would make them fit.

"I'll take them so," I told him, heading over to where the parents were. My father asked if I had found shoes.

"I did," I said.

"How much are they?"

How much? Jesus, I never even thought of asking how much. You don't think of asking how much rock star shoes cost. There's no fucking way Mick Jagger would ask a clerk, "How much do the shoes go for?"

"I don't think they are that dear," I told him, although I hadn't a bull's notion how much they cost.

He walked over to the clerk, dragging his leg a bit behind him.

"Our son picked out a pair of shoes for back-to-school?"

"Aye, he did," replied the clerk. "The lad has good taste."

"Well, we had better find out if we can afford them," said my father in a tone that made my heart sink.

He reached into his coat pocket, pulled out a paper, and handed it to the man. The man examined the paper and nodded as if he knew what it was. He told us that he had to speak with the manager and that he would be right back. He returned a few minutes later.

"This will take care of most of it," he told us, "but to get the shoes he wants, you'd have to add two quid of your own to it."

Being a good Irish Catholic lad, I only prayed when I was desperate. I immediately started mumbling something to God about not letting the clerk mention the black boots, which were bound to be cheaper than rock star shoes. I don't know if God answered my prayers or the clerk was looking to make a bigger sale, but either way, no mention was made of the boots.

"Two pounds more we would have to pay," my father thought out loud. Looking at me, he added, "That's a lot of money when we have to be buying books as well."

I really couldn't make a case against what he was saying. I knew we never had any money, and the likelihood of my mother agreeing to spend more when she expected the government to pay in full was out of the question. All I could do was to look back at him with an expression that said, "If I don't get these shoes, I will be condemned to wearing women's nursing shoes and a life of hell."

He shocked the living shite out of me when he said: "All right, we'll take them."

CHAPTER 21

DONEGAL DONKEY RIDES

I don't know which happened first: Jimmy thumping me on the arm, or him squawking about getting up to buy a telly. What annoyed me most was the fact that he had woken me out of a lovely dream I had been having. It involved eating a big, fat, juicy steak with chips smothered in brown vinegar and mushy peas. I had a lovely glass of cold milk to my mouth and was mid-gulp when I was forced to abandon my dream.

"Are we buying a telly today?" he asked me.

"Did you just punch me in the arm, you little fucker?"

"I had to," he admitted. "Sure, I asked you three times and you never answered."

"Are you mental, or what? The next time you try that, you had better run as fast as your little fat legs will carry you and shout your question down from the Moville road, for I will beat the living shite out of you if you stay within arm's reach of me."

"Right so, but are we buying the telly today?"

"Do you know what, you must have been a pirate's parrot in a previous life. You probably annoyed him as much as you annoy me, and he ran you through with his hook."

"You said we would buy a telly at the weekend."

"Yes, I know. I said *one* weekend. We could hardly buy it during the week when we are at school. It's bad enough that I have to haul around a stone weight of meat like some kind of travelling butcher without adding a telly onto my shopping list."

Every Friday, the auld fella would drive into Carndonagh and buy the week's supply of meat from Pat the Butcher. Now when I say "meat," I am using the term loosely. The weekly supply consisted of a beef heart, a beef tongue, three to four pounds of mincemeat, a few pounds of hangars, and quite often a few pounds of liver. Not exactly what you would call prime cuts. Beef hearts and tongues are quite huge, and they must have weighed several pounds each. All in all, the weekly bag of meat normally weighed in at around fifteen pounds. Mind you, it was sometimes more, since they would regularly ask for "meaty" bones for our new dog Rory. Rory was given the bones, all right, but not until after every red patch of meat had been scraped clean off them.

After my first year at Carndonagh Secondary School, my parents decided that I could be trusted to collect the family meat supply from the butcher at lunchtime every Friday. From the start of second year until I sat the Leaving Cert in 1977, I became the official meat courier. At first glance this might not seem to have been too hateful a job, but nothing could be further from the truth. To begin with, we all looked forward to the lunch time bell so that we could go up the brae into Carn and walk around.

Of course, we all believed ourselves to be hard men, and when we had four or five in a pack we felt like Hell's Angels (only without the motorbikes). Some of the pack would have been able to afford a bag of chips and maybe even a fish supper, but if I had even a couple of pennies in my pocket at any one time, I regarded myself as being fairly well off. One penny was to be used to buy a single cigarette, which would be smoked at the back of the bus on the way home.

As (bad) luck would have it, Pat the Butcher's shop was at the opposite end of the school at the dead end of the town, where there was never any action. Once in a blue moon, Pat would have the meat order ready to go and I would have hardly any delay at all. Those times were few and far between, however, and ninety percent of the time I would have to wait behind other customers in order to get our weekly meat supply. Pat always had to go out back for the heart and tongue—I suppose they weren't exactly showroom merchandise. By the time I would join up again with my posse, it was time to head back down the hill and buy a fag for later.

The packaging of the meat left a lot to be desired. Pat would put the meat order into a large white plastic bag. It wasn't totally see-through, but with the meat all squeezed in together you could easily make out big sections of a bloody heart and dark brown squishy liver. By the time I spent two hours hauling it from class to class and then rode the bus with it for another hour, the meat would have bonded together, each piece jig-sawing itself into the others until the whole thing resembled a grotesque bloody football. The blood would be squeezed out of the meat and plastered up and down the insides of the bag, making it look as if I were hauling around a severed head.

By the time I started third year, the meat-carrying job became a way of life, and I was hardly bothered by carrying the bag around on a Friday afternoon. We got used to eating it in the various forms the auld fella would cook up. We no longer referred to it as beef heart, but instead called it "roast beef." He would always preserve the tongue (most people don't know how big a beef tongue is—it kind of looks like a donkey's cock in full flight), which we called "corned beef." I got so used to hauling around the bag that, one Friday afternoon, I decided to sit down next to a cute second-year lass that I had my eye on while in possession of the big bag of bloody meat.

"Is anyone sitting here?" I asked, trying to sound suave and James Bond-like.

"No, it's free," she replied, half looking up.

I plopped myself down on the outside of the seat and dropped the army surplus satchel from Derry on my lap. There was no hiding the meat bag. It happened to be one of those unfortunate Fridays when Rory had also put in his order for some meaty bones. Not only did I have the usual bloody head-like ball pushed against the inside of the bag, silently screaming to be let out, but on top of that there was a helter-skelter effect of twisted bones striving to find freedom.

"So, what have you on for the weekend?" I asked, turning to my right once I was settled. My neighbor stared with bulging eyes and gaping mouth at the bloody, boney mess on my lap. She seemed mesmerized by the carnage. It wasn't as if she only got a peep at it, either. Since my satchel was quite shallow, the white (and bloodied red) bag was only a quarter concealed. It was the opposite of an iceberg, where most of the ice is under the surface and out of view. I realized later that she had likely been taken aback not only by the bloody scene, but by the fact that the bag was firmly centered on my crotch, out of which stretched this bone-hard foot-long protrusion. Whatever thoughts were racing through her mind, she grabbed her bag and squeezed past me and my protrusion to find a seat at the very front of the bus.

"I had a dream," I told Jimmy.

"That we would get the telly today?"

"No, you eejit, a dream that today was Saturday and I could lay in bed for a while after having worked my balls off every morning for the past week. Anyway, like I already told you, we don't have enough cash, so what I thought we could do would be to take the donkey down to Culdaff on Saturdays and Sundays and give rides to the wains until we had enough saved up for the telly." I had seen the Big Yank do it, and it brought in a good few pounds for him, so why not?

"Are we starting today?"

"Maybe, but I have to see if we can rig up the pony's bridle. Go ask your father if we can use it for Blackie." He scampered off to ask, but I was not overly hopeful that the auld fella would be terribly obliging. I would soon come to realize that he didn't want to be bothered about anything when he was writing his songs, though, and that suited me down to the ground. I didn't feel like explaining too much just yet, so I skipped breakfast and headed down to the byre to milk the cow. After I was done, I brought the bucket of milk up to the kitchen and put a dash of water on the range so that I could wash myself.

"So, you're thinking of giving rides in Culdaff with Blackie?"

"Aye."

"You'll need to be careful. He's a young donkey with a lot of life in him. Keep a good tight hold of his bridle at all times. Are you looking to go down today?"

"Aye." It didn't take much for him and I to start arguing, so I figured the best policy was to say as little as possible.

"After we have had the tea, I'll get the pony's bridle and fix it so it will work on Blackie. How were you thinking of taking him up and down to Culdaff?"

"We'll walk him down and then walk him back home when we are done."

"Jesus, that's a brave walk. It must be ten miles to Culdaff, and the same back."

"It probably is," I agreed. "He shouldn't have much fight left in him by the time we get back."

"And neither will the two of you," he said with a grin. It surprised me that he actually found something I said to be funny. I swear to Jesus, I could count on one hand the number of times I had said something that he had found to be amusing.

At noon, Jimmy and I set off walking Blackie down the Culdaff road. After two miles, I began to see that we had our work cut out for us. Jimmy was already complaining about walking, so I let him ride Blackie. It was fine on the flat road and going downhill, but when I had to climb a hill, especially after seven or eight miles, I started to feel it. That's when I got the bright idea to giddy-up Blackie so that he could help me up the hill a bit as I held on to his bridle. My brother rode nearly the whole way, so he had nothing to complain about.

I forgot that getting there was not even half the battle. By the time we hit Culdaff a couple of hours later, not only did we have to trot the bloody donkey up and down the street to drum up business, but we (which meant me) had to spend the next four hours giving children rides up and down the street. Blackie and I both ran our arses off that day. The wains in Culdaff must never have seen anyone give donkey rides before. Once the word got out that you could have a go on Blackie for a shilling, they poured out of doorways and fields to line up for a ride. Some of the wee bastards went on four and five times. Most of them wanted him to gallop, or at least trot; being the handler, I also had to gallop and trot.

I have no idea whose pockets they were robbing to get the money, but they would go away broke and come back with more coins. If I had had four or five shillings, I wouldn't be spending it on a bloody donkey ride, that's for sure. By the time we were getting ready to leave, half of the children in the town had long faces and some of the smaller ones were actually crying. This gave me the idea to advertise that we'd be back the following day.

"Don't be sad now, boys and girls," I told them. "Blackie just told me that he had so much fun here today that he wants to come back tomorrow." They started to cheer and dance in the street. You would have thought I had said I was buying everyone an ice cream.

"Go home now and gather up your money and we'll see you here tomorrow after mass."

"I didn't know we were coming back tomorrow." Jimmy looked confused.

"Neither did I, but it seems that Blackie knew."

At least Blackie was able to go home fairly much the same as he had come, which is more than I can say for myself. It turned out to be a very successful day. The problem with the success was that all of the coins we collected during the four hours we gave rides had to be carried back for ten miles—in my pockets. I must have weighed nearly twice as much on the way back as I had weighed going down. I wondered if the wains would be able to find enough money to make it worth our while to come back the following day. The other good thing about the day was the fact that we did not maim or kill any child. It was not as if we had insurance to cover any accident claim, after all.

Poor Blackie deserved some kind of treat. I had no idea what a donkey would consider a treat, but for Rory, it would have been enough dinner scraps left over so that he actually had something to eat.

I turned him into the field with the mare and pony, and slowly dragged my arse into the house in the hopes that there would be some scraps of food left over. If they hadn't fed Rory his scraps yet, he was going to be out of luck. Jimmy was already inside telling them about the big pile of money we made. I could feel it in my water that the auld fella was going to impose some kind of tax on our earnings.

"Youns had a good day then, I hear," stated the auld fella.

"I'd say we did all right," I replied, "but it was dear bought. We walked and ran about twenty-five miles—well, *some of us* walked and ran," I corrected myself, looking over at Jimmy. I added, "We haven't eaten a thing in more than eight hours. I am so hungry that I could eat a child's arse through a stepladder."

"I'll heat up some roast beef," said my mother, "and in the meantime, you can count out your money." I stuck my crotch above the edge of the kitchen table and emptied out both pockets so that nothing would fall onto the floor. It was mostly silver, with a smattering of copper coins in the mix. As the coins clattered and rolled out on to the table, I could feel bodies behind me closing in tighter to get a better look. It felt as if I had entered a dimly-lit tavern in some pirate's cove. I could sense the cutthroats breathing down my back as the house wench fetched me a tankard of grog. By the time the beef heart ("roast beef") arrived, I was halfway through counting and had already gathered nearly two pounds and fifty pence.

I estimated that the final tally would be around five pounds. Once the food started wafting up to my nostrils, however, all thoughts of money-counting went out the window. I ate the meat my mother had jammed in between two slices of scone like a ravenous dog. I didn't even look to see if Jimmy had been fed. The lazy little bastard sat around on his arse all day, and anyway, I suspected that he skimmed a shilling off one of the riders, as I could swear I had seen dried ice cream on his upper lip. After I had inhaled the food, I got back to the job at hand.

"So, what did youns wind up with?" asked the heart-serving wench as I gathered up the last pile of single shillings.

"Five pounds and two shillings." It was a small fortune. Had I been able to get a day job, I could have expected a couple of pounds.

"I think we found a new job for these boys, Daddy, what do you think?" she asked the auld fella. I didn't wait for him to answer.

"No, you couldn't do this all the time," I interjected. "For a start, the wains would only be around at the weekend, and then only when the weather would be fair. Sure you couldn't have them sitting on top of a donkey and it lashing down rain."

"He's right," said the man of the house. Jesus, Mary, and Joseph—he agreed with me without an argument. This could only mean one thing—the end of the world was surely near.

"Then there is the walk," I continued, since I was on a roll. "Fifty miles every weekend is savage. I daresay athletes preparing for the Olympics wouldn't do it. If we were to do this on a fairly regular basis, we would need help transporting Blackie and picking him up at the end of the day." For a while there, I completely forgot that this was a once-off effort to bring in enough money to buy a telly.

In my mind, I pictured having a fleet of riding donkeys all over Inishowen. Why just limit myself to North Donegal? This thing was big enough for us to go national. We would confine it to the Republic, though, and keep out of the North. It wouldn't be good publicity if your donkey wandered into the wrong area of Derry or Belfast and got kneecapped.

"I could tie Blackie onto the back of the car," offered the auld fella. I looked at him, waiting for him to say something else, but nothing else came out. For the life of me, I could not figure out what he had in mind.

The deafening silence must have made him realize that he had lost us. "We could tie him onto the bumper and drive down to Culdaff with him following us. That is what I did for your grandfather a couple of years ago when he needed to bring the cow to the bull—I tied her on to the bumper of the Morris Minor in Malin Head."

"How far away was the bull?" I asked him.

"Not very far, just a bit over the road."

"Sure, ten miles is a long way. Would the car even be able to drive as slow as a donkey walking? They are fierce slow, especially when walking uphill. Then if you decided to try and speed up, he'd be all right for a bit of a trot, but once he stopped you'd be dragging him and he could get injured. If the cops came along, we'd all be arrested."

After I said it, I realized it sounded like I was scolding him, but I could see my dream of a national donkey-riding empire slipping through my fingers before it even got off the ground. There was bound to be a license needed, and I'm sure the Gardaí would have to sign off that you were of good behavior and had never been arrested or charged with any crime. Even if I managed to slip through the cracks as a juvenile, I would always be living in fear that some investigative journalist would break the story one day that the President of RIDE (Riders of Irish Donkeys Everywhere) had been involved in an incident whereby a donkey was being pulled by a car, resulting in my father being arrested for cruelty to animals.

"All right then, smart ass. Since you're the one with all of the answers, what do you suggest?"

"Well, it would be safer and much faster to put a hitch on the back of the car." This was easier said than done, as the car was a total rust bucket—paint and dirt were the only things holding it together—but I continued. "We could borrow a horse trailer from the Smyths of Garraban for an hour. Actually, you wouldn't even need a horse trailer. I'd say he'd fit well enough into a calf trailer."

So far, neither he nor she had made any mention of being compensated for Blackie's effort. In case he did, though, I had already worked out a rough plan in my head. If we were to keep walking him down to Culdaff, I could afford to rent the donkey for one pound a day. It didn't seem like much, but if we averaged out a fiver each weekend day, twenty percent of our profit would go toward renting the donkey. He couldn't ask much more, since they had only paid thirteen pounds for the second-hand Blackie a couple of years ago. If that was not agreeable, I was willing to buy the donkey for a tenner. I figured that if it was a third-hand donkey, he'd have to knock at least three quid off the asking price. If that worked, I could have him bought outright over the course of just one weekend.

"Petrol is dear, you know, and I'd have to give something to the man who lent us the trailer," the auld fella informed me. "I'd need two pounds at the very least." What he didn't know was that I had paid close attention over the years and knew his negotiating skills by heart. I knew that if he said he would need two pounds, I could eventually get him down to one. He was lucky I was tired and was not in the mood to stand around half the night in order to save a few shillings.

"Today we were lucky enough," I advised him, "but I really had to keep going without stopping to make five pounds. I have to figure that there will be quieter days when we'd only make four. In that case, two pounds would be half of our whole day's take. The work is too hard for that. The best I could do would be one-fifty. That is fair for the both of us."

To my amazement, he nodded in agreement. "I won't have time to get a hitch on for tomorrow," he told me, "but we should have it ready for next weekend."

I went down to the room and got ready for a well-deserved rest.

"Are we giving rides again tomorrow?" asked Jimmy.

"Yes, we are. And before you ask, we need tomorrow's money before we can look for a telly."

As I crawled over the other two bodies and made my way to the inside wall, I realized that my legs felt wobbly and the soles of my feet were burning. I couldn't even begin to think about the next day. I felt like I could sleep for a week. The last thing I remember is tucking the blanket down the side of the bed between me and the cold stone wall. I believe that I was asleep before my head hit the pillow.

CHAPTER 22

PISSING OFF THE PRIEST

I woke up feeling confused. I remembered promising the pest that we would bring Blackie down to Culdaff again so that we could make more money, but it was a Sunday. How was that going to work?

For my part, I was a true believer—in capitalism. Don't get me wrong, I believed in Jesus and all, but I didn't see any conflict of interest between a man having a bit of religion and also looking to make a pound. The trouble with Ireland, and especially with Donegal in the seventies, was that the Catholic Church still ruled with an iron fist. According to the local clerics, there were six days in each week for working and one for resting, because God Himself rested on the seventh.

That was all well and good, but I didn't remember reading anywhere in the Bible (not that I ever read it, but I heard from people who did) that God had to attend Carndonagh Tech five of those days every week. If he had, he would surely have been hard-pressed to get everything that needed doing done on a Saturday. My problem, when it came to religion anyway, was that I was too practical.

On one hand, it was some kind of unforgiveable sin to work on a Sunday. But on the other hand, there was a whole shiteload of "what ifs."

What if your house (or even bus) burned down on a Sunday, should you wait until the following day to call the fire brigade?

What if you had to bury your granny on a Sunday, would you not do the decent thing and have tea and sandwiches (and maybe a glass of whiskey, Father) for the mourners at the local hotel? You could hardly tell them to go home and come back on Monday for the grub. People had to work. That was my predicament.

Another area where I would have a major problem was with the classification and use of poitín as a sin only forgivable by the Bishop himself. That point, however, struck close to home, as our grandfather was an illicit distiller himself, and he had no time for the meddlings of the law or the Church in his trade.

The cause of my confusion may not yet be clear, but I will try to make it as understandable as possible, keeping in mind that I led a life that was often anything but understandable. I suppose, as religion goes, we could be considered "fair-weather Catholics." I believe that from an early age we attended mass on all the big holy days: Christmas, Easter, and…well, definitely Christmas and Easter anyway. When we came to Ireland, we started attending more ordinary Sunday masses.

When we went to mass in Malin Head, we rarely ever even made it inside the door. Whether we hung with the locals outside the back door, or made it in, though, the Big Yank always went for the condensed version. That meant that when people started to go up to communion, he slipped out of the pew and went in the opposite direction—out the back door. It would be nearly another ten years before I would have a clue as to what took place after communion was over.

I can see how this does not sound like a breeding ground for a very stringent Catholic lifestyle, but something happened to the auld fella when he declared himself a writer. He didn't embrace the faith or "find Jesus," so to speak, but he insisted that we go to mass every Sunday morning in Bocan Chapel. I don't remember any of us being that bothered—I was the most likely voice of rebellion, but it was only an hour out of my day on a Sunday morning, so I went with the flow. I figured there was little harm in us making the transformation from fair-weather to all-weather Catholics.

It didn't seem to be a problem—until he whipped out the Sunday newspaper in the middle of mass and started reading to his heart's content. The bastard. Never before, nor since, have I witnessed a grown man sitting in the middle of church, on a Sunday morning, reading a Sunday newspaper like he was passing time along the banks of a canal. I was literally on the edge of my seat. I expected the priest to look down at any moment and single him out.

Every minute that passed was like a minute spent on death row. I gripped the edge of the wooden pew as if I was hanging off the side of Mount Everest and clinging on for dear life. The priest was probably talking, but I didn't hear it. I was staring at the auld fella and then at the priest. This back-and-forth "auld fella/priest" tennis match watching kept up until people started filing past to receive communion.

Not only did I have to worry about the priest, but there were my schoolmates to consider. How the hell would I explain what he did when I didn't understand it myself?

I don't know how we got through that first Sunday paper mass, but we did. I wouldn't give him the satisfaction of saying anything to him, but I was dying to know what had possessed him. The old lady was totally blind to any and all of his faults. To look at her, you would think that all fathers read the Sunday paper during mass. My brothers and sister were too young to notice anything out of the ordinary. My parents were always telling me that I was a terrible example for my younger brothers and sister, but all I could think now was what an unholy bloody example he was for them.

I was most puzzled by the priest's lack of interest. This was still the time when the local parish priest laid down the law more forcefully than the police. I figured that he assumed the Big Yank was mental, and everyone knows you should just ignore a mental person as best you can. Every Sunday from then on, he read the paper instead of listening to the priest.

You would think that reading a newspaper in church was bad enough, but with our auld fella there was no telling what he would think up next. You might very well ask, "What else could he possibly do to embarrass his family more than by reading the Sunday paper?" The answer was this: He decided to take on priestly powers. He brought a roll of Silver Mints sweets into the chapel with him, waited until the priest was giving out communion, and began passing them out.

Now, if you never had or seen Silver Mints, you might not grasp the significance of this. They're round, thick, white mints that melt in your mouth. They actually look like a fatter version of a communion wafer. It was no coincidence that he decided to pass around his mints at the exact time the priest was handing out communion. To further strengthen my theory was the fact that he asked his children to stick out their tongues as he placed a mint on each of them.

When I saw this, I nearly had a heart attack. Was he looking to have a showdown with the priest? Did he think he *was* some kind of priest? I would have given anything to find out what was in his head.

He told us about a game he used to play when he started driving called "chicken." Young lads would drive their cars at each other from opposite directions, and the first to swerve out of the way would be the loser. It struck me that he was now playing chicken with the priest. I did not take any of his mints, though the others all did.

⊷ ⊶

I threw on my trousers, a shirt, and a jumper and headed for the kitchen. There was a lovely smell of bacon being fried. Poor Barney had never smelled so good. The fumes quickly found their way to me, and I forgot all about donkeys, priests, and Sunday newspapers. The auld fella was standing over the black Stanley range with a towel over his shoulder, like a trainer giving boxing tips to a fighter in his corner. This pig was out for the count, though, and was not going to make it to the next round.

"There's fresh tea in the pot," he informed me without turning around.

"Grand."

"You'll be taking Blackie to Culdaff, then?"

"Aye."

"Well, you'll need a good breakfast in you. If you want to get the milking done, I'll have a fry ready for youns so you can get going as soon as you have eaten."

"Fair enough."

So far, there was no mention of having to go to chapel. If we did, it wouldn't be worth our time to go all the way home, collect the donkey, and come all the way down again. And then a terrible thought came to me. What if he intended to do some stupid shit like tie the donkey onto the back of the car and leave him tied outside of the chapel until we got out from mass? He was very capable of it. And besides, the chapel was just two miles from the main street of Culdaff. I had no intention of saying anything in case he thought it was a good idea. I even tried to get the idea out of my mind just in case he might pick up on my thoughts.

I never milked that cow so fast. She must have thought we had signed up for a cow-milking contest. I don't even remember milking her. My mind was trying to work out all of the possibilities of why the auld fella was acting civilized. I preferred him cursing and hobbling around the kitchen. That way you just stayed out of his way and you knew what you were getting: a nut job. It was more difficult trying to figure out what might be going through his head when he was quiet. I decided to shovel some shite as I pondered the mental state of the man of the house. After about fifteen minutes of shite-shoveling, I was no closer to an answer, but I had cleaned out the byre without even realizing it.

I walked up to the house to put on water for a wash. The plan of attack was going to involve speed. We would wolf down some breakfast, go and bridle up the donkey, and head off down the road toward Culdaff. Reading Sunday papers in the chapel did not figure into this plan.

Jimmy wandered up from the bedroom rubbing his eyes. "Get some breakfast into you so we can get on the road to Culdaff," I instructed him. He must have forgotten that we told the wains that we'd be back today.

"Yay! We're giving donkey rides today!"

I don't know where he got his enthusiasm from, but the donkey and I could have used some. Half an hour later we were walking over the lane and up past Frank the Postman's house. I made a mental note to bring Frank the bag full of coins as soon as I counted them so that he could change them into paper pounds. I didn't realize at the time how badly this would put poor Frank out, as there were no banks anywhere near where we lived; I thought of it as just a quick pit stop for him.

One thing was for certain: I could not trust even myself with the coins. I allowed myself to slip out the two shillings from the previous day's take of five pounds and two shillings. I fairly much knew I would blow that between Monday and Tuesday lunchtime.

I was sure that I would not break a note, though. I had worked too damned hard to bring a television into the house for my addiction to stop me now.

"Do you want chips and an ice cream cone when we finish today?" I asked my younger accomplice.

"Yes, please."

"Then you had better work for it. I'm running my arse off up and down the streets of Culdaff all day. The least you can do is to drum up some business, line them up, and make sure they have their money in their hand when I put them up on Blackie."

When we hit Culdaff, I did the Big Yank trick. I ran up and down the main street with Blackie, yelling "Donkey rides!" and "Come over and meet Blackie! Get your picture taken with Blackie!"

"Are we taking pictures today?" asked my brother.

"We are in my arse, but if someone's mother wants to take a picture of their little angel up on our donkey, sure I can stop for five seconds." Nobody took a picture, but I thought it sounded fierce professional all the same.

The riders were a bit thin on the ground for the first hour, but that was to be expected, as many of them would be coming home from mass and having Sunday dinner. I am sure that Blackie was not worried by the lack of riders after walking for the past ten-plus miles. I knew how that felt, and welcomed not having to dive headfirst into a mad rush of wains. One of our first customers was a Northern family, probably down from Derry for the day. They had a son and a daughter who wanted to ride. The parents looked like they were sizing us up and wondering if it was safe.

"Do youns come here often?" asked the father.

"Oh aye, sure we were here yesterday and the wains begged us to come back today. We live up the road a bit."

"What's the damage, then?"

"It's a shilling for each rider."

"Man dear, that's a bit steep. What's the best you can do?"

I didn't want to come down in price in case word got out. I did want the business, though, especially as they were our first victims.

"I'll tell ya what I'll do. Put the wee boy up first and then let the wee girl sit in front of him and I'll let them both ride for a shilling."

"Good man yourself," their father beamed. He didn't seem all that interested in the safety aspect once he was saving some money. I didn't trot them, though; they got a good enough deal. Trotting would be extra.

Young ones came and went all day. My mind went into autopilot, as I was worried about the end-of-year exams. I was looking forward to having the summer off, but not the exams that would come first. I didn't really improve any after the stern talk, but I knew that I had to put much more effort into taking the tests.

The number of children looking for rides started to dwindle, and at around a quarter to five I informed Jimmy that we were calling it a day. We walked over to the chipper near the Culdaff Arms and I ordered two bags of chips. I let him hold on to Blackie, as I figured the donkey didn't have the energy to wander off for the few minutes I would be inside. I would have let him order the chips, but I didn't have faith that he would have given me enough brown vinegar. I needed to drown my chips in vinegar. I loved it so much that after the chips were gone, I'd tilt the wax chip bag on one end and drink the leftovers out of the bag.

After the chips were gone, we got a 99 cone for the road. The chips and ice cream were definitely the best part of the day. The ice cream was cold and creamy, and the chocolate flake stuck up just far enough out of the ice cream to let you know it was there and that the rest of it was buried deep in the cone, waiting to be discovered. I needed some kind of reward, anyway, since I had a ten-mile walk ahead of me. Jimmy was already up on the donkey's back.

"What kind of telly do you think we should buy?"

"The kind that comes on when you push the button and you watch the shows. What do you mean 'what kind?'" The little bastard was obsessed with getting a television.

"I mean, like, will it be silver and big like Tess the Carpenter's?"

"We'll get what we can afford. That's what we'll get."

"How much can we afford, then?"

"The dollars came to around thirteen pounds, plus we got five pounds yesterday."

"Five pounds and two shillings," he corrected me.

"Five pounds and two shillings. That makes eighteen pounds... eighteen pounds and two shillings. I don't think we did as good today, and we fed ourselves into the bargain, so we probably have four pounds or a bit less. That makes a grand total of twenty-two pounds."

"Twenty-two pounds and two shillings." The little bastard sounded like some kind of government auditor. There was no way he was forgetting about the two bloody shillings. "Twenty-two pounds and two shillings," he repeated, in a semi-dream fashion. "That would keep us in ice cream cones all year long."

"You had better eat yours faster, as it is melting on Blackie's neck. Next thing you'll have wasps after us, and it's a long way to have to share with wasps."

"What's the first thing you are going to watch on the new telly?" Jesus, Mary, and Joseph—I could not wait to buy the bastarding telly just to shut him up. If they had been selling televisions on the side of the road, I would have stopped and bought one there and then.

"I'll probably watch that horror show where the two boys are walking along a quiet road and the older brother strangles the younger brother because he talks too much and then throws his body into the ditch."

"That would never happen," he said. "Sure the boy would never kill his own brother."

"I wouldn't be a bit too sure if I were you," I muttered under my breath. For good measure, I added, "Remind me someday to tell you the story of Cain and Abel."

CHAPTER 23

THE SONGWRITER SEAN O

My second year on the farm was still unforgiving backbreaking slavery, as far as I was concerned. The one good thing was that the auld fella had finally got electricity into our cottage, so we could have our telly and didn't have to light the paraffin lamp for the light. We still didn't have running water, but things got a bit more bearable.

Once we did get the telly, I watched a few films about prisoners working on chain gangs. As far as I could tell, they had it better than I did.

Take Paul Newman's film *Cool Hand Luke,* for example. Yes, they worked hard digging ditches and cleaning weeds, but I did that too. At least they got to do it in the sunshine, somewhere down south in America where it was always summer. They'd even bring you cold water to drink when you said something like, "Water, boss?" The only water I got to see on that farm was the water that pissed down on my head eleven and a half months out of twelve—and that would be in a "fairly dry" year.

I was convinced that Paul Newman and the rest of the chain gang had it much better. Never once did I see one of those hoors have to go out and milk a cow or shovel shite once they were done digging ditches. They got to lie around in their bunks smoking fags and talking about girls. No breaking their backs in the bog, cutting and footing turf for *those* boys.

They even had egg-eating contests, if you don't mind. The only time I ever saw an egg was on the odd Sunday when a fry was being made. There was me eating two eggs a month, if I was lucky, while your man Newman wolfed down fifty of them in one go—and lying on his arse while doing it.

As the auld fella got deeper and deeper into writing songs, and as his leg started to drag more and more, the portion of the work he did lessened and my portion grew.

At least I had passed my first-year exams. It wasn't by much— mostly with Ds– but I did pass. I had only one E and one F. The F was in metalwork. It seemed an appropriate grade, since I always referred to the subject as "fucking metalwork."

I even got one C, in English, my favorite subject by far. I was glad to be changing English teachers though. Not that there was anything wrong with Mr. Hannigan as a teacher. The whole thing had been my fault.

One afternoon toward the end of the year, we were lined up along the plastic wall of the pre-fab container that made up Mr. Hannigan's classroom. The bell was about to ring. I found myself at the front of the line right next to Mr. Hannigan's anorak. He always hung his coat on the same hook on the wall. The teacher was sitting at the head of the class to our right, and his coat was brushing up against the back of my left hand. I couldn't help it; my animal instincts kicked in. My left hand seemed to have a mind of its own, and before I knew it my hand had slid into the teacher's coat pocket and begun fishing for coins. The fact that it was the last class before lunch and I was broke again probably had a lot to do with putting that thought into my hand's nervous system.

My fingers went to work quickly but quietly. I could feel several coins begging to be taken. At that stage, what could I do but oblige? I took about half, and covertly slipped my hand out of the coat and into my front left trouser pocket. I don't think I took a breath the whole time. This was in a whole different league than going through Eugene Friel's coat pockets. I didn't even want to consider the punishment for taking a teacher's money, but it was bound to involve some kind of penal institution.

That bloody lunch bell must be broken, I thought to myself. I could never remember us standing around so long before. My fear was that the teacher would also get up and put on his coat, as it was lunchtime for him as well. When it finally rang, it was the sweetest-sounding bell I had ever heard. (Well, the second-sweetest. The time the money came pouring out after I got three gold bells from Doherty's one-arm bandit was definitely the sweetest.) We bolted out the door like wild mustangs.

"That was a very sly move back there." I tried not to turn too quickly. I figured the voice was talking about me, but since I was going to deny it, I didn't want to give the game away. I looked back and saw Mark McLaughlin staring at me.

"Going out the door to lunch?" I asked in as simple a way as I could.

"Don't be acting the bollix—you know what I'm talking about. Thieving from Mr. Hannigan." The bastard must have had eyes like a shagging hawk. Nobody should have been able to see it. Apparently he did, though, and the last thing I needed was anyone else finding out.

"It was an accident," I informed him as we walked down the hall.

For some reason, he seemed to find this excuse hysterical. "Shitting your trousers when you thought you just needed to fart is an accident. Shoving your hand into a man's pocket—a teacher, no less—and stealing his money is pure theft."

"So what are you now, an undercover cop?"

"No, I'm more like your partner."

"I don't have a partner—and why would I need the likes of *you* as a partner?"

"Well, a fifty-fifty partner could watch your back and make sure that you got away with your thieving. I could be your spotter."

"Look, when I called this an accident, I meant that I had never done it before. I don't know what got into me. I don't go around stealing from people."

"I don't believe you. I've seen you in Doherty's. You're mostly broke, and then every week or two you have a fistful of money. Where do you get that from?" No wonder he wanted me to hire him as a spotter. The hoor did not miss a trick.

"I work. We have a farm." I definitely didn't want to tell him about the donkey rides, or next thing you knew I would wind up with a partner who might be slippery enough to get his paws on our national donkey chain.

"We all have farms, but none of us have money. I see you carrying home the big bag of bones every Friday from the butchers. You probably tell him that the bones are for the dog, but your mother really uses them for soup." I was running thin with excuses.

"What do you want?"

"I want you to split the money from Hannigan's pocket fifty-fifty with me." *The greedy bastard. I was surrounded by hoors that sat back and let me do all the work.*

"No way. I did all the work. It would be one thing if you stood behind me blocking the view of the others, but you were just a witness. I'll give you something for having a sharp eye, but I'm not giving you half."

"You know that I would look like a hero if I told the headmaster what you did. You would get expelled, and I would get an award."

"Is that what you want to be, a rat? Surely you are more suited to being a spotter than a rat? Word would get around this school in a *day* that you had ratted me out. Do you know what they do to rats in prison?" I think I may have been watching too many Jimmy Cagney films at this point in my life, but he seemed to be considering my argument. I hoped that my reverse psychology was working.

"I still say that I'm entitled to a share."

"I believe that you are too," I agreed. "Let's count the money going up the hill to Doherty's and I'll split it 75/25."

"So, how much will I get?" Once he asked it, I knew that he had not a clue about math.

"Let's see here. Looks like seventy pence in total, so that would be fifty-five for me and fifteen for you." Obviously, I had come to this figure by rounding up for me and rounding down for him.

"It doesn't sound like much," he complained. "Did you hold back any?" He slapped my front pockets. "I know you had no money when you did what you did, so don't be trying to say that you had money of your own to start with."

"That's all of it. I didn't hold any back."

I really gave a lot of thought to siphoning off a couple of coins while walking up the hill, but I was glad that I didn't. I hadn't realized that there would be a Long Kesh strip search as part of the divvying process.

"Look at the big picture," I encouraged him. "That is fifteen goes on the penny slot machine. The odds of you winning once in fifteen pulls are very good. Besides, it is fifteen times more than you had when you came to school today. It's kind of like you got paid just to come to school, like a teacher does."

"And you'll keep me in mind for a partner when you need a spotter, right?"

"You'll be at the top of my list." *More like the top of my shit list.*

The miserable bastard blackmailed me, and he had the nerve to think I would ever have anything to do with him again? The only reason I agreed to give him some of the money was to connect him to the theft. Now that he had shared in the loot, he could hardly rat me out in the hopes of getting some kind of good student award.

For some strange reason, I didn't feel like playing the machines that day. I put in five pence worth, got nothing, and decided to call it quits. My feet were killing me. The Jagger shoes had been my exact size more than a year ago, and my feet had definitely grown since. I had to curl down my toes, especially the big one, in order to be able to fit in them at all. Normally, parents would want to be told if your feet were hurting you from ill-fitting shoes. Unfortunately, those parents didn't live in our house. I knew exactly what the old lady would say if I told her my shoes were too small: "Why don't you write to Mick Jagger and see if he can send you a bigger pair, seeing how youns both have the same taste in clothes."

I'd rather bend my toes backward and tie them like the Geisha girls did in Japan than admit to her that the shoes were too small. The worst part of every day was getting off the bus on the Moville Road and walking down to the farm. By the time I turned into the yard, I wanted to walk on my hands. This is also where I had to turn on my acting skills. I wouldn't put it past her to be out lurking by the corner of the house to see how I was walking. It was painful as all hell, but I straightened out my toes, pushed back my head, and walked in like an aristocrat.

The auld fella seemed to be in great spirits altogether. He was smiling and joking, appearing nearly normal. Jimmy filled me in first: "Uncle Daniel is coming back home to Ireland for good!"

"Well, that's a good one," I replied.

"Daddy's going to buy him a car and a caravan."

Oh, you poor misguided little bastard, I thought as I looked down on his bubbling, innocent face. *Daddy can hardly afford to put petrol in a car, never mind buy one.*

My mother didn't seem quite as happy. "It'll be good for him to get out of the Bronx. There's nothing but trouble for him there. Ever since the Hospital Sweepstakes tickets went missing, there were people out to get him. He needs to leave before he gets a bullet."

Great. Another relative goes on the run. Then it dawned on me. Could she be talking about the bloody tickets that I took without even realizing what they were? *Jesus, I hope he gets out before they shoot him, as I will have to carry that guilt around with me forever.* I still wanted to hear more about "Daddy buying him a car and a caravan," though. There was a juicy story in there somewhere; I could feel it in my water.

"So where's Daniel going to live, then?" I asked nobody in particular.

"Annie has asked me to get him a car and a caravan," volunteered the songwriter. "Your grandmother will be coming back for good next year when she retires and collects her Social Security. Seems like the plan is for them to live together in the caravan until they build a house in Malin Head."

It was a long day and my feet were killing me, not to mention that I had to feed and milk the cows yet. For some reason I was just not understanding the auld fella's good mood. He liked his father-in-law, but didn't have much time for anybody else in the family. Something was brewing; I just had to keep my ears open during the time it took to go through the fermentation process. I should have the full scoop by the time distillation began. In the meantime, I had to go play "Young MacDonald."

After I finished all my chores for the night, I went back inside and filled a basin with nice hot water to wash away the smell of the cow. I remember we used to go to school with boys who lived on a farm, and they always smelled like cows. They probably had to do the same work as I did now, but just didn't bother washing properly. The other thing you had to be very careful of was to always wear a cap. Your head tended to drift down as you milked, and before you knew it you'd be resting your hair on the cow's belly.

As I washed myself by the front door, the auld fella sat up in his chair at the top of the table and the corner of the range. He held a mirror, or rather a piece of a mirror, with his left hand as he trimmed his whiskers with his right. He had started growing a beard when we moved out to the farm, and he seemed to be shaving it into a goatee.

"I'll take the basin when you are done with it," he told me. "I want to see how this looks when the rest is shaved. I've decided on a stage name: Sean O. It's from the Gaelic version of our name. The goatee forms an 'O,' so it will be like my symbol, like a trademark."

"Oh," said I.

"That's right, Sean O," said he.

"Oh. Sean O."

"No, there's only one O, after the Sean."

"Oh...oh, right, I get you." I could have kept this going all night. I decided to mess with him a bit more. "So when will you be changing everything over into the new name?"

"What do you mean?"

"I don't think you can be going around with two names, sure the Gardaí will be thinking you are some kind of international criminal mastermind."

"I think they have more to be worrying themselves about."

"Oh now, I wouldn't be too sure. What is it called when you use a different name than what is on your documents...an alias, that's it. Sure all criminals have aliases."

"But I'm just writing songs, not out robbing banks."

"There's another thing to consider as well; what happens when you really start to become successful and famous? You will be getting royalty checks for your songs. The music industry will know you as Sean O and make your checks out to that name, but when you try to cash them in the bank, you won't have a scrap of anything to show that it's really you."

"Jesus, I hadn't thought about that. I don't know where to start." He'd opened the door enough for me to let myself in.

"I'd suggest you go into Carn Garda Station as soon as you get a chance and talk to the sergeant. Tell him about your new venture as a songwriter, but make sure you let him know that you are going to be hugely famous and will be writing number one hits for the likes of Johnny Cash, Willie Nelson, Big Tom, and Dana. That means you will need a stage name, and you have already picked it out: 'Sean O.'"

"Do you really think I need to go to the cops?"

"Of course you do. Don't you know that this whole country is run by the parish priest and the local Garda sergeant? Sure they have forms in Garda stations for every conceivable aspect of our lives. You go in there and say, 'My name is Sean O and I am a future songwriter to the stars. Have you got a form I can fill out that will let me legally use my stage name when I am famous? Oh, and do I need to change the name on my driver's license?'"

"That doesn't sound too difficult."

"It's not. The best place to start must be with the law of the land. Once you have those boys on your side, you're right."

"What about the parish priest?" I was starting to feel like we had the whole father/son role reversed.

"Well, I'm afraid I can't help you there. We never did have much of a relationship with that man."

"We went down to Bocan Chapel often enough?"

"Yes, we went to Bocan, but what was our intent going there? Did we go to listen to him do his job, or did we go there to get a jump-start on the Sunday news?"

Silence. I had had my entertainment for the night. No use in beating him up too badly.

"I think the important thing is to get the law to understand your future plans. I wouldn't worry too much about the parish priest. After all, you don't often hear of them getting involved with music, except for a folk mass. They can be nice."

"That's it, then. I'll go to the Gardaí in Carndonagh and get this sorted."

"Oh, and make sure that you get plenty of official-looking stamps on whatever official forms they give you. It is possible that this is the first time they will genuinely have come across this type of request way up here. In that case, get the sergeant to write out some kind of letter, on official paper, claiming that he knows you, has been told who you will become, and advises all others to acknowledge both of your identities. That should do it."

I surprised myself that I could be so convincing when it came to giving advice, especially when I pulled it squarely out of my arse without any advanced warning.

CHAPTER 24

GETTING CAUGHT WITH A FAG

U nfortunately, none of Sean O's songs made it into the Eurovision song contest in 1972. I wished that one of them had made it, and won it as well. The winning Eurovision song must have made the writer a fortune, as that thing would be played virtually non-stop in every country. It also catapulted the careers of the singers. I remember when ABBA won with "Waterloo," and whatever they came out with after that turned to gold. Not only would we be quite well off, but the chances would be good that he could write other songs that the group would record and they too would be successful.

It would have meant no more beef hearts or tongues for a while, and no more milking bloody cows either. I might have even been able to stop raiding peoples' pockets for change. One thing is for sure: I would have been able to get a pair of shoes that weren't two sizes too small for me. It would soon be the summer holidays and I had been seriously crippled for more than a year. I developed a strange way of walking that distributed the pain around my feet more evenly. It involved curling my big toes downwards whilst simultaneously drawing the tops upwards from the inside and then walking as much on my heels as possible.

I probably looked deformed. It's likely that nobody said anything because they took pity on me. On one of those cripple-walk days, I joined a group of other boys, probably six or seven of us, to walk around the town on our lunch break. I don't know why I did it, but I smoked my one cigarette that afternoon instead of saving it for the bus ride home. I suppose it made me feel like one of the tough boys, even though my gait would have you believe that I should be in some kind of home for children with polio.

As we walked across the Diamond on our way back to school, I heard a blood-curdling voice shout out, "J.P., is that you?"

For many years afterward, my biggest regret in life was turning around in that moment. There were the two of them staring back at me, my mother with a look of genuine shock on her face. I immediately threw away the cigarette—much too late—and walked over to the car.

"Get in," she growled.

I sat in the back with the younger wains. Her backhand blow came as a surprise. Fortunately, it glanced off my chin.

"What are you doing smoking?" she asked.

How do you answer that? You smoke because you smoke. She should know—both of them should, since they both smoked when we were young.

"I was just trying it out. I didn't really like it." That seemed to buy me some time to think.

"Who were those ones you were with?"

"Just some boys from my class."

"Where are they from?"

"Some are from Clonmany, others from Moville, and a couple from around Glen Togher."

"I never saw anything good come out of Clonmany yet," she interjected. The auld fella was quiet and appeared satisfied with her interrogation.

"Why are you walking like some kind of damned cripple?" I sneaked a sideways glance at the auld fella to see what he thought of that remark, but he was giving nothing away.

"The shoes are too wee for me."

"And whose fault is that? You know damn well you should have gotten your shoes a couple of sizes bigger so that you could grow into them."

"Can I go now?"

"What's your big hurry? Are you missing your useless Clonmany friends?"

"No. The bell goes in less than five minutes, and I'll be in trouble if I'm late."

"Trouble is nothing new to you. You're in trouble right now. When does your Group Cert start?"

"The week after next." She started to turn around more in her seat, and I figured she was looking for the knock-out blow. I pressed my back as far into the seat as possible.

"We're going to be keeping a close eye on you. You'll never know when we are behind you—just like today. If you don't pass those exams with flying colors, you will not have to ever worry about dress shoes again, since all you'll ever be wearing will be Wellington boots."

That was one evil woman. Christ knows what she would have done if she had known about the gambling.

"Now can I go?"

"Go. No more fags. You can smoke when you have a job, and *that's* not happening for a while."

It's a good thing she didn't ask how I could afford the one she caught me smoking. With that, I got out of the car and they took off out the Moville Road. What in the name of Jesus were they doing in Carn on a Thursday? They could have at least come in the following day and saved me the bother of having to cart around the bloody mess that would be our weekly dinner.

She was right about one thing. I would never know when they were around. I would have to start sneaking about more myself. Peering over a book or looking through a hole cut in the middle of a newspaper might be useful devices from here on out.

The bells ringing from Carn Church meant that I was already late. I had to hoof it downhill. I must have been some sight, running on my heels with curled toes. I must have looked like I was in training for the Paralympic games as I dashed down the brae to the school.

At least it was woodworking class, so it took a while for them to get their pieces of wood and arrange their tools. I apologized to the teacher, telling him that my parents had met me uptown and kept me late. He had that look on his face with the upward eyebrows that said, "I know you are telling me a load of shite." I didn't care. If he decided to check up on the excuse, I was sure they would be glad to fill him in on their findings.

Just as I had the year before, I knew I was in academic trouble. I had spent all year just coasting along, having the craic. Now it was time to face the music. I had no doubt that my Group Cert would be covered in F grades. Since my birthday was in September, they only needed to keep me in school through third year, and could pull me out at sixteen if I didn't have the excuse of good grades to keep me enrolled. As much as I tried, I could think of nothing worse than being stuck on the farm on a full-time basis. It was bad enough to be there all summer and then on the weekends for the rest of the year, but I was quite sure that I would be ready for the lunatic asylum if that were to be my everyday life.

The worst part was the fact that there was only so much you could do with a handful of fields. They could threaten me with working on the Houton family farm in Malin Head all they liked; that would have been a completely different story. The Houtons had 100 acres of good land—three farms together, actually. Whenever Daniel needed anything, he just wrote to his sister in America and next thing you know, he would have a new tractor, a new cattle shed—anything he wanted. He was talking about getting a new Land Rover. Apparently he had outgrown the wee car that his brother-in-law had bought for him.

Speaking of the car and caravan, I had managed to find out why the auld fella was so happy about buying them. In all fairness, he did find a lovely clean car for Daniel. It was a Ford Anglia, all black, with chrome strips along the side. The car looked like new. Of course he had to make his commission, and it was quite hefty. I think the car cost something like 500 pounds. When he first started to talk to his partner-in-crime about it, I heard him say that he would add on 100 "for their troubles." A week later the 100 had grown to 150, and the last I heard, the new sale price was 775 pounds. For all I know, it could have easily topped the 800 mark before the final figure made its way across the Atlantic.

The caravan was a gold mine for him altogether. It was owned by some Northern folks and kept down at Culdaff beach. Apparently they fell upon hard times and had to sell their holiday home. They originally asked about 700 for it, but the two of them beat up this poor family so much that they agreed to sell for 350. My father even got them to throw in the kitchen table and chairs. Of course, we didn't need to fear that this lower price would affect his commission rate.

His first thought was to tell his sister-in-law that he paid 800 for it, which allowed him to more than double his money. (I'm not sure where he got the money to buy it in the first place. Maybe he had to borrow that on the Q.T. and pay it back once it was sold.) The more he thought about it, though, the more he believed that 800 was too little. He reasoned that a 100-pound commission was not worth anyone's while, especially on an original price of 700. He liked the sound of 950 better. I had absolutely no say in his dealings, but I often felt sorry for my aunt, who worked seven days a week in New York City as a private nurse, paying not only her own living expenses and those of her elderly mother, but who dealt with a constant stream of (often-inflated) bills back in Ireland.

The other reason that I would have jumped at the idea of working on the Houton farm was because of the craic I could have. My grandfather was certifiably insane, and my uncle was not too far behind. The older Houton was into devilment—making poitín, and making fun of his old friends—while my Uncle Daniel was into having a good time and "chasing tail," as he called it. When I first heard him use the phrase, all I could think of was chasing rabbits as a younger boy, but I knew he was far too old to be chasing after rabbits. Then I saw him in action, right under my very nose, so to speak.

Heather Patterson was a local Protestant girl (he and I seemed to share a fondness for Protestant lassies) who could have been a professional model. She was tall and slim, and had long straight black hair that went all the way down to her waist. She was probably finishing up secondary school just as I was starting, so she was four or five years older than me. Not that she would have been too old for me. I had a history with older Protestant girls, as evidenced by my neighbor in the Maheramore house; they seemed to like younger men, and I was all right with that. When Daniel zoomed in on Heather, she was around eighteen and he must have been about thirty.

When it came to chatting up women, he had balls the size of coconuts. He didn't need the right setting or for certain music to be playing. He could just stop them in the street and start talking to them. That's what he did with Heather. He and I were going down to the local shop to buy fags as she was walking over the lane by her house. He had never seen her before, but as he passed her, he nearly went over the ditch from trying to see her in his rear mirror.

"We're going back," he informed me. He threw the car into reverse and backed up until he was beside her.

"What's your name?" he asked her.

"Heather."

"Just like...just like the heather, growing wild. Are you wild, Heather?"

I started to squirm in my seat. I never heard anyone talk to a girl like this, especially one they did not know. She looked down and giggled.

"This is my nephew J.P. They are neighbors of yours." I looked out of the car and she looked in as we both said hello.

"Would you like to go for a ride sometime?"

Oh Jesus, now he did it. He just met the girl and he is talking about riding already. I could see she was uncomfortable, so I leaned over and told her, "When an American says a 'ride,' he means to go out in the car for a drive." This calmed her, and she started to smile again.

"You mean you guys have your own language here?" Daniel asked.

"We have two," I told him, "Donegal English and Irish."

"I remember a bit of Irish from when I went to school in Malin Head," he informed us. "Pog mo thoin."

"Very nice," I told him. "You never lost it."

He grinned like the Cheshire Cat, as he thought I had complimented him. He eventually tore himself away from Heather, and we carried on to the shop.

"Hey, what was all that about going for a ride?" he asked me.

"In Ireland, when you say you want a ride, it means that you want sex. You are riding a girl when you are having sex with her."

"So what's wrong with that?"

"Nothing."

"Then why did you have to explain to her that when I said 'ride,' I meant going out in the car?"

"Because that *is* what you meant. Besides, she was uncomfortable with you just stopping her on the road and talking about having sex."

"So do you think she's the shy type?"

"I don't really know. The family are hardworking farmers, as are all the Protestants around Donegal."

"She's a Prod, then?"

"Aye."

"She may be hotter to trot than a Catholic girl."

"Maybe. I'll tell you one thing. She's built more for speed than comfort."

Daniel started to laugh so hard that he went into convulsions. He couldn't keep driving and had to pull the car over into a gap in the ditch.

"Christ, lad, the things you come out with. What do you know about a girl being built for speed?" He was still laughing.

"Because I had sex with a Protestant girl myself, and she was definitely built for comfort. Her tits were so big it took both my hands to properly hold just one of them."

"Man, you are a dark horse. Did you take her for a ride?"

"Sure, how could I take her out in the car when I was only thirteen years old? Not to mention I'd have to steal the old man's car."

"No, I meant did you have her to ride...you know?"

"Oh, now I get you. You'll have to learn how to use the word properly. You would just ask, 'Did you ride her?' Or, 'Was she a good old ride?' Just remember those two things and you'll be all right."

"You know what we should do? We should go down to McGrory's in Culdaff some night they have a band and see if we can't find us a couple of chicks."

"I'm all for it, but you will have to convince my old ones to let me go. It might be a better idea to say you want me to help you out on the farm some weekend. You could collect me after school some Friday, and we could go either Friday or Saturday night."

"My man, I like the way you think. You are a devious bastard just like myself."

He decided that since we were already "out on the town," we needed to go over to the Orchard Bar to shoot some pool. Hell, he was the adult in charge, so I was not arguing. We went in and there were only a couple of locals at the bar, as it was so early.

"What are you drinking?"

"I'll have a bottle of Coke." He came down to the pool table with a bottle of Coke and a glass of what looked like whiskey.

"I'll put in the money and you can rack them up."

That was a good choice, seeing as I didn't have any money.

He was a damn good pool player. He did that fancy American thing where he made a circle with the forefinger and thumb of his left hand and put the cue stick through the opening. After the first game, a local woman who had been at the bar came to watch.

"You want to see a trick shot?" he asked her.

"Sure."

He set up the cue ball behind a triangle of other balls and explained how he would jump the ball in the air over them all and then bring the cue ball back to hit the triangle and knock the first ball into the corner pocket. I felt sorry for him, as there was no way he was going to do it. He lined himself up and, after he took a drink of the whiskey, he hit that white ball and made it pop right up in the air. Not only that, but it slammed into the opposite cushion and spun back toward the triangle. I stood there mesmerized as everything he predicted began to take place.

Slowly but surely, the cue ball hit the triangle. The balls moved a bit, but the cue ball had stopped, and there was no way it was going to make a ball go into the corner pocket. Well, at least he had got most of it right. I must have looked like I had given up, as the next thing I heard from behind me was, "Wait for it..." I did. What I saw next shocked me. The very last ball in the triangle was pushed by the ball behind it and slowly started rolling toward the pocket. Just when I thought it had lost all momentum, it dangled over the hole and dropped into the pocket in slow motion. Everybody in the bar must have been watching, as they all broke into applause.

"You're very handy with that stick," the girl told him.

"I can work my stick really well," he told her with a smile.

I noticed a man sitting at the bar turn around every few minutes to look at the two of them. I had seen him around the neighborhood before, but I didn't know if the woman was with him or not. If she was, we could have a problem. Like his father, Danny Houton, Daniel liked women, whiskey, and fighting. Any of the three could get him in trouble, but the whole three together, at the same time, could spell disaster. When I heard the man at the bar raise his voice a bit and say something about a "Yank," I figured it was time to get going. I was afraid that sooner or later, Daniel was going to try out his newfound knowledge of the verb "to ride," and when the buck at the bar heard that, it might be too late to stop a fight.

I stood next to him and whispered in his ear, "We need to get going." He still had a silly grin on his face and was looking at the woman who had admired his stick work.

"What's the hurry?"

"Your sister is making dinner, and if we are not back in time, she will be in a horrible mood. There won't be much chance of them letting me go to Malin Head for the weekend if we get back late and she smells alcohol. Remember, the thought, smell, or sight of alcohol affects her like a cross does a vampire."

That made him laugh. "My nephew reminded me that we have an important dinner date," he told the woman.

"Oh, so your wife is waiting for you?"

"No, nothing like that. I never had a wife. I am a free spirit who can't be tamed."

The woman leaned in closer to him. "Maybe we'll see about that." Daniel laughed and finished his drink. I was glad to get him back out into his Anglia.

"Shit, I forgot to buy fags."

There was no way we were going back into there. "Pull over here to the wee shop, sure they have fags." He got out and came back five minutes later with twenty Majors.

"Do you want one?" he asked me.

"I'll take it for later," said I, sticking it in my shirt pocket.

I knew better than risk the chance of Sarah the Sniffer smelling tobacco on me. At least Daniel could hide the smell of the whiskey with the cigarette, not that he seemed worried about it. Sarah may have been my nightmare, but she went much easier on her baby brother—the lucky bastard.

CHAPTER 25

GAELTACHT GIRLS

"You ungrateful, useless bastard," shouted the auld fella as he dragged his leg through the door, waving around some papers above his head.

I did not know for sure that that his greeting was aimed at me, but I was certainly one of the most likely suspects. I quickly did a mental note of the past few days and tried to remember if I had broken anything and left it for someone else to take the blame. That was kind of my trademark. For some reason or other, I had the worst luck when it came to breaking things. Windows, glass bottles, light bulbs—if it was made of glass, I only had to look at it and it broke. My mother used to say that I was like a "bull in a china shop." Actually, I was not that awkward. Most time, it was a matter of being in the wrong place at the right time.

Unfortunately, my breakages were not reserved only for glass. I broke the wooden handles off shovels, hatchets, hammers, and even a sledgehammer once. You would think that I would not get into much trouble, as I clearly broke the handles off from working so hard, but that did not matter to my auld fella. The way he saw it, I broke things on purpose.

I don't remember what I had broken the first time I got a bad beating for it, as it was probably before I started school, but what I learned over the years was that when something broke, the best approach was to push it back together the best I could and hope that it would fall apart in someone else's hands. That was easy enough with tools, as wood can be pushed together many times, but glass items needed a bit more creativity, not to mention glue.

Maybe he was yelling because I had cut too big a piece of Barney when I fixed myself breakfast one morning? Nothing came to me. As far as I was concerned, I was actually the model citizen. Ever since the summer holidays began, I had been working my arse off in the hay fields and in the bog. Whatever had been bothering him had come in the post. He couldn't wait for the post to be delivered like everybody else. He had to go collect it and open it before he got home. After all, he reasoned, if Warner Brothers Studio had picked one of his songs as a backing track for a film, he wanted to know as soon as possible.

"What's wrong?" my mother asked him.

"I told you he would never amount to anything. Here are the results of the Group Cert—he failed it."

Oh shite. I forgot about the results. I can't say I was surprised. What the hell was the Group Cert anyway? Nobody they knew, or even themselves, had passed the "Group Cert." It wasn't as if having the bloody Group Cert was going to land me a job as a barrister. Still, passing it would have made my life easier.

"Is this true?" she asked me.

"I don't know. I never did it before. I had no idea what to expect."

I wanted to tell her that it was impossible to concentrate on two weeks of exams wearing shoes that were two sizes too small, but I was quite sure she would have come after me with a knife, or at least a two-by-four.

"What are we going to do with you? Unfortunately, you are too old to be put up for adoption." She really knew how to make a boy feel wanted.

"The way I see it," my father chimed in, "we can either pull him out of school next year and let him work the farm with me, since he has already demonstrated that he has no interest in schooling, or we can transfer him to the college."

I nearly laughed when he said that I could work the farm with him. If I matched what he did, we would both have a two-hour work week. The college sounded a bit scary, but it was probably the only real option.

To say that mine were not the most warm-hearted of parents would have been like saying Hitler wasn't such a great humanitarian, but I had to admit that they tried the best they could when it came to education. They knew I was screwing up in school, and they weren't going to turn a blind eye. Probably the fact that I was the eldest and had an influence on all of the other poor little bastards who came after me had something to do with it as well. My last year in grade school, they decided to send me to the Falcarrach Gaeltacht in West Donegal during the summer. While all the other children started learning Irish in baby infants class, I didn't start until I went into fourth grade, which meant that the rest of my classmates had a five-year learning advantage on me.

The tutor they hired helped, but I was still struggling along trying to come to grips with it, and the Gaeltacht college sounded tough. You weren't allowed to speak any English. You would stay in a local home with a few other boys and the Bean an Ti and Fear an Ti (the literal translation of this was "man and woman of the house"), and could never speak a word of English. If you didn't know the Irish equivalent, you had to work around it until you were told the word, then you had to commit it to memory. There was no fear of the locals tempting you to speak English either. They looked down upon it as an inferior language, the likes of which was forced upon the Irish through persecution. If you were ever caught speaking English, God help you. I never did understand what that meant, but if you needed help from above to get out of it, it couldn't be good.

Once we arrived down at the Gaeltacht, I realized that it wasn't as bad as it was made out to be. Nobody would speak English to you (you would have to whisper in English to the other boys after lights out and hope you weren't caught), but you learned songs in Irish and all kinds of dances. There was some kind of ceile dance every night after class.

Unfortunately, even there I managed to get into bother. Mind you, it didn't happen until the very last night of our stay. We discovered that it was tradition for the boys to break out of their house on the last night and make their way to the girls' house. After a couple of weeks, we all had a fairly good idea of where the other half lived. For days we had planned how we were going to do it, at what time, and what road we would take. It was like planning a prison break.

Unfortunately, the Fear agus Bean an Ti also knew about the tradition, and they were determined that no boy would get out of their house that night. Around midnight, myself and two other boys got up quietly, got dressed, and attempted to sneak down the stairs and out the front door. The Fear an Ti was sitting on a chair with his back to the door, half-snoozing while sitting up. There was no way we were getting out by traditional methods. Then it hit me. I signaled to the other two to go back to our bedroom. Once there, I went over to the bedroom window, opened it and told them, "This is our way out."

"You must be mad," they said, nearly at the same time.

"We are only on the second floor, and the ground below is soft. I'll lower myself out the window and drop down. When you see that I've cleared the house, you both follow."

I could tell by the looks on their faces that they would never make good commandos. I dropped down anyway and waited below for my comrades. They must have been making too much noise, for the next thing I knew the bedroom light came on. I realized that meant the people in the house knew about our escape. I turned on my heels and bolted across the back yard toward the main road.

I had no idea what to expect, but I really didn't think that the man of the house would get in his car and hunt me down. I was wrong; that is exactly what he tried to do. Even though I was on my own personal mission, I believe that it was a matter of pride for them that no boy from *their* house would get past them. Unfortunately for them, they didn't plan on a wild hoor from Inishowen jumping out of a second-story window. The whole night involved climbing over and hiding behind ditches and trying not to get lost in a bog hole. Every time I saw a car's headlamps in the distance, I would hit the ground and make myself invisible. Some of them would have been men coming home from the pub, but I had no intention of getting caught and being dragged back in.

Eventually after a lot of climbing, sliding, hiding, and crawling, I made it to the girls' house. I felt like a long-distance runner who had finally crossed the line. Their house turned out not to be so protected, since the girls normally would stay put and the boys would make their way to them. I went around the back and quietly tapped on the bedroom window. One of the girls came over to open it and I crawled in.

"Who else got here?" I asked them.

"Just you. It seems that you are the only one to make it out tonight." A couple of them giggled, and I could see that they appreciated the effort.

"You have to be careful, though," a young girl from Ballyshannon told me. "There has already been a teacher by here a wee while ago. They know you got out, and they are mad. It seems that they were full sure that nobody could get away with it this time."

Another one passed me a Mars bar. I was glad for it, as I hadn't eaten since the 6 o'clock tea and had used a lot of energy running on the roads and through the bogs. The lights of a car suddenly shone on the house and stopped at the front door.

"Quick, get under my bed," said a girl whose bed was in the corner. "You won't have time to leave now. Somebody make sure that window is tightly shut, or they'll suspect something."

I actually didn't really believe that there was a posse of teachers out hunting for me until the bedroom door opened and a man shone in a torch on the beds to do a head count. I had thought about lying in the bed. Good thing I was under it—unless he decided to look under the beds, in which case I would be a dead man. He didn't look any more, though, and slowly turned and left the room. After a few minutes, the car pulled out. I slid out from under the bed, and they all sat up in theirs.

"You are just like one of the Western film outlaws," the Ballyshannon girl told me.

"I just hope that I don't wind up with a noose around my neck and the other end of the rope thrown over a tree, like what happens to some of those outlaws," I joked.

"You're very brave," another girl chimed in.

I was enjoying living the life of an outlaw. Never once did I give any serious consideration to how it would all end. As a matter of fact, that was pretty much my lifestyle summed up in one sentence: *"He never thought about how it all might end."*

Seeing as how this was my first official jailbreak, I was not sure what tasks needed to be carried out. As I watched all these young girls in bed, the thought occurred to me that if there was a Protestant girl in the audience, we might make a couple of new tasks of our own.

"So what do I need to do now?" I asked them all. A couple of girls had been to the Gaeltacht in previous years, so they were the experienced ones.

"Well, in the past any of the boys who managed to break out would go to one of the girls' houses and check on them to make sure they were all safe. Then they would carry notes that any of the girls wanted to pass to the other house."

Make sure they were all safe? Did they not realize that they had just let an Inishowen fox into their henhouse?

"I see," I said, trying to sound thoughtful and insightful. "So do youns have messages that you want me to carry across the enemy lines, risking body and soul?"

Several of them fished under their pillows and pulled out letters. It seemed like they were prepared for the midnight rendezvous. The Ballyshannon lass kneeled up in her bed. She seemed like the group spokeswoman.

"Because you are such a brave lad and did not consider your own safety or the punishment that might befall you amárach, just like what happened to our brave heroes during the Easter week uprising in 1916 when they were marched out of the GPO and executed, it is only right and fitting that we send you off with a kiss."

I liked the idea of being kissed by so many girls, but the goodness was knocked out of this thought a bit by the remark that I would face punishment the next day. I didn't have a clue what that punishment might be. I thought that the possibility of my being executed come morning, was fairly remote, but they did use the phrase; "God help you if you were caught." Still, I would have to cross that bridge when I came to it. Right now there were girls to be kissed. They had me stand in one spot, and they came up and kissed me and returned to their beds. It kind of reminded me of the condemned man's last meal. The Ballyshannon lass was the last in line—I'm sure she did it on purpose. No peck on the cheek for her. She wrapped both arms around my neck, stuck her body into mine, and sucked on me like I was *her* last supper. Her kiss lasted nearly as long as all the others' put together.

If I had had sense, I would have stayed in contact with that wee one. As it was, I had a job to do. It was a dirty job, but somebody had to do it, and once again, that someone was me. I tucked the letters down into my pockets, listened to the most covert way to get to the next house, and left through the window like a thief in the night.

My plan of attack for the next house was much the same as the first. I would use the road when I could, but as soon as I saw lights coming from any direction, I was over the ditch and diving for cover. Alternating between walking and diving tends to slow you down on your journey. It felt like I had been walking for hours, but I didn't have a clue what time it would be. I just hoped the girls would still be up. It would be a bit of a kick in the teeth if they were all asleep and I had no way to prove that I had successfully carried out my mission.

After a few more bends in the road, I saw a couple of houses off to the left. I was sure that one of them was their place. I crept up to the house, going wide so as not to be seen by anybody who may be inside looking out. Fortunately, it was also a bungalow. It would have been a right pain in the arse to be reaching around for pebbles, trying to hit a window on a top floor in order to get their attention.

I got low to the ground and hunched under the windowsill, slowly raising my head to see if there were girls inside. I didn't see any movement, and didn't know whether to tap on the glass or not. What if the owners of the house were in the room I was tapping on? They had to be in one of those rooms. I moved along to the next window to see if that was a better possibility. There was a bathroom window between the two rooms. The second room looked like it had two rear bedroom windows. That might be a good sign that it was a larger room used for lodgers.

I slowly raised my head again and started to peer into the window. If a local Garda had come upon me crouching around the back of a house looking into a girl's bedroom in the middle of the night, I'd probably not be going home the next day, as they would take me away for sure. I don't know if my eyes were playing tricks on me, but I thought I saw the image of a girl in a white night dress, like a ghost in a horror film. I reached into my pockets and pulled out a couple of letters to show her. She waved me toward her. The window slowly opened, and she helped me in. The scene was like that of the other house, only these girls were even more excited. They had heard the landlords talking about a boy who broke out and saying every one of our teachers was out looking for him.

At first I felt like a proud rooster, but then I realized that these teachers wanted to be in their beds, or in a pub, or anything but chasing after some eejit who was making their last night miserable. I pulled the letters out of my pockets and handed them to the one girl.

"They had me carry these letters to youns."

I was really starting to feel the night on me now, especially when I realized that I didn't have a plan for going back into the house.

"What are you going to do now?" one of them asked.

"I've been asking myself the same question. I definitely have to go back. I'm getting a lift back home to Inishowen with one of the teachers tomorrow."

"That's not going to be a fun trip," another added. "Do you think he will tell your parents?"

"Oh, I'm sure he will. I'm also sure that I'll get a right hammering, but you know what? It was worth it. It's tradition that the boys break out on the last night, and if I didn't do it tonight, it could have ended the tradition. I just hope some other boy gets out again next year." I was, however, secretly enjoying the fact that I may have been the last one ever to escape.

"Do you know how to get back to your house?"

"I haven't a bull's notion."

"Well, it's going to take you a brave wee while. If you go through the fields, the long way around, it would probably take you until daybreak. But if you stick to the roads, you should get there before then."

"Oh, I'll stick to the roads all right. They'd be doing me a favor if they came upon me now and took me back to the house." None of them offered to start a kissing ring this time, but I could see by the look in their eyes that I had made the night special for them.

"Slán agus beannacht, ladies."

With that, I made my escape back out through the window, hoping that it would be the last window I climbed through that night. Then I walked and walked until I thought I couldn't walk another step. Even though I was terrified of the reception I was going to get, it was good to finally see the two-story house up ahead. I hoped that I could go to bed for an hour before being interrogated. I knocked on the door and took a deep breath. I heard a stirring right behind the door and remembered that the Fear an Ti was sitting up against it. Although it hadn't done him much good earlier, it seemed like he was sticking to his guns.

A few seconds later, he opened it, and I looked into the face of a man who I was sure would have liked to tear the head off my shoulders. He looked down over his big thick brown moustache, saying nothing. After a couple of seconds of staring at me with his big dark eyes that never blinked, he moved to one side and I walked past him up to the bedroom. Even as I walked away, I could feel his eyes drilling holes into the back of my head. I whipped off my clothes and jumped into my bed. After what felt like ten minutes, one of the boys who had planned on breaking out as well was standing over me.

"Come on, get up," he whispered. "We only have a wee while to get some breakfast before we have to leave to go home."

I rolled out of bed and into my clothes. The first thing I noticed were my aching feet. I went downstairs, staring at the floor the whole time. Nobody spoke. I ate whatever I could reach. If the butter was too far away, I ate the toast dry. If I couldn't reach the milk, I drank the tea black. After a few moments of this unhappy breakfast, I went up to my room and gathered my stuff. I took it downstairs and waited by the front door. Nobody said goodbye, or good luck, or *anything*. The Fear an Ti was still looking at me over his big bushy moustache.

That was only ten minutes, and it felt like two hours. I wondered what the two-hour drive home would feel like. I would find out momentarily

The teacher who was to take me home pulled up, got out, and opened his boot. He put my bag inside. There was nobody else in the car. I thought there would be at least one other person. He turned to the Fear and Ti and told them, "Slán." Then we both got into the car. We drove all the way from Falcarragh to Carndonagh without one word between us. When we got close to home, I showed him where I lived. He stopped, got out, and opened the boot again.

This is where he tells them what a trouble-maker I've been, and that I am never allowed back to the Gaeltacht for the rest of my life, I thought. But he didn't. He handed me my bag, and as he wished me Slán, I saw that he had a small smirk on his face.

"You'll probably be the last boy to ever get out on the last night," he told me, and then he was gone.

I was dumbfounded. He had actually *respected* my breakout, and confirmed that I was to be the last one ever to get away with it. I wanted to run in and tell everybody, but I realized almost immediately that not everyone was going to appreciate my efforts at creating a place in Gaeltacht history.

I would have to be satisfied knowing that there was a wee girl in Ballyshannon who would gladly wrap herself around me, and would probably never forget her outlaw from Inishowen.

CHAPTER 26
"OLIVER!"

The one good thing about getting caught that day in Carn was that there was no denying my feet were in bits. The parents got me a new pair of shoes (well, the government got me a new pair) for going back to school. They were the policeman/priest's black brogues, but they were a good two sizes bigger than the Mick Jaggers, so there would be no more walking like a polio victim. Changing to Carndonagh Community College was also a good move, despite the fact that I got held back a year. I could sense that it made me a better student and got me away from the slot machines.

Carndonagh College was located between two places—the convent out past the hospital on the Glen Togher Road, and the Colgan Hall. I stayed put when it was lunchtime at the convent, as it would take most of my break just to walk downtown.

Welcome additions were the girls. The classes were evenly split between boys and girls, which was new to me; and the Carndonagh girls had bigger breasts and were curvier all around than what I was used to.

Plus our teachers were characters—for example, our Latin instructor, who we called Yogi Bear. Yogi was a small, round man nuttier than a fruitcake. One time when we were discussing great Roman orators, he came to class dressed in a toga with an olive-leaf crown. He would get so carried away at times that he seemed to forget we were even there, and would have animated conversations with himself, complete with arm waving and full-blown disagreements.

I noticed almost immediately that nearly every subject was being taught at a much higher level. The two years of French I took at the Tech couldn't hold a candle to the first-year French that my classmates knew. I understood full well that this was my last chance at school, however, and there was no way I would blow it this time. Besides, we were able to have the craic during class, as teachers seemed to look upon us differently than they did with the Tech students. The only thing I didn't like was the fact that I should have been moving on to third year but was just starting second. A good consolation prize was there was no Group Cert at Carndonagh, and I had the next two years to prepare for the Inter Cert.

The other discussion I heard at the college, which nobody talked about at the Tech, was that of honor subjects. Several of my Carndonagh College classmates had already chosen their honor subjects, which they would sit for the Leaving in four years. One lad wanted to be a dentist, and he set himself up for five or six honor subjects. The more honors you received (C and above on the higher paper), the more points you would be awarded, and there were a set number of points required to study medicine, law, etc.

I put myself down for three honors: English, biology, and chemistry. I wanted to be a journalist. I figured the competition for that may not be as stiff as that of some of the other occupations.

The one real spanner in the works with the new school was the Friday meat run. No matter what combination of locations was thrown at me, I had to find a way to get that meat on the evening bus. The best situation was when we changed class at lunchtime to the Colgan Hall. They'd give you a bit of extra time to eat your lunch, as they knew you had to walk down to change classrooms. No more slots for me; I'd beat it over to Pat the Butcher, grab the bloody bag as quickly as possible, and leg it to my classroom. Of course, a new school meant a whole new line of questioning: "What have you in the bag?"; "My *mother* gets the meat for our dinner;" and "Are you going to carry that around all day?" There were days when I would have liked to grab a hold of that big bloody beef heart and jam it into some fucker's gob.

The students going to Carndonagh College were much more well-off than those who went to the Tech. Christ knows, they were all in a better way than me, but that required only having a few pennies in one's pocket every day. That never really posed a problem, though. How you handled yourself was always more important than what you had in your pocket.

The one thing all us boys had in common was our fixation on the girls. There was one girl, Ann Marie McLaughlin, who had the finest tits we had ever seen. Not that we had ever seen them—we had to make do with the lumps that stuck out from under her jumper. No matter what she wore, her breasts were always bursting to get out. Although I had no clue about breast size then, thinking back, they must have been a 40D. As Benny Hill would say, "You didn't get many of them to the pound."

No matter how horny we made ourselves from looking at the girls, it didn't take long for deflation to set in thanks to the tiny, round, pink-faced, horn-killer nun who delivered the next class.

The only boy who didn't feel that way was Liam Hannigan—a sick little bastard. Hannigan used to fantasize about how the nuns looked under their habits. He talked about fishnet stockings and lacy underwear to the point where you would jam a Biro in your ear just to not have to listen to him anymore. Some said that his brother who had been in England had brought back perverted magazines, and that's why he was the way he was. The rest of us figured he was just a sick, perverted fucker.

⭑━⟡ ⟡━⭑

It was during my time at Carndonagh College that I became more exposed to music and began to feel a greater appreciation for it. I had mostly heard local Donegal music and country bands from Ireland. My parents did have an early Johnny Cash album, which I would listen to over and over again. Even way back then, I thought the American singer was much stronger and better than any of our country singers in Ireland. Then one day a classmate, Jimmy Toland, told me about this American singer called Neil Diamond. He said that there were no singers in Ireland covering his records, but that there was a country-western singer called Brian Coll who could yodel and sing like a Yank. As it so happened, he was booked to play the Lilac Ballroom that weekend.

On Friday evening, after I hauled the big bloody red bag of meat back to the farm, I planted the Lilac Ballroom seed into my parents' heads. I was hoping against hope that they would let me thumb into Carn. Once there, I could line up a lift back with some neighbor. No such feckin' luck.

"I heard that Brian Coll boy on the radio," exclaimed the auld fella. "I think I may have a song that would suit him." I didn't fully understand what he was saying, but I had a bad feeling in me water.

"Sure, maybe you should take the song into the Lilac for him to hear, then," replied his crazy-ass woman.

"Aye, I think I will. Do you want to come in with me then?" asked the songwriter from the bog, looking in my direction.

For a minute, I didn't know what to say. I wanted to go, but who the hell wanted to go to a dance with their auld fella? If I said no, though, I'd be house-bound. I figured I could get a lift in and then disappear into the crowd. There should be a few hundred people, so maybe I could steer clear of him.

"Aye, I wouldn't mind," I replied.

"Right so," said he, "yourself, myself and your brother will go into Brian Coll."

My brother? Ah, fuck that. Sure, the wee hoor was only 12. Would I have to babysit him? How would I pull a bird if I was babysitting a wain? I fretted the whole weekend, not knowing what it would look like when the "Blessed Trinity" all arrived up outside the Lilac Ballroom.

As it turned out, the auld fella had other plans. He drove around the back of the hall and walked up the back steps. He was carrying a tape recorder, which probably contained a tape of Eugene Friel singing one of his songs to the melody of an old Donegal song.

The auld fella wrapped his knuckles on the heavy wooden door and shouted "Oliver!" I was confused. If he was looking for Brian Coll, then surely he should have shouted "Brian." I later realized that he had done this on purpose. Oliver was the owner of the Lilac Ballroom, and by shouting out for the owner, those inside would think that the person outside had a legitimate reason for coming in. Sure enough, it worked. The door opened, and the auld fella didn't need an engraved invitation to enter. His show-band music-writing career had begun.

"How's it going?" he asked, sticking his hand out to one of the bandsmen who was getting ready to go on stage.

"Aye, all right," replied the musician, eyeing my young brother and me with a confused look on his face.

"I'm Sean O, a local songwriter, and I have a song I think may be a good fit for Brian." Man, he had some balls. He didn't even know what Brian Coll looked like, and here he was making it sound as if he were his personal songwriter.

"Oh aye, well Brian's still getting ready—sure, I'll tell him you're asking for him when he comes out."

There was a lot of commotion going on between four or five guys dressed in suits, and another few in t-shirts and jeans. I could hear a band playing onstage already. I couldn't tell how the auld fella felt, standing there with his tape player in his hand, but I felt like a right prick.

After about fifteen minutes, a tall guy in a suit sucking deeply on a cigarette came over and announced that he was Brian Coll. "I hear you brought me a song," he said.

"I did," said the auld fella. "I specialize in ballads, and I think I have one that will suit you very well. I'm Sean O, by the way."

"Well, thanks for coming in, Sean, but we are about to go on stage in a couple of minutes. Why don't you hang around here and listen to us, and when we're finished we'll have more time to chat."

"That's grand," replied O.

After about five minutes, the music in the main ballroom stopped and someone announced Brian Coll and the Buckaroos. They all ran out on to the stage, and in no time they were belting out the "Wabash Cannonball."

"Are you going out to listen to them?" the auld fella asked me. I was dying to get out and had been wondering how I could do it without too much notice.

"I wouldn't mind."

"Go on out, so."

I tucked my head into my chin and opened the door that led from backstage to the front right of the stage. In those three seconds, I had walked into a different world. There were women and men, music and laughter. Men were dancing with girls, and girls were dancing with each other. The saxophone blasted notes into my left ear so loud that I thought it might bust my eardrum, and as I passed by the huge speakers, I could feel the bass guitar throbbing in my veins.

I kept walking and never looked back. It was as if I had walked away from that other world, and I was free for as long as the band played. Deep down, I knew that this was borrowed time, but I would enjoy every minute of it until the warden called me back to the jailhouse.

I must have looked a right eejit, walking around the floor staring, but it was all new to me. It didn't take me long, though, to figure out what I was supposed to do. The women and girls all stood around in a large circle at the edge of the dance floor, looking toward the band. The men then would walk around anti-clockwise (for whatever reason), with their back to the band, and scope out the women. When they saw one they fancied, they'd either hold out their hand so that the girl they were eyeing could take it, or else they would nod at the woman and jerk their head backwards toward the band. I learned that both of those methods were the universal (or at least Donegal) way to ask a bird out to dance.

Just when I figured I must have been the youngest hoor in the ballroom, I spotted Toland. I walked up behind him and gave him a punch to the kidneys. He spun around like a madman.

"You fucker," he greeted me.

"How are they hanging now?" I asked him.

"I didn't know you were coming. How did you make it in?" he asked me.

"It's a long story. A family member gave me a lift."

"Did you pull a bird yet?" he asked me.

"No fucking way. Sure, they are all way older than us. They'd be looking for men with jobs."

"Well, you don't want to find one to marry, just to ride for the night."

"Jesus, you make it sound so easy. What should I do, saunter up to one like James Bond and say something like, 'Would a ride be out of the question?'"

"You really don't have a clue, do you? Have you ever pulled a bird in your life?"

"I did. I had sex with a Protestant lass, if you must know."

"A Protestant? Jesus, what was that like?"

"It's a long story. I lost a shoe during it."

"I want to hear more."

"You'll have to buy the book. Now tell us what we need to do to score here."

"All right, so here is the way I do it. You spot a bird that you fancy and ask her out to dance. Always make sure that you ask her out at the start of the set. That way you get to dance three times with her unless she walks off. During the dance you ask her the usual questions: her name, where she lives. Then when the third song finishes, you ask her if she would like to go up to the mineral bar for a Club Orange and packet of salt and vinegar crisps. Never mention cheese and onion, as you don't want to be kissing a bird with onion on their breath at the end of the night."

"Club Orange *and* a packet of crisps? Sure, that is like taking her out for a meal. I don't have that kind of money to spend on a bird."

"Then my advice to you is to start saving up. My motto is 'You have to set aside if you want the ride.' No girl wants a cheap hoor, you know."

"I wouldn't have taken you for the poetic type."

"I look upon it as a gift," he replied, taking my jab as a compliment. "Now let's walk around the hall and see if we can spot a couple of girls who aren't looking for a wealthy farmer."

As we walked toward the front of the stage, I knew that we would be walking by the side door that I had passed earlier. I didn't want to look, but I couldn't control myself. I was hoping that I would not see anybody I was related to, but that was not to be. Standing at the door was the bold Sean O, with my brother by his side. The auld fella was staring straight ahead. Perhaps he was working out how he was going to convince a professional singer that the scratchy song on his hand-held recorder would be a future hit. My brother saw me almost immediately and started to jump and wave at me. I did my best to look away and not let on that I knew them.

"Who is that auld fella with the midget?" Toland asked me. "Is the midget waving at us?"

"I don't think he's a midget," I replied. "He looks like a wain."

"Jesus, what would a wain be doing out at this time of night? You know what? I think the auld fella's wife must have run off on him, and he took the midget—or the wain—out with him to find her. That must be it. Sure that auld fella could hardly pull a bird with a wain standing next to him."

I wanted to get as far away from this entire situation as possible.

"Look at those two over there," I told Toland. "They look like they might be hot to trot."

"All right," said Toland, "remember the plan. When I ask them up to the mineral bar, we are in good shape if they agree to go."

"I won't be in good shape," I told him. "I have only twenty pence in my pocket."

"All right, you ask out the skinny one, as she probably doesn't eat that much. Don't ask her if she wants crisps, just ask her what she wants to drink. Then you buy her a Club Orange or Cidona, and tell her that you aren't thirsty. I have enough for two bags of crisps, so I'll pass mine around to the two of you."

The plan sounded decent, so I went with it. Maybe it was beginner's luck, but the two lassies agreed to dance with us and then to go to the mineral bar upstairs after the set finished. Toland looked cool and calm, but I was shitting bricks. We didn't discuss the next phase of the plan. I would be totally fucked if the auld fella came looking for me in the mineral bar when it was time to go. All I could hope was that Brian Coll would spend enough time with him to allow me to have a quick snog up against the side wall of the hall.

I don't know how long we sat up there, but the next thing I knew they were playing the National Anthem. It was time to test the next phase of the plan: "Lock Lips." Lo and behold, both girls agreed to walk out with us, which was a fairly good indication that we'd get to kiss them and possibly do some fondling. Toland and his partner walked off to the side of the hall, and I followed a distance behind.

My girl was feeling friendly enough until I forgot myself and thought I was kneading the Protestant neighbor's big tits. Unfortunately, the skinny girl did not have big tits, and she pulled my hand away. Still it was a good night—a great night, actually—and when she said she needed to find her lift home, I slipped around the corner without even looking for Toland. I knocked on the band's door, where the auld fella and my brother were waiting for me to appear.

"We were wondering where you had got to," said the auld fella.

"Ah, I met one of the lads from school. How did Brian Coll like the song?"

"He liked it a lot. He told me to bring a few more next time they come around."

I had a feeling that I was going to be able to work this show-band angle. Maybe it wasn't such a bad thing to have a songwriter in the house after all.

CHAPTER 27
MELODY FARM

Now that the auld fella was trying to be a songwriter, we could look forward to getting into the Lilac Ballroom most weekends for free. I say *most* weekends because there were some bands he just had no business visiting with his songs. Bands like Horselips (traditional Celtic rock) or Brush Shields (rock) fell into that category. Saving the fifty-pence entrance fee was a big deal when we barely had a pot to piss in. It might not sound like a lot, but before decimalization, fifty pence was called "ten shillings," and it wasn't a coin—it was a paper note. Paper notes were regarded as serious currency.

Another fairly good thing was that I was always guaranteed a lift in and, unfortunately, a lift back out. Getting in was grand, but I would have far preferred getting back home with someone else at the dance, or just thumbing back. Riding in and out with the auld fella was not the type of thing I wanted to be leaked out onto the street. Besides, if you pulled a bird and she offered you a lift with her friends, you were totally bollixed. You sure as hell could not say that your father was standing inside the hall waiting to take you home. This is where the pros of having a songwriting father start to wear thin and the cons take over.

In the beginning, it was a bit unnerving to be outside the back door of the Lilac Ballroom in pitch black, watching the auld fella hammering on the door and calling out for Oliver. I was full sure that the time would come when some musician would open the door and tell us to fuck off. I wondered what he would do then. Would he go around the front and pay one pound and fifty pence for the three of us to get in? Would he even have thirty bob on him? As it so happened, we never found out; they always opened the door.

After the first meeting with any band, we'd be greeted like long-lost brothers the next time we saw them. The main sticking point for me was just after the band went on stage. I always slipped out as stealthily as I could so that nobody would recognize me. To make matters worse, as time went on, more and more of my classmates started going to the dances. I didn't even have a decent cover story as to why I would was coming out through the back of the stage, as my friends would all know that I wasn't with any of the bands. Even if someone did spot me, I hoped against hope that they wouldn't recognize the auld fella.

What happened next caught me completely off guard. Apparently Sean O was so desperate to be recognized as a songwriter that he started his own aggressive marketing campaign. Unfortunately for me, I turned out to be the campaign. For some reason or other, he decided that he would gain fame as a result of me telling everyone in school that he was now a songwriter.

As much as I tried to understand this strategy, I could not see how it made an ounce of sense. First, it was not as if I could ask my classmates if they had heard any of his songs being played on the Larry Gogan National Radio Show. All of his songs were confined to tapes, and only saw the light of day when he popped them into the portable tape recorder and played them for somebody. The one thing you never did growing up in Donegal (unless you were a half-wit) was to invite people to take the piss. I could only imagine how a conversation like that would go:

Me: "Lads, did I tell you that my auld fella is a songwriter now?"
Lads: "What was he before?"
Me: "Well, a farmer, I suppose."
Lads: "What songs has he written?"
Me: "You wouldn't have heard of them yet, but one is called 'The Grass is Greener in Donegal.'"
Lads: "Who sings it, then?"
Me: "Eugene Friel. He has a farm outside of Malin Town. The auld fella writes the words and Eugene puts music to them."
Lads: "So, what you are saying is that those two old farmers think they are Lennon and McCartney? Oh, wait a minute—I think I heard one of your auld fella's songs playing on the radio: 'Shite is Brown in the County Down.'"

No good could have come from me talking about the auld fella writing songs. Sooner or later, someone was bound to get punched in the face.

Second, even if my schoolmates did not think it was hilarious that my father was writing songs, what positive impact could they possibly have? Hardly any of them would have had the money to buy records, and even if they did, they would have wanted to listen to popular groups such as Status Quo, Queen, David Bowie, The Rolling Stones, or Thin Lizzy.

I hoped that he would not come up with the idea of me bringing his tape recorder into school and charging ten pence to listen to Eugene Friel singing "The Grass is Greener in Donegal" (sung to the tune of "The Wild Colonial Boy"). I am afraid that I didn't have much faith in his chances of ever becoming a famous songwriter. Still, that didn't stop him from quizzing me about how many fellow classmates I had told about his songs every day when I came home from school. I felt like some kind of missionary, sent out to the jungles of Africa, in order to spread the good word: "Sean O has risen (at about 10:30 in the morning); Sean O has written; Sean O will write again."

"So then, how many did you tell today?" he would ask me as soon as I walked in the door.

"I don't rightly remember. I sort of lost count."

"One or two, three or four?"

"Yeah, maybe around four."

"What did they say?" Was he fucking serious? I wanted so badly to shout out, *"They didn't give a shite!"* I thought back to when I was young and he would tell the neighbors that I, his own son, would never amount to anything. It made me feel like telling him that he was mad in the fucking head, that his songs would never amount to fuck all. But I fought back the urge. He sat there waiting for a reply.

"They said, 'Is that right?'" I knew that he did not like answers that kept him guessing. That was a good way to mess with him without him catching on.

"Is that right?" he mumbled to himself a couple of times.

His interrogations bothered me most on Fridays. The last thing I needed on meat-courier Fridays, after lugging a big bag of bloody meat around the school for several hours and then down the lane for a mile and a half after getting off the bus, was to be quizzed by the Song-Writing Stormtrooper. It made it all the worse knowing that he had sat around on his arse all day.

At the risk of sounding too harsh on the auld fella, it must be remembered that he was a fair old piece of work in his day. Unfortunately for me, "his day" was when I was at my most vulnerable. They say that old people usually mellow in their old age, and the Big Yank did show signs of being less violent after he got our mother pregnant for the fifth time (his banjaxed leg didn't seem to hold him back in that department). The fact that the last two children they'd had were both girls may have helped to soften him up a bit. Of course, more mouths to feed meant that there would be even less on the table come dinnertime.

As our baby sister joined us on the farm, the second-hand black-and-white telly I had bought (with the money made from giving donkey rides and stealing from the uncle's pockets) just about gave up its ghost. The picture tube must have been going on it, since you couldn't see anything on the screen during the day and only faint pictures at nighttime. It got so bad, in fact, that my brothers and I resorted to watching it from under a blanket, which we threw over the telly and our three heads. Now that we had become somewhat hooked on it, the idea of going without a television was not a pleasant thought.

The television didn't start acting up as a result of us abusing it, either. It was not like we were watching it nonstop. With only two stations, we got to watch television for a couple of hours in the evening on a school night, and just a bit longer on Friday nights and Saturdays.

We had heard about someone getting a color television, which seemed like the most incredible thing we could imagine. We had to imagine it, of course, as we had never actually seen one.

There was also no way that we would ever be able to afford one. Since they had just come out new, we would not be able to buy one second-hand anytime soon. The idea of a color television got me to thinking: Why not just turn our black-and-white into color?

"What do you think about having a color telly?" I asked Jimmy one Saturday morning after I had finished milking the cow.

"Are we getting one?"

"Well, we can't afford to buy one, but I have an idea how we could make one."

"How?"

"The Pattersons brought over a bottle of Lucozade when they visited last week and the bottle should still be out in the scullery. We will peel the orange plastic paper off the bottle and Sellotape it to the top half of the telly."

"Then we'll have a color telly?"

"Not exactly," I told him, "because everything will just be orange, but the next time we get sweets that are wrapped in purple or blue plastic paper, we'll save up the wrappers and then tape them to another part of the screen. When the whole screen is covered, we'll be able to watch everything in color."

"We could use tin foil for silver color," he added. That was the trouble with my brother. You'd try to have a sensible conversation with him, but sooner or later he would come out with something that made him sound like a total eejit.

"Tin foil?" I asked him. "What kind of an amadan would put tin foil on their television screen? How in the name of Jesus are you going to be able to see through tin foil? Are you going to poke holes in it?" I went out through the kitchen and found the empty bottle of Lucozade. I carefully removed the plastic wrapper and located a small roll of Sellotape on the mantelpiece. I had the materials needed to turn a black and white telly into a color one. Well, an orange one, anyway.

"All right, now you stretch out the Lucozade paper as tight as you can and I'll tape it to the sides of the box. Mind you don't tear it, though, as we'll need to tape over the tear and that will probably make that area harder to see." By the sound of it, you'd have thought I had been converting television screens all my life. I taped the ends nice and tight. It didn't look half bad.

"Now for the big test," I told him, turning it on.

"What will we watch?"

"Sure, it doesn't matter. Whatever comes on will now have color to it." As it so happened, an old Western film was on. I knew, once I saw it, that the color was a big mistake. It was hard enough to see before, but now that I had added another layer of plastic over the screen, you had to put your face about three inches from the television to make anything out. I wasn't about to admit my mistake, though.

"I can hardly see a thing," Jimmy complained.

"What do you mean?" I asked him, "Sure there's a horse and a cowboy. Obviously it's a Western." He stuck his face closer to the screen.

"I've never seen an orange horse before," he mumbled. I briefly thought about punching him in the head, but I knew he was right, and me acting like the auld fella would fix nothing.

"Wait until we save up the sweet wrappers and we can add blue, purple, and green," I told him. "Then we'll be like those rich people who get to watch their color television."

There weren't a lot of ways to make money in North Donegal at age 15. Giving donkey rides was definitely successful, but it half killed me that summer, and I don't think it made the donkey any too happy either. Asking my parents for the money was never an option, and since I was too young to drive (and didn't know how to, anyway), it was next to impossible to travel anywhere to find some paying work.

Around this time I heard some lads at school talking about how they were joining the Army Reserve for a couple of weeks in the summer and getting a lot of money to train at Finner Camp in Bundoran. The reserve unit was called the FCA. Apparently recruits completed the same training as full-time soldiers did, but only for two weeks, and every now and again they had to report for a weekend of drill. It was said to pay something like sixty pounds for the two weeks, which I considered to be a small bloody fortune. Some of the boys from town whose parents had good jobs or owned businesses looked down their noses at those of us who joined the FCA, which they called the "Free Clothes

Association." I would soon be 16, and while normally one needed to be 18 to join, I heard that could be waived if my parents signed some forms. There were even stories of 15-year-olds getting in.

I figured that my parents would not have any problem signing the forms, as it was a win-win proposition for them. First, I would be away from home for two weeks, so that was two weeks less food they would have to put out. Second, I would make money which I could use to buy my own school clothes (they probably did not know about our plans to replace the old telly). I was quite sure, as well, that there would also be a "third." That would be the fact that my father would most likely ask to "borrow" a portion of the sixty pounds for something like car insurance, road tax, or something else he should have been providing himself. I also knew only too well that it would never be paid back.

By the time July and the training camp weekend rolled around, I was chomping at the bit to make my escape. I wasn't even sure which excited me the most— making money or firing guns. My parents loaded everyone into the Ford Cortina and drove to the Diamond in Carn, where I planned to catch a bus down to Bundoran. I didn't even look back at them as I made my way to the bus. The last thing the auld fella said to me was, "Don't forget to tell them about my songs!" We were becoming trained killers, and he expected me to sit around in the evening telling them about his songs?

The two weeks away from home absolutely flew by. By day we learned to shoot rifles, throw (dummy) grenades, and even fire an RPG-type rifle. After we had the evening tea at the base, we'd jump into our civilian clothes and walk the mile into town to check out the girls. Bundoran was a fairly tough town, and the locals didn't like the soldiers who were based there or the part-timers like us who came to train. They'd often throw out dirty comments as you passed them on the street, and we learned to always go places in bunches. I didn't care, though. For two weeks

I got to fire guns, eat regular meals, and never once did I have to milk a poxy cow.

When I returned home, I felt like an explorer who had conquered a new world. I didn't mind the fact that I had to thumb a lift out from Carn or walk down the long road to get to the farm. I saw something I wasn't expecting when I turned down our lane: a sign had been erected atop the ditch by the gatepost declaring that the farm's name was now "Melody Farm." Melody fucking Farm. I wondered if that meant I could go around whistling tunes and practice dance moves instead of milking cows and shoveling shite. Wouldn't that be lovely? Somehow or other, I had a strong feeling in my water that nothing was going to change for me.

Yet something *did* change during those two weeks. I had no doubt now that my life would amount to much more than shoveling shite on a farm. I think the auld fella saw the change, too, as he never again asked me to spread the word about his songs. The strange thing was, I kind of missed him not asking. It was nearly as if he had lost faith in me—which was ironic as all hell, since through all of the years of him bad-mouthing me he never seemed to have an ounce of faith in me anyway.

I still tagged along with himself and Jimmy when they went to the Lilac Ballroom, though. Fifty pence was nothing to be taken lightly. I even tried to convince myself that if I picked up a bird and she offered me a lift, I would tell the auld fella that I was all right and that he should carry on without me.

In my head it sounded reasonable, but I knew it would be a different story when it came to saying it for real.

CHAPTER 28

DREAMS, WHAT DREAMS?

After repeating second year and changing schools, I began putting a bit more effort into my studies. It wasn't that I was becoming some kind of great scholar, but the idea of spending the future out standing in my father's fields did not appeal to me. Ireland may have once been referred to as "the Island of Saints and Scholars," but she earned that reputation without any help from me. I did just enough to get by.

For me, school was like a prisoner's work-release program. I didn't really want to be there, but it was sure as hell better than 24-hour-a-day incarceration with the jailers. I went there to have a laugh with the lads, ogle the girls, and, of course, bring home the meat every Friday. I never gave much thought to how smart or dumb I was. The fact that I could coast most of the year, entertaining my classmates, while still passing exams (the Group Cert being the exception), was a fair indication that I could have achieved far greater results had I taken school seriously.

The '75 Inter Cert results showed that I was making a bit of progress. I not only passed it, but got a few honors as well. Even though I was taking three honors classes, I surprised myself by actually getting all three. The surprise was mainly due to the fact that I had started studying only two weeks before the exams started. This was the first year that the Tech and Carndonagh College merged into a new school. Apart from having a brand new school building, the merger meant that we got to turn our attention to a whole new class of female. They were women—not girls—taking a new secretarial course being offered by the school, with ages ranging from 19 to early 20s. We discovered that they were mostly from Buncrana and Derry—a fact that explained their beauty. They were fully-developed in every sense of the word.

I don't know if they were made to do it, but they always went to lunch as a group. Even if we didn't see them go out, we made sure to be there when they came back. We would take up spots in the very middle of the school's common area, and the women would have to pass right by us to access their room. When these girls walked by us, it was as if time slowed; they seemed to strut past in slow motion. We all stood frozen in place, hoping for a sideways glimpse or a bit of a smile as they graced us with their presence.

I thought I was the only one who breathed in deep through my nose as they floated by, in order to catch a lungful of their womanly perfumes, but I soon found out that everyone else was doing the same thing. Long hair, perfect arses, and breasts that cried out "Come squeeze me!" captivated our teenaged hearts and minds at the end of every lunch break. It must have been obvious, too—I am sure we were all glued to the spot with our jaws hanging open. I can't say for certain how any of us looked, of course, as I never took my eyes off those women until the last gorgeous arse disappeared into the classroom. I often wondered what businesses they would wind up working for. Whoever it was would have the sexiest secretaries in Ireland.

⊷⊷ ⊶⊶

Now that the Inter Cert was behind me, I was able to drop the subjects in fourth year that I did not care about and concentrate on those remaining for the last two years. This was life or death, since the grades you achieved in the "Leaving" would determine what you would most likely do for the rest of your life. I would like to say that this realization changed me, and the way in which I applied myself, in the most important school years of my life so far, but that would be a gross exaggeration. I was, in fact, even more reckless than in previous years.

The first two subjects I decided to change were French and Latin. Two years of Latin did nothing to convince me that the language had any merit in the 20th century. I found it about as exciting as shoveling shite out of the cow barn. I did like French, and would have continued it for the Leaving, but my first year of French at the Tech had not prepared me for the much higher standards of the College. After three years, I was still trying to play catch-up.

I liked languages, however, and was not prepared to go from learning four (English, Irish, French, and Latin) to just two. Well, there was that *plus* the fact that I discovered that the Spanish teacher was an absolutely gorgeous bird. I looked into it and discovered that I was allowed to take Spanish during my two final years. I actually enjoyed the Spanish class, but I enjoyed imagining all the things I could be doing with my teacher more. The pièce de résistance was my discovery that I was the only male student in the whole class. The class was made up of me and twenty-one female students (some of whom were not half-bad). I am glad to say that the teacher took a shine to her only male student and from day one christened me "Juan." I am also happy to report that Juan could do no wrong—even when I was caught day dreaming, or when it was discovered that I had not completed a homework assignment.

Word eventually leaked out that I had the entire female population of fourth-year Spanish class to myself.

"How did you manage that, you jammy bastard?" asked Kieran McCullough.

"It's not what you know, but *who* you know," I replied smugly.

"That was some fucking coup you pulled there," wee Danny Doherty informed me. "Not only have you all the birds to yourself, but their teacher is a right ride."

"Of course she is," I replied. "Sure, isn't she a Derry woman? I reckon there are better rides in Derry than the rest of Ireland combined." With the languages out of the way, I set my sights on deciding which other classes I needed to drop and which could be salvaged. I enjoyed science, but since it was being broken up into chemistry, biology, and physics, I decided that I needed to drop the one which was the most taxing on my brain. That, of course, would be physics. There was no way I was going to have any craic if I had to concentrate on getting a passing grade in physics. Chemistry and biology were a piece of cake in comparison.

Next, I swapped out geography for art; I didn't see too much relevance in geography anyway. We lived on a small island in the middle of the Atlantic Ocean. The rest of the world didn't seem to want to get involved with us, apart from the tourists who came to visit Ireland in the summer. I figured that those who couldn't find work in Ireland would get jobs in America, Australia, or God-between-us-and-all-harm; England. So why was it important to know about all of those other countries?

There was no room for boredom in my school life, so even if I had a fondness for a subject, it needed to be cut from the team if it was taught by a boring teacher. This led to my dropping history. History was taught by the most boring bastard ever to tie a pair of shoes. Mr. Kearney was very knowledgeable about all things historical, but he didn't have a clue as to how to make them interesting. I daydreamed more in his class than any other. When he would teach about a centuries-old war, I would picture myself in that war, fighting for whoever was the underdog. I swung a curved sword during skirmishes in the Ottoman Empire. I pushed through the crowd on the bridge in Sarajevo, looking for the assassin of Prince Ferdinand, who kicked off the First World War. Unfortunately, my daydreaming didn't do much to help me get a good grade come exam time, so history and its boring pre-senter had to bite the bullet.

⊨⊰ ⊱⊨

At least passing the Inter Cert did give me the courage to push my luck and try to get the auld fella to give me driving lessons in the car. It wasn't that I was in a mad rush to drive anywhere, but I had heard Jimmy talking about how our father was going to teach him to drive. I figured that I should be getting lessons first, as I was three years older than him. Besides, he couldn't even apply for a provisional license yet. I dropped a few hints around my mother that it was about time I learned how to drive. I figured that I would stand a better chance if she pleaded my case to the big judge. Eventually he got the hint and, after a few weeks, told me that I could apply for a provisional license and he would teach me driving.

Apart from the odd goat or pig slaughter, there wasn't much excitement on the farm, so the possibility of being able to drive was a huge deal. The timing was just about perfect, as I would have money in my pocket after coming back from the two weeks' training in the FCA. I could see that hurdle a mile away—the old man telling me that we couldn't afford petrol for the lessons— and knew that if I gave him a pound for petrol, he wouldn't have any excuse.

Now, if you could have seen the cut of our car, you'd be asking yourself how any young fella could get excited at the thought of driving it. It had to be at least fifteen years old, which would have been perfectly fine had it been a classic, or even been looked after properly. Neither of these categories applied to the auld fella's Mark II Cortina.

I don't know what the mechanics of the car were like. I'm thinking they were not good overall, since it broke down often, but the worst part was the driver's floor. Basically, there was no floor. More than half of it was rotted out and had been replaced by a giant, gaping hole. My mother flat-out refused to drive it, as she was afraid that she would fall through the floor someday. The auld fella's solution was to jam a flattened-out biscuit tin lid into the hole and drive around like that. He didn't even bother to solder or weld the tin lid into the hole; he just jammed it in and put his feet on top of it. Then again, I suppose there wasn't much chance of his gigantic feet falling through the hole.

Whenever it rained (which was about six and a half days of every week), the rainwater from the road would shoot up through the hole and wet feet and legs. I used to wonder if he felt it in both legs. Since he had multiple sclerosis and dragged one leg behind him, I figured that there was a good chance he wouldn't know when that leg was wet unless he examined his trousers. It must have been like his leg was asleep all the time.

I decided that I would wear my Wellington boots whenever I got a lesson. Holes aside, wet feet seemed a small price to pay for learning how to drive a car.

I was proud as punch the day I got my provisional license. It was the first real sign that I was ready for the outside world. It was as if I could see light at the end of the tunnel—and for the first time, it wasn't just a train coming the other way. I now had an official government document that gave me the right to drive on the road. I wanted to frame it and put it up on the wall.

I wasn't looking for much. I didn't need to learn how to drive on Route 66 or the Autobahn, and I certainly didn't need a fancy car. A car with big gaping holes in the floorboard would do just fine. The only thing I needed was a driving instructor, and that was a done deal, since the auld fella had said himself that he would teach me.

I am not sure which days of the week are best for driving lessons, but when it came to mine, the auld fella couldn't seem to decide which day would work. When it rained, it was too wet and would probably annoy his one good leg (though this had never seemed to bother him in the past). When it was dry, he had more important things to do that could not get done in the rain. I never discovered what those things were, as I was under the impression that I was the one doing all the work, no matter what the weather was like.

I came back from Finner Army Camp with a load of money in my pocket (well, it wasn't actually in my pocket. Living with my parents and brothers was kind of like living with a bunch of pirates. To be sure of keeping my possessions, I buried them.) It was enough to pay for petrol for my lessons, but that didn't seem to matter. The days turned into weeks, and the weeks into months, and I still had not gotten a single lesson. Apart from being kept in this limbo state of driving deprivation, the worst part was the fact that my provisional license would expire after six months. Five months had already slipped by, and not once had my father made an attempt to take me out for even a half hour in his miserable rust bucket of a car.

Why in the name of sweet Jesus did he tell me to apply for the provisional and that he would teach me? I wondered bitterly. He knew the rules. He knew that the provisional was good only for six months. Even if he had had a change of heart and decided to make up for lost time, there was no chance that I could learn how to drive a car and pass my road test in four weeks. I felt more than let down. I felt betrayed. I busted my arse on that farm everyday doing a man's job—*his* job, for fuck's sake.

My mother was not much help when I told her the provisional license had expired. "So why didn't you ask your father to take you out in the car?"

"You make it sound like he didn't know all along that I was waiting for him. Sure, wasn't he sitting right there at the head of the kitchen table when I opened up my new provisional license and showed it to all of youns?"

"That's between the two of you, then. You know I won't drive that car for fear that I may fall through the floor."

"I wish he could fall through the fucking floor," I shot back.

She didn't appreciate my remark. "That's no way to speak about your father. You know that he has a lot on his mind. Anyway, why are you in such a hurry to drive? It's not like you have anywhere to go."

"I'm not staying around here to be a farm worker all of my life."

"So, you're too good for the farm now, is that it?"

"Milking cows and shoveling shite is not my calling. There are other things I want to do."

"Well, I don't know what your 'calling' would be. I haven't seen any sign of you being fit to do anything other than milk cows and cut turf."

"I want to be a writer. I want to go to the journalism college in Dublin and write for a living. Now you know."

"A writer? More like a comedian. What would you know about writing? There's only one writer in this house, and that's your father."

"Jesus, has he brainwashed you as well? Do you really think the auld fella can write anything worth a shite? When have you heard any of his songs on the radio?"

"It's only a matter of time before they are playing on the radio. He has given songs to half of the bands in Ireland. Sean O will be big one day; you wait and see."

Jesus, the lunatics had taken over the asylum. I didn't bother my bollix answering back. It sounded more like she was trying to convince herself than me. I had a father who couldn't be bothered spending a half hour with me once in six months and a mother who thought that the sun, moon, and stars shone out of his arse. I had really hit the jackpot with these two.

Why couldn't I have been like Tarzan and raised by apes? Even a pack of wolves would have taken more interest in raising me. I promised myself that one day I would escape and learn everything I needed to know about life. I could skip the pig and goat killing bits. What I really needed to know was how to drive.

CHAPTER 29
SON ON THE RUN

I began fourth year at Carndonagh Community College with the intention of enjoying myself as much as possible. As a matter of fact, I secretly dedicated it "The Year of Craic." Though most of my other schoolmates were preparing to take the Leaving Cert in two years' time, I figured that I could have fun in fourth year and then get serious in the final year. As far as I was concerned, I was being fierce conservative altogether. My usual *Modus Operandi* (I suppose that Latin did have its uses) was to begin studying for exams two weeks in advance. By that reckoning, a whole year of study should give me perfect scholarly results.

As I concentrated on how best to amuse myself during the year, my mother dedicated her time to steering me toward a job. "Steering" was putting it mildly. It was more like she was fixated on getting me out of the house and off the list of mouths to be fed.

"Have you given any more thought to what you want to do when you leave school?" she would ask, repeatedly, at any given time of the day or night.

I had long since given up on telling her what I really wanted to do. She had no time for any idea that involved creativity. She was focused on finding me a job that I would have for life, one that would allow me to retire after punching in my thirty years.

"If I could get enough points in my Leaving to win a scholarship, I would like to study law. There's a new course starting next year at the Regional College in Letterkenny called the Legal Executive Course."

She gave a sarcastic chuckle. "*You* get a scholarship? Are you daft? Sure, you only ever scrape a passing grade in your exams at the best of times. You'd better get your head out of the clouds and realize that you'll be damned lucky to get any kind of a job."

Good old dream-crushing Sarah. She could always be relied upon to bring a body down. I should have learned my lesson long ago. I had no business telling her my innermost dreams.

"What you need to do," she continued, "is get a respectable job in the bank like Master McDonagh's son. You'll have a steady paycheck guaranteed for thirty years and a low rate mortgage for a house. If you keep your nose clean and tend to your job, you might even get promoted to manager one day before you retire."

I was forced to listen to her vision of me becoming a bank teller for months on end. She had no interest in what I wanted, but my joining the bank would serve two purposes for her. First, I would have a job that paid enough for me to get a flat, which meant that she would no longer have to feed me. Second, it would bring "respectability" to the family. She would be able to hold her head high around the village if she had a son who was a bank official.

After a few months of listening to her rant and rave about how wonderful it would be to have me working in a bank, I couldn't take anymore. I probably should not have let her know how I really felt, or perhaps should have tried to explain it in a more reasonable manner, but I couldn't help myself. I let her have it with both barrels.

"You want me to work in a bank, is that right?" I asked her one Saturday afternoon as she pushed her weekly bank-brainwashing routine on me.

"You want me to get a job that is respectable? One that will make all your neighbors look up to you? Is that it?" I continued.

I could see a light flickering in her eyes and the faint trace of a smile on her lips. She must have thought that she had broken me, and that I was finally ready to give in and do what she had decided I should do.

"I'll tell you what will happen if I took a job in the bank to make you happy." We were locked on each other—her anticipating that she was going to be the mother of a bank official, which in turn would give her a leg up in the community and me getting ready to launch the nuclear warhead that I had been holding back for months.

"If I went to work for a bank, handling other peoples' money, day after day, working with boring fucking bankers, wearing boring fucking suits, for the rest of my life—I'd go mental.

"No, wait, even worse. I believe that one day I would crack and rob the fucking bank. That's right, I'd scoop up as much money as I could and I would go on the run. I wonder what your neighbors would think of you having a bank robber for a son?"

"You...wouldn't...couldn't...do that," she stammered. "Sure, the police would think you were in the IRA. They're the ones robbing banks and post offices these days."

"I could, and I would. As a matter of fact, you just gave me a good idea. As I ran out of the bank with a bulging sack of money, I would shout out to my ex-coworkers, 'Up the Republic and the Provisional IRA!'"

She looked like she had seen a ghost. I, on the other hand, was wound up tight as a Swiss clock. I actually got a thrill out of the thought of going to work in a bank and then robbing it just to annoy her.

"You'd get caught and locked up for the rest of your life."

"I don't give a shite. I'd head to Brazil like Ronnie Biggs and live the rest of my life on the run in the sun. Even if I didn't get that far, I dare say I would have plenty of peace in Portlaoise prison, with no one to annoy my arse trying to get me to work in a poxy *bank* for the rest of my life."

There was pure silence. I was waiting for a screaming retort, but she had nothing. I must have been fairly convincing. Actually, I was not acting in the least. The thought of being stuck in a bank for thirty years seemed like a jail sentence to me, and if I went along with her choice of employment, I had a feeling it would not end well. Having a son who might get locked up for bank robbing and being a member of the Provisional IRA had a mellowing effect on my mother's quest for finding me a respectable position. She certainly never mentioned me going to work for a bank again, or proposed any idea that would involve me working in any kind of financial institution.

I figured it was just as well. After all, I had picked up some bad habits when I was the chief cashier for the auld fella's canteen and when I collected money as his horse conductor. I think I would be tempted to skim off a little commission each day in the bank. They would hardly miss a few pounds here and there.

I likened it to working in a sweet shop. You could hardly be expected to work around sweets all day without dipping in every now and again. Sure, that would be nothing more than a fringe benefit.

It now seemed that I could fairly much plan out my own future. Not that this meant I would be assured of getting my first career choice, by any means. We had had a Careers Day in the school at the start of fourth year, run by Father Logan. He had a little room where you could go in and pick out blue government pamphlets for each career choice. The pamphlets provided basic information about what each job entailed, be it nursing, teaching, engineering, etc. If you wanted to know more, you would then ask Father Logan, as he was the careers counselor.

Being the inquisitive sort, I did wonder how a priest would know about all the jobs out there. Now, if you had it in your mind to join the priesthood, and you wanted to know what to expect before taking the plunge, then no doubt he would be your man, but he couldn't have known much about anything else.

"What advice can you give me about becoming a journalist, Father?" I asked when it was my turn.

"I would say that it would be quite difficult to get into," he said, "as there is only one school of journalism in Ireland, down in Dublin."

"Then it is like other professions, where the better you do in the Leaving, the higher chance you have of being accepted?"

"Yes, I suppose that would be the case, but I believe they only accept about a dozen or so new students every year. Do you have any journalists in your family?"

I could feel the dream of writing for a living slipping through my fingers. It sounded as if having a connection to writers might give me a better chance of getting accepted at the journalism school. I didn't like the idea that was swirling around inside my head, straw-like. Should I grasp at it or just give up?

"My father is a writer." There. I said it. It was too late to take it back. The cat was out of the bag now, and there wasn't much to do but to see how it would all play out.

"Interesting."

I didn't know what that meant. Was it good or bad? The suspense was doing my head in.

"Does he write for one of the local papers?"

Now I realized that I had really made a mistake. I didn't know how he would react if I told him he wrote songs for showbands and banged on the back door of the Lilac Ballroom to come in and peddle his wares. I briefly considered lying and telling him that he wrote for the *Derry Journal.*

"Ah no, he actually writes songs."

"I see."

Fuck me. He was at it again. What did that mean?

"I believe that most of those who are accepted into the School of Journalism each year actually come from families where the father is the editor of a regional or national newspaper."

Good old Ireland. If you wanted to vote or get a decent job, you had better follow in your auld fella's footsteps. That was all well and good for those whose fathers paved the way before them, but what about the rest of us poor hoors? What if you had a head case for a father? What then? Then you were totally fucked.

"If you like to write and you think you'll have a good Leaving Cert result, why don't you consider becoming a teacher?"

I knew the answer to that one. The auld fella had actually attempted to recruit me into the field of teaching the year before, ordering me to tutor my brother Jimmy, who was having a difficult time with school. I don't know why he suddenly thought I was capable of becoming a teacher, but apparently that was to be one of my new after-school roles. It was just a little something to throw in there to kill time in between busting my balls on the farm. I suppose they figured that I was bored with so much free time on my hands.

One thing that this temporary, unpaid tutoring position taught me was that one needed to have all kinds of patience to be a teacher. When my brother could not understand what I was trying to teach him, I shouted it at him. Saying it louder didn't help one bit. It didn't take long for him to get frustrated and stop listening to me, at which point I would respond by giving him a clip alongside of his head. I could hardly be blamed for turning to violence, as that is the way my first teacher in Ireland handled situations of disobedience or laziness. The clip only made matters worse, though; he normally swung back, and next thing you knew we were slugging it out. I didn't think I was cut out for teaching.

"No offense, Father, but I don't really see myself as a teacher. If there is not much hope for me becoming a journalist, I think I'd like to study law."

"That is a good choice," he agreed, "but you will have to have a good few honors in the Leaving, as it takes a lot of points to get a law scholarship."

"I'm taking only three honors," I informed him, "and that would not be enough to get a place in Trinity or UCD. There is supposed to be a new course in Letterkenny Regional College called the Legal Executive Course that allows you to become an apprentice with a law firm after two years. Then you can eventually sit the exams to become a qualified solicitor."

"Well, it certainly sounds like you have done your homework," said the priest with a smile. "I am sure you will do just fine, and the best of luck getting into that new course. By the way, I believe that it is only being held in Letterkenny, so you will be competing against students from all over Ireland."

Jesus Christ, why did I always have to set my sights on getting accepted somewhere that would be a huge fucking challenge? I couldn't help but think that I was setting myself up to fail, and I was full sure that when I did, Doomsday Sarah would be there with her commentary.

⚓ ⚓

I decided that, as third-level education was not right around the corner at the moment, I might as well focus on having the craic. Mind you, though, I was not always fully aware that I even *was* having the craic. Take, for example, the time that I decided to walk on top of the bridge instead of along the footpath after returning from my lunch hour uptown. I don't know what kind of mental notion I took, but I decided that it would be fierce fun to mount the bridge railings, which were only about a foot and a half wide, in order to cross the bridge, holding my arms out horizontally like a tightrope walker. Getting across safely without plunging thirty feet or more into the river was by no means a safe bet. The other hairy part was the fact that when you did the high-wire act over the Carn River, you exposed yourself for the entire world to see.

I will never forget this last performance. There I was with my arms extended out to each side, gingerly placing one foot in front of the other and trying to ignore the swollen river, which raged below on my immediate right. I had just looked up to see how much further I had to go to reach safety when my eyes locked on to the head honcho of Carndonagh Community College, Father Peter McDermott.

Big Peter, as we referred to him, drove a wee mini car, and his six-foot-three-inch, seventeen-stone frame filled every inch. He seemed to have his face plastered up against the front wind-shield, and I had no doubt that he saw me as clear as a bell. He looked a little shocked that I would pull such a daredevil stunt right in his face. Not that there was any law against walking on top of a bridge. It's just that it was not something normally done by sane individuals. I had actually been enjoying the stunt before Big Peter drove by. I climbed down off the bridge when I reached the end and sauntered back to Carndonagh College without giving much more thought to the big fella in the wee car.

Every summer before school finished, we had a sports day. It was a bit like the Fifteenth of August in Malin Head, except that there was no tobacco juice getting spat in anybody's ears. There were always those who would win multiple medals, but most of us competed in only one or two events. During the summer of '76, I decided that I would create my own category. Sponsored events were the norm—sponsored walks, sponsored fasts, sponsored anything. I decided that I would seek sponsorships from my fellow students to streak across the sports field naked on the last day of school.

Word of my sponsored streak started to spread like wildfire. I soon realized that I was going to need support to make the streak a reality. I didn't nominate any popular charity to receive the money collected, as I figured that I was as deserving a charity as any. Also, if things turned out badly, I might need all the help I could get to start a new life in an undisclosed location. All of the girls in fourth-year Spanish were behind me—so much so, in fact, that they created actual sponsorship cards and volunteered to distribute them around the school. This thing was taking on a life of its own. Students I didn't even know were approaching me in the halls and asking me if I was really going to streak.

One week before the sports day was scheduled to take place, I walked into Spanish class, feeling like a celebrity. Just as class began, Big Peter's secretary came on the intercom and announced that I was to report to the office. My heart sank. I had no idea why I was being summoned but knew it could not be good. The class was silent as I left. I presented myself in front of the secretary, who picked up the phone and spoke softly to the person on the other end.

"Father McDermott will see you now," she informed me. I knocked on the big priest's door and entered. He was standing ramrod tall in front of his desk. His black cassock made him look even bigger, since it draped all the way from his neck to the tops of his shoes.

"What are you playing at?" he roared at me. Jesus, I had never been roared at by a man in a dress before. I didn't know what to say.

"You don't have much to say now, do you?" he roared again. He was right. I couldn't think of anything to say under these circumstances. I thought about asking him why I was there, but figured that might drive him totally mental altogether.

"You have one more year left here," the man in black informed me. "For that year, I don't want to hear about you organizing sponsored streaks, walking on top of bridges, robbing orchards, or taking part in any other prohibited activities. Do I make myself clear?"

I would have needed to have my head examined if I did anything other than agree with him at that stage. "Yes, sir...Father... Father Sir." I was confused as all hell.

"Get out of here and get back to your class," he ordered. I didn't have to be told twice. I was glad that my knees had held up during the interrogation, as they had begun shaking the moment I walked into Big Peter's office. All the girls looked up from their books when I walked back into class. Even Ms. Harkin seemed interested in knowing what had happened.

"Everything all right, Juan?" she asked me. I couldn't bring myself to speak just yet, so I nodded as I walked to my seat at the back of the room. "Is the sponsored streak still going ahead?" Jesus, the whole school must have known about it— even the bloody teachers knew. Although I was shocked by Peter's outburst and the fact that our Spanish teacher knew my plans, I was glad to see that Ms. Harkin had a small smile on her face. As soon as the class ended, the girls turned around in their seats and started to quiz me on what had taken place in the office.

"You looked white as a sheet when you walked in, so you did," Siobhain Farren informed me.

"What did they say to you?" asked Marjorie McCullough.

"Big Peter tore into me," I shared. "Told me that he'd beat me to within an inch of my life if I went ahead with the sponsored streak."

"What will you do now?" one of them asked.

"What can I do? Sure, I have no choice but to cancel the streak."

"Ah, you can't do that," a couple of them complained.

"How can I not?" I asked them. "Have any of youns ever stood in front of that big hoor in the black dress when he was threatening to knock your block off? If I streak across the field after getting that warning, I had better keep running, as there is not going to be any safe spot left in Ireland for me. I wonder, do priests down here have authority across the border?"

Collette O'Neill, a fiery-looking redhead, stared at me as I tried to soften the streak-cancellation blow to the rest of the girls.

"Do you know how much work we put into getting sponsorships for you?" she asked me forcefully, in a manner that would have made Big Peter proud.

"I know youns have worked fierce hard at it." What else could I say?

"We have made up 200 sponsorship cards by hand and raised nearly ninety pounds so far. My own mommy gave fifty pence out of this month's children's allowance money, and *she* won't even be there to see it."

I was kind of glad to hear that Mrs. O'Neill wouldn't be seeing me buck-arse naked, but I was flabbergasted that they had raised that amount of money. Maybe doing it and then going on the run would not be such a bad idea after all. I figured that ninety pounds (and even more by the time the day came around, as it was still nearly a fortnight away) was bound to last a brave wee while across in the six counties.

"Jesus, youns have done fierce well getting that amount of sponsorship money. How much more do you think you can raise between now and the sports day?"

"We'd raise a good bit more," Collette continued in her self-appointed role as spokeswoman for the fourth-year Spanish class, "but it's not just about the money. You could even donate that to charity. Hundreds of students are looking forward to seeing you streak. If you don't, then you will be letting down a lot of people."

Donate the money to charity? Ah, come here, there was no need to go that far. I had heard it said that God helps those who help themselves. I needed all the help I could get, so I surely didn't want to go vexing God by not following His rules. Besides, it was going to take money to go on the run. It would be a full-time job. It wasn't like you could do it for a week or two and then decide to go back to your normal way of life, hoping that everyone would have forgotten why you disappeared in the first place.

"I'm very grateful for everything you girls have done," I assured them, "but I had no idea that the whole bloody school—and probably half of Inishowen—would get wind of this streaking business. If I go ahead and do it after getting a formal warning, there is no telling what might happen. I know damned well that Peter will throw me out of school. When that happens, my parents will most likely kick me out of the house, and I'll be homeless. Streaking would be great craic for a few minutes of entertainment, but how am I going to live without a job—since I won't have a Leaving Cert—or any place to lay my head? How long would ninety pounds—even though it is a small fortune—last me?"

I was hoping that they would see the seriousness of it all and tell me that they supported my decision to cancel the streak.

"So, you're saying that you'll do it if we can raise more money, then?" asked O'Neill.

"I'll tell you what." They pushed their heads in closer as I lowered my voice. "Go ahead and see how much more you can raise, but do it very secretly. We don't need teachers getting wind that it's still going ahead. And keep your ears open. I'll not guarantee that it will happen, so don't be telling anybody that it is a done deal."

Thoughts were racing through my head. If I could get a mask—maybe a balaclava—and put it on to hide my identity, nobody could prove that it was actually me streaking...unless I was tackled, of course. That was something you saw all of the time on English football pitches. British policemen would rush out onto the field and tackle a streaker, taking him away by force. The British bobbies wore those big helmets that you could hide a small child under, and when they caught their streaker, one of them would always take off their hat and cover the man's mickey with it. They'd always get confused when they had a woman streaker, as they didn't know how to cover everything with one hat. They'd start off on one of her boobs and then switch to the other boob, then sometimes drop it down before bringing it back up to cover a boob again.

What if they had Gardaí at sports day? That would be a sure sign they planned to arrest me. If they caught me, would a Garda cover my mickey with his hat? By the time the day rolled around, word may have reached the RTE or UTV studios, and the television stations might have cameras on hand. What the hell would my mother say if the neighbors saw me on the telly, buck-arse naked, with my mickey covered by a Garda's hat?

Despite the great danger involved and the likelihood of getting caught, I still wanted to do it. I wasn't sure if it was more for the thrill or for the thought of making at least 100 pounds for a few minutes' work. If it was to be done, then it would have to be planned better than it had been up to that point. Using a getaway car might give me the best chance of escape. The obvious problem with that option, though, was that I lacked a car. Even if I knew someone who would be crazy enough to loan me their car and leave it unlocked at the sports field gate with the engine running, I wouldn't know how to drive it away.

Then I got to thinking that I could have someone behind the wheel of the car. As I approached, they'd throw open the passenger door and we'd take off like mad hoors. That was easier said than done, as well. Who would a man get that would be willing to act like a bank robber in a black-and-white gangster film? I figured that Uncle Daniel might be up for the challenge. Somehow or other, I didn't think it would be his first time running from the law. But then again, I was afraid that his Ford Anglia might not have the power to outrun the police all the way across the border into Northern Ireland.

After proposing and then shooting down options, I began having serious doubts about my chances of coming up with a decent escape plan. As much as I hated to admit it, getting caught in the act was becoming more of a reality. Perhaps I needed to think up a defense for getting caught? Ignorance of the law was definitely out of the question. I could see Big Peter in my mind's eye telling the police, "I *told* him that he needed to behave himself and forget any idea he had of streaking. He *knew* he shouldn't do it."

There was always the temporary insanity plea. I thought I could get a long line of people—spearheaded by my own family—to testify that I was not quite right in the head. It would probably work, but maybe too well. Knowing my luck, the hoors would lock me up in a mental asylum and throw away the key. Still, I settled on taking this route in the event that I was caught.

In the meantime, I would plan how to best streak across the crowded field without getting caught. After all, as Collette O'Neill had said, hundreds of students were looking forward to it.

Collette O'Neill. *She* was who I could use as my accomplice. I knew by the look in her eye that she was determined to see me succeed. I would have her wait behind the Colgan Hall with a pair of trousers and a spare shirt. I would then run across the field, in a mask, through a gap in the ditch, and scamper into the clothes. Collette and I would then walk innocently around the wall and back into the field in broad daylight. Anybody who saw us would think that we went for a quick court. If the police investigated the streaking and questioned witnesses, they would be told that the streaker was a tall, thin male (a description which would apply to about fifty percent of all fourth-year boys). He had been wearing a mask, the witnesses would say, and when he ran, his mickey bobbed up and down (or back and forth, depending on your point of view).

I figured that I had an airtight case. Of course I would be the main suspect, but I had a witness (O'Neill), and nobody would expect a girl to be involved in the streaking. The more I thought about it, the more excited I became. Big Peter would blow a gasket, since he would be 100% sure that I was the streaker but wouldn't be able to prove it. The only thing that might have been somewhat identifiable would be my mickey, but I didn't think he would go so far as to order every fourth-year boy on the field to drop their trousers and line up for a mickey inspection.

Then I started to wonder if the police might do that. After all, isn't that what they did when they had criminal suspects and witnesses? They would line up six or seven men and have the witnesses try to pick the bad guy out of the lineup. What if they had witnesses who were girls? Would they really have you stand in a line with your cock hanging out and ask the girls if that looked like the mickey they saw running by them earlier?

I was the first one get up on the morning of sports day. It would have been difficult to smuggle extra clothes in my small book bag, and I couldn't risk anyone in the house seeing me, so I decided to wear two pairs of trousers and two shirts into school. I had gotten a friend to get me a balaclava (ski mask) to hide my face. I didn't ask where he got it, but he went into Derry every weekend, so I assumed it was there. I was glad that he was the one taking it into school, as it would have been very difficult to explain why I had a balaclava in my bag in the middle of summer. The weather may not have been tropical in North Donegal, but there was still no bloody chance of getting snow and freezing winds in June.

Although it was the last day of school before the summer holidays, and lunch had been moved forward by an hour, we still had normal classes up until lunchtime. I don't know if it was the extra clothing or the fact that I was nervous, but I was sweating bullets after the first hour. As soon as the lunch bell rang, I darted into the jacks and pulled off the under layer of clothes. I had brought in a plastic bag to put them inside and quietly pass along to Collette. Seamus McGuinness was waiting to walk uptown with me. When the coast was clear, he would give me the balaclava, which I would stuff into my jeans pocket. He also volunteered to grab the clothes that I planned to throw off just before I ran out of the school and across the field.

As we walked out the front door, we met my Spanish teacher walking in. "Hola, Juan," she said, adding something that sounded like, "Están policia aquí ahora," and raising her eyebrows.

"What did she say to you?" asked McGuinness.

"She told me that there were cops at the school." I had never seen cops at a sports day over the past three years, so I knew they were there for me. It was one thing outrunning a teacher. But if a Garda caught you, you had a serious problem.

"I have to call off the streak, Seamus."

"Do you think they are here for you?"

"I wouldn't put it past Peter. The hoor has no sense of humor whatsoever. I don't fancy whipping out my mickey in a lineup."

He looked at me strangely.

"I won't be needing the balaclava now," I said. "I have too much to do down here. You go on ahead, and I'll stay behind and do damage control."

"Slán, so," he replied, adding, "An Phoblacht abu, Comrade."

My first move would be to break the news to Collette. I wasn't looking forward to that. I figured she would go ballistic when I broke the news.

To my surprise, she took it quite well. "We knew when we saw the blue bottle they were out to get you. Let them watch like hawks this year and waste their time. When they are not expecting anything next year, BAM! We'll streak right past them, shaking our wobbly bits."

"Our?"

"Of course," she said, "next year I am going to streak with you."

Oh God, I thought, *there really is a God.*

CHAPTER 30

AER LINGUS WANTS ME!

My fourth-year summer "holidays" were much like all my other summer holidays, in that they involved even more backbreaking work than the other holidays. Farm machinery was a very rare sight on our farm, as most everything was done by hand. It wasn't done that way due to any kind of romantic notion that the hand was the best machine, or that we wanted to work in sync with Mother Nature. We might have been naturalists, but Woodstock hippies we were not. The fact of the matter was that we could not afford anything that might have made life any easier.

My desire to get as far away from the farm as I possibly could, as soon as I possibly could, was reinforced by every bar of moist turf I cut and every cock of hay I jammed onto the end of a pitchfork. Looking back, I realized that I might have been a little harsh on the land. After all, a small patch of godforsaken land could only do so much. The real culprit and the one that made life unbearable for a small Irish farmer in North Donegal, was the bastarding weather.

Year after year, I would watch the auld fella play Russian roulette with the weather. Come summer (it is quite comical to even use the word "summer," as many a Donegal summer was little more than an early winter), we would wait for a reprieve from the lashing rain, then decide whether the grass was to be cut and saved for hay or if we should wait to see if a "dry spell" may be coming. I think an official dry spell in Ireland was, and still is, two consecutive days without rain.

Of course, I didn't have the luxury of sitting around waiting to see what the weather would do. Turf banks could still be pared and turf cut in damp weather. Backbreaking work was less hateful when the sun was shining, though.

When we got desperate enough, the decision to cut fields of grass would have to be based on a half-decent day. Hay was needed to get us through the winter, no matter how poor the quality. I could not keep track of the number of days and weeks that I worked in acres of hay fields, turning the long grass over (by hand rake, of course) to dry on one side, only to have it rain and set me back to day one. The longer the hay sat out in the fields, and the more it was flipped back and forth to keep it from rotting, the more washed-out and tasteless it became.

The cows, horse, and donkey never complained—the poor bastards had to eat whatever was put in front of them—but I could taste the difference. When the grass was first cut, I could never resist popping a long blade into my mouth, chewing and sucking on the semi-green stalk. By the time it was put into a big winter stack, at the end of a wet summer, it would be grey and brittle. One might as well be chewing on a bristle from a straw broom.

⟫⟨ ⟩⟪

Toward the end of fourth year, I realized it was time to plan my future and my escape. Although I had no reason to believe that I had what it took to make a top-rate pilot, I applied for a pilot's exam when Aer Lingus announced a national hiring campaign.

"So you think you can fly a plane, then?" asked Sarah, like she was some kind of pre-employment screener for Aer Lingus.

"Not at the moment," I said, "but I have a fair idea that they'd train me how to do it."

"Sure, you can't even drive a car."

That really got me going. "No thanks to your husband," I said. "If Aer Lingus hired me, I'd have faith that they would actually give me lessons."

"You'd better mind your tongue and be careful how you speak about your father."

I don't know if they called in everybody to take the exam, but I received an official notice in the mail to attend the Aer Lingus pilot's exam in Dublin a week after school ended for the year. It was to be held on a Saturday morning. Not just any Saturday morning, mind you, but the Saturday morning after our school disco in Redcastle. I had never been to Dublin, and didn't have a bull's notion how to get there or what I would do when I arrived.

Surprisingly, the auld fella actually organized the getting down and back. "Your Uncle Daniel will drive you to the exam this Saturday," he told me. "Youns will have to leave about four in the morning to get there by nine."

Jesus, that was going to be tight. The disco wouldn't be over until two, so it would be nearly three in the morning by the time I'd manage to get a lift back to the house. What if I met a quare one and we had a wee court? In that case, I might not make it in time to leave for Dublin. I should have asked Daniel come to the disco to pick me up and we could have headed straight down.

"I'll be going to our school disco in Redcastle the night before," I informed my father. I watched out of the corner of my eye to see how he would react. He must have known that life on the farm was difficult for a young fella and going to the end-of-year disco was a big thing.

He kept stirring the pot of sauce on the range. "What time will that be over?" It was coming. I could feel it in my water.

"Around half one." I knew they wouldn't play the National Anthem until two, and we'd be hanging around looking at the girls for at least a half hour after that.

He was about to tell me that I needed to stay home and get a good night's sleep so that I'd be fresh for the exam the next morning. I knew it.

"Well, then," he said, "you'd better get as much sleep as you can on the way down in the car."

I had been prepared to come back with an argument for how I could go to the disco and still make the exam next morning— I could feel the words taking shape in my mouth and making their way onto the end of my tongue—but I stopped myself just in time. "I will, aye."

⊱⋅ ⋅⊰

That Friday evening I put on the only decent clothes I had for going out. I knew they'd also be what I'd wear to Dublin the next day. Daniel was up at the house having dinner and sleeping over to make sure that he'd be on time in the morning. He looked up from his dinner plate when I came out of the room.

"Looking sharp, my man," he greeted me with a wide grin. "The girls better watch out tonight with you on the prowl."

"He'd better behave himself," his sister shot back.

"Oh come on, Sarah, you know how these pilots are. They have a woman waiting in every airport!" Great, that's all I needed: Daniel cracking jokes and the old lady not one bit pleased.

"I'd better head over the lane, so," I said to nobody in particular. "The minibus will be around shortly."

"I'll see you in the morning," Daniel shouted after me. "Don't do anything I wouldn't do!"

"There's not much you wouldn't do, you hoor, you," I muttered to myself.

Walking over that lane at night to the Moneydarragh Road was like hurtling through an army obstacle course. Unless we didn't get rain for a couple of days at a time (which would have been classed as a "dry spell," of course), you'd slip and slide and hope that you could stay upright without being covered in muck. Thankfully, I made it through in an upright position, and didn't have to wait long after that for the bus to arrive. Half-blinded by the driver's headlamps, I couldn't make out any of the faces inside. I heard a couple of the girls giggling though, and figured that some of the lads were getting their "speak" in early. The smell of Old Spice wafting up off the lads was so heavy that you could stir it with a spoon.

"How's about ya, mucker?" someone roared from the back of the bus. I was still making my way down the aisle looking for a seat.

"Is that you, McGuinness?" I asked the dark bus.

"No, it's Eamon De Valera."

"I thought youns would have gone straight from Moville. What has you coming over this way?" McGuinness was on his own, so I took a seat beside him.

"I was wondering that myself," he replied, "but the driver told us he had some bog men to collect out here in the middle of nowhere, so here we are."

"Well, I'm delighted for you. It's about time you broadened your horizons and ventured out of the concrete jungle. Speaking of big towns, I'll be in the biggest one tomorrow meself."

"What are you doing in Letterkenny?"

"Letterkenny, my bollix. I'm headed down to Dublin, to take the Aer Lingus pilot's exam."

"Fuck off. They're going to let *you* fly a plane?"

"Well, they're not letting me fly one tomorrow. They're just letting me take the entrance exam. If I pass it, I'll get called back for an interview."

"Well, this calls for a toast," he exclaimed, as he put his hand inside his coat pocket and pulled out a small bottle.

"What have you got there?"

"Smirnoff Vodka. Here, have a slug."

"I couldn't drink that," I told him. "If the old lady smelled it off me when I got back home, she'd crucify me."

"Sure, that's the best thing about vodka, nobody can smell it off your breath." He handed it to me and I raised it slowly to my mouth. I sipped a bit; it stung like a fucker. I handed it back to him.

"What do you think?" he asked eagerly.

"I'm not sure. Aren't you supposed to put something into it, like red lemonade?"

"Coke, actually. But what do you think this is, a feckin' pub?"

"So save it until we get to the disco. We'll get a bottle of Coke and mix it. Are you sure that nobody will be able to smell it?"

"What do you smell off me?" he asked.

"Old Spice."

"See? It works. I've already had three swigs out of it." When we got to the disco, we paid our fifty pence to get in and headed to the bar, where we bought a bottle of Coke each. After a few minutes we went into the jacks, where McGuinness poured one bottle of Coke into the vodka bottle, put the lid back on the vodka, and shook it like he was fixing a bottle of milk for a baby. He took the other full bottle and poured half of the Coke into the empty Coke bottle. He then poured the contents of the Smirnoff bottle evenly into each Coke bottle. I had a feeling it wasn't his first time doing this.

"Sláinte," he said, grinning, as he held up his Coke bottle and crashed it into mine. I took a big gulp, and continued drinking after he had stopped. He tapped me on the arm.

"Christ, man, go easy. We have the whole night ahead of us. You don't want to wind up on your ear this early." I don't know if it was the vodka, or the fact that another school year was over, or that maybe, just maybe, I might become a pilot and escape the farm, but the music made me feel like moving (I can't say that I felt like dancing, as I didn't know how to dance. But I did know I wanted to move.) I tapped my feet and nodded my head to the infectious beat of Status Quo. I don't know how long I stood standing there up against the pillar, but the vodka had long since run out. I saw McGuiness sitting at the edge of the dance floor, chatting up a bird, and I went over to him.

"Do we have any more Coke?" I asked him. The girl gave me a strange look. I wasn't sure if she thought I was walking strangely (it felt like the dance floor was tilting up a bit to one side) or, if she wondered why I just didn't go get my own Coke. She didn't know that ours was far better.

McGuiness shook his head. Fuck it. We must have finished it. I tilted my way across to the men's jacks and looked in the mirror. Jesus, I couldn't get myself into focus. My face was moving around in the mirror. I had to put my face nearly up against the glass. When I did, I saw that the white parts of my eyes weren't white, but red. They looked bloody, like the eyes of a herring or a mackerel that had been two days out of the water.

There was no bloody way I could go back to the house looking like that. I didn't think the old lady would be up at 3:00 in the morning, but she might get up before we left at 4:00. I started to throw water on my eyes like a mad hoor. I even started to drink it from the tap to dilute the vodka. The second time I pushed my head down to the tap for water, I misjudged the distance, or the tap moved around on me, and I wound up busting my lip on the metal. Now I had blood in my eyes *and* blood on my teeth. I was a right bloody mess. It was already half one. I had to get myself straightened out in the next half hour.

I went into a stall and wrapped a fistful of toilet paper around my hand. I then bared my teeth and stuck a fistful of toilet paper between the inside of my top lip and front teeth. The paper felt dry for only a moment before it was soaked. I pulled out my hand and saw that blood had seeped through. I needed something cold, so I balled up the rest of the paper and gave it a quick run under the cold water tap. I then squeezed it into a smaller ball and jammed it behind my lip. The cold water felt better.

The door opened and McGuiness walked in. He looked at me and then at the sink. I looked down. Apparently I had been concentrating so intently on my lip that I didn't realize I had dripped blood onto the white sink and splattered it all over the sides. It looked like someone had just slaughtered a pig.

"What the fuck are you doing, cutting your wrists?"

"I busted my lip."

"Who'd you get into a fight with?"

"I wasn't fighting, for fuck's sake. I was trying to clear up my eyes that were all red from the vodka and I hit my lip on the tap."

"Jesus, you're a right mess. You'd better get cleaned up before you go into that interview tomorrow."

"Interview, my bollix. If the old lady sees me like this, the interview will be the least of my troubles."

"Just don't tell her I gave you vodka. There's no need for us *all* being in the shit."

"I'll be better if can keep throwing cold water on my face and sucking on wet toilet paper for the next half hour."

"If you stay here for another half hour," McGuinness warned me, "you'll be walking home. The bus driver sent me in to fetch you. We are all on the bus ready to go. I've saved you a seat."

"Shite." I grabbed a fistful of toilet paper and ran it under the cold tap before belting out the door. I was really glad that the bus was dark, as I wasn't a very pleasant sight. I was definitely not expecting the entire bus to break out in applause as I made my way down to the seat.

"How are you going to fly a plane and be bleeding all over yourself?" McGuinness asked me.

"Sure, I told you we won't be trying to fly any planes tomorrow. This is only the entrance exam."

"No, I know that, but you must bleed very easy all the same. There's no way that you can keep running out of the cockpit mid-flight to get wet tissue for your bleeding."

I tilted my head back on the seat as I pressed the wet paper tightly to my mouth. The best thing to do with McGuinness was to ignore him altogether. I was glad to see that we were going though Moville first and taking the long way home. That would give me more time to sort myself out. I just hoped that Daniel would not be in a talkative mood on the way down.

At around a quarter to 3:00, the bus dropped me off at the end of our lane. The whole area was in total darkness except for *our* bloody house. There was no mistaking it—the kitchen light was on. I couldn't make out anybody moving around, but then again I did not have a very clear view through the gaps in the ditch.

I wiped the damp toilet paper across my face and hoped that I had been able to clean off all signs of blood. I didn't know if I still looked like a fish going on his third day out of water.

I stopped to get rid of the toilet paper and destroy the evidence. I found a squishy bit of mud, dropped the balled-up paper, and buried it in the mud with my shoe. It disappeared like it had been sucked down into quicksand. I turned the corner of the ditch and headed for the back door, where I let myself in as quietly as I could. So far, so good.

"Is that you, J.P.?" Oh Jesus, Mary, and Joseph—she was up.

"Aye." I whipped out my last piece of unused toilet paper and held it up to my nose as I walked into the kitchen and headed through to the bedroom.

"Have you a nosebleed?"

"I do," I said, holding my head back so that I didn't have to look her in the eye. "I'll just lie down on the bed for a few minutes so that I'll be ready to go when Daniel gets up."

"I'll be getting him up in about a half hour. Don't you be talking going down to Dublin. You need to get sleep."

It looked like I had made it past the first obstacle. If I could rest my eyes for a half hour, I might not look so bad, but I did not know how long it would take to clear up completely. After what felt like five minutes, I realized that someone was shaking me.

"Hey J.P., it's time to get up. We'll be hitting the road in a few minutes."

For a split second, I wondered why Daniel was telling me to get up in the middle of the night. Then the fog started to lift and I remembered that we were heading down to Dublin. I sat up, scratched my head a bit and made my way into the horrendously bright kitchen. I could barely open my eyes enough to see out. Daniel looked like he must have gotten fifteen hours of sleep, and as he looked at me and got ready to say something, I could see a grin getting ready to break across his face. I shot him a deranged stare as my eyes went from slits to bulging. I shook my head as much as I could without the old lady noticing. It felt like my brain had come loose from its sockets and was banging up against the inside of my head. He got the hint.

"All right, Sarah, I've got to get this pilot down to Dublin. We'll see you later this evening." I slipped in front of Daniel and headed for the scullery. I must not have looked that well, judging from the look on Daniel's face.

"Are you not going to eat some scone?" my mother called after me.

"No, I'm grand," I replied without turning around.

"Here, Daniel, take this down with youns. I'm sure you'll get hungry after that long drive."

I figured that she was giving him a few slices of scone for the road. I wasn't going to chance looking back, though. I would have loved a cup of tea, but there was no way I could chance her getting a good look at me. I was full sure that I'd be all cleared up by the time we drove back home. I sat in the front passenger seat as Daniel handed me a flask and a lump of tin foil that I presumed contained buttered scone.

"As soon as we get out to the main road, I'm going to pour out a cup of tea and have it with this scone," I told him. "I'm hungry as a hoor."

"So why didn't you eat before you left? We had time."

"I saw the look you gave me," I told him. "There was no way I was taking a chance of your sister getting a good gawk at me."

"You look a bit worse for wear, all right," he shared. "Were you in a fight?"

"No, I was drinking vodka."

"Good man," he laughed. "You've got the Houton blood, all right."

"Jesus, don't mention a word of that when we get back, or I'll have as much blood *on* me as *in* me."

"Your secret is safe with me," he assured me. "Anyway, they won't know what you're getting up to in airports all over the world after you become a pilot."

"Hopefully not, but I haven't got the job yet. I think I'll close my eyes a bit before I pour out some tea."

$$\bowtie$$

The sun shining in my eyes made me sit upright from my slumped position. It was still dark. How the hell was the sun shining when it was still dark? The car was stopped, and Daniel had the window rolled down, talking to someone. It was a soldier. We were at a British checkpoint in the North. Another soldier was standing outside the passenger's door, shining his torch on my face.

"Where are you going at this hour?" asked a soldier on the driver's side of the car.

"We're heading down to Dublin," Daniel replied.

"Are you from Dublin?"

"No, we're from Donegal."

"Donegal. Purpose of your trip?"

"My nephew is taking an exam to be a pilot."

"Open up your boot."

Daniel got out of the car and opened up the boot of the Anglia. The soldier moved things around to see what he had back there. Jesus, I hoped that grandfather had not hidden one of his goat-killing guns underneath the spare tire. British soldiers did not take too well to Irishmen carrying guns. They tended to shoot them on sight without asking any questions. I knew that there would not be enough time to explain that the gun must belong to my crazy grandfather.

"Open up the bonnet now," said the soldier. They walked around to the front. Daniel opened up the bonnet and the soldier peered down into the engine.

"Let them through," the soldier called up ahead.

We drove forward very slowly, with our lights off.

"How long was I asleep?" I asked Daniel after we had cleared the checkpoint.

"About two hours. You were out for the count. That one soldier was shining the torch right up against the window in your face. I think he thought you were dead. You have dried blood around your mouth."

The closer we got to Dublin, the more nervous I started to feel. I should have been excited, but I began to think that my mother was probably right. Why would they hire some young lad from a farm in the arsehole end of Donegal to be a pilot?

All was not a lost cause, though. Even if didn't wind up passing the exam, it was still great to finally see Dublin.

It was as big as they said it would. There were a lot of buildings, like in Derry, but no armored cars or army tanks on the streets. I had never seen so many people in one spot. We parked the car, got out, and walked up O'Connell Street. It was around half eight, and I didn't have to be at the exam until nine. We walked up one side of the wide street, crossed over, and strode back down the other. Daniel was smiling and saying hello to the pretty girls.

"Hello, beautiful, do you want to show us around Dublin?" he would ask. That man had some balls. Some of the girls smiled back, but others looked scared and seemed to walk faster to get away.

"What time is it now?" I asked him.

"Ten to nine."

"Right so, I'd better go in to this test. I have no idea how long it will take. I'd say a couple of hours, anyway. Where should we meet?"

"Let's meet back here, outside of Cleary's store, at noon. Whoever gets here first, will wait for the other."

"Right so," I said. "Wish me luck."

"Good luck. Get the job so you can take your poor old uncle out for a drink."

"I'll do my best."

At 11:30 am I handed in my finished exam and made my way back to Cleary's. I had found the exam fairly easy, though I didn't actually expect to pass it. I couldn't even bring myself to daydream about getting hired as a pilot, as I would be too disappointed when I was not called for an interview.

I couldn't help thinking, though, that the best part of being a pilot would be looking down at fields from the sky and knowing that I'd never again have to be on the ground working in one.

CHAPTER 31

INTERVIEW COCK-UP

I turned 18 shortly after beginning my final school year in Carndonagh. As Dickens said, "It was the best of times, it was the worst of times." Whatever you want to say about 18 being an age of wisdom, it is surely an age of foolishness. I don't know who in their right mind would consider someone a man, based on reaching the ripe old age of 18. In my case, though, there were other events that got me to thinking that my time had come.

One of those was my sponsored streak. Of course, the streak did not actually take place, but that was more of a technicality than anything else. I made sure that word got out that I was a marked man and the police had the evil eye set on me. Nobody seemed to hold it against me. As a matter of fact, there were a few not-too-hateful-looking birds who came forward to let me know that they had supported my decision and thought I was fierce brave. One of those supporters was Trish Harkin. I definitely wanted to hold it against her, and I did, for a short while.

As far as I was concerned, Trish Harkin had everything that a man could want. She was tall, slender, had long golden hair, and had stick-out boobs and a nice rounded arse. A man did not have to rely on his imagination too much in the late 70s, as girls wore tight tops and high-waisted trousers with tight arses. For some reason or other, Trish thought I was a rock star. I didn't know if it was because of my Mick Jagger shoes, my decision to streak, or a combination of the two, but at any rate, her and I went at it hot and heavy for a while. Keep in mind that "hot and heavy" in Ireland meant kissing and groping each other a bit up against a wall on your lunch hour or, when you could manage it, on a Saturday night at the Lilac.

For a while there, it looked as if my final year would be quite tolerable after all. I was getting that much closer to seeing what the world had in store for me, there was a remote possibility of my becoming a pilot, and best of all, Trish Harkin wanted to be with me. As far as I was concerned, Trish was the one. When it came to women, I was no Don Juan, but I did have my moments. Well, maybe more like *a* moment, and it had been with a Protestant girl, but I didn't have anything against Catholics. Sure, wasn't I one myself?

Toward the end of September, I received an official brown envelope in the post. It was from Aer Lingus. I just knew it was one of those letters letting me know that they appreciated me taking part, but unfortunately I was not being called to Dublin for the interview. The auld fella opened the letter. He seemed to be the only one who could open an envelope properly. I don't know what age you needed to be in order to be deemed competent to open your own letters. This was definitely not the house you wanted a girl to send you a love letter.

"Aer Lingus is calling you back to Dublin for the interview."

"Come again?" For a minute there, I nearly thought he said that Aer Lingus wanted me to *come to Dublin for an interview.*

"Aer Lingus wants you to go back to Dublin for an interview."

"Can I see that?"

It wasn't that I didn't believe him. I was just in such a state of shock that it wasn't making sense. *Am I really going to be a pilot?*

"It says here that they want me to appear before an interview board at 11:30 am next Friday."

They were both silent. For a pair of hoors who had put so much stock in my getting a good pensionable state job, they didn't have much to say now. Maybe I wasn't quite as stupid as they always said I was. Maybe they were actually feeling guilty for putting me down all the time, and now that I had proved them wrong, they had to eat their words.

"You can daydream about being a pilot all you want while you milk the cow," the old lady snapped, breaking me out of my reverie. "She won't milk herself."

I don't believe the word "congratulations" had ever made it off of Sarah's tongue in her life. If I had given much thought to why she was the way she was, it probably would have just driven me mental. I ignored her, deciding then that I would put everything I had into getting the pilot's job. If I didn't get picked, it certainly wouldn't be for want of trying.

I milked the cow on autopilot—so to speak. As I pulled and squeezed, I tried to work out how I thought the interview might go. I had never been interviewed for anything, so I hadn't a bloody clue what to expect. I figured that they would ask me why I wanted to be a pilot. The honest answer would be "so that I can get off that fucking farm and have a life." I knew that I couldn't afford to be honest, though. I'd have to make up some sob story about how as a young boy I would continually look up at the sky and think how wonderful it would be to devote my life to flying people around the world.

The cow's dry tits alerted me to the fact that milking time was over. I carried the bucket up to the house and put water in a saucepan to have a wash. I figured it was good to start planning the trip, so I asked the auld fella about going back to Dublin.

"Will you be talking to Daniel about taking me back down to Dublin?" He shot a look over at my mother. That was not a good sign.

"I don't know if he'll be able to take you," he answered, without looking at me.

"He's got a cow about to calve," added his sidekick.

"How will I get down?" I wanted this so badly, I'd walk if I had to.

"I'd say the bus from Derry would be your best bet." There was something about the way he said it that made me think they wouldn't even be taking me to Derry. Were they afraid? Derry and Belfast were both being blown to bits all the time during the troubles of the mid-70s. Surely my parents weren't afraid to drop me off? They certainly weren't timid about bringing us up to the North when there was smuggling to be done. That would be very rich, if they were worried about the danger now and me old enough to handle myself much better than I could have done nearly ten years before.

"Do you know what time the bus leaves Derry?"

"According to the timetable, it leaves at 6:00 in the morning."

"Jesus, that's cutting it close. The bus is supposed to take around five hours to go down. Sure, I'd be getting into Dublin at 11:00 am—the same time as my interview —and that would be without any bomb scares or shootings all the way through the North."

"I'm sure they'd understand if you were a bit late," said Sarah casually. "They'll be listening to the news down in Dublin and know how dangerous it is in the North. Just let them know if your bus gets detoured because of an overnight bomb or rioting along the way." I felt like asking her how I'd get word to the interview board if the bus is blown up.

"Daniel said he'd drop you off at the bus in the morning," added the auld fella.

It felt like I told half the school that I was going down to Dublin for the interview that week. A lot of my fifth-year classmates were sorry that they had not signed up for the exam, and more than a few said that there was no way that Aer Lingus would ever hire a mad hoor like me to fly their planes. Trish was excited for me, but I think she was worried that my going away might be the end of things between us.

"Will you forget all about me when you become a pilot?"

"How could I do that?" I asked her. "Anyway, wouldn't you come down to Dublin every weekend to visit me?"

"You know how difficult that would be. It takes a half day to go to Dublin and another half day to come back. Then, what if you are flying to America or Australia at the weekend? You may as well be on the moon. On top of that, my parents would never allow me to go to Dublin every weekend."

"Let's not think about all that just yet. I may only be flying back and forth to Heathrow, and coming home for the tea every evening!"

I must have said something right, since she threw her arms around my neck and kissed me, pulling my head in closer. She didn't even push me away when I squeezed her arse with both hands. Neither of us was in any hurry to break away. She kept her hands clasped around my neck, but pulled her head back a bit to look at me.

"Promise me that you'll do your best to get that interview. It's very important."

"Of course I will. There's no bloody way I want to spend my life trying to scrape an existence out of a few fields."

It was true and all. I was ready to fight tooth-and-nail for this job. Not only was it to be my ticket out of backbreaking, unforgiving farm work, but I had an added incentive now that I could see how important it was to Trish that I become a pilot.

My first hurdle was to find decent clothes to wear to the Interview. I didn't own a suit, or even anything that could be made to look like one. Daniel had a lot of things to wear, but even if his clothes weren't crazy-looking Yankee clothes, he was five feet nine inches and I was six foot two and a half. On top of that, he had a solid build, while I had less meat on me than the "dog" bones I brought home every Friday evening. I could get no help there.

I always wore Wrangler jeans and a denim jacket. I had one shirt with a collar. Everything else was t-shirts and jumpers. I had bought a pair of dress trousers with my FCA money, as well as a cream shirt with a collar. I'd have to wear that. I could borrow a tie from Daniel, but what could I wear over the shirt? A jumper wouldn't look right. I don't know how much a jacket would cost or what I could find that would match a cream shirt and high-waisted, light-blue-pinstriped navy blue trousers.

Then there was the question of cost. I had to make the money from the army last me the whole year (and the auld fella would have to get his cut along the way). There was no bloody way I could spend half a year's stipend on a jacket to make me look respectable for a day.

"I don't see why you can't wear that jacket you were sent from America," chimed in my mother.

As much as I hated to admit it, I might have no choice but to wear it. The main problem was its color. It was bright yellow. It was also nylon. I didn't know if that would be acceptable to wear to such an important interview. It was possible that a man could get away with wearing a yellow jacket in Dublin or London, but in Donegal, you may as well streak and wear nothing, as you'd get the same reaction. In the end, I decided that I would wear the yellow jacket and pray that I didn't look like an overgrown parrot.

Daniel came over on Thursday night, just as he had when I had gone to Dublin to take the entrance exam. We had to leave the house before half five to make the Derry-to-Dublin bus at 6:00 am. As I've mentioned, he was *not* a morning person.

"Man, you're going to make me old before my time, getting me up at this hour of the morning," Daniel told me as we sipped our tea that morning.

"I'm not fond of getting up in the dark myself," I told him, "but I'd rather get up in the dark to fly a plane for a lot of money than to milk a bloody cow for nothing. Besides, the only drink I can offer you now is milk, and I have a fair idea that you'd like something stronger than that eventually."

Daniel broke into a huge grin. "My man, I've said it before and I'll say it again. I like the way you think. Are you ready to head for Derry?"

"Aye, ready as I'll ever be." I put on the yellow nylon windbreaker and stared at my reflection in the kitchen window. I don't think the red polka dot tie Daniel brought me did my get-up much justice, but then again, it would be hard to know what *would* have gone with such a mix-and-match ensemble. I didn't have time to be studying myself. It would be nearly 6:00 by the time we reached the Derry bus. I just hoped the soldiers at the checkpoint did not want to go through everything in the car, or I might miss the bus. I didn't have a plan B. I had only enough money to take the bus down and back, plus a burger after the interview. I'd probably hitchhike back down from Derry, since nobody had mentioned picking me up when I got back.

Fortunately, it was plain sailing going up, and I made the bus with a few minutes to spare. The driver was a fairly old fella, and it felt like he was giving me strange looks when he thought I wasn't watching. I decided I wouldn't bother telling him I was going for a pilot's interview, as I was pretty sure that I was not dressed like a pilot. I was hoping to sleep on the way down, but was too nervous. Just my luck, there had been a big bomb blast near Enniskillen during the night, and the soldiers were going through every car with a fine-toothed comb. We must have wasted a good half hour waiting to get through the checkpoint.

It was nearly 11:30 by the time we reached Dublin, and I had a good fifteen minute walk to get to the Aer Lingus building. I was too nervous to walk, so I ran. I saved a good five minutes or more by running, but when I got there, I was sweating like a Clydesdale pulling a plough. I found the floor where the interviews were being held, and sat down in a hard chair with several other young men. I think I must have been one of the youngest there. I was definitely the sweatiest.

I had no choice but to wipe off my face with the sleeve of my jacket. The nylon did not make a good job of mopping the sweat up, so I was basically transferring rivers of wetness from one side of my face to the other.

Nobody spoke a word, so I didn't either, although I was dying to know what I should do next. I thought about knocking on the door to let them know I was there, but what if I interrupted their questions and they got thick with me?

After about half an hour, the door opened and a young fella walked out. He was wearing a suit. I looked at the others. They were all wearing suits. I was the only one in a parrot's getup. I thought about getting up and leaving. As I was deciding what to do, an old man who looked like he was at least 70 with white hair and glasses came out of the room, looked at a sheet he had in his hand, and then looked at me. More accurately, actually, he squinted at me. I didn't know if it was my wet face that confused him or the tropical-colored bird jacket that I had had the audacity to wear to the interview of a lifetime.

"Who are you?" he barked at me.

"John Sexton," I said, and added, "Sir." He looked back down at his paper.

"Sure, you were supposed to be here over an hour ago."

"I'm sorry sir, but the bus down from Derry was late because of a bomb going off last night."

"Bomb? What bomb? There are no bombs in Dublin." I figured it was wiser to say nothing, so I just let him talk. "Well, you won't be coming in now. We are stopping for our lunch. Come back at half one and we will see if we can fit you in." He started to walk back into the room, then turned and added, "You may have to come back another day."

I hoped that he was just trying to scare me. I was pretty sure that I wouldn't be coming back down again unless it was to start training with them. I headed out to O'Connell Street to find the cheapest burger I could get. My mind started thinking. If I didn't get going into the interview room until half one, how would I make the bus back to Derry at two-something? I didn't know if there was a later bus. What if I missed it? I definitely didn't have the money to stay anywhere. My only hope was to impress them so well that they'd know right away that I was meant for the job and cut the interview short.

I was so nervous that I couldn't concentrate on looking at the girls walking by. I went back up to the floor and sat outside the interview door, hoping they might come back early and decide to call me in. They must have come in another door, as nobody passed me.

At 1:25 pm, the door opened and the same old fella told me that I could come in. When I stood up, he looked at my jacket and my trousers, and then at my shoes, which were black brogues. It was obvious that they were not proper dress shoes, but I was glad that they were black and not the fancy Mick Jaggers. If I had shown up in brown and black shoes, with striped orange shoelaces, they would definitely have thought that I was taking the piss.

There was a long wooden table at the back of the room. Two old men sat at either end, with an ancient-looking old woman in the middle. The other man and woman looked old enough to be the parents of the 70-year-old. They had been talking amongst themselves when I walked in, but now they stared in silence as I walked up to the table. They all seemed to be mesmerized by the bright yellow jacket.

"You were supposed to be here over two hours ago," said the old woman, looking at my face, down at my jacket, then back to my face.

"Yes, I'm sorry. The bus took longer to come down from Derry. I'm sorry."

"You live in Derry?" she asked with a look of shock on her face.

"Oh, no, Ma'am. I live in Donegal, but I took the bus to Dublin from Derry."

"Pilots have to be on time, if planes are to fly on time," the old man's father scowled at me. The three of them then muttered something between them.

The old man I had first seen asked, "So why do you think you would make a good pilot?"

The fucker. I was all ready for the "Why do you want to be a pilot?" question.

"Well," I answered slowly to buy myself more time. "I am very healthy and fit. I also have fierce good eyesight."

"Go on."

"I'm not afraid of heights." I was starting to pull answers out of my arse now.

"Have you ever been on an airplane?" The old woman asked me.

"No, Ma'am."

"Then how do you know you wouldn't be afraid to fly? A lot of people are afraid of flying." She was getting under my skin. I wanted to ask the old bitch if she ever milked a goat or shaved a pig.

"No offense, Ma'am, but I am not afraid of anything." That made her raise her eyebrows a bit. She then pointed at a model of an Aer Lingus plane on the front of their desk.

"What model of plane is this?" she asked me. The only plane I had ever heard mention was a Boeing 707, so I had to go with that one.

"That's a Boeing 707," I said without hesitation. To this day, I don't know if I was right or wrong.

"Can you tell us the difference between a diesel engine and a petrol engine?" asked the old man who seemed to be in his 90s.

If my auld fella had let me drive the car, or even the tractor, I might have been able to come up with at least a half-intelligent answer, but under the circumstances, I had no choice but to bluff my way through it.

"Well, it's like this. You will find that most of the farm equipment, such as tractors, diggers, JCBs—things like that—run on diesel, and most of the cars on the road run on petrol. Now there are some diesel cars as well, but they cost much more to buy, so there are fewer of them."

The three of them sat staring at me for what felt like several minutes. None of them said anything or made any movement— they just stared. It may have been my first interview, but I knew damn well that they weren't staring at me because they were enthralled by my technical answers. They were most likely just wondering how this fucking eejit ever passed the entrance exam in the first place.

"What do you like to do in your spare time?" asked the old lady. I nearly broke out laughing at that. I wanted to ask her, *"What spare time?"* However, I was delighted that we had got past the difficult questions and thought maybe this was a good sign.

"Well, I read a lot, listen to the radio, and I also like to write creatively."

"Who are your favorite authors?" she asked.

This was the time to make up for any wrong answers I may have given. I could tell by their accents that the three of them were from Dublin, so I figured I would score a bull's eye if I talked about a Dublin writer.

"I read mostly what my father has collected," I told her. "I have read a series of books by a Tibetan monk called Lobsang Rampa, but my favorite writer of all is from right here in Dublin." That seemed to perk her up.

"James Joyce?" she asked with a faint hint of a smile.

"No," I said, "Brendan Behan."

"Brendan Behan…Brendan Behan?" She asked it twice like she couldn't believe I would read Brendan Behan. I had been so focused on trying to impress them that I failed to notice her smile slowly turning into a scowl. I dug my grave even deeper.

"Yes, I have read nearly everything he has written," I proudly replied.

"You actually enjoy his dirty language?" This was where I should have seen the writing on the wall. I should have told her that I did not appreciate his language one bit and that I only read him because I had nothing else to read.

"I think it's entertaining and also very authentic, as he writes the way people talk."

"I can assure you," she said, with a little shake of her wizened head, "that the decent people of Dublin do not talk that way. Maybe they do in the English prisons where he spent his youth, after he was caught trying to plant bombs in England for the I.R.A., but the *rest* of us know how to speak properly."

As she was talking, I could hear the sound of carpenters hammering in my head. They were the final nails being hammered into my pilot's coffin. All of the relics then leaned in toward each other and muttered like a bunch of old ladies in the post office on a Friday morning.

"You are free to go now," said the old woman. "You'll be notified in due course."

I don't even know if I thanked them. It may have been my first interview, but I knew I had blown it badly. I made my way down the stairs and out into the street.

⟻⊹ ⊹⟼

After asking directions to Busaras, I walked over to the main bus station for the long journey back to Derry. I walked up to the ticket counter.

"What time does the bus leave for Derry?"

"You know that leaves in the morning?" the ticket man asked me.

"What morning?"

"Tomorrow morning. The last bus North left about a quarter of an hour ago." Lovely. I wasn't getting the job and now I couldn't even get a bus. What the hell was I going to do in Dublin overnight? I had never been away from home overnight, except for the time I went to the Gaeltacht to study Irish. And even there, I had a bed.

"Can I stay here?" I realized this sounded strange, but I had nowhere else to go.

"You cannot," replied the ticket man, looking at me like I was mental. "You'll have to find yourself a B&B and come back for the 9 o'clock bus."

I was totally fucked. Not only did I not have money for a bed for the night, but I didn't even have enough to get myself something decent to eat. I would have to walk around the streets of Dublin all night and be back in the morning for the bus. If one of my mates had told me they were going down to Dublin to walk around all day and night before riding the bus back the next morning, I would have thought it sounded like right craic and been all for it. Now I was scared. People seemed to be getting stabbed and kicked to death in fights every night after the pubs and clubs closed on O'Connell Street.

I walked away from the bus station and toward O'Connell Street, as I didn't know any other street. I walked up one side and down the other until it got dark. I could tell you every item that every shop had in their front window. At around 7 o'clock, I was getting hungry, so I went into a shop and bought a pint of milk. I was hoping that would keep me going until the morning. I reckoned I would have just enough for another pint of milk, when it started to get light, and the bus fare home.

I soon began to notice that people did not dress as wildly in Dublin as I had thought. I caught a lot of people staring at my yellow jacket. At about 11 o'clock, I started getting fierce tired, so I found myself a piece of a cardboard box, laid it down in a doorway, and then sat myself down on it. It actually felt decent. I pulled my knees up to my chest and rested my head on top of my knees. I must have fallen asleep for a few minutes, waking up only when I heard someone talking to me. I looked up and saw a man and a woman staring down at me. The woman fumbled in her purse, pulled out a ten-pence coin and handed it to me. "Get yourself something to eat," she told me, as they stumbled down the street, arm in arm.

Jesus, they thought I was homeless.

Well, actually, I was. I had made money begging without even trying. I hoped that more people would feel sorry for me, but that drunken couple were the only ones who did.

I was cold, hungry, and tired. Sitting in a doorway on O'Connell Street did not provide me much shelter from the cold night wind, so I moved around the corner to Henry Street. I found a shop that had a nice angled doorway. (It's funny how doorways have absolutely no significance until they become a place of shelter.) I took my cardboard seat, threw it over the low security gate, and climbed over to make myself somewhat comfortable.

I had just settled in and was hoping for some kind of a night's rest when a pair of policemen turned the corner and shone a torch in my face.

"What are you doing in there?" asked one in a broad country accent.

"I missed the last bus to Derry and I can't afford a B&B, so I'm trying to get a bit of sleep."

"Ah, Jesus, you can't sleep in that man's doorway. You'll have to move it along," his partner informed me.

Had I been a bit more street smart, I would have informed them that I was staying put. That way, they would have arrested me and brought me back to their barracks, where I would at least have been safe and probably warm for the night. They may even have fed me.

Instead, I took my cardboard with me and moved further down the street. The police were a curse, but a blessing as well. True, they would not let me sleep in a doorway, but if I ran into a few local gougers and they decided to give me a kicking, I liked knowing the boys in blue were not far away. I was careful to not go too far down the street. Nothing good could come of lying in a dark doorway in Dublin City in the middle of the night. I picked a door that was close to the other one. I didn't expect much sleep, but I couldn't be walking the streets all night.

I must have dozed off, as I woke up with a stiff neck and freezing in my parrot's costume. I was hoping that it was nearly time to go wait for the bus. I kicked away the cardboard, re-tucked the tail of my cream shirt into my high-waisted pin-striped trousers, and went looking for some place where I could find another pint of cold milk. I found a wee shop that must have catered to late-night drinkers. I took a pint of milk up to the register and asked the man what time it was.

"Half two," he replied.

"Are you sure?" I asked him. I was expecting him to say maybe seven, or at least half six. I still had more than six hours to go. He looked at his watch.

"It's 2:32," he replied with a bored look. Feck it. I was up now. I may as well start walking around.

That was the longest night I had ever spent.

At 7:00, I walked over to the bus station. I was fed up to the gills with O'Connell Street. Busaras was open and I took a seat inside on a bench. I was dog-tired, but afraid to nod off in case I missed the bus again. I was looking forward to a nice hot cup of tea when we stopped for a break in Monaghan, thanks to the drunken woman who had given me the ten pence.

I was a happy pup when I finally got to stand in line to board that bus for Derry. I didn't even feel bad that I had blown the interview. It's not like I had wanted to be a pilot all my life anyway. I wondered if Trish Harkin would still want me if I was a bus driver. I got on and handed the driver the money.

"How do you like driving a bus?" I asked the driver. He looked at me and then at my parrot's outfit. He probably thought I was taking the piss.

"Are you in school?" he asked me.

"I am," I said, "up in Donegal."

"Donegal? Well, then," he said, handing me a receipt and a couple of coins, "either finish school and become a teacher, or be a fisherman. Sure Donegal men make loads of money at the fishing."

I thanked him and made my way to the back of the bus. I wondered how Trish would feel about me being a fisherman. It would be good to make loads of money, but I didn't think she'd like me to smell like fish all the time. I'd tell her about the outcome of the interview as soon as I got back; I didn't have to wait for the results. Judging by the way I got on with those old fossils on the interview board, I knew damn well that I had no chance of ever being a pilot with Aer Lingus.

It didn't take me long to fall asleep on the bus. I dreamt that I was on a plane, flying somewhere, and it kept jerking like it was running out of fuel. My feet were fierce cold, and when I looked down I saw there was a huge gaping hole in the floor with a biscuit-tin lid jammed inside it. I looked around for someone to tell, but there was no sign of anyone working. I opened the seat belt, carefully stepped around the hole, and made my way up to the front of the plane. This took a while, as the plane was shaking and spluttering. I still couldn't find anyone who was working. I knocked on the pilot's door. I thought I heard someone say "Come in," so I opened it.

Inside on the Captain's chair sat my auld fella. He was wrestling with the steering wheel. He turned around when I walked in.

"What the hell are you doing here?" I asked him.

"Flying the plane," he said, like he did it every day of the week.

"Jesus, you're not making a very good job of it," I told him. "Sure, it's spluttering and spitting like an auld fella with TB."

"I think it's because I filled it with diesel and it should have been petrol," he informed me as he wrestled with the steering wheel. "If you see that girl out there who goes around with the tea, can you send her in? I'd love a cup of tea."

Tea? Tea! We're getting ready to crash and all he can think about is tea?!

The man sitting next to me on the bus was shaking my shoulder to wake me.

"We've stopped in Monaghan for a cup of tea," he said.

Jesus, my feet were freezing. I was half afraid to look down, but when I did, I was glad there was no hole. Coming out of the fog of sleep, I made my way inside the wee canteen, and was ecstatic to realize that I had enough money for a Cadbury Snack to go along with my tea. It didn't fill me by any means, but it was the first solid thing I had eaten in nearly twenty-four hours. I wasn't looking forward to the walk I would have once I got off the bus in Derry City Centre. Nobody would pick me up, since you'd never see anyone thumbing inside the city. I'd have to walk all the way to the border in Muff before I could start thumbing. That had to be a good four or five miles.

It wound up taking me half as long to get home from Derry as it did to get from Dublin to Derry. I was totally shagged after my ordeal.

"What the hell happened to you?" my mother asked as I struggled through the door.

"I was late for my interview, and by the time I got out of it, the last bus to Derry had already left. I had to wait around Dublin until this morning."

"Well, there's plenty for you to do now after all your gallivanting around Dublin. You can bring a couple of bags of turf down, and after that the cow will need to be brought in for milking."

I wasn't exactly expecting them to throw me a surprise party, but I half expected that they'd be glad to see me, having had no contact with me since the day before. Fortunately, Trish was much happier to see me on Monday.

"I'm so glad you got back," she told me as she hugged me tightly at lunchtime. "So, when will you start flying?"

"As soon as I can afford a ticket to go somewhere."

"I don't understand. I thought you got to fly for free when you are a pilot...and your girlfriend would fly free too," she added with a grin.

"Maybe if I was a pilot, but I really don't think they will be hiring me."

"Why not? Sure they won't give out the results yet, will they?"

"No, but I have a fairly good idea that I won't be on the list. The interview didn't go well. I don't think they hire many fellas from the country. Probably mostly Dubliners get the job."

"Well, I'm keeping my fingers crossed for you. Tell me the minute you hear something, as mammy is waiting to know too."

"Your mother is waiting to know? What does she want to know for?"

"I told her about you. She wasn't too happy at first, but she softened up a bit when I told her you were going to be a pilot for Aer Lingus."

"How does she feel about fishermen?"

"I haven't a clue. Why do you ask?"

"Ach, I was just wondering." I couldn't put my finger on it, but something didn't seem right. What did she go telling her mother about us for, anyway? I'd be damned if I would ever tell my auld ones about Trish. No good could come of it.

When the envelope did come from Aer Lingus a fortnight later, I knew what it was going to say before the auld fella read it out. The only way I was getting on a plane was if I bought the ticket myself. The lads were right; they weren't going to let a mad hoor like me fly their planes.

Trish didn't take it the news well. Apparently, neither did her mammy.

"Mammy says that I can't see you anymore."

"Because I didn't get the job with Aer Lingus?" She didn't reply.

"There are loads of other jobs, you know. Tell her I'll get another one—an even better job."

"I tried saying something to her, but she wouldn't listen to me. She said that your family has nothing, and that you are not good enough for me."

"And what do you say?" More silence.

"You know what, Trish? You tell your mammy she can kiss my arse. I don't know what makes her think she is the Queen of Sheeba, living in a semi-detached in Ard Colgan. Ard fucking Colgan, Trish. Not exactly Beverly fucking Hills." I was mad as a bull. She started to walk off.

"Good luck with waiting for a pilot to fall from the sky into your lap."

I shouldn't have said that. I didn't mean that I wanted a plane to crash. I had nothing against pilots just because I wasn't picked. *One day I'll show her mammy*, I thought. *One day.*

CHAPTER 32

GATE PAINTING BLUES

During my fifth and final year in secondary school, I realized one thing: It was time to concentrate on my studies instead of just having the craic. Jimmy had already dropped out of school to become an apprentice carpenter to a master craftsman. My parents figured there was no sense in him spending another couple of years in school when he could be learning a trade.

I, on the other hand, had long since forgotten about my dream of being a pilot. It was no great loss, since you can't lose what you never had.

Not having any other backup plan, and needing to put a bit of distance between myself and the farm (especially those in charge of it), I applied for admission to Letterkenny College to study law in their new Legal Executive Program.

Nothing changed at home. I still had my chores, and still snuck into the Lilac Ballroom most weekends. Many of my classmates were now starting to congregate there, and the auld fella was still pushing his songs to visiting bands. The only difference now was that he started to wear a gold hoop earring. I thought it would look better on me, and since he had bought a pair, I asked him what he was going to do with the other one.

"I'm not going to wear it," he said. "I just need the one."

"Well, give it to me and I'll wear it."

"You can have it if you want," he replied without giving it much thought.

No other fifth-year boy (and no boy in any other year, for that matter) in school had an earring, and I knew that it was going to make a lot of tongues wag. I didn't know if I would get into trouble for wearing it, but after all, we had never been told we could not. No doubt Big Peter would be none too pleased when he heard about it, but I wasn't endangering my life on a bridge or waving my mickey around on a sports field, so what could he say? My only real concern was how to get it into my ear. The auld fella had gotten my mother to put his in, using a cork behind his ear and a sewing needle to make the hole. She had used some kind of antiseptic to clean the ring before she pushed it in. Maybe I should have asked for the earring earlier on so she could do the same for me, but I didn't want her stabbing me with a needle anyway. I hadn't had pleasant experiences being near her when she was armed with a weapon in the past.

Around that time, I started to see a wee girl from Carn town. She was in the year behind me. We would meet up most lunch hours uptown and shoot pool. We would also court up against the wall of the pool hall when nobody was watching. I told her about the earring, and she said she would put it in for me the next day at lunchtime.

The next day I was on the edge of my seat waiting for the lunchtime bell. As soon as it sounded, I belted off like a madman up the hill to the pool hall. I got there at exactly 1:07 pm. Marjorie Gill was already there, sitting on the edge of a pool table at the far end of the room. I went over and pulled her into me close. She opened her legs and put her hands around my neck.

"Did you ever do it on a pool table?" she asked me.

"I tried," I said, "but the sheep was confused. She kept trying to eat the green felt on the table, thinking it was grass."

She gave me a playful push back. "You bloody farmers and your sheep."

"Hey, easy on with that farmer talk. I am not a farmer. I am being held against my will on a farm and made to do work by my captors. One day I will be a free man."

"All right, farmer-against-your-will, are you ready to get an extra hole?"

I took a dignified stance and raised my left arm out, addressing a non-existent forum. "I shall lend you my ear. Literally."

She looked confused, like I was mental.

"Julius Caesar? Willy Shakespeare?" I ventured.

"Which ear?" she interrupted.

"The left one, of course. Left for straight, right for gay."

"Okay, give me your right ear."

"Hey, hey. If we had this place to ourselves, you'd know exactly why it was going in the left ear."

"Promises, promises." She reached into a bag she had set down on the pool table and took out a cork. She then took out something wrapped up in a cloth. It turned out to be a big needle.

"It looks like everyone uses a cork and needle to pierce ears," I remarked.

"That's what my friends and I use. Did some of your other classmates get pierced too?"

"No," I replied proudly, "I'll be the first fella in Carn School to wear an earring. My auld fella got his pierced a wee while ago."

"Your auld fella? Really? He's not in a band, is he?"

"No, but he's started to write songs."

"Fancies himself as an Elton John then, does he?"

"More like Mental John, I'd say." I made myself laugh so hard that my head bobbed up and down, and Marjorie had to tell me to hold still. When I was still enough, she plunged the needle into my earlobe and stuck it into the cork behind my ear.

"Jesus Christ," I yelled out just as a couple of first-year boys walked in the door. They looked at us and then at each other, not knowing whether to stay or run back outside.

"It's all right, boys," Marjorie called down to them. "We're nearly finished here. Play away."

"That wasn't so bad now, was it?" she asked me.

"Jesus, it wasn't so good either. Now what?"

"Give me the ring."

I gave her the gold earring, and she fidgeted with it until it was in. I could feel her spinning it around.

"You must keep moving it around in the hole every day," she advised me, "or else it will get stuck and fester, and you'd have to go to the doctor."

I was dying to see it. "I'm going into the jacks to look in the mirror," I told her. I wasn't sure what to expect. I didn't know if I'd look like an English rock star or a pirate. Either one was good, I reckoned.

I liked it. I had started to let my hair grow at the end of fourth year, and now that it was long, it suited the earring perfectly. I decided I looked like a rock star. I didn't have the facial hair for a pirate.

"Magic!" I told Marjorie when I came out of the jacks. "I can't wait to show the lads."

"Make sure none of them pull on it, or they could rip your earlobe. That goes for your slave masters too." She gave me a sexy wink and headed home for her lunch.

I was so excited to be the first male student to wear an earring that I didn't hang around the town, but instead beat a hasty retreat back to school. I kept brushing my hair back on the left side, so that the ring would be good and visible. When I got back to the common area walk-through, I took up a spot along the wall so that my right shoulder was against the wall and my left ear was on display. A couple of my fellow fifth year schoolmates started to drift back after lunch. My mind wasn't on any conversation, as I was waiting for them to comment on the new look. McGuinness was the first to notice.

"What the fuck is that you have in your ear?"

"What, this?" I tried to sound as laid-back as I could possibly manage. "Yeah, well I figured that it was a good look for me."

"Aye, you look like you should be in a band. I'd say the birds will like it. Jesus, I might get one myself." Just then, the flock of secretarial girls came drifting down the hall in a pack. McGuinness was obstructing my view. More importantly, though, he was obstructing the secretaries' view of my earring.

"For fuck's sake, McGuinness, move your arse so I can get a good look at those secretarial birds."

I tilted my head a bit so that the sun would catch my left side and might shine on the gold ring. Most of the women just strutted past in slow motion as time stood still, but I think one did sneak a peak over and give a little smile.

"Did you see that?" I asked McGuinness. "That wee one with the hair down to her waist smiled at me."

"I think she was laughing at the way you were grinning with your eyes closed and head tilted back, rocking back and forth. You looked like your man Stevie Wonder."

"My eyes weren't closed. They were just narrowed, with the sun in them. That's a good sign, if the earring makes me look like a singer. Birds go for men in bands."

Several more of my classmates came around to comment about the earring. When the bell rang to signal the end of lunch, I made my way to my English class with Paddy McDaid. Paddy would call all the girls by their surnames and refer to us either as "mister so-and-so" or "fella." He continually walked around the classroom as he taught. About ten minutes into the class, he walked past me and I felt something touch my left ear. I turned around and saw Paddy beside me, pushing back the hair over my left ear with his pen.

"What have we here, fella?"

I wasn't sure what kind of answer to give. I couldn't tell if he approved or disapproved, but I knew he was likely to let me know before too long.

"It's an earring, Sir." I definitely didn't mean it to sound smart. Paddy looked like he boxed in his younger days, and I had no doubt he could still beat the shite out of any of us if he felt the need.

"Indeed. I kind of figured that's what it might be. Have you joined a band?"

"No Sir, I just thought I'd try it to see how it looked."

"Oh, I'd say it's rather fetching. What do you say, ladies?" The girls in the class sniggered and tried to get a look at it. "Just remember, fella, even if you do join a band, the chances are you will have to write your own material to be very successful. Even though some music may sound like drivel, the really good songs are by writers with an excellent grasp of the English language."

"Yes, Sir."

"All right then," Paddy continued as he jumped right back into business, "give me some examples of why King Lear may have been 'more sinned against than sinning.'"

<hr />

As the end of the school year approached, I began to wonder what I'd do for a bit of spending money during the summer and beyond. I had shot myself in the foot, so to speak, with the FCA and figured I was now *persona non grata*. The summer before I had gone out with a few of the lads after training and drank pints of beer, which I wasn't used to. When I got back to camp, I was fairly much three sheets to the wind. That in itself would not have been a major crime, as they often saw soldiers having one too many, especially young fellas who were not used to drinking. When I signed back in at the guard house after pub closing, however, I was told by the private doing guard duty that he was working my shift as I was supposed to be pulling guard overnight. After that, I didn't get any notification for the monthly drill. Even though I was never officially fired, I didn't feel like I could go back.

I wasn't too bent out of shape about my part-time army career having been cut short, as I would have had to cut my hair to a respectable length and get rid of the earring. I decided to get over the Leaving, and then see if I could pick up some manual labor somewhere within biking distance. It was bad enough being broke as a boy, but as a teenager I had dances to go to, and usually needed a few bob to spend on a bird, so being broke was a bit of a disaster. Halfway through the final exams, the auld fella gave me a bit of unexpected good news.

"When you're done with your exams, Denis Harkin could use some help painting the field gates and his shed."

"Did he say how much he was paying?" I couldn't trust the old fella's wheeling and dealing. For all I knew, he had struck up a deal that would involve Harkin giving my father bales of hay or a load of turf in exchange for me working the summer for him.

"I didn't really ask. I figured you've been doing so much talking about getting a job that you'd be happy with whatever he offered."

"I need the money, all right. I'll go over there on Saturday and see what he needs done." I was dying to know how much I would be getting paid, but whatever it was, it would be more than I'd get sitting around the house waiting for the results of the Leaving to come.

The finals were rough on the system. I stayed up every night until after 2:00 in the morning, cramming as much as I could into my memory for that day's exam. Of course, I still had to get up at around 7:00 in order to do all of my chores. By the time Saturday arrived, I didn't feel like going to talk about work, but I knew it had to be done. Dennis showed me a couple of the gates leading into his fields, rusty metal that didn't seem to have ever been painted. The shed was a massive hay shed in which he kept his tractor and farm machinery. The big roof was bowed in a semi-circle and had originally been red, but it was so faded that it too looked rusted.

The Harkins were one of the few local families who made a decent living from farming. You could tell by the amount of machinery they had, as well as the size of their shed. The feckin' thing was gigantic. It must have been at least three, if not four, stories tall. I didn't fancy working on the steep sloping sides of the roof, and I would have to paint every square inch. It was not safe for somebody with no painting experience. However, beggars could not afford to be choosers.

"I figure it will take about a fortnight for you to paint all of the gates and the roof of the shed," he told me.

"Is that it, then? That's all the work you'll have for me?"

"Is that not enough?" he asked, laughing. "Well, if it's more work you want, I think I can find other jobs for you to do...a couple more weeks' worth, anyway. I hear you're doing the Leaving. What will you work at after you get your exams?"

"I'm looking to get into Letterkenny College to study law."

"Good man. We'll have to watch out for you, and not vex you, or you might sue us."

I wasn't as interested in small talk as I was in finding out how much money I could expect for the work. "So, Dennis, how much does this painting job pay, then?"

"Well, it's not so much a painting job as it is throwing a bit of paint on to keep off the rust. Sure, we won't fall out over it anyway."

It wasn't what I wanted to hear, but it didn't sound like I was going to get a figure out of him. I wish I could have, for then I could have tried to negotiate a better deal if he offered too little. At least he was friendly with my auld fella, and that meant he probably wouldn't take advantage of me. Anyway, it wasn't as if I could charge like a tradesman. At the end of the day, I knew fuck-all about painting.

"Let me know when your exams are done and you can come over the first fine day for the painting," Dennis instructed me.

"Aye, right so."

About a week and a half later, on a Thursday, I finished my last exam. It was a strange feeling to be done. Really done.

There was no big celebration. It was a bit anticlimactic, actually. I had spent practically my whole life (that I could best remember) in school. Being in fifth year kind of gave you bragging rights: we were at the top of the food chain. Now that we were out, another wave of students would feel what it was like to be where we had been this past year. It was also bloody unsettling not to know what the future would bring, or if we would even *have* a future.

I couldn't accept that scratching around on a few acres of rush-filled fields could be considered a future. I think the fact that my younger brother was already out in the workforce made it a bit harder as well. Being the eldest, I felt like I should have been the one to do everything first.

The first thing I did on that Friday morning was absolutely nothing. I didn't get up early to milk the cow. When the auld fella went through his usual early morning ritual of cursing and shouting to get Jimmy up for work, I just pulled the pillow tightly around my ears and willed myself back to sleep. I knew the cow would eventually need milking, but feck it, I had never heard of a cow bursting due to not being milked on time.

When he woke me at 10:00 to let me know that Sarah and he were heading in to Carn to go shopping, I simply told him, "Good luck."

I felt him standing above me, expecting more of a conversation. "You're going to milk the cow, right?"

I felt like telling him that just because he dragged his leg, it didn't stop him from sitting under the cow and milking her. It wasn't like the Cow Milkers' Union of Ireland (that would probably be the "CMUI," if such a thing existed) would picket the front gate of our farm if he (a non-unionized milker) extracted a couple of pints of the white stuff.

"Aye."

A few minutes later I heard the Cortina pulling out of the street. I smiled when I realized that it was Friday—meat day. That was no longer my concern, however, as I had officially been retired as the meat courier. I got dressed and made myself a spot of breakfast. I wandered down to the byre with my milk bucket, singing "Whiskey in the Jar" (replacing the word "whiskey" with "cow juice") as I milked the cow. I figured that I would cycle over to the Harkins' after I was done and let Dennis know that I would be ready to start the next day as long as it kept dry. I decided that even if I got along well at the painting, I would not look for more customers, as the weather in North Donegal did not lend itself to outside painting. There were wet spells when a painter would not be able to use a brush for weeks at a time. It was definitely a fair-weather occupation.

After I drove the cow (I was good enough to drive a cow, but not a car) out to the back field, I washed and cycled over to Harkin's yard. I didn't bring anything, as I didn't plan on staying. I needn't have worried, as Dennis had all the brushes, white spirits, and bright blue paint a man could use.

I was to paint the gates first and then tackle the shed. He didn't actually use the word "tackle," but that is how I felt about taking on that monstrosity. Dennis thought more in terms of "throwing on a bunch of paint."

The more well-off farmers always had round robust bars in their gates. You had to make sure your paint covered the whole

360 degrees around. The less well-off farmers had flat metal gates. They did the same job, but were more flimsy. Then there was the likes of us who couldn't afford bought gates, and had to tie fence posts to barbed wire or squares of wire. We could never just flip back a bolt and push a gate open. We had to unlatch the wire loop off the top and roll back the gate one step at a time.

Unfortunately, Denis and I had a difference of opinion as to when I should start work. He was of the opinion that since I was already there and it wasn't raining, I may as well get stuck in right away. I learned two things about painting gates that first day. The first is that a novice painter will wind up with as much paint on himself as the gates. The second is that you work up a ferocious appetite. I started around 11:00 am, and by the time he checked on me at 1:30 pm I was already so hungry that I could have eaten a child's arse through a stepladder. Thankfully, the Donegal tradition of feeding your workmen was alive and well in the Harkin household, and I was told to come in for a bite of dinner.

"I see you're hard at it," Dennis remarked as he checked the gates for quality.

"Oh aye, you never know how long it will stay fair. I wanted to get as much done as I could, seeing as how I am already here."

My sarcasm seemed lost on him. "Do you think we'll have enough paint?" He was asking the wrong one, asking me. "Only, I wasn't figuring on you painting yourself as well," he said, grinning.

I hadn't bothered to think about it before, but when I looked down, I saw that I had bright blue paint all over my shirt, trousers, shoes and, as I was to find out, my hair. "It's those round gate bars you know, you have to slap the brush hard and get underneath to get the undersides done."

"Good man, I'm glad you are so thorough and getting everything covered. It's just that you look like one of those punk-rock boys with the blue hair. You should leave it like that," he said, laughing his arse off. "It will probably be all the fashion at the College."

I reached my hand to the top of my head and felt patches of hard hair. I must have looked a right sight.

"Come on in and we'll have our meal."

I didn't have to be asked twice. Five big floury Donegal spuds and a fried mackerel later, I was back to work. I think I painted six or seven gates by the end of the day. The end of the painting day, that is. I had plenty of chores still waiting for me back at my captors' place. Somehow or other I would have to find time to cut and spread turf as long as the weather stayed fair. I shouldn't have fretted about fitting it all in, however, as I would have help organizing my chores calendar.

"Look at the state of you," was my mother's greeting when I had cycled back. "Did you get any paint on the gates or were you just painting yourself? You'd better not expect me to scrub that paint off your clothes. You should have thought about that before you threw it all over yourself."

"It's my first painting job, you know."

I was too tired to listen to her telling me that I was as useless at painting as everything else. I was feeling sore from being bent over all day, and the clothes were starting to harden. I decided that I would just keep them for painting and wear the same ones every day. The hair would have to be washed, though. If I couldn't get all of the blue oily paint out with white spirits and soap, I knew it would have to be cut out.

"I hope you don't scare the cow when you go out to the field to drive her in. Did you forget that the turf still needs cutting? It should all be cut and spread out by now."

Jesus, Mary, and Joseph, that woman could go on and on without having to come up for air. For the past month I had been up studying until the wee hours of the morning, getting by with four hours of sleep if I was lucky, and then working for hours on the farm before turning around and doing it all over again. My first day off turned out to be my first day at work. She made it sound like I was sitting around all day on my arse doing nothing.

"I know that I'll be expected to paint all day tomorrow, so the first chance I would get would be Sunday."

"Well, we can't wait another week, so if you don't finish the cutting tomorrow, you'll have to go to the bog after you finish at Harkin's place."

She liked using the royal "we." She also liked to make it sound as if painting all day, milking, feeding, and cleaning out after animals was easy. After I had that all done, it would be no bother for me to spend another couple of hours of back-breaking work cutting and spreading turf. It was times like these when I wished I was on a chain gang in Mississippi. There was no sign of any food being cooked, and I felt like asking her how I was expected to do all of this work without eating. I was too tired to respond, though, so just dragged myself out to the field.

Saturday morning came around way too early. I slept like a dead man once Jimmy shut up about the smell of white spirits emanating from my hair. I was determined to get the paint out at all costs, even if it meant dousing my hair with enough spirits to wash every paintbrush in Ulster. Jimmy didn't care for the long hair, but even though I couldn't play an instrument, I still liked looking as if I should be in a band. Maybe I would even get a job as a roadie. God knows I must have met most of the roadies in Ireland, having a weekly backstage pass to nearly every band in the country.

I picked up my trousers from the end of the bed, and was surprised to see that they were so hard they could nearly stand up on their own without help from my legs. It made walking feel strange. I wanted to walk straight-legged. I'd have to force them to bend, though, as there was no way to ride a bike without bending your knees.

There was no sign of rain yet, so after I had washed some scone down with a hot mug of tea, I headed off to Harkin's yard. Dennis was pulling and hauling at machinery. I got my painting supplies and took off down the fields to finish painting gates.

It was a repeat of the day before, only with an earlier start. The other difference was that I found a cap to cover my hair. It would be a long day, and I didn't fancy spending an hour scrubbing the life out of my head that night.

After about four hours of solid painting, I started looking over my shoulder to see if there was any sign of Dennis calling me in for food. It was hard to work on just bread and tea, but good luck finding anything else to eat at my house in the morning. After all, Barney was good while he lasted, but all good things come to an end.

Dennis finally drove his tractor to the bottom fields where I was painting and brought me for the meal. I was excited to see his wife filling the frying pan with Doherty's Special Mince. I had nothing against fish, mind you, and that's what you'd expect to have on a Friday, but my jaws were watering for some meat and it didn't get much tastier than Doherty's. It looked like she split the entire pound of mince between Dennis and myself, and just when I thought it couldn't get any better, she scooped big spoonfuls of fried onions on top.

"I'd say you'll be finished with the gates by today. What do you think?" Dennis asked.

"I'm not sure how many you have altogether."

"You've done around a dozen now, and I'd say there was about twenty to begin with, so you shouldn't have much more than eight or nine."

"I should be able to finish them all if I stay until around seven. Sure, anything I don't finish I can do Monday, and then start on the shed roof."

"I was kind of thinking you might be able to start on the shed roof tomorrow after Mass." I wasn't expecting him to say that. He was starting to sound like our auld lady.

"Jesus, Dennis, I don't know if I can come back tomorrow. My mother wants me to finish cutting the turf bank. If I don't, I'll have to do it every evening after I finish here working for you."

I figured I'd add in something else to strengthen my argument: "Anyways, I'd have thought you wouldn't want the neighbors to be seeing so much work going on, with it being Sunday and all." I didn't know why, but this seemed to perk him up.

"I was thinking about that," he said, "and the good part about being up on that high roof is that probably none of them will look up at it, so no one will even know it's being painted."

The bastard had me there. It looked like I would be working all the hours of the day and evening for the next while. I was sure that our auld lady was going to go bonkers when I told her I had to work for Harkin the next day. I may have to share some of my wages with her to keep the peace. That was the worst part: As hard as I was working, I'd still have to share what little I'd be getting paid. For the first time in my life, I hoped that we'd get one wet hoor of a day so I could get a bit of rest.

"All right, let me finish a bit earlier, say around six, so that I can do some work in the bog. If I don't finish the gates today, I'll start on them tomorrow before the roof."

"Just make sure that whatever gates you have to leave for tomorrow are way down at the bottom of the field. I don't want the neighbors to see us painting anything from the road."

I don't know why he said "us," since *he* wasn't going to be seen working on a Sunday. He didn't even want it to be known that he had someone working for him. It wouldn't surprise me a bit if a neighbor asked him who was painting for him and he acted shocked.

I decided to say nothing when I got back, and instead headed straight to the bog after the milking was done. The old lady
caught me before I headed back out. If I had not stopped to wolf
down some leftover potatoes and carrots, I may have missed running into her.

"Where are you off to?"

I was hardly going to a dance with my painted trousers and
shirt. "I'm headed to the bog to cut turf."

"I thought you were going to be doing that tomorrow?"

"So did I, but Dennis said I needed to paint tomorrow."

"You won't be finishing the turf tomorrow?"

"The only way I could do that would be if I didn't go down to
mass with youns. I could cut first, and then go over to him and
paint."

I was hoping that she would go for it. I had no desire to sit
in the chapel watching the auld fella reading the Sunday paper.

"That might be best," she replied. "The turf needs cutting.
And before you know it, the hay will need to be cut and saved as
well."

Jesus, she wasn't happy unless she was assigning me work every minute of the day. I couldn't begin to imagine what they'd do
when I eventually left.

I headed out to the bog in the back of the house, which was a
fierce handy place to have a bog. As hard and all as the work was,
I looked forward to getting out there by myself and enjoying the
peace and quiet. There was nobody shouting. I was like a turf-
cutting Donegal monk. Bend, push, lift and throw. Repeat. I cut
for about an hour and a half and called it quits, as I'd be back out
in the morning when the holy rollers went to mass.

Curtainless windows and morning light acted as my alarm
clock. Mind you, on a Sunday morning in July, I would have
preferred if the day could have had a lay-in as well. I slipped
out of the bed and into my hard clothes. I didn't mess with any

breakfast—there'd be time for that when the floorless car of worshipers headed out.

Anyway, I still had a couple of loose cigarettes stashed away, and since I didn't get much of a chance to smoke a fag these days, I brought one out with some matches to the bog. I'd light it when I saw the car's arse turn out the lane. I smoked half of it and stubbed it out, saving the other half for a painting break. They'd only smell paint off me when I got back, and besides, I had one of the auld fella's communion mints for emergency purposes.

A couple of hours later, I was back in Dennis Harkin's yard. This was the big day when I'd paint the shed roof. Dennis had everything laid out on a small table at the front of the shed. There was no sign of life, and I figured that they all had gone down to Bocan chapel as well.

There was a ladder propped up against one side where the ditch was higher, and I could get to the top by using just the one ladder. It was still tricky, since I had to carry up the gallon of paint and brush while holding on for dear life. It dawned on me that I hadn't climbed a roof in quite a while. I was definitely out of practice. I didn't feel like a conqueror anymore, more like someone who would be far happier down on the ground.

I carefully stepped along until I came to the middle and found a place to lay down my tools where there wasn't so much of a bend, and so a lower chance of them sliding off. That was where I made base camp.

I didn't have a plan other than promising myself not to fall off and break my neck. I dipped the brush into the paint, got down on my hands and knees, and slowly made my way over to the side of the roof. I slapped the paint up and down until the brush ran out of paint, then made my way back over to the can and re-dipped. That was when I realized it was going to take a long bloody time to paint the roof.

After about a half hour, I began to feel more confident and less worried about falling off. That, and the fact that the corrugated metal was digging into my kneecaps, led to my decision that it would probably be safe enough to walk upright.

I concentrated fairly well for the next hour, and hardly noticed when the Harkins' car landed in the street. I actually didn't even know if it was them, since I couldn't see out over the roof where the car had stopped. A few minutes later, Dennis' head popped up over the edge of the roof. It looked funny, since there was no sign of the rest of him, just his head.

"How are you getting' on now?" he asked.

"Grand," I said.

"The wife will be puttin' on the food shortly. I'll give you a shout when it's time to eat."

"Right so."

I brought the paint down closer to where I was using it, so I'd have less distance to walk back to dip. I also took a chance at bringing it closer to the bend in the roof since the tin roof had ridges, and I figured there was less chance of it sliding off. This saved me a few feet of walking. I was starting to feel the hunger now that Dennis talked about eating. Sunday dinner was bound to take a bit longer to make, but I was really looking forward to a bit of grub. Actually, I was doing more than just looking forward to it. I started to fantasize about it. I figured that wealthy farmers must eat well on Sunday. There was bound to be a nice piece of meat, maybe chicken. What if they had lamb? Oh Jesus, if they had lamb I'd be in heaven. If they had lamb, they'd also have mint sauce.

The brush was dry again, and I was not too far from the paint can. I decided to stretch out and reach into the can instead of going to the bother of getting up and walking. The dinner probably wouldn't be much longer. Thankfully I had a long reach and could do it. I just needed another inch or two and I'd be dipping into the paint. Just when I felt that I couldn't reach any further, the brush made it in. I slowly pulled it out and looked to my right to see where I'd be painting. As I turned, I jerked the can and it tipped over. I turned around in time to see the entire contents of the can—about three quarters of a gallon—coming at me like a bright blue river of lava racing down the side of a tin volcano.

My first thought was to get away from the paint before I got covered, so I scurried backward, pushing with my hands. After a couple of quick pushes back, my left foot pushed against air. I realized that I was about to go over backwards off the edge of the roof. I panicked and froze to the spot. I knew that falling off that roof would probably spell my death, and not knowing what else to do, I stayed glued there. The thick blue paint came at me and covered my whole chest and shoulders. I had to lift up my chin so that I wouldn't get it in my mouth. Whatever didn't make it past my chest diverted to the sides and began to run down along my torso toward my waist. In a few minutes it covered me.

I was glued to the spot – or more accurately, painted to the spot. When the shock subsided, I tried raising my upper body, but my hands were slippery with paint. If worst came to worst, I could wait until Dennis called me in to eat, but I'd rather he didn't see me helpless like this.

I slowly dragged myself forward with my elbows. Next I brought up my knees. That allowed me to crawl towards the ladder on my hands and knees. When I reached the edge of the roof by the ladder, I knew I needed to turn around and go down backwards, but my knees were so weak that they were trembling.

Somehow or other, I found it in me to step on the top rung and very gingerly started to make my way down. When I was halfway, Dennis walked out to tell me that dinner was ready. He asked me something about the painting, but I couldn't focus. I needed to feel the ground beneath my feet. When I finally planted them down, I turned around to answer him.

"Good God of Almighty, what happened to you?"

I looked down at the blue mess that used to be me.

"I had an accident. The paint spilled on me and I nearly fell off the roof."

"Is the paint all gone?" he wanted to know.

"It is."

"How much of the roof did you paint?"

"I don't know...maybe the top quarter...I thought I was going to fall off and get killed."

"Jesus, lad, that paint should have at least covered half of the roof, maybe more. Paint's not cheap, you know. You can't be goin' around throwin' it about the place."

"I'm sorry. Are we havin' the dinner now?"

"The dinner? Sure, I couldn't let you into the house in that state. You'd have paint on everything. You'll have to head off home."

With that, he turned around and headed back into his house, leaving me standing there covered in blue paint. I got on my lilac and black bike, with blue dripping, and pedaled away as best as I could. I figured that I must have looked like I had crashed into a bloody rainbow. Thankfully there wasn't anybody at the house when I got back, so I stripped down and started to scrub myself with white spirits. When that ran out, I used diesel. It made a better paint remover than a Molotov cocktail ingredient, but it did burn like a bitch anywhere I had a cut or scratch.

By the time the mass crowd got back, I was half presentable. I didn't wait around to be asked why I wasn't at Harkin's, but headed straight out to the bog. My sides were sticking together with hunger, but I'd have to wait until we all ate together.

The following day was half-decent looking, so I figured that I'd go over and get a couple of hours in before it rained. It was windy, so that at least would make the paint dry quicker. I didn't overly fancy being up on that big roof with the wind blowing, but

I'd just have to be more careful and not take chances by over-stretching for paint. Dennis was in the shed tinkering with the tractor's engine.

"I don't think it will stay dry for too long," I told him, "so I figured I'd get a bit done anyway."

"Ah, I don't think you should be going back up," he told me.

"How will it get finished?"

"I'll have to get someone else to finish the job. It's a big roof, and the hardest parts are still left to do."

"What else have you for me, then?"

"I can't say I have anything for now. I'll pay you for the time you were here."

He put his hand in his pocket, fished out a five-pound note and handed it to me. I looked at it, waiting for him to pull out something else. That was it. Five miserable pounds for spending three days getting covered in paint and nearly breaking my neck. I didn't even thank the cheap bastard. I turned my bike around and cycled away. I was in no hurry to get back, so I cycled slowly. A working man's laboring wage would be around ten pounds for the day. I wanted to turn around and argue for more money, but I figured he would gyp me out of it saying that I had no experience or skills.

Still, I was expecting to get near it, maybe six or seven quid for each of the two full days, and around three quid for the half day. I would have still been disappointed to have been let go, but at least I would have had around fifteen pounds in my pocket. Five was a pure insult. I painted every bloody gate on his farm and a quarter of his dangerous roof. Even the clothes that were destroyed by the paint could not be replaced with five quid. I was not looking forward to walking into the house with the news.

"What are you doing back so soon?" asked my auld fella. "Is it raining over there?"

"It's not. Your friend Dennis told me that I was done and he had no more work for me."

"You must be a really fast painter to have finished that big shed so soon. You should have paced yourself and got the rest of the week out of it," he quipped.

I waited to see if there'd be any more questions. If there weren't, I wouldn't volunteer any additional information. He seemed preoccupied with reading the Sunday paper. He must not have got through it all at mass.

"By the way," he said, "how much did you get for the painting job?"

"Five pounds."

"Five pounds a day? Jesus, he didn't overpay you, did he? He could have spared another pound or two a day, I would have thought." I was afraid he'd later find out and then accuse me of lying to him.

"Actually, he paid me five pounds total, not five pounds each day."

"Five pounds in total? Are you pulling my leg?" It was a popular expression, but under the circumstances, I thought it ironic that he'd use it. It occurred to me that had I been under the kitchen table and pulling the sick leg, he wouldn't even have known it.

"He had to give you more than five pounds," joined in the auld lady with a suspicious look in her eye. I was in no mood for a cross-examination, and the fact that she thought I was holding back money that I had earned from the fruits of my own labor was starting to rub me the wrong way.

"Here, I'll tell you what. I'll empty out my pockets and you can count it for yourself, seeing as how you don't think I am capable of knowing what a five-pound note looks like."

I pulled the insides of my pockets out like a rabbit's ears and the crumpled five-pound note fell out on the table.

"Do you see anything else?" I asked her. "How much does that look like to you?" I could feel my heart racing and my blood running faster, as if I were about to get into a physical fight. I felt more ready to attack than defend.

"Take it easy," the auld fella instructed me. "There's no need to bark at your mother."

"I'm fed up being treated like the hired help around here. Then when I get screwed over by a friend of yours, she makes it sound like she's taking his side and calling me a liar. I nearly fell off your friend's roof yesterday and broke my neck. Of course that was *my* fault, too. That's why he fired me. How the hell do you think I could have finished that big hoor of a roof in a day? He didn't even have the decency to invite me in for a couple of spuds after it, and me shaking from the shock. He handed me that five-pound note like he begrudged me getting it. If I didn't need it so badly, I would have told him to wipe his arse with it."

I stopped to catch my breath. I had not taken a breath throughout my entire tirade. They both looked like they were in a state of shock. I turned around and headed out to the bog. I had a lot of energy to burn off after my rant, so I figured I'd put it to good use. Nobody came near me. As a matter of fact, my parents fairly much stayed out of my way after my blowout. I don't know if they got together and agreed to it, or if they saw something in my eyes that day that told me I was near the breaking point. I actually felt like something was going to snap.

I stayed out of their way as well, and took to visiting the local farms on my bike every day after I finished my chores to see if anybody had any work for me. I kept looking for weeks, but it was hard times for all small farmers, and nobody had any money to spare. Besides, every house was full of children, so they all fairly much had their own built-in workforce.

CHAPTER 33

GOODBYE TO SCHOOL
AND ELVIS

I 'll never forget the week that the Leaving cert results came out. I received the best and worst news of my life, all in the same week.

I was hoping to be able to go down to Malin Head for the Fifteenth of August sports day. Daniel said he would come up and collect me after breakfast and I could stay over on my Aunt's farm for a few days. I was really looking forward to it. Since it would be the first time that I would be attending without the rest of the family, I could knock around with Daniel, my grandfather, and their drinking friends.

After breakfast I went to do the milking, feeding, and cleaning, and the auld fella drove down to the Post Office to collect the mail like he did every day. By the time I was finished and getting ready for the off, the old man had returned.

"There's an official brown envelope here addressed to John Sexton," he stated.

"Well, it's either for you or me then."

He peeled back a corner and stuck in his forefinger, sliding it along the length of the envelope like a letter opener. He studied the paper inside.

"It's for you," he said, handing it to me. I didn't like the look on his face.

I could see straight away that it was the results of the Leaving cert. I opened the letter slowly so I wouldn't get too quick a shock by seeing how badly I had done.

To my surprise, I had passed every subject, and had got two out of the three honors.

Could that be right? I read it again, more slowly.

There was no mistake. I had passed the Leaving cert.

It felt like an anvil had been lifted off my chest.

"I passed the Leaving," I muttered to myself.

I don't know if anybody responded, as I was in my own dream world. I had basically waited six years for this day.

I felt a bit like a dog that chases after a car. When he catches it, what does he do with it? He definitely doesn't drive it. What was I now to do with this coveted certificate of completion?

I'd have to wait and see if I was going to get a scholarship for the Legal Executive Course. I was now more anxious than ever to see what the morning post would bring.

Two days after he brought me the good news, the old fella returned home from collecting the post and handed me the daily paper. We only ever got a Sunday paper and the local *Derry Journal* every Friday. I was shocked to see him with a Wednesday edition of the *Irish Independent*. I would never have asked him to buy me a paper.

I opened it. What I read on the front page immediately emptied my lungs of air. "The King is Dead." Elvis had died. How could the king of rock and roll be dead?

I read through the article in a state of shock. I was hoping that it was some kind of hoax, but they had pictures of thousands of grieving fans outside of Graceland. I can't explain it, but I felt like a good friend had died, and I was in mourning just like those people in Memphis.

I kept out of everyone's way that day, and thankfully they kept out of mine. Later in the evening, when my head had cleared a bit, I began to think about it all. It was only then that I realized what my father had done. Unbeknownst to me, he was aware of my love for Elvis. Even though it may not sound like much, we couldn't afford a daily newspaper, and for him to bring one back so that I could read and re-read it until most of the ink from the paper was transferred to my fingers was probably one of the most thoughtful things he had ever done for me. I would never have known he had it in him.

Another person who surprised me by his kindness was my brother Jimmy. The following week, I received a letter saying that I won my scholarship to attend Letterkenny College, but I had no money on which to live. He and my parents must have gotten together and discussed the matter, coming up with the solution that Jimmy would give me half of his apprenticeship earnings each week. This would give me three pounds to buy food from Monday to Friday, and I would thumb home every Friday evening.

Every Monday morning around 7:00 am, I would make my way over to the foot of the Redcastle Mountain and hold out my thumb until someone would stop and pick me up. I never got there in one straight shot. The lift could be for five miles or twenty—I just never knew.

I didn't like taking the shorter lifts, as they would usually drop me on a part of the road where fewer cars went by, but when it was freezing cold or raining, I took anything I could get just to be inside a warm car. A drive straight down to Letterkenny would probably take an hour, but when I thumbed, it could easily take from four to six hours, and the same to get back on a Friday evening.

Despite having to live on baked beans, toast, and tea for most of the time, I was enjoying everything about college life. Learning was not such a chore, since I really liked studying law. I began to look forward to being able to practice law one day, and this eased the disappointment I had felt knowing that I would not be a journalist.

Toward the end of September, the old lady cornered me when I got back from college at the weekend and told me that the national police force, An Garda Siochana, were having a recruitment drive and that a walk-in exam was taking place at the Golden Grill ballroom in Letterkenny. I asked her why that would be of any interest to me.

"Do you know how many attorneys and people with degrees are walking around unemployed these days?" she asked me back. I had no idea, but that didn't stop her. "What would be the use of going to school for all those years only to be on the dole?"

"I don't think every one of them is on the dole," I shot back. "And besides, I have no desire to be a policeman."

"It's a good stable government job. You'd be making a living right after training, and you could go far if you put your mind to it. Sure, the commissioner is a Donegal man. Why don't you just do the exam anyway? Then after you pass it, you could always say that you could have been a Garda if you had wanted. The Golden Grill is just across the street from your college."

She kept going on and on about joining the police all weekend. By the time I reached Letterkenny on Monday afternoon, I had decided to go and take the bloody exam just to get her off my back. I don't even remember what the exam was like, since I had absolutely no interest in it. A couple of weeks later when I returned home on a Friday evening, she handed me a brown government-looking letter. It didn't seem to have been opened (although I had witnessed her steaming open a letter before and resealing it), and was addressed to John Patrick Sexton. I was quite surprised to read that I had passed the Garda exam and was scheduled to take a physical and psychological exam in the Phoenix Park Garda HQ the following week.

My mother was standing by waiting for my decision.

"All right," I told her. "I did the exam like you wanted, so now you can tell the neighbors that your son could have been a Garda, but instead he went back to studying law."

"Ah, you'll have to go down to Dublin, seeing as how they have you on their list. There are probably thousands of disappointed lads all over Ireland who didn't pass the exam and would love to have the opportunity to go to Dublin. It doesn't mean you have to take the job. You can always say that you went all the way, and at the end of the day it wasn't for you."

And there was me thinking that the old man could sell sand to the Arabs. He was a novice compared to her.

"It's during the week, and I'll miss out on classes. Besides, I have no way of getting to Dublin. Three pounds barely buys enough food to last the week as it is, and there is no money left over for bus fare."

"Well, leave it with your father and we'll see if he can organize a lift down. If you were sick, you would wind up missing some classes, so it's not the end of the world. Wait until you see. You'll thank me later."

I don't know why she thought that. I was only going along with it to keep her quiet.

I was packing up my clothes on Sunday night for the trip back to college the following day when the auld fella broke the news. "Your appointment in the Phoenix Park is Friday morning, so I got you a lift to Dublin from a fella I know who has a truck going down Thursday night."

"Where would I stay when I get there, if it is at night?"

"Your brother has agreed to give you an extra three pounds this week. We can kick in another two quid, so a fiver should get you B&B. If you thumb back here on Thursday morning, you can buy a bus ticket back from Dublin with the money you would have spent on food for two days at college."

They seemed to have thought of everything, which left me with little excuse not to go along with it. The following Thursday found me standing at the front gates of Letterkenny college with my thumb out at noon. I should have probably started thumbing earlier, but I wanted to take at least one class, and it wasn't like I was going to need time to prepare for a physical and psychological. I arrived home at 6:00 pm. A huge plate of food was put in front of me nearly as soon as I stepped into the kitchen. That was a first.

"I was talking to the sergeant in Moville on Monday," the auld fella shared, "and he said that somebody as tall as you needs to be a certain weight and chest measurement. You need to eat as much as you can between now and tomorrow morning so that you are not too underweight."

"I think I probably should have started this weight gain program a little earlier than today," I replied. "Like maybe a year or two ago."

"That is why I got you these to eat on the way down," he continued, handing me a huge bag of bananas.

"There must be a stone weight of bananas here." I would not have eaten that many in a year.

"Ten pounds, to be exact," the auld fella replied. "I read somewhere that boxers who were struggling to make a higher fighting weight would eat loads of bananas before they were weighed in and that would do the trick."

He was dropping me off at the Greencastle pier at 9:00 pm, as I was getting a lift down to Dublin in a fish lorry. I was hoping that I wouldn't have the smell of fish on me by the time I got there. I went into the bedroom after dinner to change into the clothes that I'd be wearing to the exams. I stripped off my shirt and looked at my bare torso reflected in the glass. I held out my arms to each side and sucked in my cheeks. With the long hair and visible rib cage, I looked like a Donegal Jesus. I figured that it was a complete waste of time going down to Dublin if the police were looking for young fellas with a decent amount of meat on their bones, since there were slim pickings on me. Armed with a big bag of bananas, though, we headed off to meet up with a lorry load of Dublin-bound fish.

My father spoke to the driver of the lorry. He grunted something back that I couldn't hear since the wind was howling around my ears. He then told me to climb into the cab and that they'd see me Friday night. I don't know if we had held back the driver, but he started to drive off as I was closing the cab door. I joked about nearly losing my bananas, but he totally ignored me. As a matter of fact, he didn't say a single word to me the whole way down. For nearly four hours, I stared out the window and ate bananas.

When we finally arrived in Dublin at 1:00 am, he stopped on a dark street and told me that this was where I needed to get off. I asked him where I was and he muttered, "the Bridewell." He may as well have said "Timbuktu" or "Shanghai," for all the good that information did me. I walked around the cobblestone street looking for a bed and breakfast, but there wasn't a light on anywhere or a sinner to be seen. After about an hour of walking around, I started to think that he must have dropped me off in the most remote part of Dublin he could find. I had not a clue how I would ever find Phoenix Park once it was daylight.

After another half hour, I came across a Garda station. I went in clutching my half bag of bananas and rang the bell on the counter. A big broad Garda with a droopy moustache opened the hatch and stared at me.

"I just got a lift down from Donegal," I told him. "I'm going to the Garda Headquarters in the morning to take a physical and psychological exam, and I was supposed to find a B&B around here for the night. Do you know where it's at?"

"Is that fish you have in the bag?" the big cop asked me.

"No," I said, "it's bananas. You probably smell fish because I got a lift down in a fish lorry from Greencastle pier." He looked confused. I don't know if it was the fact that I smelled like fish at 2:00 in the morning or that I was carrying around five pounds of bananas.

"Well, there's no B&B around here, I can tell you," he said. "If you want a place to stay until the morning, you can use one of our interview rooms." He opened the door into the office and I followed him.

"That would be great."

"What time do you have to be at the Phoenix Park?" he asked me without turning around.

"Nine o'clock."

"All right, I'll leave a note for the morning relief to come and fetch you around 8:00. That will give you plenty of time to walk up and sign in at the front gate. It should take about forty-five minutes from here."

I thanked him again and closed the door behind him. The interview room was very basic. It had a large wooden desk with three chairs around it. There was a big wood press in one corner of the room. I left my bananas on the table and sat down in a chair. I realized that even though I was dog tired, there was no way that I was going to be able to sleep upright. I got up on the table and stretched out, using my arms as makeshift pillows. I didn't expect to sleep that way either, but I was dead wrong. I actually slept well—too well. I woke up to find that it was bright out. I didn't know the time, but had a bad feeling that it was too bright to be early.

I grabbed my bananas and walked out into the room behind the public office. A Garda sitting behind a typewriter looked up, surprised to see me.

"Who are you?" he asked.

"I came down from Donegal late last night. I'm doing the physical and psychological at Garda Headquarters this morning. Do you know what time it is?"

He looked at his wrist. "It's a quarter to nine."

"Jesus Christ, I'm late. I'm supposed to be there by nine. Can you tell me how to get there?"

He pointed his arm towards the door. "Go down by the River Liffey and make a right. Keep going straight until you come to the big gates of the park. Go through the gates and bear to your right. That will take you to the top of the park. You'll see the front gates of HQ and all of the buildings behind it. Tell them who you are and where you are going at the gate house, as you'll have to sign in." As an afterthought he added, "You'll never make it by 9 o'clock, you know."

I didn't even stop to thank him. I bolted out the door and headed to the right like he told me. There was no way I could afford to walk up at this stage. I started to run. Then I realized that I still had a half bag of bananas to get through. Somehow or other, I managed to run, peel, chew and swallow bananas at the same time. I must have been a sight for sore eyes, running through the park, throwing banana skins over my shoulder as I stuffed my face. By the time I arrived at the front gate, I was sweating like a Clydesdale after pulling a plough all day. I went into the guard house and told the cop on the gate why I was there. He gave me a strange look when I swapped the half-eaten banana from my right hand to my left so that I could use the pen to sign in. I picked up the rest of the bananas and walked over to the building where the physicals were being held.

When I entered the waiting room, I saw a bunch of young men sitting around looking like they had wandered into the wrong building. Nobody was saying much apart from the odd comment. I didn't have time for talking, as I still had nine or ten bananas to eat.

After about fifteen minutes, a woman dressed a bit like a nurse came into the room with a clipboard and called out my name and another name. Shite, I had only managed to get through three more bananas. It would have to do.

I turned to the fella on my left, intending to give him the remaining bananas, but he looked well-fed and I didn't think he would have any trouble making the weight. I passed the bag to my right, as that fella was scrawny and as undernourished-looking as myself.

"Eat as many of these as you can before they call your name. It will make you a bit heavier when they weigh you," I whispered.

We followed the nurse down the hall, and each of us went into a separate room. I waited there for about ten minutes before the doctor came in. He was a very old-looking man with a stethoscope around his neck. He made me stand on a scale and wrote down my weight. Next I stood with my back to a chart, so I assumed he was recording my height. He listened to the front and back of my chest, and then shone a light into my ears and eyes.

"You have an irregular heartbeat," he said, and then he told me to strip down to my underwear and sit on the examining table. He took a rubber hammer and hit my knees a few times and around my ankles.

The next thing surprised me: He told me to stand up and drop my drawers. He made me look over my right shoulder and cough as he grabbed me by the balls. I tried to force my eyes to look to the left to see what he was at, but I couldn't see much without turning my head. The next thing I knew, he was telling me to get dressed and go back out to join the other boys in the waiting room.

I went back to where I had been sitting and noticed that the skinny boy was no longer there. The poor bastard didn't get a chance to eat many bananas.

After about twenty minutes, he came back into the room and sat in his old seat. He had a big grin on his face.

"You look like you had a good time in there," I told him.

"The doctor gave me a great compliment," he informed me. "He asked me to drop my jocks, and then he grabbed my family jewels and told me that I had a 'good cock.'"

"And what did you say to that?" I asked him.

"I said, 'Thank you, Doctor.'"

"Are you sure he told you that you had a good cock?" I asked him. "That doesn't really sound like something a doctor would say."

"I know," he said. "That's what makes it all the better. When you think about it, he must see hundreds of cocks every year during these types of examinations."

"I don't want to burst your bubble, but I think what he probably said was 'have a good cough.'"

He considered that for a minute. "Jesus, you might be right," he agreed. "I *thought* he looked at me a bit funny when I thanked him."

"I hope he is not the same one doing the psychological," I told him, "or he might have some extra questions for you."

The psychological exam was as tame as the physical one. They asked a few questions about why I wanted to be a policeman and how it might feel to have to shoot someone or arrest someone I knew. Unlike the questioning by the Aer Lingus board, this time I told them exactly what I thought they wanted to hear. I thought about the whole thing on the bus back up to Derry. I didn't know why, but I realized that I had actually tried to do well. God knows

I was not interested in being a policeman. After all, I only did it to keep the old lady off me back. However, the thought of being out there on the streets keeping the peace appealed to me. My mother was waiting for me when I got back. Unlike before, she was actually interested in hearing about how the exam had gone.

"Aye, it was all right," I informed them.

"Is that all—just all right?" she asked.

"Well, they never let on how they are thinking. The doctor did say that I had an irregular heartbeat."

"Did he say anything else?"

"No."

"I wonder what he was thinking?"

I had done my duty, and on Monday morning I was back on the road thumbing down to college. I didn't expect to be bothered with any more joining-the-police talk. Even if I did want to be a pilot, or a cop, at that stage I didn't think they were going to hire 19-year-old lads for such a serious position. At least, I felt that way for a few weeks.

One Friday evening about a month later, though, I walked in the front door to find another brown envelope. I was convinced it would be a letter thanking me for taking part but letting me know that I had not been selected. I was quite shocked to find out that it was quite the opposite. I was being called back to Dublin to do the final interview. The fucking banana trick had worked.

"There's really no point," I told the old lady.

"What do you mean, no point?"

"Sure, I don't want the job. Remember, I only did it so that I could say later that I could have been a Garda but I didn't want it."

"You've come this close now," she said. "Sure you have to go the last little bit. When they tell you that they are taking you, that's when you can say 'Thanks, but no thanks.' You can't quit now."

In a warped way, I could see her point. I must have been losing it when she seemed like the sensible one. One thing I was certain about was that there was no chance she was going to talk me into taking the job if, by some weird cosmic shift in the universe, those in authority (and obviously not in their right minds) deemed me suitable to don the uniform of a policeman.

"Here's the deal." If she wanted me to do the interview badly enough, I figured that I could chance my arm and dictate the terms. "I'm not going back to Dublin smelling like fish. I'll need a few quid for the return bus or train trip, whatever is the cheapest. I'll clean up the best that I can, but there is no chance that I will cut my hair." I was growing fond of my Jesus look, and besides, winter was coming in. I would need as much head and facial hair as I could grow to protect me against hours of standing out in the cold twice a week waiting for lifts.

On top of all that, I knew that I had more chance being elected President of Ireland than being selected to join the police, and I didn't want to waste a year of growing my hair for a half hour of a wasted interview.

"Nobody else will go for an interview to be a Garda looking like a hippie."

"Then if the interview board is smart, they should be picturing me working undercover, since nobody would ever expect an Irish cop to look like Jesus. I could go deep undercover like the cops on the telly do when they work in places like the Bronx and Miami."

"I still think you will look like you're doing drugs to them, but we'll find a way to get the bus fare between now and then. Don't go up there acting like you don't care whether they pick you or not. It will all have been a waste of time if they think you are not taking it serious."

"I'll lie and tell them that I wanted to be a cop since I was in grade school. I won't even breathe a word about the time that my Uncle Daniel beat up a New York City cop with the officer's own gun, and he had to go on the run and come back to live in Ireland."

"Oh Jesus," she sighed. She even thought I looked like him now. I saw her eyes widen as she envisioned my letting the secret slip in the interview. "Don't even think about that, never mind laugh about it. If that was to ever be found out, I am sure they would come and arrest him even after all these years." I had no intention of ever mentioning it to anybody outside of the family, of course, but it was entertaining to see how worked up she got at the thought of it slipping out.

Just as before, I went back to college life and was as happy as a pig in shite (or at least a pig that didn't have to dodge a crazy man's knife). I put the whole idea of joining the police force out of my mind. The same could not be said for my mother. She somehow rounded up the bus fare for me to be able to go back to Dublin for the interview. I didn't let on to anyone from my class why I was going to Dublin, but instead let them think that I was going down to have a good time.

Surprisingly, the interview was not terribly intense. They seemed impressed by the fact that I had won a scholarship to the new Legal Executive Course. I didn't share my own belief that I must have scraped in by the skin of my teeth.

Not that I was waiting with bated breath, but when I didn't hear any news from the boys in blue by the beginning of December, I assumed that they had already chosen those who would eventually become the guardians of the peace. I was actually very surprised that I had made it as far as I had, since there were definitely more law breakers in the family than law abiders. I could only imagine what some of my classmates back in Carndonagh would have to say if they had known that I was applying to be a cop. The first thing they would have done would be to tell me to fuck off. Actually, when someone was skeptical, they'd usually say it in the form of a request, as in, "Would you ever fuck off?" Next thing they'd do would be to piss themselves laughing.

The week before we paused for the Christmas break, I had a hateful time getting back home from Letterkenny. I waited outside the college gate from 1:00 pm on, and did not get a single car to stop until after 3:30. It was starting to snow a little. If I ever needed a quick lift, it was that Friday.

To make matters worse, girls would come out to the gate, stand there for ten minutes, and a car would stop and pick them up. I even saw a priest stop and pick up a girl who had barely got to the edge of the footpath. I knew damn well he had seen me standing there as he approached.

By the time I got home around 6:30, I was frozen to the bone. I didn't want to talk to anyone. I just wanted to hug the range and thaw out enough to feel like I had rejoined the living.

I caught the auld fella staring at me like he wanted to say something significant. I was too tired, cold, and hungry to play guessing games, so I ignored it the best I could. Nothing he could have said would have made me feel any worse, except maybe to tell me that I now had to thumb into Carn to collect the bag of meat.

They must have decided between them that the old lady would be the spokesman. She came over to the range, opened the top lid, and threw in a sod of turf.

"We have some news," she said, half glancing at me. I didn't know if she waited for dramatic effect, or if they expected me to be curious. When she didn't get a response, she continued. "The Garda sergeant in Moville who took your application came by in the squad car this afternoon."

"Did one of our relatives die?"

"No, they did not. It was good news. He said that he got the results for the next training class of new Guards in Templemore, and that you are on the list."

It sounded like she had said that they had chosen me to train to be a Garda. That couldn't be right.

"I'm on the list to go to training to be a Garda? Are you sure that is what he said?"

"Of course I am sure. He said to offer his congratulations to you when you got home from college, and for you to call over to the Garda station so that he could tell you what you needed to know about starting training."

My mind was reeling. How the hell did they decide to pick me to go to training?

I tried hard to concentrate, wondering if I had been exposed too long to the cold and the likelihood that it had done a number on my mind. I even considered the possibility that I was still standing on the side of the road in the dark somewhere, and that I was now experiencing some kind of mental mirage.

Strangely, I did not automatically reject the whole idea of joining the police, either verbally (as I did every step along the way through the process) or to myself.

"When my fingers thaw out, I'm going to make a mug of tea."

"Well, aren't you excited?" She sounded way too excited. She must have forgotten the part where I only agreed to go through with all of this for the neighbors to know that I could have been in the police if I chose to.

"Oh, aye."

I didn't have the energy to debate it. The fact that I was not in a rush to reject the notion scared me a little. Maybe I would feel different when I thawed out.

I don't know if my parents were expecting to see Vatican-like smoke bellowing out of the chimney, but I could feel their eyes follow me to the turf basket as I got up to fill the range with turf. I didn't let on, but I felt a little shell-shocked the whole weekend realizing that I had actually been one of a select few to successfully make it into training for the National Police Force of Ireland.

I was peeling a pot of spuds for the Sunday dinner when it hit me. I wondered what those old bastards on the Aer Lingus interview board would think if they knew that one of their rejected trainee pilots could one day have the power to pull their car over and summons them to court for having a flat tire, or a bald head, or for living past their sell-by date. It made me want to be stationed in Dublin.

Oh, there was more—and this was definitely the pièce de résistance—what would old lady Harkin have to say when she found out that her daughter could have been going out with a member of the force? I would have given anything to be able to see the old bag's face when she got that tidbit of news.

I figured it would be smart to at least hear what the sergeant had to say about the training so I could make an informed decision. I was getting ready to thumb over to Moville on Monday when the auld fella offered to give me a lift. Either he was really mellowing in his old age, or else he was anxious to get me off the dinner roster.

I didn't ask him to come into the police station, but he followed me in, and thankfully he was well-behaved throughout the meeting. Then again, he wasn't the type to feel relaxed in a cop shop.

"That went well," he said once we got out on the street. "I can't believe that you will be starting training as early as February."

"I know." The fact that he used "will" instead of "could" had not gotten by me.

"Did you hear what he said about lads waiting for years to get selected, and how even then some of them will never get called?"

"I did."

I was surprised by the fact that I would have to start training in mid-February if I decided to take the job. That would only leave me a little over a month to enjoy college life. I thought of little else during the whole Christmas break. I knew it would prove to be one of the biggest decisions of my life. I also knew that I would not let anyone know until the last minute.

Either way, Jimmy would be the first to know what I had decided to do. If I stayed on in college, he would probably have to continue to support me for most of the next two years. (I would be forever grateful for his support, without which it would not even have been possible for me to go to college, scholarship or no scholarship.) I always felt like this was way too much to ask, although I didn't even have to ask him, as he did it anyway. That is why I decided to tell him first.

When I arrived back home the first weekend of February, I made the announcement that I would not be returning to college on Monday morning, and that I would be preparing to go to Templemore Garda Training Center that following week. I think that everyone was more surprised than anything else. They all figured by then that I was going to turn down the offer. It was definitely one possibility, and quite a strong contender at the beginning.

When I weighed up the pros and cons, I liked the idea of not having to spend the rest of the winter freezing in the dark for hours on end and not having to sponge on my brother's generosity any longer. The long arm of the law had reached out and beckoned.

CHAPTER 34

BROKEN FENCES

B ecoming part of the "respectable establishment" served a couple of different purposes for me. Mainly, it gave me the freedom for which I had longed. There had been other avenues of escape which I could have pulled off, and the rebel in me had given these quite a bit of thought. At the end of the day, though, I chose the option which would not necessitate having to break ties with my younger brothers and sisters. Being an exile from my parents did not cause me that much concern, but the prospect of having a 4-year-old baby sister I might not get to know until much later in life ate at me.

Succumbing to a Government job came at a price, however. It did not instill within me an overwhelming sense of pride or a powerful feeling of accomplishment—and it should have. Being chosen to train as a member of the Garda Siochana was somewhat akin to winning the lottery for most young Irish males. There were thousands of hopefuls throughout the country waiting to receive that official brown government envelope informing them that they were to follow in their father or grandfather's footsteps. I took the job almost begrudgingly.

My new position also served the purpose of showing my father how wrong he had been. However, all those years of being put down, ridiculed, and belittled seemed to me to warrant a greater reward. Writing was in my blood, especially poetry, and down deep I thought that maybe one day I could be thought of as a William Butler Yeats or a Patrick Kavanagh. Needless to say, fighting and getting into trouble were also in my blood, so the idea of being in wars, perhaps as an underdog fighter for a worthy cause or a foreign war correspondent like Ernest Hemmingway, also appealed to me.

My first two years on the job were rocky. I was not adored by every Sergeant I worked under. Toward the end of my first year and while still on probation, I was dragged up in front of a stone-faced Superintendent. The man must have been within an ass' roar of 70 years of age. He also had not aged well. He didn't talk to me; he barked at me.

"Can you give me one good reason why I should not fire you?" he asked, writing in a file (probably my "about to get fired" file).

Unfortunately, I could not think of a decent answer, even though my livelihood depended on it. The truth was that I needed a job, but I didn't think that would impress him. Not only did it lack any kind of passion for the profession, but the fact of the matter was that half of the fucking country needed a job in the recession-torn Ireland of the late 70's and early 80's.

Standing in front of my would-be executioner, my mind started to involuntarily flash back to the events which led to my current predicament. Two weeks before I had gone on leave and toured around Ireland with my girlfriend Martina, who would later become my wife. For some inexplicable reason—alcohol may have been involved—I allowed her brother, a hair dresser, to give me a perm. My hair, which was always thick and was then longer than it should have been, came out looking like a stack of hay. I remember laughing and saying that I looked like a white Jimi Hendrix. To top it off, I started growing an unofficial moustache—in those days a policeman had to apply for permission through the chain of command to grow hair on his face.

Desiring to milk every last minute of my time away from work, I failed to get my hair cut or shave off the illegal facial hair before showing up for work, in uniform, the day I reported back. Had I been assigned to an undercover narcotics unit, my new look would have been perfect. Unfortunately for me, a large bomb had been detonated close to our headquarters the morning of my return, and by the time I reported for roll call at 2:00 pm all hell had broken loose.

The Superintendent who was now deciding my fate was in charge of the operations that very same day. He chewed the Station Sergeant's arse off for allowing one of his uniformed men to report for duty looking like he had just returned from touring with the Rolling Stones.

I know this because after roll call the Station Sergeant cornered me. "You must have balls the size of grapefruits to be showing up for work looking like a roadie from a rock band. The Superintendent just chewed me out." He then turned to the Station orderly, whose job it was to record all comings and goings in the station log book. "Don't mark Sexton down on duty until he goes to the barbershop to get a hair cut and shave."

I somehow managed to survive that incident and make it through probation. My fiancée Martina wanted me to get stationed in Mayo, or at least the West of Ireland, so she could be close to her parents. Having busted my arse to get as far away as possible from my own parents, I willingly agreed to look for a transfer back down to Mayo. Besides, Martina's parents actually seemed to like me, and it didn't hurt that I came with the "respectable government job" that every Irish mother seemed to value so highly. After my having served a year "on the border," the transfer was approved and I was posted to Castlebar, the capital town of County Mayo.

Everything was working out better than it had done at any other time in my life, so even though I was only 21 and Martina was 19, it seemed natural to get married that same year I returned to Mayo. Martina's parents were as different from my own parents as day and night. With Pat and Mary I could laugh and joke around; we all regularly went out to the pub together. And I never felt like I was walking on eggshells waiting for the next row to break out, as was often the case back home in Donegal.

The only time things got a little shaky was during the wedding planning. Martina and I both had steady incomes, so I wanted us to be independent and pay for our own wedding. Neither of us had many relatives—my only close ones in Donegal apart from my immediate family were my grandmother and Uncle Daniel. Martina's parents were both only children, so they had no siblings or children of siblings to invite. However, her mother wanted to invite all of their neighbors. It caused a bit of friction when I put my foot down and vetoed the neighbors, but since we were not asking for money from anybody it gave us the upper hand.

Unfortunately, that was not to be the only hurdle. My father—who for some reason I could never fathom was not a fan of Martina—blankly stated that if I invited my grandmother and uncle to the wedding, he would not go, and he would not allow any of my brothers or sisters to attend either. I was beyond shocked by his ultimatum. There was never any doubt that my grandmother and uncle would attend. I had already asked them, and they were looking forward to it. Now just because my old fella did not like his mother or brother-in-law, he had hijacked his own son's wedding.

My shock soon turned to outrage, but I knew the selfish bastard meant every word of it, so I had to succumb to his bullying tactics. Having to drop my Houton family members was something with which I knew I would never fully reconcile, nor would I ever understand why my mother could not have backed me up when it involved her own mother and brother. I didn't see any of my family prior to the church. The Donegal dictator had decided to drive down that morning, so he never met any of my in-laws until after the wedding ceremony. I barely remember speaking to him at all. What I do remember was that he arrived to my wedding without wearing a tie. The Irish wear their finest clothes when attending a wedding, and for a man back then to show up to his son's wedding without a tie was nearly as unheard of as if he had shown up in a pair of Speedos.

"Do you not have a tie?" I asked him.

"No," he said.

"If youns had let me know, I could have brought one from my flat." I had to think fast. It was Sunday morning, and the only place open would be the local paper shop.

"Jimmy, could you lend your father your tie? I'm sorry you won't have one, but it's worse for him to not be wearing one." I was sorry that Jimmy would now be tieless and him the Best Man, but I was adamant that I would get a tie around the old bastard's neck. For once, I managed to get my way.

At the reception my mother told me they did not have a wedding present for us, but they would get us one later. Six years later, we were still waiting on it. At least the auld fella had the decency to not ask me for a loan to buy the present.

I am not sure how I ever managed to get my new bride to agree to travel up to Donegal on our honeymoon so that I could work on the farm saving hay and turf for my ungrateful father. Lucky for him I had young school-going siblings in the house, or I am quite sure I would have left him to his own devices to keep warm during the winter. Martina never once complained when we returned year after year.

We were exceedingly happy. My new Mayo family looked upon me as another son. Our daughter Sandra was born two years later, in 1982, and I don't think any father ever felt prouder to be taking his wife and newborn home from the hospital. The

Mayo grandparents fawned over their new granddaughter as if they had never seen another child.

In all fairness, my mother was also very fond of her first grandchild. My father acknowledged his granddaughter, but he was fairly noncommittal, which was no shock to me. I didn't need him to make a fuss. Sandra had plenty of people who would show her their love. It was his loss.

One thing about being a proud new father was that it made me reflect upon my early childhood. As I held my little Sandra, I could not begin to contemplate how a grown man could inflict pain and suffering on an innocent little child. I reached out to my brother Jimmy, who had gotten married shortly after me and also had a daughter. I reminded him of the oath to which we had both sworn as young boys. I made him reconfirm that as long as he would live, he would never physically hurt any of his children. We had both been through too much to ever mistreat our children.

Life continued to be more than good, and it only got better when, four years after Sandra was born, Martina gave birth to our son Jason in 1986.

After having served on the Irish police force for eight years, I applied for a three-year sabbatical. This type of leave had previously been granted to teachers and other State employees, but had never been available to Gardai until a recent expansion of the rules. I jumped on this chance to ditch the job for a bit and do something fresh and exciting.

I was still in my 20's, and since the Garda Siochana was very much run by old men, young guys found it next to impossible to get ahead, either through promotion or specialized units. I figured if I was lucky enough to be chosen as one of the "guinea pigs," I'd head off to the US Department of Justice in America... and still be considered young when I got back.

As part of the application, I needed to write an essay explaining why I wanted the leave of absence. I stated that I wished to travel to the US to study law enforcement procedures and operations, and bring this knowledge back to be used by the Garda. They must have liked this reason, as my career break was officially approved to take effect the following month.

I hardly expected that my becoming an Officer of the Law would have a life-changing effect on my relationship with the auld fella. But I figured it would at least bring him some amount of peace, especially considering the interest he showed when I was deciding on whether or not to go for training. I was also quite sure that my mother would be thrilled with my choice. However, as usual, I expected more of them emotionally than they ended up giving.

When my sabbatical was granted, I let my family in Donegal know that I, Martina, and the kids would be taking off to America for a few years. Since it was a brand new program, they didn't fully understood what I was doing. My mother seemed to think I was resigning from the Garda Siochana—an action to be met with raised eyebrows from her friends and neighbors.

Our son Jason had been born in the middle of the winter, and my parents hadn't yet seen the latest addition to the family. I decided to introduce him and at the same time talk to them about our big move.

I totally didn't expect the reception, or lack thereof, from my father. He refused to acknowledge any of us, and sat staring out the kitchen window in his head-of-the-table throne which nobody but he dared to sit in.

"So this is the bold Jason," said my mother as she held out her arms to hold her first grandson.

"Aye, we christened him John Jason," I told her.

"He is the latest John Sexton," my wife said, smiling.

"Since youns call me JP, maybe he'll wind up getting called JJ," I joked. There was still no acknowledgement from the auld fella.

We had some tea and scones, and tried making small talk. But the more time dragged on, the more painful it became watching Jason's grandfather stare out the window like he was expecting Johnny Cash to come waltzing into the driveway to ask him if he could record a few of his songs. After several hours of this cold shoulder torture, I had had enough.

"Let's get out of here," I said to my wife.

"Where are youns going?' asked my mother.

"Far away from this ignorant bastard," I replied, nodding to indicate the auld fella as I picked up the baby.

"Ah, don't go," pleaded my mother.

"Let him go," bellowed the auld fella. "He's always running away."

I felt the blood bubbling in my veins and the hairs standing up on the back of my neck.

"You sour-faced old fucker," I said, "you have no right to open your mouth. We brought our baby son all the way up here from Mayo just so you could meet him and to say goodbye, but you just sat there staring out the window like some kind of lunatic. Nothing I ever did was good enough for you, was it? Did you ever stop to think what kind of a life I had growing up? Do you think for one moment that I wanted to be milking cows every morning before I went to school and as soon as I got home—or that I wanted to carry buckets of water from the well to scrub myself clean enough to not be laughed at in school for smelling like shite?

"Cutting turf and working in the fields every minute of the day is man's work. I was only a boy when I had to carry your load. Not once did you ever have a kind word for me or let me know what a good job I was doing for the family.

"And you know what, I am not even sure if you have Multiple Sclerosis. Maybe you have been faking it all of these years just to get out of doing the work."

"I did my fair share," he shot back, still staring out the window.

"Fair share? Is that what you call driving to the post office every morning to collect the letters? Even when I left home, I didn't turn my back. How many times a year have I come back to help save the hay and cut turf in the bog? Did you conveniently forget that we came up here during our honeymoon, working in the fields all day so that your cows would have food and youns would have heat in the winter?"

"You don't need my permission to go," he barked. "You always do whatever you want."

"I'm not asking for your fucking permission. You don't have any say in what I do with my life. But the least you could do is to look into the eyes of your own grandson and wish him well."

"Go on, get out of here," were his last words.

"Oh, I'll get out of here, all right. And you will wait many the long day before you will ever see me come back. As a matter of fact, you can go and fuck yourself. The next time we see each other will be in Hell."

With that, I turned my back and walked out the door.

My mother's sisters would later tell me that the reason he was pissed off with us and did not look at his new grandchild was because he was mad I was leaving and would not be around to do work around the farm. He probably never liked my wife for the same reason—he thought of her as taking me away from Donegal.

The next time I saw him was not in Hell, but three years later... stretched out in his coffin. It was the quietest and frailest I had ever seen him. I stared down at him, glued to the spot, half-expecting him to start arguing over something that only he could find a reason to argue. The silence out of him was deafening.

That was when it dawned on me. It was too late for any more arguments...or for reconciliation. Neither of us would ever get the chance to mend those broken fences.

Forty-eight hours after burying my father, I was back in New York City, trying to come to terms with what had happened.

Ironically, the place where I was attempting to make sense of it all was in a jail on Riker's Island. A place where madness reigned supreme.

GLOSSARY

Acting the maggot Clowning around
Agus And
Amadan Fool
Amárach Tomorrow
Anorak Year-round coat
An Phoblacht Abu Up the Republic
Banjaxed Broken, busted
Banshee Wailing cry, sometimes heard when someone is about to die
Blue Bottle Police
Bog Place where turf is cut and harvested; also slang for toilet
Boot of the car Trunk
Bonnet of the car Hood
Busaras Main bus depot in Dublin
Cakehole Mouth
Caravan Mobile home/trailer
Cidona Non-alcoholic carbonated apple drink
Clay Pipe Centuries-old man's tobacco pipe made from clay
Collecting the Post Collecting the mail
Craic Fun, entertainment

Crisps Potato chips

Daft Silly

DDT A poisonous powder used to kill lice that was later banned

Dear Expensive

Dog's Dinner A mess

Eamon de Valera Former President of Ireland

Eejit Idiot, fool

Fags Cigarettes

Family Jewels Male genitals

Feck More polite version of "fuck"

Few Bob Few shillings

Flat An apartment

Footpath Sidewalk

Footing Turf Placing turf into little stacks to aid drying

Fortnight Two weeks

Fret To worry

Garda Irish Police (short for Garda Siochana or Guardian of the Peace)

Getting your speak in Letting a girl know you fancied her

Group Cert The first major exam in Second year

Gurn Complain, whine

H-Blocks British designed jails used during internment in the North

Hold Your Tongue/Hold Your Whist Don't say anything

Hoor Whore, applied equally to men and women

Hoor's Melt A worse version of hoor

Jacks Bathroom

Jocks Y-fronts

Jumper Sweater/pullover

Leaving Cert Final exam in secondary school

Long Kesh/The Maze British prisons in Ulster where torture was rampant

Lorry Truck
Mickey/Willy Penis
Mineral bar Place in a dance hall that sold only non-alcoholic drinks
Myxomatosis Disease used to cull and kill rabbits over-running the country
The Phoblacht Illegal nationalist newspaper, mostly sold by hand in pubs
Pish Old Donegal term for piss
Pog mo Thoin Kiss my ass
Potin (pronounced "pocheen") Illegal Whiskey/Moonshine
PROVOS Provisional Irish Republican Army
Quare One Girl/Girlfriend
Ra Short for I.R.A.
Get the Ride Have sex
Right Ride Sexy
Sasanach Irish word for the English
Shagged Tired, or having sex
Skittery Diarrhea-like
Slan agus beannacht leat Health and blessings, said to someone departing
Slan Goodbye
Snog Kissing session
Spuds Potatoes
Stations of the Cross Religious ceremony involving the blessing of a house
Taking the piss Making fun of someone
Telly T.V.
The Troubles Period of guerilla warfare in Ireland from about 1968 to 1998
To "Get Thick" To become annoyed or mad
Turf Prehistoric fossil fuel hundreds of thousands of years old

Turf Mole Turf dust

Wee Court (pronounced "Coort") Making out with a girl

Whin Bush Green prickly bush with needles and yellow flowers when in bloom

Youns Donegal version of you (pl.)

ABOUT THE AUTHOR

In Ireland we have a phenomenon known as a "spoiled priest." Unlike a spoiled child, it has nothing to do with a priest throwing a temper tantrum.

A "spoiled priest" refers to somebody who either had thoughts about becoming a priest, or who even went into the Seminary, but for one reason or another, decided not to go through with it.

I suppose I could be considered something of a "spoiled writer." The difference between the two though, is that a writer can never truly walk away from his/her writing. In much the same way, a writer is different from a recovering alcoholic, since we never want to recover and give it up for good.

I always knew I had a writing problem. No matter what far-flung corner of the world I might find myself in, or what manner of insanity might have engaged me at the time, I always felt the pull of yet to be born words and sentences scrambling in my mind, begging to be paperized. For me, the desire to write has always haunted me from the inside and served as a reminder that it would catch up with me one day and to resist would be futile.

The poet Maya Angelou captured it beautifully when she said; "There's no greater agony than bearing an untold story inside of you."